LONGMAN STUDY GUIDES

GCSE

Science

Di Barton

LONGMAN

► LONGMAN STUDY GUIDES

SERIES EDITORS: **Geoff Black and Stuart Wall**

Titles available

Biology	Mathematics
Business Studies	Mathematics: Higher Level
Chemistry	Music
Design and Technology	Physics
Economics	Psychology
English	Religious Studies
English Literature	Science
French	Sociology
Geography	Spanish
German	World History
Information Technology	

Addison Wesley Longman Limited
Edinburgh Gate, Burnt Mill, Harlow,
Essex CM20 2JE, England
and Associated Companies throughout the World.

© Addison Wesley Longman 1997

First published 1988
Third edition 1997

ISBN 0582-30498-9

British Library Cataloguing-in-Publication Data
A catalogue record for this book is available from the British Library.

Set by 30 in 9.75/12pt Sabon
Produced by Longman Singapore Publishers Pte
Printed in Singapore

CONTENTS

► EDITORS' PREFACE

Longman Study Guides have been written by the people who set and mark the exams – the examiners. Examiners are aware that, owing to lack of practice and poor preparation, some students achieve only the lowest grades: they are not able to effectively show the examiner what they know and understand. These books give excellent advice about exam practice and preparation, and will help you to organise a structured revision programme, all of which are essential for examination success. Remember: the examiners are looking for opportunities to *give* you marks, not take them away!

Longman Study Guides are designed to be used throughout the course. The self-contained chapters can be read in any order appropriate to the stage you have reached in your course. The examiner guides you through the essential parts of each topic, making helpful comments throughout.

We believe that this book, and the series as a whole, will help you establish and build your basic knowledge and examination technique. For additional help with exam practice and revision techniques, we have published a series called **Longman Exam Practice Kits**, which are available from all good bookshops, or direct from Addison Wesley Longman.

GEOFF BLACK AND STUART WALL

► ACKNOWLEDGEMENTS

I am grateful to the following Examination Groups for permission to reproduce questions which have appeared in their examination papers. However, the answers, or hints on any answers, are solely the responsibility of the author.

EDEXCEL Foundation (London)
Midland Examining Group (MEG)
Southern Examining Group (SEG)
University of Cambridge Local Examinations Syndicate (UCLES)
Welsh Joint Education Committee (WJEC)
Northern Ireland Council for Curriculum, Examinations and Assessment (NICCEA)

I would like to acknowledge the major contribution made by Mike Evans to the following chapters: Atomic structure and bonding; Useful products from oil and metal ores; The Periodic Table; Chemical reactions; and The reactivity series and acidity. I would also like to acknowledge the contributions made by Stuart Farmer to the chapter on Variation, inheritance and evolution.

I would also like to thank Geoff Black and Stuart Wall for their help and guidance during the preparation of this book.

DI BARTON

This book has been written as a course companion for use throughout your GCSE course in Science. The first chapter gives advice about preparing for the examination including information about revision, coursework and the skills that you will need to demonstrate. Chapter 2 focuses on the National Curriculum for Science (assessment objectives, tiers of entry and the examination papers) and the syllabuses of each of the main examination boards. You should read these first two chapters carefully as they give invaluable advice which will be useful throughout your Science course.

Each of the remaining chapters, 3 to 18, deals with an important aspect of the National Curriculum for Science. Each chapter begins with a **Getting Started** section which is an introduction to the chapter. This includes a **Topic Chart**, a table which, at a glance, provides a breakdown of the chapter into key topic areas. The chart can be used to check your study and revision progress over the two years. A Topic Chart looks like this:

TOPIC	STUDY	REVISION 1	REVISION 2
Life processes			
Levels of organisation			

Each topic is then explained in the **What you need to know** section – the core of the chapter. This section gives you the important facts about the topics. Under some of the headings, a statement from the National Curriculum is given in italics, together with a reference back to the National Curriculum, as outlined in the Appendix at the end of Chapter 2. We have also identified where part of the topic is for the Higher Tier only, see below:

H   The **liver** produces **bile** which helps to:

▶ **emulsify** (break up) large globules of fats (lipids) and form smaller droplets; these are broken down by lipase into **fatty acids** and **glycerol**;
▶ **neutralise** the hydrochloric acid from the stomach enabling other enzymes, which require higher pH values, to work on the food molecules.

To help you practise what you have just learnt, there are then a series of examination questions followed by suggested answers. Try not to look at the answers until you have attempted to answer the questions yourself.

In each chapter there is also an examination question with a typical student's answer: some of the responses are excellent A grade answers whereas others may have faults or weaknesses. These answers will help you to see what problems are identified by examiners and where you could improve your own examination answers.

At the end of each chapter there is a summary box which briefly identifies the key points about topics covered in the chapter. You should check that you know, and understand more fully, each of the key points listed.

Revision, Examinations and Coursework

▶ **GETTING STARTED**

Just as a tennis player learns new techniques and trains for a tournament, so there are a number of techniques that you can develop which will help you to improve your performance in the examination, and gain more marks. For example, you can practise answering questions to a set time limit, and without using books to help you, before the exam. You will then be better prepared to cope with the actual conditions you will meet in the exam.

Examination questions are written by examiners to find out how much you know and understand. They also test your ability to handle information and to apply what you know to new situations. You are often given information in a question to help you answer the question, so a lot depends on reading the question fully, and making use of all the available facts. You will gain marks only for answering the questions which are set by the examiner, not for answering your own version of the question!

Coursework is the work that you will have completed at school or college prior to the written examination. This work will have been marked by your teacher and you may have had some feedback about how well you are doing. Remember that Coursework counts for 25% of your total assessment in Science, and that the written Terminal Examination (together with Module Tests where applicable) counts for 75%.

TOPIC	STUDY	REVISION 1	REVISION 2
Revision			
Coursework			
Final examination papers			
Module tests			
Words of instruction			
Diagrams			
Spelling, punctuation and grammar			
Language and literacy skills			
Mathematical skills			

WHAT YOU NEED TO KNOW

▶ **Revision**
1. Make a plan.
2. Active revision.
3. Practise.
4. Revise with a friend.

Make a plan and start early

▶ **Plan** your revision so you have time to study your notes on all the topics in the weeks leading up to the exam.

▶ Use the syllabus descriptions in Chapter 2 to help you make a complete **list of topics**.

▶ When you decide to start your revision, count **how many weeks** there are before the exam and **how many topics** you have to revise.

▶ Work out the numbers of hours you have each day for revision – you do have to eat, sleep and relax as well! However, make good use of 'holiday' time and weekends.

▶ Make a revision plan to revise a set number of topics **each week**; choose some easier topics and some more difficult topics which may need more revision time.

▶ You will need to **return** to revising some topics nearer the exam; this is where summaries of key facts are useful.

Active revision

▶ Make your revision as **active** as possible to keep it interesting. For example, look at your notes and write a **summary of the key facts** about a topic on a separate card or sheet of paper; this is far more effective than just reading through your notes over and over again.

▶ Try to **memorise the key facts** and write down what you can remember without looking at your summary; check back to the summary to see which points you forgot and learn these again.

▶ To improve your **concentration**, divide your revision time into short blocks, say of half an hour at a time, and then have a few minutes' break.

▶ At the start of your revision time, quickly check back on the topic you revised during the last session to **reinforce your memory**.

▶ At the end of your revision time, feel a sense of **achievement** by marking on your check-list those topics you are happy with and make a note of those you would like to look at again.

Practise

▶ Practise drawing **diagrams** from memory.

▶ Cover up the **labels** at the side of a diagram with a piece of paper and see how many labels you can remember.

▶ Draw a **flow chart** and leave blank spaces to fill in from memory.

▶ Practise **answering the examination questions** at the end of each chapter to test yourself the day after you have revised a topic.

▶ **Mark your own answer** using the examiner's marking scheme to see where you could have gained more marks.

Revise with a friend

▶ Ask a friend to **test** you on key facts.

▶ **Compare summaries** of key facts.

▶ Try to **tape record** information using a cassette recorder; you can then listen to the tape as a change to reading notes.

▶ **Explain** a difficult idea to a friend, or even to your teddy bear!

▶ **Mark** each other's answers to the examination questions – experience what it is like to be an **examiner**!

The usual scheme of assessment is that *Experimental and Investigative Science* (Sc 1) is assessed by **coursework** throughout your GCSE course, and *Life Processes and Living Things* (Sc 2), *Materials and their Properties* (Sc 3) and *Physical Processes* (Sc 4) are assessed by final **written question papers** and, if you are following a **modular** course, short written **module tests** as you complete each module.

▶ **Coursework**   The **coursework component** of all Science courses, both Double and Single Award, is worth 25% of your overall assessment for Key Stage 4. Coursework assesses those skills grouped under the heading of **Experimental and Investigative Science (Sc 1)** (see Chapter 2). The assessments will be based on practical work carried out during the topics you are studying. For example:

▶ **Life Processes and Living Things (Sc 2)**
Humans as Organisms: Food tests to identify the presence of starch, fats, proteins and simple sugars.
Plants as Organisms: Investigating the effect of light on the growth of seedlings.
▶ **Materials and their Properties (Sc 3)**
Rates of Reaction: Investigating the effect of temperature on enzyme catalysed reactions.
Changing Materials: Determining the formula for magnesium oxide.
▶ **Physical Processes (Sc 4)**
Electricity and Magnetism: Measuring the efficiency of an electric motor.
Energy Resources and Energy Transfer: Investigating how insulation affects heat loss from a container of hot water.

There are normally two different methods by which you can be assessed on practical skills. One way is by your teacher watching you carry out a particular practical, perhaps involving you in the handling of apparatus or in following instructions. The second method is by your teacher assessing what you have written during a practical investigation.

The work you hand in for assessment may include your observations and a presentation of your results, perhaps as a chart or graph. Your teacher can then use your written work to assess your ability to make and record observations. You are usually assessed on more than one occasion for a particular skill, so don't worry if you haven't done too well on any one particular piece of work. You may be assessed on the same skill at a later date, or you may be able to arrange this with your teacher. The best person with whom to discuss the standards you have reached on your practical assessments is your teacher at school. He or she may not be able to tell you the actual mark for any particular skill, but may be able to give you some guidance about how you can improve your level of performance in a particular skill area.

Points to remember when submitting coursework:

▶ There should be a clear heading or title, and an introduction which describes the investigation, and shows that you understand what the investigation is about.
▶ You should have your name, the date and your form or set clearly written on the work.
▶ Underline the headings and subheadings.
▶ All diagrams, charts, graphs, photos, etc. should have a heading and labels.
▶ List all relevant equipment and apparatus.
▶ Describe any safety precautions which you have taken, for example wearing safety goggles, using small amounts of chemical substances, using a fume cupboard.
▶ Present your results as a chart or graph. Refer to, and make use of, your results when writing up your coursework.
▶ Describe any problems you had during the investigation and suggest possible solutions.
▶ Identify possible sources of error and suggest further investigations.
▶ List any references that you may have used.

You will find it useful to keep all your coursework in a folder, as the exam boards usually look at the coursework from a random selection of about 10% of candidates from a centre. Your work may therefore go to an examiner, called a coursework moderator, who is responsible for ensuring that standards are similar between different schools.

You will be given credit for your performance under four headings:

1. **Skill area P** – planning experimental procedures.
2. **Skill area O** – obtaining evidence.
3. **Skill area A** – analysing evidence and drawing conclusions.
4. **Skill area E** – evaluating evidence.

These skills are assessed by matching your performance when doing an activity to a number of statements (mark descriptions) which describe levels of performance in each skill area. This scheme of assessment forms a 'common element' across all of the Science Syllabuses of the Examining Groups.

Table 1.1 Sc1 assessment criteria. Skill area P – planning experimental procedures

Programme of study requirements

Candidates should be taught:

(a) to use scientific knowledge and understanding, drawing on secondary sources where appropriate, to turn ideas suggested to them, and their own ideas, into a form that can be investigated;

(b) to carry out preliminary work where this helps to clarify what they have to do;

(c) to make predictions where it is appropriate to do so;

(d) to consider the key factors in contexts involving a number of factors;

(e) to plan how to vary or control key variables;

(f) to consider the number and range of observations or measurements to be made;

(g) to recognise contexts, e.g. *fieldwork*, where variables cannot readily be controlled and to make judgements about the amount of evidence needed in these contexts;

(h) to select apparatus, equipment and techniques, taking account of safety requirements.

Mark descriptions

The mark descriptions are designed to be hierarchical.

All work should be assessed in the context of the syllabus.

		Candidates	Increasing demand of activity
2 marks	P.2a	plan a simple, safe procedure	
4 marks	P.4a	plan a fair test or a practical procedure, making a prediction where appropriate	
	P.4b	select appropriate equipment	
6 marks	P.6a	use scientific knowledge and understanding to plan a procedure, to identify key factors to vary, control or take into account, and to make a prediction where appropriate	
	P.6b	decide on a suitable number and range of observations or measurements to be made	
8 marks	P.8a	use detailed scientific knowledge and understanding to plan an appropriate strategy, taking into account the need to produce precise and reliable evidence, and to justify a prediction where appropriate	
	P.8b	use, where appropriate, relevant information from secondary sources or preliminary work	

Table 1.2 Sc1 assessment criteria. Skill area O – obtaining evidence

Programme of study requirements
Candidates should be taught:
(a) to use a range of apparatus and equipment safely and with skill;
(b) to make observations and measurements to a degree of precision appropriate to the context;
(c) to make sufficient relevant observations and measurements for reliable evidence;
(d) to consider uncertainties in measurements and observations;
(e) to repeat measurements and observations when appropriate;
(f) to record evidence clearly and appropriately as they carry out the work.

Mark descriptions
The mark descriptions are designed to be hierarchical.
All work should be assessed in the context of the syllabus.

		Candidates	Increasing demand of activity
2 marks	O.2a	use simple equipment safely to make some observations or measurements	
4 marks	O.4a	make appropriate observations or measurements which are adequate for the activity	
	O.4b	record the observations or measurements	
6 marks	O.6a	make sufficient systematic and accurate observations or measurements and repeat them when appropriate	
	O.6b	record clearly and accurately the observations or measurements	
8 marks	O.8a	use equipment with precision and skill to obtain and record reliable evidence which involves an appropriate number and range of observations or measurements	

Table 1.3 Sc1 assessment criteria. Skill area A – analysing evidence and drawing conclusions

Programme of study requirements
Candidates should be taught:
(a) to present qualitative and quantitative data clearly;
(b) to present data as graphs, using lines of best fit where appropriate;
(c) to identify trends or patterns in results;
(d) to use graphs to identify relationships between variables;
(e) to present numerical results to an appropriate degree of accuracy;
(f) to check that conclusions drawn are consistent with the evidence;
(g) to explain how results support or undermine the original prediction when one has been made;
(h) to try to explain conclusions in the light of their knowledge and understanding of science.

Mark descriptions
The mark descriptions are designed to be hierarchical.
All work should be assessed in the context of the syllabus.

		Candidates	Increasing demand of activity
2 marks	A.2a	explain simply what has been found out	
4 marks	A.4a	present findings in the form of simple diagrams, charts or graphs	
	A.4b	identify trends and patterns in observations or measurements	
6 marks	A.6a	construct and use appropriate diagrams, charts, graphs (with lines of best fit), or use numerical methods, to process evidence for a conclusion	
	A.6b	draw a conclusion consistent with the evidence and relate this to scientific knowledge and understanding	
8 marks	A.8a	use detailed scientific knowledge and understanding to explain a conclusion drawn from processed evidence	
	A.8b	explain how results support or undermine the original prediction when one has been made	

Table 1.4 Sc1 assessment criteria. Skill area E – evaluating evidence

Programme of study requirements
Candidates should be taught:
(a) to consider whether the evidence collected is sufficient to enable firm conclusions to be drawn;
(b) to consider reasons for anomalous results and to reject such results where appropriate;
(c) to consider the reliability of results in terms of the uncertainty of measurements and observations;
(d) to propose improvements to the methods that have been used;
(e) to propose further investigation to test their conclusions.

Mark descriptions
The mark descriptions are designed to be hierarchical.
All work should be assessed in the context of the syllabus.

	Candidates		Increasing demand of activity
2 marks	E.2a	make a relevant comment about the procedure used or the evidence obtained	
4 marks	E.4a	comment on the accuracy of the observations or measurements, recognising any anomalous results	
	E.4b	comment on the suitability of the procedure and, where appropriate, suggest changes to improve the reliability of the evidence	
6 marks	E.6a	comment on the reliability of the evidence, accounting for any anomalous results, or explain whether the evidence is sufficient to support a firm conclusion	
	E.6b	propose improvements, or further work, to provide additional evidence for the conclusion, or to extend the enquiry	

▶ Final examination papers

The final written question papers are taken at the end of your GCSE course usually in May or June of Year 11 and are worth 75% of your marks, unless you are taking a **modular** course where the terminal exam is worth only 50%. As described in Chapter 2, all the Examining Groups set examination papers which are similar in style and format, consisting of compulsory, structured questions, which are answered on the question paper in the spaces provided. The papers for the Foundation Tier and Higher Tier may contain common questions or part questions targeting the overlapping grades CC and DD. The papers aimed at the Higher Tier have more opportunity for extended writing and calculations.

Structured questions

'There are examples of structured questions at the end of each chapter.'

A structured question usually starts with an introductory sentence telling you what the question is about, followed by the '**stimulus material**' as described below, followed by a series of short sub-questions (a), (b), (c) and so on which require a few words or a few sentences for an answer. Sometimes the sub-questions are further divided into say, (b) (i), (b) (ii) etc.; you will usually need to have answered (i) before doing (ii). Most structured questions have an '*incline of difficulty*' which means that sub-question (a) may be easier to answer than sub-question (b) or (c). However, if you are unable to answer part (a) for example, you should go on to attempt (b) or (c).

Points to remember when answering structured questions:

▶ Your answer should aim to **fill the space** that is provided, but you can write more if you wish. If a question asks you for '**three** changes' there are usually three lines for your answer with the numbers 1, 2 and 3 on the lines.

▶ Use as many **scientific words** as possible so that the examiner can see evidence of your knowledge and understanding in Science and can award you marks.

▶ If you are asked for the answer to a calculation, always include the **units** for any number that you write: for example, the rate of doing work is 10 W or 10 watts, not just 10.

▶ At the end of the space for your answer the marks allocated for each sub-question are shown so if you are asked to 'suggest **two** things' two marks will be allocated.

Remember the general rule:

'one correct fact usually gains one mark'.

Stimulus material used in structured questions

Structured questions are usually based on a particular **topic** or **theme** from the syllabus, such as '*circulation*', '*reactions*', '*waves*'. The questions are usually based on '**stimulus material**' such as one of the following:

▶ A **diagram** of some apparatus that you may be familiar with, for example, an electrical circuit or a part of the human body.

▶ A **table** (chart) showing information, for example about the heights of pupils in a class, or the results of heating different materials.

▶ A **graph**, for example showing the motion of a car over a period of time, or the rate of a reaction.

▶ A **photograph** or sketch with some explanatory information.

▶ Some written information, for example a **newspaper article**.

Questions involving extended writing

These questions are usually more common on the Higher Tier papers. The questions:

▶ may ask you to 'explain how something happens' or to 'suggest reasons' for a particular observation;

▶ usually require a longer answer in the form of a few sentences;

▶ may allocate up to *6 marks* for your answer;

▶ are often aimed at assessing candidates for grades CC to A*A*.

You may find it helpful to write the main points of your answer in pencil on the question paper before answering the question. Check you have matched the number of points you have made to the marks allocated and remember to cross out your rough notes.

▶ **Module tests**

The number and frequency of Module Tests vary from syllabus to syllabus (see Schemes of Assessment for each syllabus in Chapter 2). They contain short, structured questions (described above) and some use **multiple choice** (or objective) questions.

Multiple choice or objective questions

Each question has a '**stem**', which is the main part of the question. The stem may include diagrams or tables of figures and you need to read the stem carefully to obtain as much **information** as possible before you read the list of suggested answers called '**options**'. These options are usually labelled A to E and only *one* of them is the *correct answer*, which is the '**key**'. The incorrect answers are the '**distractors**'. One way of approaching this type of question is to look for the correct answer and to ignore the distractors. Alternatively you can work through the list of options and *reject each distractor* until you are left only with the 'key'. Look at the following example.

'Example of a multiple choice question'

Many types of different waves and rays bombard the Earth. Which one of the following makes us feel hot?

A gamma rays   **B** infra-red rays   **C** radio waves   **D** visible rays   **E** X-rays

You may know the correct answer to this (key = **B**), or you may be able to reject each of the distractors. For example, you may know that radio waves are involved in communication and so **C** can therefore be *rejected* as an answer to this question, and so on.

In the exam, you may be able to use rough paper or the question paper to work out your answer. You mark the answer that you have chosen on a special answer grid using a soft HB pencil. You can then rub out an answer if it is wrong and make a new mark. Remember, there is only *one* correct answer to each question, and every question carries one mark. If you get stuck on a question, leave it and go on to the next. You may have time to come back to that question later and at least have a guess at the answer before the

'Check your answers'

exam ends. When you have completed as many questions as possible, you should *check* each of your answers carefully, making sure that you have put your answer against the number on the grid which corresponds to the question you have answered. Try to use all the time you have in the exam in this positive way instead of just doing nothing!

▶ **Words of instruction**

In examination questions there is usually a '**word of instruction**' in each sub-question. This is used by the examiner to tell you how to answer the question in a certain way. For example, if you are asked to '*Explain*' then writing a descriptive list will not qualify you for the marks.

One syllabus describes four groups of words of instruction. Depending on the context, some words may appear in more than one group.

I. 'State . . .', 'List . . .' 'Name . . .', 'What . . .', 'How . . .', 'Describe . . .', 'What is meant by . . .'

These words are about *recall of information*. (Remember about *20%* of the examination will test factual recall.)
For example:

'*Name* the part labelled **A** on the line provided.'
'*What is* the function of valve **D**?'
'*State* the feature you can see on the diagram.'

2. 'Explain . . .', 'Complete . . .', 'Why . . .', 'Construct . . .', 'Which . . .'

These words are about using recalled information in a *wider context*.
For example:

'*Explain* why the wall of the left ventricle is more muscular . . .'
'*Explain* the advantages of using . . .'
'*Complete* the table by writing the property in the space provided.'

3 'Suggest . . .', 'Work out . . .', 'How would you know that . . .'

These words are used to assess your ability in *problem solving*, *interpretation*, *evaluation*, *data handling* and in *communication* of scientific ideas and principles. '*Suggest*' is one of the most commonly used words.
For example:

'*Suggest* two reasons why . . .'
'*Suggest* how this change could have happened.'

4 'Calculate . . .', 'Predict . . .', 'Discuss . . .'

These words are usually used on Higher Tier papers and are concerned with asking you to **apply knowledge**, **interpret**, **evaluate** and **process information**.
For example:

'*Calculate* John's acceleration between points X and Y.'

It may be helpful to identify and underline the word(s) of instruction in the question before you start to write your answer.

▶ **Diagrams**

You may be asked to draw diagrams to show apparatus, or possibly diagrams to show something like a magnetic field pattern or the arrangement of the planetary bodies in a solar eclipse.

▶   Use a *sharp* HB pencil.
▶   Try to make the diagram fit the space allowed on the exam paper, or use about a third to a half page of A4 if answering on lined paper.
▶   State the *magnification/scale* (if relevant).

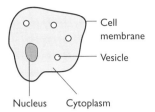

Animal cell

Cell membrane
Vesicle
Nucleus
Cytoplasm

Fig. 1.1 How to use radial labelling lines around a diagram

▶ Write a *heading* above the diagram to state what it is showing.

▶ Use *labelling lines* to label the different parts of the diagram clearly. For example, Figure 1.1 opposite shows how you can use radial *labelling lines* around a diagram. Alternatively, as in Figure 17.3 (page 326), you can use a *list of labels* at the side of a diagram.

▶ Include as much *accurate detail* on the diagram as possible.

▶ When you draw apparatus, only draw the *relevant parts* of the apparatus and omit standard equipment such as retort stands, Bunsen burners, etc. The diagrams in this book may be useful to study for guidance.

Look at the *number of marks* allocated for the diagram. Five marks may mean that it's better to only spend about five minutes on a diagram. You can always come back to it if you have extra time at the end.

▶ Spelling, punctuation and grammar

The assessment of spelling, punctuation and grammar is allocated 5% of the marks on the **coursework** component. The marks are awarded in accordance with the following criteria:

▶ **Threshold performance**: Candidates spell, punctuate and use the rules of grammar with *reasonable accuracy*; they use a *limited* range of specialist terms appropriately. **1 mark**

▶ **Intermediate performance**: Candidates spell, punctuate and use the rules of grammar with *considerable accuracy*; they use a *good range* of specialist terms with facility. **2 marks**

▶ **High performance**: Candidates spell, punctuate and use the rules of grammar with almost *faultless accuracy*, deploying a range of grammatical constructions; they use a *wide range* of specialist terms adeptly and with precision. **3 marks**

▶ Language and literacy skills

You should be able to **communicate effectively** in written English by using grammatically correct sentences. You should develop the following skills throughout the course:

▶ recording and storage of information in an appropriate form;

▶ using and understanding information gained from various sources;

▶ communicating ideas to others;

▶ summarising and organising information in order to communicate adequately;

▶ using appropriate language to explain the results of observations in a variety of contexts;

▶ using and interpreting scientific nomenclature, symbols and conventions.

▶ Mathematical skills

The Mathematical skills required by each syllabus vary slightly. Usually you are allowed to use calculators in all written papers but check on the regulations stated in the syllabus. The Examining Groups assume you will have the ability to:

Foundation and Higher Tier

'Some useful mathematical skills'

▶ add, subtract, multiply and divide whole numbers

▶ recognise and use expressions in decimal form

▶ make approximations and estimates to obtain reasonable answers

▶ use simple formulae expressed in words

▶ understand and use averages

▶ read, interpret and draw simple inferences from tables and statistical diagrams

▶ find fractions or percentages of quantities

▶ construct and interpret pie-charts

▶ calculate with fractions, decimals, percentage or ratio

▶ solve simple equations

▶ substitute numbers for letters in simple equations

▶ interpret and use graphs

▶ plot graphs from data provided, given the axes and scales

▶ choose by simple inspection and then draw the best smooth curve though a set of points on a graph

Higher Tier only

▶ use appropriate limits of accuracy
▶ recognise and use expressions in standard form
▶ manipulate simple equations
▶ select appropriate axes and scales for graph plotting
▶ determine the intercept of a linear graph
▶ understand and use inverse proportion

A note about graphs

If you are asked to draw a graph in the exam there are some important points to remember:

(a) use the axes and scale if they are given in the question;
(b) if the axes and scale are not given in the question then decide on a scale that will fit the figures given in the data;
(c) the x axis goes along the bottom or on the horizontal, the y axis goes upwards or on the vertical;
(d) the factor that changes regularly, such as time, goes on the x axis;
(e) label your axes, and indicate the scale used;
(f) write a heading on your graph;
(g) draw either a smooth curve through the points on the graph or the best-fitting straight line.

Marks are usually given for:

▶ use of appropriate scale and correct axes;
▶ correctly labelled axes and title;
▶ accurate plot of points;
▶ best straight line or best smooth curve.

The GCSE Key Stage 4 Syllabuses

▶ **GETTING STARTED**

Science has become an essential subject for all learners to study either as a single or a double award for Key Stage 4. The double award Science courses usually involve you in twice the amount of time for a single subject and lead to two qualifications. The double award is a good foundation for studying separate Sciences and some of the newer modular Science courses at A level or AS level.

The syllabuses from the examination groups are all based on the requirements of the National Curriculum for Science. However, the syllabuses do vary in their interpretation of what you should study. It is well worth checking with your teacher exactly which syllabus you are studying and at what level so that you do not attempt to revise topics which may be at a higher level than you need. The addresses of the examination groups are given on page 25 should you require further information.

At the end of each chapter there are some questions from the different examination groups, and outline answers. There are also some typical student answers with comments from an examiner. Some of the examination questions are based on past papers for GCSE Key Stage 4, others are based on the sample assessment material for the revised Key Stage 4 Syllabuses. However, all the questions are of a similar style and assess similar abilities and will give you good experience in answering examination questions.

Remember you need to be actively involved in your revision, and to take responsibility for planning and organising your revision time. Meeting deadlines for submitting course-work has become part of your school life. Try to plan your revision so that you meet the examination deadline as well.

TOPIC	STUDY	REVISION 1	REVISION 2
The National Curriculum for Science			
GCSE Key Stage 4 Syllabuses			
Aims			
Assessment objectives			
Tiers of entry			
The written examination papers			
Your final certificate			
London EDEXCEL Foundation			
Midland Examining Group (MEG)			
Northern Examinations and Assessment Board (NEAB)			
Northern Ireland Council for Curriculum, Examinations and Assessment (NICCEA)			
Southern Examining Group (SEG)			
Welsh Joint Education Committee (WJEC)			
Addresses of the examination boards			
Appendix: Details of the four study programmes Sc1–Sc4			

WHAT YOU NEED TO KNOW

▶ **The National Curriculum for Science**

The National Curriculum for Science, which applies to all school-age pupils, is organised on the basis of **four key stages**. You may have already taken National tests at Key Stages 2 and 3. Now you are ready for Key Stage 4.

The National Curriculum describes **programmes of study**, which set out what students should be taught, and **attainment targets**, which set out the expected standards of performance as described by **level descriptors** of increasing difficulty. An example of a statement in the **programme of study** is '*Pupils should be taught how variation may arise from both genetic and environmental causes*'. The **level descriptor** for level 7 states '*Pupils identify characteristics between individuals, including some features, such as eye colour, that are inherited and others such as height, that can also be affected by environmental factors*'.

There are **four programmes of study/attainment targets** each weighted at 25%:

1. Experimental and Investigative Science (Sc 1)
2. Life Processes and Living Things (Sc 2)
3. Materials and their Properties (Sc 3)
4. Physical Processes (Sc 4)

Experimental and Investigative Science (Sc 1) is assessed by **coursework**, which represents 25% of the total assessment and relates to the subject content of *Life and Living Processes (Sc 2)*, *Materials and their Properties (Sc 3)* and *Physical Processes (Sc 4)*.

▶ **GCSE Key Stage 4 Syllabuses**

Each Examining Group produces Science syllabuses that divide the programmes of study in different ways. The usual pattern is to use the main headings, Life and Living Processes (Sc 2), Materials and their Properties (Sc 3) and Physical Processes (Sc 4), and devise topics or units of study which describe the knowledge, skills and understanding that an examiner can expect of candidates. It is very important that you, as an examination candidate, should obtain a correct, up-to-date copy of the syllabus for the Science course you are studying. Ask your teacher the following:

▶   the name of the Examining Group;
▶   the precise name and number of the syllabus.

You can then contact the Examining Group (see below) for an order form and price list (publications list), and order a copy of the syllabus and past question papers.

▶ **Aims**

The **aims** are a description of the purpose of the Syllabus. They are often long-term goals which cannot always be assessed in a written examination.

▶   to stimulate curiosity, interest and enjoyment in science and its methods of enquiry;
▶   to acquire a systematic body of scientific knowledge and to develop an understanding of Science, including its power and limitations;
▶   to develop abilities and skills that are relevant to the study, practice and application of science, which are useful in everyday life, and which encourage safe practice;
▶   to develop experimental and investigative abilities;
▶   to develop an understanding of the nature of scientific ideas and activity and the basis for scientific claims;
▶   to develop an understanding of the technological and environmental applications of Science and of the economic, ethical and social implications of these.

It is hoped that you will achieve these long-term aims during your GCSE Science course.

▶ **Assessment objectives**

The **assessment objectives** are a statement of the skills and abilities which you should develop as a result of studying Science. You will be assessed on these objectives by coursework and in the written examination.

There are **three** main assessment objectives

▶ experimental and investigative Science (25%);
▶ knowledge and understanding (60%, about one-third for recall);
▶ communication and evaluation (15%).

Objectives related to Experimental and Investigative Science (Sc1) (25%)

Candidates must be able to carry out experimental work in which they:

▶ plan procedures;
▶ use precise and systematic ways of making measurements and observations;
▶ analyse and evaluate evidence;
▶ relate this to scientific knowledge and understanding.

The assessment of Experimental and Investigative Science will be by coursework through-out your GCSE course. You will be assessed by your teacher on your performance in each of four skill areas linked to the above statements:

Skill Area P – Planning Experimental Procedures;
Skill Area O – Obtaining Evidence;
Skill Area A – Analysing Evidence and Drawing Conclusions;
Skill Area E – Evaluating Evidence.

The contexts for the teaching and assessment of these four skill areas are taken from Life Processes and Living Things, Materials and their Properties and Physical Processes.

For each skill area there are mark descriptions provided for your teachers to judge which mark on a scale of 1 (low) to 8 (high) best fits your performance during each piece of assessed coursework.

Objectives related to Sc 2, Sc 3 and Sc 4

Knowledge and Understanding (60%)

▶ Recall, understand, use and apply the scientific knowledge set out in the syllabus (about one-third recall).

Communication and Evaluation (15%)

▶ Communicate scientific observations, ideas and arguments using a range of scientific and technical vocabulary and appropriate scientific and mathematical conventions.
▶ Evaluate relevant scientific information and make informed judgements from it.

The scheme of assessment in each Syllabus describes how each of these objectives will be assessed by the different components of the examination. The target weighting for the assessment of **recall** (remembering facts) is about 20–25%. It is important that you, as a candidate, realise that the written examination paper is not going to test only recall of facts but also your understanding and application of those facts, as well as your ability to communicate.

The assessment of Life and Living Processes (Sc 2), Materials and their Properties (Sc 3) and Physical Processes (Sc 4) will be by written examination papers, usually at the end of the course. These question papers are set and marked by the examiners (often teachers!) employed by the Examining Group.

▶ **Tiers of entry**   All the schemes of assessment consist of **two** tiers of entry:

▶ **Foundation Tier** – recommended for those candidates who expect to achieve **grades GG to CC** inclusive.
▶ **Higher Tier** – recommended for those who expect to achieve **grades CC to A*A*** inclusive.

You can only be entered for **one tier**, so the grades that you are expected to obtain should lie within the range of grades for that paper. If you are expected to reach grade CC where the target grades overlap, you should enter for the tier which you feel most confidence in obtaining.

Take note: if you enter for **Higher** Tier and obtain **insufficient** marks to be awarded DD you will be **ungraded** (U). If you enter for **Foundation** Tier and achieve **higher** marks than CC you will only be awarded CC. Discussion between you, your teacher and your parents should help to decide on the most realistic entry option for you.

▶ **The written examination papers**

All the written final examination papers set by the Examining Groups are similar in format and style. They all have the following.

▶ **Compulsory, structured questions** which are answered on the question paper. The Foundation Tier papers contain more short answer questions. The Higher Tier papers have more opportunity for extended writing. For example, you may be given several lines on which to compose your answer and awarded, say, 4–6 marks.

▶ The **number of marks** allocated for each answer is given in brackets on the question paper.

▶ **Spaces and lines** are left for your answers so you can see how much you need to write.

▶ There may be calculations of appropriate complexity for that level of paper.

Where the assessment is only by final written papers and coursework, the written papers are worth 75% of the total assessment and the coursework is worth 25%. In the modular schemes the Module Tests are worth 25%, and the value of the written papers is reduced to 50%.

▶ **Your final certificate**

In Science **Double Award** scheme a candidate's result will be reported as **two identical grades** on the scale GG to A*A*, for example CC (never different levels such as BC). In Science **Single Award** a candidate's result will be reported as a single grade on the scale G to A*. The number of marks required for a particular grade is agreed each year by the Examining Group and depends on the difficulty of the examination paper. There is no stated 'pass mark' for a particular grade. The same **standard**, however, will be maintained from one year to the next, so grades AA achieved in 1998 will be of the same standard as those achieved in the year 2001!

THE SYLLABUSES OFFERED BY EACH EXAMINING GROUP

▶ **London EDEXCEL Foundation**

Formerly the University of London Examinations and Assessment Council.
London offers the following syllabuses from 1998:

Science (Combined) Double Award 1524 [Single Award 1527]
Science (Modular) Double Award 1531 [Single Award 1538]

Scheme of Assessment Science (Combined) 1524 and 1527

Table 2.1

Tier	Type of assessment	Component number and AT	Duration **D** Double **S** Single	Weighting
Foundation	Written	01 (Sc 2)	**D** 1 hr 30 mins **S** 1 hr	25%
Foundation	Written	02 (Sc 3)	**D** 1 hr 30 mins **S** 1 hr	25%
Foundation	Written	03 (Sc 4)	**D** 1 hr 30 mins **S** 1 hr	25%
Higher	Written	04 (Sc 2)	**D** 1 hr 30 mins **S** 1 hr	25%
Higher	Written	05 (Sc 3)	**D** 1 hr 30 mins **S** 1 hr	25%
Higher	Written	06 (Sc 4)	**D** 1 hr 30 mins **S** 1 hr	25%
Both	Coursework	07 (Sc 1)	–	25%

Syllabus content Science (Combined) 1524 and 1527

Table 2.2 S: Single award (only part of some topics studied for single award).

Life Processes and Living Things (Sc 2)	Materials and their Properties (Sc 3)	Physical Processes (Sc 4)
Life Processes **S**	Particles and Atomic Structure **S**	Mains Electricity **S**
Cell Activity **S**	Bonding **S**	Energy and Potential
Nutrition in Humans **S**	Representing Reactions **S**	Difference in Circuits **S**
Circulation **S**	The Reactivity Series of Metals **S**	Electric Charge
Breathing and Respiration	The Periodic Table **S**	Magnets and Electromagnetism
Nervous Co-ordination **S**	The Chemistry of some	Electromagnetic Induction **S**
Hormonal Co-ordination **S**	Elements and their	Movement and Position **S**
Maintaining the Internal	Compounds **S**	Forces and Movement **S**
Environment **S**	Extraction and Uses of Metals	Forces and Shape **S**
Nutrition in Green Plants	Useful Products from Crude	Wave Properties **S**
Water Relations and Transport	Oil **S**	The Electromagnetic Spectrum **S**
Control of Growth in Plants	Rates of Reaction **S**	Light **S**
Variation **S**	Energy Changes **S**	Sound
Inheritance **S**	Reversible Reactions	The Solar System **S**
Evolution **S**	Ammonia and Fertilisers	The Rest of the Universe **S**
Humans and the Environment **S**	The Earth and its Atmosphere	Energy Transfer **S**
Ecosystems		Work and Power
		Energy Resources and Electricity
		Generation **S**
		Radioactivity **S**

Syllabus content for Modular Double Award (1531) and Single Award (S) (1538).

Table 2.3

Module number	Module title
1	Body Maintenance **S**
2	Inheritance and Survival **S**
3	Understanding Ecosystems
4	Chemicals and the Earth
5	Materials Chemistry
6	Chemical Patterns **S**
7	Science in Sport
8	Electricity and Waves in the Home **S**
9	Applications of Sound and Electricity
10	Energy and Gravitation **S**

Scheme of Assessment Modular Double Award 1531 and Single Award 1538

These syllabuses are assessed by module tests (25%), final written papers (50%) and coursework (25%). There are ten module tests for Double Award and five for Single Award.

▶ **Module tests:** (20 mins) 20 multiple choice questions.
▶ **Final Written papers: (S) single award (D) double award**
  Foundation Tier (1 hr 30 mins):
  1F tests modules 1, 2, 6, 8, 10 (S, D); **2F** tests modules 3, 4, 5, 7, 9 (D).
  Higher Tier (2 hours):
  1H tests modules 1, 2, 6, 8, 10 (S, D); **2H** tests modules 3, 4, 5, 7, 9 (D).

▶ **Midland Examining Group (MEG)**

Midland Examining Group offers the following syllabuses from 1998:

Science Syllabus A (Co-ordinated) Double Award 1794 [Single Award 1795]
Science Syllabus B (Suffolk) Double Award 1777 [Single Award 1778]
Science Syllabus C (Salters) Double Award 1774 [Single Award 1775]

Scheme of Assessment Syllabus A (Co-ordinated) 1794 and 1795

The Scheme of Assessment may vary slightly between syllabuses but Table 2.4 below the format used for Science **Syllabus A (Co-ordinated) Science** 1794 and 1795.

Table 2.4

Tier	Type of assessment	Component number and AT	Duration **D** double **S** single	Weighting
Foundation	Written	1 (Sc 2)	**D** 1 hr 30 mins **S** 45 mins	25%
Foundation	Written	3 (Sc 3)	**D** 1 hr 30 mins **S** 45 mins	25%
Foundation	Written	5 (Sc 4)	**D** 1 hr 30 mins **S** 45 mins	25%
Higher	Written	2 (Sc 2)	**D** 1 hr 45 mins **S** 1 hr	25%
Higher	Written	4 (Sc 3)	**D** 1 hr 45 mins **S** 1 hr	25%
Higher	Written	6 (Sc 4)	**D** 1 hr 45 mins **S** 1 hr	25%
Both	Coursework	7 (Sc 1)	–	25%

Syllabus content Syllabus A (Co-ordinated) 1794 and 1795

For **Syllabus A (Co-ordinated) Science** the content is arranged in 28 teaching blocks for Double Science and in 17 teaching blocks for Single Science (S), as shown in Table 2.5.

Table 2.5

Life Processes and Living Things (Sc 2)	Materials and their Properties (Sc 3)	Physical Processes (Sc 4)
Introducing Biological Principle **S**	Introducing Chemistry **S**	Electric Circuits **S**
Digestion **S**	Metals and the Reactivity Series	Energy Transfer **S**
Respiration	Periodic Table and Atomic Structure **S**	Forces S
Breathing	Geological Changes	Wave Properties **S**
Circulation and Transport **S**	Rates of Reaction **S**	Using Waves **S**
Communication and Control **S**	Structure, Bonding and the Mole	Radioactivity **S**
Energy Flow and Cycling of Elements	Oil **S**	The Earth and Universe **S**
Inheritance and Evolution **S**	Earth Cycles	Using Electricity **S**
Living Things and their Environment **S**	Equilibria and Industrial Processes	Electromagnetism

NEAB offers the following syllabuses from 1998:
Science (Co-ordinated) Double Award 1201 [Single Award 1203]
Science (Modular) Double Award 1206 [Single Award 1208]

Scheme of Assessment Science (Co-ordinated) 1201 and 1203

Table 2.6

Tier	Type of assessment	Component number and AT	Duration **D** Double **S** Single	Weighting
Foundation	Written	1F (Sc 2)	**D** 1 hr 30 mins **S** 1 hr	25%
Foundation	Written	2F (Sc 3)	**D** 1 hr 30 mins **S** 1 hr	25%
Foundation	Written	3F (Sc 4)	**D** 1 hr 30 mins **S** 1 hr	25%
Higher	Written	1H (Sc 2)	**D** 1 hr 30 mins **S** 1 hr	25%
Higher	Written	2H (Sc 3)	**D** 1 hr 30 mins **S** 1 hr	25%
Higher	Written	3H (Sc 4)	**D** 1 hr 30 mins **S** 1 hr	25%
Both	Coursework	7 (Sc 1)	–	25%

Syllabus content Science (Co-ordinated) Double Award 1201

Life Processes and Living Things

Table 2.7

Theme	Topic
1. Life Processes and Cell Activity	1.1 Basic Principles 1.2 Transport across Boundaries 1.3 Cell Division
2. Humans as Organisms	2.1 Nutrition 2.2 Circulation 2.3 Breathing 2.4 Respiration 2.5 Nervous System 2.6 Hormones 2.7 Homeostasis 2.8 Disease 2.9 Drugs
3. Green Plants as Organisms	3.1 Plant Nutrition 3.2 Plant Hormones 3.3 Transport and Water Relations
4. Variation, Inheritance and Evolution	4.1 Variation 4.2 Genetics and DNA 4.3 Controlling Inheritance 4.4 Evolution
5. Living Things in their Environment	5.1 Adaptation and Competition 5.2 Human Impact on the Environment 5.3 Energy and Nutrient Transfer 5.4 Nutrient Cycles
Materials and their Properties	
6. Classifying Materials	6.1 States of Matter 6.2 Atomic Structure 6.3 Bonding

Table 2.7 Continued

Theme	Topic
7. Changing materials	7.1 Useful products from Oil 7.2 Useful products from Metal Ores 7.3 Useful products from Rocks 7.4 Useful products from Air 7.5 Representing Reactions 7.6 Quantitative Chemistry 7.7 Changes to the Atmosphere 7.8 Rock Types 7.9 Tectonics
8. Patterns of Behaviour	8.1 The Periodic Table 8.2 Acids and Alkalis 8.3 Metals and Non-Metals 8.4 Compounds of Alkali Metals and Halogens 8.5 Rates of Reactions 8.6 Reactions involving Enzymes 8.7 Reversible Reactions 8.8 Energy Transfer in Reactions
Physical Processes	
9. Electricity and Magnetism	9.1 Potential Difference in Circuits 9.2 Energy in Circuits 9.3 Mains Electricity 9.4 The Cost of Using Electrical Appliances 9.5 Electric Charge 9.6 Electromagnetic Forces 9.8 Electromagnetic Induction
10. Forces and Motion	10.1 Representing and Measuring Motion 10.2 Forces and Acceleration 10.3 Frictional Forces and Non-Uniform Motion 10.4 Force and Pressure on Solids, Liquids and Gases
11. Waves	11.1 Characteristics of Waves 11.2 The Electromagnetic Spectrum 11.3 Sound and Ultrasound 11.4 Seismic Waves
12. The Earth and Beyond	12.1 The Solar System 12.2 The Universe
13. Energy Resources and Energy Transfer	13.1 Thermal Energy Transfer 13.2 Efficiency 13.3 Energy Resources 13.4 Work, Power and Energy
14. Radioactivity	14.1 Types, Properties and Uses of Radioactivity 14.2 Atomic Structure and Nuclear Fission

Scheme of Assessment Modular Double Award (1206) and Single Award (1208)

These syllabuses are assessed by **module tests** (25%), final written papers (50%) and **coursework** (25%). Half of the modules are assessed by module tests and half by terminal examination. This means that in Double Science there are **twelve modules** (1–12) to be followed but only **six module tests**. In Single Science there are **six modules** (13–18) to be followed and **three module tests**. The tests consist of compulsory objective questions and can be taken at either tier.

For Double Award the six module tests are:

1. Humans as Organisms
2. Maintenance of Life
5. Metals
6. Earth materials

9. Energy
10. Electricity

For Single Award the three module tests are:

13. Life and Living Processes
15. Materials from Oil and Ores
17. Energy and Electricity

For **Double Award** there are **two** terminal written papers for each Tier, each lasting 1 hour 30 mins. Paper 1 (F and H) will assess:

4. Inheritance and Selection
8. Structures and Bonding
12. Waves and Radiation

Paper 2 (F and H) will assess:

3. Environment
7. Patterns of Chemical Change
11. Forces

For **Single Award** there is **one** terminal paper for each Tier, lasting 1 hour 30 mins. The paper will assess:

14. Environment, Inheritance and Selection
16. Patterns, Structures and Bonding
18. Forces, Waves and Radiation

▶ **Northern Ireland Council for Curriculum, Examinations and Assessment (NICCEA)**

NICCEA offers the following syllabuses from 1998:

The Sciences: Double Award (Modular and Non-Modular)
The Sciences: Single Award (Modular and Non-Modular)

These syllabuses are designed to meet the requirements of the Northern Ireland Regulations and the Northern Ireland Programme of Study for Key Stage 4 Science.

Scheme of Assessment Science Non-Modular

The Scheme of Assessment follows a similar pattern to those of the other Examining Groups. The table (Table 2.8) shows the format used for Non-Modular Double and Single Award.

For the double award, the written papers have two sections, A and B. Section A consists of 12–15 short answer questions and section B has 3–4 structured questions There is a similar format for the single award.

Table 2.8

Tier	Type of assessment	Component number and AT	Duration D Double S Single	Weighting
Foundation	written	1 (Sc 2)	**D** 1 hr 30 mins **S** 1 hr	25%
Foundation	written	2 (Sc 3)	**D** 1 hr 30 mins **S** 1 hr	25%
Foundation	written	3 (Sc 4)	**D** 1 hr 30 mins **S** 1 hr	25%
Higher	written	1 (Sc 2)	**D** 1 hr 45 mins **S** 1 hr 30 mins	25%
Higher	written	2 (Sc 3)	**D** 1 hr 45 mins **S** 1 hr 30 mins	25%
Higher	written	3 (Sc 4)	**D** 1 hr 45 mins **S** 1 hr 30 mins	25%
Both	coursework	(Sc 1)	–	25%

Syllabus content for Double Award Non-Modular and Modular

- ▶ Sc 2: Living Organisms and Life Processes (Module A)
  The Living World – Environment and Genetics
- ▶ Sc 3: Using Materials and Understanding Reactions (Module B)
  Patterns, Problems and Processes
  Metals, Non-metals and their Compounds
  Organic Chemistry
  Science at Work
- ▶ Sc 4: Forces and Energy (Module C)
  Waves, Light and Sound
  Electricity and Magnetism
  Earth in Space

Scheme of Assessment Modular Double Award

- ▶ Module tests: 25%
- ▶ Terminal Examination: 50%
- ▶ Coursework: 25%

There are **three module tests** of 45 minutes each consisting of 12–15 short answer questions, based on modules A, B and C. A total of 75% of the marks on the **final written papers** are allocated to the topics not tested on the module tests. At the **Foundation** level the final written papers last 1 hour and have 4 structured questions and the **Higher** level papers last 1 hour 30 minutes and have 5–6 structured questions.

Single Award Modular

For the Modular Single Award, based on Science at Work, the **module tests** are weighted at **50%**, and the **terminal examination** at **25%**. There are six module tests each of 45 minutes, consisting of six short answer questions, based on the following modules:

- ▶ Staying Alive;
- ▶ Maintaining the Species;
- ▶ Materials;
- ▶ Chemical Reaction;
- ▶ Energy in Space;
- ▶ Light, Force and Energy.

▶ Southern Examining Group (SEG)

SEG offers the following syllabuses from 1998 onwards:

Science: Double Award 2610 [Single Award 2600]
Science: Modular Double Award 2630 [Single Award 2620]

Scheme of Assessment Science 2610 and 2600

The topics match the standard format of the National Curriculum and the Scheme of Assessment is shown in Table 2.9.

Syllabus content Science 2610 and 2600

The content of this syllabus is shown in Tables 2.10, 2.11 and 2.12, where the teaching blocks for Single Science are indicated by **S**.

Table 2.9

Tier	Type of assessment	Component number and AT	Duration **D** double **S** single	Weighting
Foundation	Written	2 (Sc 2)	**D** 1 hr 30 mins **S** 1 hr	25%
Foundation	Written	3 (Sc 3)	**D** 1 hr 30 mins **S** 1 hr	25%
Foundation	Written	4 (Sc 4)	**D** 1 hr 30 mins **S** 1 hr	25%
Higher	Written	5 (Sc 2)	**D** 1 hr 30 mins **S** 1 hr	25%
Higher	Written	6 (Sc 3)	**D** 1 hr 30 mins **S** 1 hr	25%
Higher	Written	7 (Sc 4)	**D** 1 hr 30 mins **S** 1 hr	25%
Both	Coursework	1 (Sc 1)	–	25%

Table 2.10 Sc2 Life Processes and Living Things

Theme	Topic
1. Life Processes and Cell Activity	1.1 Life processes **S** 1.2 Cells **S**
2. Humans as Organisms	2.1 Nutrition **S** 2.2 Circulation **S** 2.3 Breathing 2.4 Respiration 2.5 Nervous system **S** 2.6 Health **S** 2.7 Hormones **S** 2.8 Homeostasis **S**
3. Green Plants as Organisms	3.1 Photosynthesis 3.2 Water and mineral salts 3.3 Plant hormones
4. Variation, Inheritance and Evolution	4.1 Growth **S** 4.2 Reproduction **S** 4.3 Inheritance **S** 4.4 Evolution **S**
5. Living Things in their Environment	5.1 Adaptation and competition **S** 5.2 Energy flows and cycles in ecosystems 5.3 Humans and the environment **S**

Table 2.11 Sc3 Materials and their Properties

Theme	Topic
1. Classifying Materials	1.1 Solids, liquids and gases **S** 1.2 Elements, compounds and mixtures **S** 1.3 Atomic structure and isotopes **S** 1.4 Bonding
2. Changing Materials	2.1 Chemical reactions **S** 2.2 Quantitative chemistry 2.3 Changes to the atmosphere 2.4 Useful products from air 2.5 Geological changes 2.6 Useful products from metal ores and rocks 2.7 Useful products from oil **S**
3. Patterns of Behaviour	3.1 The reactivity series **S** 3.2 Acids and bases **S** 3.3 The Periodic Table **S** (including transition elements) 3.4 Rates of reaction **S** 3.5 Enzyme reactions 3.6 Reversible reactions 3.7 Energy transfer in reactions **S**

Theme	Topic
1. Electricity and Magnetism	1.1 Electric charge 1.2 Energy in circuits **S** 1.3 Power 1.4 Electromagnetic forces 1.5 Electromagnetic induction **S** 1.6 Transformers 1.7 Mains electricity **S**
2. Forces and Motion	2.1 Speed and velocity **S** 2.2 Force and acceleration 2.3 Force and non-uniform motion **S** 2.4 Force and pressure on solids **S**, liquids and gases
3. Waves	3.1 Characteristics of waves **S** 3.2 Light **S** 3.3 The electromagnetic spectrum **S** 3.4 Sound
4. The Earth and Beyond	4.1 The solar system **S** 4.2 The wider Universe **S** 4.3 Evolution of the Universe and stars
5. Energy Resources and Energy Transfer	5.1 Energy resources **S** 5.2 Energy transfers **S** 5.3 Work, power and energy
6. Radioactivity	6.1 Characteristics and detection **S** 6.2 Effects and uses **S**

Scheme of Assessment Modular Single Award 2620 and Double Award 2630

These syllabuses are assessed by **module tests** (25%), final **written papers** (50%) and **coursework** (25%).

There are **nine module tests** for Double Science and **five module tests** for Single Science as shown in Table 2.13. The tests consist of multiple choice questions and last for 20 minutes each. They can be taken at either tier and in any order of modules, on dates set by the Examining Group.

For **Double Award** there are **two** terminal written papers for each Tier:

▶ *Foundation Tier*: Papers 2 and 3 last 1 hour 30 minutes.
▶ *Higher Tier*: Papers 4 and 5 last 2 hours.
▶ Papers 2 and 4 test modules 1–5; Papers 3 and 5 test modules 6–9.

For **Single Award** there is **one** terminal written paper, testing modules 1–5, for each Tier:

▶ *Foundation Tier*: Paper 2 (same as paper 2 Double Award) 1 hour 30 minutes.
▶ *Higher Tier*: Paper 3 (same as paper 4 Double Award) 2 hours.

Syllabus content Modular Science 2620 and 2630 (S)

Module number	Module title	Attainment target
1	Maintenance of Life **S**	Sc 2
2	Maintenance of the Species **S**	Sc 2
3	Structure and Changes **S**	Sc 3
4	Force and Transfers **S**	Sc 4
5	Energy Sources **S**	Sc 3 & 4
6	Vital Exchanges	Sc 2
7	Bonding and Materials	Sc 3
8	Using Power	Sc 4
9	Universal Changes	Sc 3 & 4

▶ **Welsh Joint Education Committee (WJEC)**

WJEC offers the following syllabuses from 1998:

Science Double Award, Single Award
Science Modular Double Award, Single Award

Scheme of Assessment Science Double Award, Single Award

Table 2.14

Tier	Type of assessment	Component number and AT	Duration **D** double **S** single	Weighting
Foundation	written	1 (Sc 2)	**D** 1 hr 20 mins **S** 45 mins	25%
Foundation	written	2 (Sc 3)	**D** 1 hr 20 mins **S** 45 mins	25%
Foundation	written	3 (Sc 4)	**D** 1 hr 20 mins **S** 45 mins	25%
Higher	written	4 (Sc 2)	**D** 1 hr 40 mins **S** 45 mins	25%
Higher	written	5 (Sc 3)	**D** 1 hr 40 mins **S** 45 mins	25%
Higher	written	6 (Sc 4)	**D** 1 hr 40 mins **S** 45 mins	25%
Both	coursework	–	–	25%

The question papers are divided into two sections, A and B, with 30 marks for each section. Section B of the Foundation paper is the same as section A of the Higher Tier paper.

WJEC Syllabus content Science Double Award

Table 2.15

Biology	Chemistry	Physics
B1 Basic organisation of animals and plants	C1 Particles and atomic structure	P1 Energy and potential difference in circuits
B2 Trapping and transfer of energy	C2 Elements and the periodic table	P2 Mains electricity
B3 Release of energy by living organisms	C3 Compounds	P3 Electric charge
B4 Transfer of materials in living organisms	C4 Bonding and Structure	P4 Electromagnetic forces
B5 Transfer of information	C5 Rates of reaction	P5 Electromagnetic induction
B6 Genetics	C6 Energetics	P6 Force and acceleration
B7 Variation and Evolution	C7 Chemical calculations	P7 Force and non-uniform motion
B8 The impact of human activity on the environment	C8 The extraction of metals	P8 Force and pressure on solids, liquids and gases
B9 Maintenance of a healthy steady state	C9 Rocks	P9 The solar system and the wider universe
	C10 The air	P10 Characteristics of waves
	C11 Crude oil	P11 The electromagnetic spectrum
		P12 Sound and ultrasound
		P13 Seismic waves
		P14 Energy transfer
		P15 Work, power and energy
		P16 Radioactivity

WJEC Syllabus content Modular Double Award, Single Award

There are thirteen modules listed below in Table 2.16, nine modules which are common modules (CM) to Single and Double Award candidates. The remaining four (DM) modules are to be followed by candidates entered for Double Award only.

Table 2.16

Module	Title	Related AT (Sc)
CM1	Life Processes	2
CM2	Maintenance of Health	2
CM3	Genetics, Evolution and the Environment	2
CM4	Chemical Patterns	3
CM5	Chemical Reactions	3
CM6	Energy Resources: Uses and Implications	3
CM7	Forces and Motion	4
CM8	Basic Electricity	4
CM9	Energy Transfer	4
DM10	Planet Earth	2, 3, 4
DM11	Exchange Mechanisms in Plants and Animals	2
DM12	Chemical Bonding, Quantitative and Industrial Chemistry	3
DM13	Physics in Action	4

WJEC Scheme of Assessment Modular Double Award Single Award

There are seven module tests for double award common modules CM 1, 2, 4, 5, 7, 8 and Double Module DM 10; and six module tests for Single Award, common modules CM 1, 2, 4, 5, 7, 8. Each test consists of structured questions and lasts for 30 minutes.

Terminal examination 50%
In Science: Double Award the terminal examination will consist of two papers for each of the two tiers. Paper 1 will be common to that of the Single Award examination.

Table 2.17

Paper	Tier	Duration	Coverage	Marks per paper	Weighting
1	F	$1\frac{1}{2}$ hours	Modules CM 3, 6, 9	90	20%
	H	2 hours		120	
2	F	$1\frac{1}{2}$ hours	Modules 11, 12, 13	120	30%
	H	2 hours		150	

In Science: Single Award the terminal examination will consist of one paper for each tier.

Table 2.18

Tier	Duration	Coverage	Marks per paper	Weighting
F	$1\frac{1}{2}$ hours	Modules CM 3, 6, 9	90	50%
H	2 hours		120	

▶ **Addresses of the examination boards**

LONDON
EDEXCEL Foundation (formerly University of London Examinations and Assessment Council)
Stewart House, 32 Russell Square, London WC1B 5DN
Tel: 0171 331 4000
Fax: 0171 631 3369

Order a publications catalogue from:

EDEXCEL Foundation Publications
River Park, Billet Lane, Berkhamsted, Herts HP4 1EL
Tel: 01442 876701
Fax: 01442 876809

MEG
Midland Examining Group
Syndicate Buildings, 1 Hills Road, Cambridge CB1 2EU
Tel: 01223 553311
Fax: 01223 460278

NEAB
Northern Examinations and Assessment Board
Devas Street, Manchester M15 6EX
Tel: 0161 953 1180
Fax: 0161 273 7572

Order a publications catalogue from:

NEAB Publications
12 Harter Street, Manchester M1 6HL
Tel: 0161 953 1170
Fax: 0161 953 1177

NICCEA
Northern Ireland Council for Curriculum, Examinations and Assessment
29 Clarendon Road, Belfast BT1 3BG
Tel: 01232 261200
Fax: 01232 261234

SEG
Southern Examining Group
Stag Hill House, Guildford, Surrey GU2 5XJ
Tel: 01483 506505
Fax: 01483 300152

WJEC
Welsh Joint Education Committee
245 Western Road, Cardiff CF5 2YX
Tel: 01222 561231
Fax: 01222 571234

IGCSE
International General Certificate of Education
University of Cambridge Local Examinations Syndicate
1 Hills Road, Cambridge CB1 2EU
Tel: 01223 553311
Fax: 01223 460278

When contacting the Examination Groups you will need to ask for the Publications Department and request an order form or publications catalogue to be sent to you. On the order form indicate exactly which syllabus you require and be prepared to send a cheque or postal order with your order.

▶ **Appendix: Details of the four study programmes, Sc1–Sc4**

Experimental and Investigative Science (Sc1)

Contexts derived from **Life Processes and Living Things, Materials and their Properties** and **Physical Processes** should be used to teach pupils about experimental and investigative methods. On some occasions, the whole process of investigating an idea should be carried out by pupils themselves.

References to these sections of the National Curriculum are given in square brackets throughout the text in the following chapters.

1. Planning experimental procedures
Pupils should be taught:

(a) to use scientific knowledge and understanding, drawing on secondary sources where appropriate, to turn ideas suggested to them, and their own ideas, into a form that can be investigated;
(b) to carry out preliminary work where this helps to clarify what they have to do;
(c) to make predictions where it is appropriate to do so;
(d) to consider the key factors in contexts involving a number of factors;
(e) to plan how to vary or control key variables;
(f) to consider the number and range of observations or measurements to be made;
(g) to recognise contexts, e.g. *fieldwork*, where variables cannot readily be controlled and to make judgements about the amount of evidence needed in these contexts;
(h) to select apparatus, equipment and techniques, taking account of safety requirements.

2. Obtaining evidence
Pupils should be taught:

(a) to use a range of apparatus and equipment safely and with skill;
(b) to make observations and measurements to a degree of precision appropriate to the context;
(c) to make sufficient relevant observations and measurements for reliable evidence;
(d) to consider uncertainties in measurements and observations;
(e) to repeat measurements and observations when appropriate;
(f) to record evidence clearly and appropriately as they carry out the work.

3. Analysing evidence and drawing conclusions
Pupils should be taught:

(a) to present qualitative and quantitative data clearly;
(b) to present data as graphs, using lines of best fit where appropriate;
(c) to identify trends or patterns in results;
(d) to use graphs to identify relationships between variables;
(e) to present numerical results to an appropriate degree of accuracy;
(f) to check that conclusions drawn are consistent with the evidence;
(g) to explain how results support or undermine the original prediction when one has been made;
(h) to try to explain conclusions in the light of their knowledge and understanding of science.

4. Evaluating evidence
Pupils should be taught:

(a) to consider whether the evidence collected is sufficient to enable firm conclusions to be drawn;
(b) to consider reasons for anomalous results and to reject such results where appropriate;
(c) to consider the reliability of results in terms of the uncertainty of measurements and observations;
(d) to propose improvements to the methods that have been used;
(e) to propose further investigation to test their conclusions.

Life Processes and Living Things (Sc2)

Work on the ways in which animals and plants function as organisms should be related to cell structure and the underlying chemical reactions. Relationships between inheritance, variation and evolution should be considered. Work on energy transfer within an ecosystem should be related to pupils' knowledge and understanding of energy transfer in other systems.

1. Life processes and cell activity
Pupils should be taught:

(a) the life processes common to plants and animals;
(b) that organ systems are adapted for their roles in life processes;
(c) that plant and animal cells have some similarities in structure;
(d) how substances enter and leave cells through the cell membrane by diffusion, osmosis and active transport;
(e) that the nucleus contains chromosomes that carry the genes;
(f) how cells divide by mitosis so that growth takes place, and by meiosis to produce gametes.

2. Humans as organisms
Pupils should be taught:

Nutrition	(a)	the structure of the human digestive system;
	(b)	the processes involved in digestion, including the roles of enzymes, stomach acid and bile;
Circulation	(c)	the structure of the human circulatory system, including the composition and functions of blood;
Breathing	(d)	the structure of the thorax;
	(e)	how breathing, including ventilation of the lungs, takes place;
Respiration	(f)	that respiration may be either aerobic or anaerobic, depending on the availability of oxygen;
	(g)	that an 'oxygen debt' may occur in muscles during vigorous exercise;
Nervous system	(h)	the pathway taken by impulses in response to a variety of stimuli, including touch, taste, smell, light, sound and balance;
	(i)	how the reflex arc, which involves a nerve impulse carried via neurones and across synapses, makes possible rapid response to a stimulus;
	(j)	the structure of the eye and how it functions in response to light;
Hormones	(k)	the way in which hormonal control occurs, including the effects of insulin and sex hormones;
	(l)	some medical uses of hormones, including the control and promotion of fertility and the treatment of diabetes;
Homeostasis	(m)	the importance of maintaining a constant internal environment;
	(n)	how waste products of body functions are removed by the lungs and kidneys;
	(o)	how the kidneys regulate the water content of the body;
	(p)	how humans maintain a constant body temperature;
Health	(q)	the defence mechanisms of the body, including the role of the skin, blood and mucous membranes of the respiratory tract;
	(r)	the effects of solvents, alcohol, tobacco and other drugs on body functions.

3. Green plants as organisms
Pupils should be taught:

Nutrition	(a)	the reactants in, and products of, photosynthesis;
	(b)	that the rate of photosynthesis may be limited by light intensity, carbon dioxide concentration or temperature;
	(c)	how the products of photosynthesis are utilised by the plant;
	(d)	the importance to healthy plant growth of the uptake and utilisation of mineral salts;
Hormones	(e)	the hormonal control of plant growth and development, including commercial applications;
Transport and water relations	(f)	how plants take up water and transpire;
	(g)	the importance of water in the support of plant tissues;
	(h)	that substances required for growth and reproduction are transported within plants.

4. Variation, inheritance and evolution
Pupils should be taught:

Variation	(a)	how variation may arise from both genetic and environmental causes;
	(b)	that sexual reproduction is a source of genetic variation, while asexual reproduction produces clones;
	(c)	that mutation is a source of genetic variation and has a number of causes;
Inheritance	(d)	how gender is determined in humans;
	(e)	the mechanism of monohybrid inheritance where there are dominant and recessive alleles;
	(f)	that some diseases can be inherited;
	(g)	that the gene is a section of DNA;
	(h)	the basic principles of cloning, selective breeding and genetic engineering;
Evolution	(i)	the fossil record as evidence for evolution;
	(j)	how variation and selection may lead to evolution or to extinction.

5. Living things in their environment
Pupils should be taught:

Adaptation and competition	(a)	how the distribution and relative abundance of organisms in a habitat can be explained in terms of adaptation, competition and predation;
	(b)	how the impact of human activity on the environment is related to population size, economic factors and industrial requirements;
Energy and nutrient transfer	(c)	how food chains may be described quantitatively using pyramids of numbers and pyramids of biomass;
	(d)	how energy is transferred through an ecosystem;
	(e)	the role of microbes and other organisms in the decomposition of organic materials and in the cycling of carbon and nitrogen;
	(f)	how food production can be managed to improve the efficiency of energy transfer.

Materials and their Properties (Sc3)

Work on the properties of materials should be related to pupils' knowledge of structure and bonding. Work on chemical reactions should emphasise patterns and predictions made from these patterns, including how knowledge about chemical reactions is applied when new substances are manufactured.

1. Classifying materials
Pupils should be taught:

Atomic structure	(a)	that solids, liquids and gases are all composed of particles;
	(b)	that atoms consist of nuclei and electrons;
	(c)	the charges and relative masses of protons, neutrons and electrons;
	(d)	about mass number, atomic number and isotopes;
	(e)	about a model of the way electrons are arranged in atoms;
	(f)	that the reactions of elements depend upon the arrangement of electrons in their atoms;
Bonding	(g)	that new substances are formed when atoms combine;
	(h)	that chemical bonding can be explained in terms of the transfer or sharing of electrons;
	(i)	how ions are formed when atoms gain or lose electrons;
	(j)	that ionic lattices are held together by the attraction between oppositely charged ions;
	(k)	that covalent bonds are formed when atoms share electrons;
	(i)	that substances with covalent bonds may form simple molecular structures or giant structures;
	(m)	the physical properties of some substances with giant structures and some with simple molecular structures.

2. Changing materials

Pupils should be taught:

Useful products from oil	(a)	how oil deposits are formed;
	(b)	that crude oil is a mixture of substances, most of which are hydrocarbons, which can be separated by fractional distillation;
	(c)	the use as fuels of some of the products from crude oil distillation;
	(d)	the products of burning hydrocarbons;
	(e)	that there are different groups of hydrocarbons;
	(f)	that alkanes are saturated hydrocarbons, and alkenes are unsaturated hydrocarbons containing one double covalent bond between carbon atoms;
	(g)	that hydrocarbon molecules can be cracked to form smaller molecules, including alkenes;
	(h)	that addition polymers can be made from alkenes formed during cracking;
	(i)	some uses of addition polymers;
Useful products from metal ores and rocks	(j)	that metal ores are found in the Earth;
	(k)	that the way in which a particular metal is extracted from its ores is related to its reactivity;
	(l)	an example of how a reactive metal can be extracted by electrolysis;
	(m)	an example of how a less reactive metal can be extracted by reduction with carbon or carbon monoxide;
	(n)	an example of how a metal can be purified by electrolysis;
	(o)	that a variety of useful substances can be made from rocks and minerals;
Useful products from air	(p)	how nitrogen can be converted to ammonia in industry;
	(q)	how nitrogenous fertilisers are manufactured, and their effects on plant growth and the environment;
Representing reactions	(r)	to represent chemical reactions by word equations;
	(s)	to represent reactions, including electrolytic reactions, by balanced equations using chemical symbols;
Quantitative chemistry	(t)	to use chemical equations to predict reacting quantities;
	(u)	to determine the formulae of simple compounds from reacting masses;
Changes to the atmosphere	(v)	how the atmosphere and oceans evolved to their present composition;
	(w)	how the carbon cycle helps to maintain atmospheric composition;
Geological changes	(x)	how igneous rocks are formed by the cooling of magma, sedimentary rocks by the deposition and consolidation of sediments, and metamorphic rocks by the action of heat and pressure on existing rocks;
	(y)	how the sequence of, and evidence for, these processes is obtained from the rock record;
	(z)	how plate tectonic processes are involved in the formation, deformation and recycling of rocks.

3. Patterns of behaviour

Pupils should be taught:

The Periodic Table	(a)	that the Periodic Table shows all elements, arranged in order of ascending atomic number;
	(b)	the connection between the arrangement of outer electrons and the position of an element in the Periodic Table;
	(c)	that elements in the same group of the Periodic Table have similar properties;
	(d)	that there is a gradual change in the properties of the elements from the top to the bottom of a group;
	(e)	the properties and uses of the noble gases;
	(f)	the properties and reactions of the alkali metals;
	(g)	the properties, reactions and uses of simple compounds of the alkali metals;
	(h)	the properties, reactions and uses of the halogens;
	(i)	the properties, reactions and uses of simple compounds of the halogens;

	(j)	similarities between transition metals and characteristic properties of their compounds;
	(k)	some uses of transition metals;
Rates of reactions	(l)	that there is great variation in the rates at which different reactions take place;
	(m)	how the rates of reactions can be altered by varying temperature or concentration, or by changing the surface area of a solid reactant, or by adding a catalyst;
	(n)	that reactions can occur when particles collide;
	(o)	that the rates of many reactions can be increased by increasing the frequency or energy of collisions between particles;
Reactions involving enzymes	(p)	how the rates of enzyme-catalysed reactions vary with temperature;
	(q)	the use of enzymes in the baking, brewing and dairy industries;
Reversible reactions	(r)	that some reactions are reversible;
	(s)	how the yield of products from reversible reactions depends on the conditions;
	(t)	that some manufacturing processes are based on reversible reactions;
Energy transfer in reactions	(u)	that changes of temperature often accompany reactions;
	(v)	that reactions can be exothermic or endothermic;
	(w)	that making and breaking chemical bonds in chemical reactions involves energy transfers.

Physical Processes (Sc4)

The links between electricity and magnetism, between forces and motion and between light, sound and other waves, and the relationship of energy to these areas, should be made clear. Work on the solar system and the wider Universe should relate to pupils' knowledge of physical processes.

1. Electricity and magnetism
Pupils should be taught:

Energy and potential difference in circuits	(a)	how to measure current in series and parallel circuits;
	(b)	that energy is transferred from batteries and other sources to other components in electrical circuits;
	(c)	that resistors are heated when charge flows through them;
	(d)	the qualitative effect of changing resistance on the current in a circuit;
	(e)	how to make simple measurements of voltage;
	(f)	the quantitative relationship between resistance, voltage and current;
	(g)	how current varies with voltage in a range of devices, including resistors, filament bulbs, diodes, light-dependent resistors (LDRs) and thermistors;
	(h)	that voltage is the energy transferred per unit charge;
	(i)	the quantitative relationship between power, voltage and current;
Mains electricity	(j)	the difference between direct current (d.c.) and alternating current (a.c.);
	(k)	the functions of the live, neutral and earth wires in the domestic mains supply, and the use of insulation, earthing, fuses and circuit breakers to protect users of electrical equipment;
	(l)	that electrical heating is used in a variety of ways in domestic contexts;
	(m)	how measurements of energy transferred are used to calculate the costs of using common domestic appliances;
Electric charge	(n)	about common electrostatic phenomena, in terms of the movement of electrons;
	(o)	the dangers and uses of electrostatic charges generated in everyday situations;
	(p)	the quantitative relationship between steady current, charge and time;
	(q)	about electric current as the flow of free electrons in metals or of ions during electrolysis;

Electromagnetic force	(r)	that like magnetic poles repel and unlike magnetic poles attract;
	(s)	that a force is exerted on a current-carrying wire in a magnetic field and the application of this effect in simple electric motors;
Electromagnetic induction	(t)	that a voltage is induced when a conductor cuts magnetic field lines and when the magnetic field through a coil changes;
	(u)	how simple a.c. generators and transformers work;
	(v)	the quantitative relationship between the voltages across the coils in a transformer and the numbers of turns in them;
	(w)	how electricity is generated and transmitted.

2. Forces and motion
Pupils should be taught:

Force and acceleration	(a)	how distance, time and speed can be determined and represented graphically;
	(b)	about factors affecting vehicle stopping distances;
	(c)	the difference between speed and velocity;
	(d)	about acceleration as change in velocity per unit time;
	(e)	that balanced forces do not alter the velocity of a moving object;
	(f)	the quantitative relationship between force, mass and acceleration;
	(g)	that when two bodies interact, the forces they exert on each other are equal and opposite;
Force and non-uniform motion	(h)	the forces acting on falling objects;
	(i)	why falling objects may reach a terminal velocity;
Force and pressure on solids, liquids and gases	(j)	how extension varies with applied force for a range of materials;
	(k)	how liquids behave under pressure, including simple everyday applications of hydraulics;
	(l)	how the volume of a fixed mass of gas at constant temperature is related to pressure.

3. Waves
Pupils should be taught:

Characteristics of waves	(a)	that light and sound can be reflected, refracted and diffracted;
	(b)	the conditions for total internal reflection and its use in optical fibres;
	(c)	about longitudinal and transverse waves in ropes, springs and water;
	(d)	that waves can be reflected, refracted and diffracted;
	(e)	the meaning of frequency, wavelength and amplitude of a wave;
	(f)	the quantitative relationship between the speed, frequency and wavelength of a wave;
	(g)	that waves transfer energy without transferring matter;
The electromagnetic spectrum	(h)	that the electromagnetic spectrum includes radio waves, microwaves, infra-red, visible light, ultraviolet waves, X-rays and gamma-rays;
	(i)	some uses and dangers of microwaves, infra-red and ultraviolet waves in domestic situations;
	(j)	some uses of radio waves, microwaves, infra-red and visible light in communications;
	(k)	some uses of X-rays and gamma-rays in medicine;
Sound and ultrasound	(l)	about sound and ultrasound waves, and some medical and other uses of ultrasound;
Seismic waves	(m)	that longitudinal and transverse waves are transmitted through the Earth, producing wave records that provide evidence for the Earth's layered structure.

4. The Earth and beyond
Pupils should be taught:

The solar system and the wider Universe

(a) the relative positions of the Earth, Moon, Sun, planets and other bodies in the Universe;

(b) that gravitational forces determine the movements of planets, moons, comets and satellites;

(c) how stars evolve over a long time-scale;

(d) about some ideas used to explain the evolution of the Universe into its present state.

5. Energy resources and energy transfer
Pupils should be taught:

Energy transfer

(a) that differences in temperature can lead to transfer of energy;

(b) how energy is transferred by the movement of particles in conduction, convection and evaporation;

(c) how energy is transferred by radiation;

(d) that insulation can reduce transfer of energy from hotter to colder objects, and how insulation is used in domestic contexts;

(e) the meaning of energy efficiency and the need for economical use of energy resources;

Work, power and energy

(f) the quantitative relationship between force and work;

(g) to calculate power in terms of the rate of working or of transferring energy;

(h) the quantitative links between kinetic energy, potential energy and work.

6. Radioactivity
Pupils should be taught:

(a) that radioactivity arises from the breakdown of an unstable nucleus;

(b) that there is background radioactivity;

(c) that there are three main types of radioactive emission, with different penetrating powers;

(d) the nature of alpha and beta particles and of gamma radiation;

(e) the meaning of the term 'half-life';

(f) the beneficial and harmful effects of radiation on matter and living organisms;

(g) some uses of radioactivity, including the radioactive dating of rocks.

(Reproduced with courtesy of HMSO, Crown copyright.)

3 Humans as organisms

▶ **GETTING STARTED**

Chapters 3 to 6 of this book will take you through the main topics and points needed to cover Attainment Target 2: Life and Living Processes. Taking responsibility for your own body, for what you eat, and for how fit you are, is an important part of your everyday living. If you have a basic understanding about how your body works, you will be more able to understand the importance of a balanced diet, regular exercise and relaxation, and the need to avoid cigarette smoking, excessive alcohol and dangerous drugs. In this chapter we look at the basic structure of your body, and then consider nutrition, circulation and respiration in more detail. The chapter concludes by reviewing the main functions of the skeleton in supporting the body and giving the muscles a firm attachment when they contract to move bones.

TOPIC	STUDY	REVISION 1	REVISION 2
Life processes			
Levels of organisation			
Organ systems			
Cell structure and function			
Movement of substances			
Nutrition			
Circulation			
Respiration			
Breathing			
Nervous system			
Hormones			
Excretion			
Homeostasis			
Health			
The skeleton			

WHAT YOU NEED TO KNOW

▶ **Life processes**   *'life processes common to animals and plants'* [2.1a]

1.   **Movement.** An animal can move its whole body; plants usually open and close petals or 'move' leaves and shoots towards the light during growth.
2.   **Nutrition.** Taking in substances from the surroundings: animals actively search for food, plants manufacture food by photosynthesis.
3.   **Respiration.** The release of energy from food inside the cells, usually by combining it with oxygen.
4.   **Excretion.** The removal of unwanted, poisonous substances produced by chemical reactions in the cells.
5.   **Growth.** An increase in size of the organisms due to forming new cells.
6.   **Reproduction.** The production of new individuals from the existing organisms.
7.   **Sensitivity (irritability).** The ability to respond to a stimulus such as temperature, light intensity, chemical substances.

To help you remember these seven processes, think of a nonsense sentence of seven words, each starting with the first letter of each process. For example, **M**any **N**aughty **R**abbits **E**at **G**reen **R**hubarb **S**hoots.

▶ **Levels of organisation Cell → Tissue → Organ**

▶   Animals and plants are made of millions of tiny **cells**, such as red blood cells and nerve cells in animals, and epidermal cells in plants.
▶   Collections of cells that work together are called **tissues**, for example muscle tissue in animals and xylem tissue in plants.
▶   Different kinds of tissues are grouped together as **organs** to carry out certain functions. For example, the heart in mammals, and the leaf in plants.
▶   Organs are then grouped together to form **organ systems** as described below.

▶ **Organ systems**   *'adaptation of organ systems for their role in the life processes'* [2.1b]

The seven organ systems in your body are:

▶   The **circulatory system**: a series of thin tubes filled with blood which flows to every cell in the body pushed by a powerful pump, the heart. The blood in the arteries, veins and capillaries carries oxygen, glucose and amino acids to every cell, and carries waste products, such as urea and carbon dioxide, away from the cells.
▶   The **respiratory system**: the trachea (windpipe) and lungs. Takes in oxygen and removes carbon dioxide.
▶   The **digestive system**: the mouth, oesophagus (gullet), stomach and intestines. Breaks down and absorbs food taken into the body.
▶   The **excretory (urinary) system**: kidneys, ureters, bladder and urethra. Removes harmful waste produced by the body. For example, urea produced by the liver is removed by the kidneys.
▶   The **skeletal system**: the bones and the muscles attached to them. Protects and supports the organs and muscles, and enables the muscles to move the body.
▶   The **reproductive system**: in females – the womb (uterus), the ovaries and the vagina; in males – the testes and penis. Enables you to make eggs or sperm to pass on genetic information to create the next generation.
▶   The **nervous system**: the brain, spinal cord and sense organs – eye, ear, nose, tongue, skin. The brain controls all the organs in the body and enables you to respond to the information received by the sense organs.

Fig. 3.1 outlines the seven organ systems.

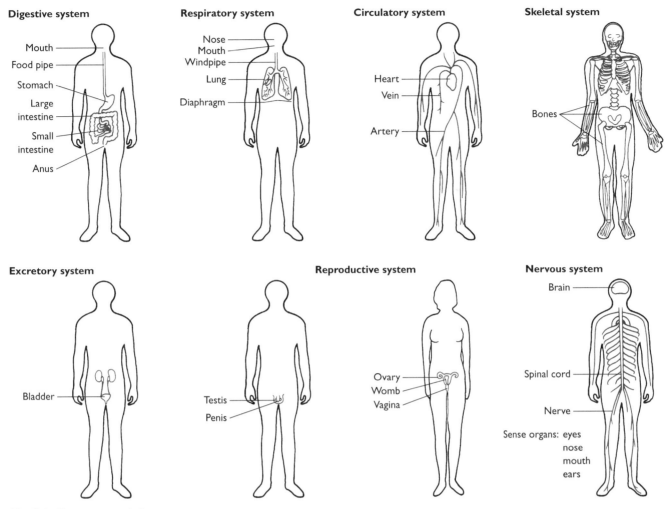

Fig. 3.1 Organ systems in humans

▶ **Cell structure and function**

Structure

'similarities in structure between plant and animals cells' [2.1c]

Plant and animal cells contain: nucleus, cell membrane, cytoplasm and mitochondria.

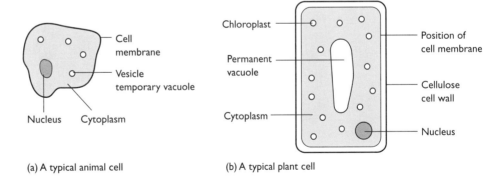

(a) A typical animal cell   (b) A typical plant cell

Fig. 3.2 Types of cell

Table 3.1 The key differences between the two types of cells

'Comparison of plant and animal cells'

Feature	Plant cell	Animal cell
cell wall	present	absent
cell vacuole	present as large	present as small
	permanent vacuole	temporary vesicle
chloroplast	present	absent
shape of cell	regular	irregular

Functions of parts of the cell

▶ Cytoplasm – this is where chemical reactions take place under control of enzymes.
▶ A cell membrane – this allows movement of substances in and out of the cell.
▶ Nucleus – this contains chromosomes which carry the genes (genetic information in the form of a chemical called DNA) to control the cell's characteristics.
▶ Mitochondria – these are where energy is transferred.

▶ Movement of substances H

'how substances enter and leave cells through diffusion, osmosis and active transport' [2.1d]

▶ **Diffusion**: the movement of molecules from a region of their *higher* concentration to a region of their *lower* concentration, along a concentration gradient. For example, in the lungs, **oxygen** in the air in the alveoli **diffuses** through the wall of the alveolus, through the wall of the blood capillary and into a red blood cell.
▶ **Osmosis**: the diffusion of water molecules from a region of *higher* water concentration to a region of *lower* water concentration through a partially permeable membrane. For example, in a root hair cell surrounded by water, the *water* will move into the cell cytoplasm by **osmosis** and the cell will become turgid.
▶ **Active transport**: the movement of molecules by chemical activity into and out of cells, across a membrane from a region where they are in a *low* concentration to one of a *high* concentration. This process requires the expenditure of energy in metabolism and occurs where diffusion is too slow to meet the demands of the cells. For example in the *uptake of salts* from the soil into the root hair cells.

'See Chapter 4 Green Plants as Organisms for more information and diagrams'

▶ Nutrition

'the structure of the human digestive system' [2.2a]

Use Fig 3.3 to help you identify and learn the parts of the digestive system. You need to know the mouth, salivary glands, oesophagus (gullet), stomach, small intestine, large intestine, pancreas, liver and gall bladder.

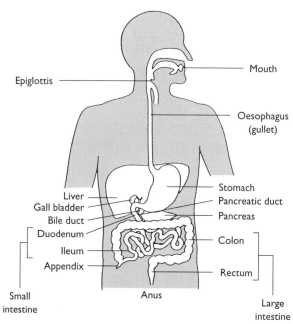

Fig 3.3 The human digestive system

Digestion

'the processes involved in digestion including the role of enzymes, stomach acid and bile' [2.2b]

'Large molecules are broken down to smaller molecules'

Digestion is the breakdown of **large insoluble** food molecules of carbohydrates, proteins and fats into **smaller soluble** molecules. The small soluble molecules can then be **absorbed** into the blood stream and transported to the cells. **Enzymes** increase the **rate** of breakdown of food molecules but work within limited **pH** ranges, so the **acidity** of various parts of the digestive system is important.

▶ **Starch** is digested to **maltose** (a sugar) by **salivary amylase** in the mouth and small intestine; it works best at body temperature and at a pH of between 6 and 7 (neutral).
▶ **Proteins** are digested to **amino acids** by **proteases** in the stomach and small intestine; **pepsin** works at a lower pH created by stomach acid.
▶ **Fats** are digested to **fatty acids** and **glycerol** by **lipase** in the small intestine; bile neutralises the hydrochloric acid from the stomach enabling enzymes, which require a higher pH, to work.

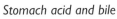

Fig. 3.4 The villi in the small intestine increase the area for absorption

Stomach acid and bile

The lining of the stomach secretes **gastric juice** which contains dilute **hydrochloric acid** (about pH 2) and the enzyme pepsin. The gastric juice:

▶ creates an **acidic pH** so that **pepsin** can break down large **protein** molecules into smaller molecules;
▶ **sterilises** the food by destroying most of the bacteria.

The **liver** produces **bile** which helps to:

▶ **emulsify** (break up) large globules of fats (lipids) and form smaller droplets; these are broken down by lipase into **fatty acids** and **glycerol**;
▶ **neutralise** the hydrochloric acid from the stomach enabling other enzymes, which require higher pH values, to work on the food molecules.

Names of enzymes usually end in **-ase**.

Food tests

These tests help to identify the different types of foodstuff which may be present in a sample of food. You have probably carried out simple food tests in the laboratory to see if carbohydrate, protein or fat is present in a food. The summary chart will help you to remember these food tests.

Table 3.2 Summary chart of food tests

'Some useful food tests'

Type of Food	Substance used	Positive Result
starch	iodine solution	blue-black colour
reducing sugar	add Benedict's solution and warm tube gently	green/red colour
protein	Biuret test: add sodium hydroxide solution then a few drops of copper sulphate solution	violet/purple colour
fat	rub food on to filter paper	a transparent grease stain forms

Balanced diet

The cells in your body are made from many different elements, such as carbon, hydrogen, oxygen, nitrogen, sulphur and phosphorous. Plants and animals obtain these elements from their environment in different ways: by photosynthesis and by absorbing minerals from the soil in the case of plants; by eating plants or other animals in the case of animals.

Human beings require a *balanced diet*, which should include some of each of the seven main types of food shown in Table 3.3:

Table 3.3 Balanced diet

'Items in a balanced diet'

Type of food	Reason	Source
Carbohydrate	glucose, sucrose } for energy starch	jams, sweets, bread, potato
Protein	amino acids – for growth and repair of cells	meat, cheese
Fats	fatty acids – storage and energy	butter, oils
Vitamins	A, B, C, D – good health	fresh vegetables and fruit
Minerals	e.g. iron, calcium – good health	fruit, green vegetables
Fibre (Roughage)	to help bowel movement	vegetables
Water	for all the reactions in the body	fruit and vegetables

If you eat too much energy-containing food, the surplus is stored as fat which can make you overweight and can increase the stress on your heart. Too much saturated (animal) fat in your diet can also increase the risk of heart disease as the fat can be deposited inside the blood vessels and block them. An average 15-year-old girl needs about 10,400 kilojoules of energy each day whereas an average 15-year-old boy needs about 12,100 kilojoules of energy each day.

Your daily dietary requirements will vary according to age, pregnancy, illness, and how active a person you are. For example, if you do a lot of exercise you will use up a lot of energy and will need more carbohydrate and fats which can be broken down to supply energy to your muscle cells. A young person who is still growing will need more protein than an adult, who has stopped growing, to supply amino acids for the growth of extra body cells to make more tissues and muscles.

Deficiencies

Many people in under-developed countries suffer from a lack of one or more of the different types of food in their daily diet. For example:

▶ a lack of **protein** causes a disease called **kwashiorkor** and children are unable to grow and develop properly;
▶ a lack of **vitamin A** causes 250,000 children to go blind every year and many more suffer severe **eye problems**;
▶ a lack of **vitamin D** causes soft bones, which can lead to a condition known as **rickets**;
▶ a lack of **iodine** in the diet causes children in less developed countries to suffer **mental retardation**;
▶ a lack of **iron** in the diet causes **anaemia**.

Food additives

Food additives include chemical preservatives, artificial colourings and flavourings. They are added to improve the colour and taste of food as well as the 'shelf life', i.e. how long it will last.

Some additives, however, may have long-term effects on people and may cause allergic reactions in children. For example, **tartrazine**, an orange colouring found in fruit drinks, is thought to cause **hyperactivity** in some children.

All food must state the substances they contain. Chemical preservatives are described in terms of an international code of E numbers. For example many jams contain E220, which is sulphur dioxide.

INGREDIENTS:
CHERRIES, SUGAR,
WATER, COLOUR
E124, FLAVOURING,
PRESERVATIVES E211, E220.

Fig. 3.5 Food label

▶ Circulation

'the structure of the human circulatory system including the composition and functions of blood' [2.2c]

The blood system, arteries and veins

The blood system is a **transport system,** which carries blood to and from every cell in the body. The blood is pumped by the **heart** in a series of tubes or blood vessels called **arteries** and **veins,** which divide into very tiny blood vessels, the **capillaries.** Fig. 3.6 shows the structure of these blood vessels.

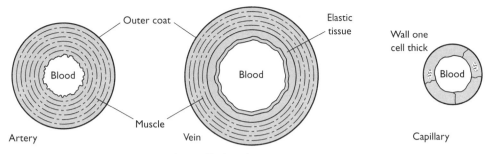

Fig. 3.6 The arteries have much thicker walls than the veins

Arteries carry the blood *away* from the heart under pressure and so have thick muscular walls. **Veins** have much thinner walls, and possess valves to help blood flow one way *towards* the heart. The blood in the veins is at a lower pressure than blood in the arteries so the muscles of your arms and legs contract to help squeeze the blood back to the heart.

Table 3.4 compares the structure and function of the three types of blood vessel.

Table 3.4 This chart [H] compares arteries, veins and capillaries

'Check you know the differences between arteries and veins'

Comparison	Artery	Vein	Capillary
Internal (lumen) diameter	Fairly narrow; can expand (= pulse)	Fairly wide	Very narrow; red blood cells squeeze through
Wall structure	The wall is relatively thick and also elastic, to withstand pressure	The wall is relatively thin; there are valves to keep blood moving in one direction	Wall is composed of a single cell layer; gaps between cells allow exchange of materials with surrounding tissues
Blood direction	Blood flows away from the heart	Blood flows towards the heart	Blood flows from arteries to veins
Blood pressure	High	Low	Very low
Blood flow rate	Rapid, irregular	Slow, regular	Very slow

The heart
The heart is basically two muscular pumps that work side by side. Each side is divided into two chambers, an **upper atrium** and a **lower ventricle**. The **right atrium** takes in deoxygenated blood which has been round the body, and the **right ventricle** pumps the blood to the lungs, via the pulmonary artery. The **left atrium** takes in oxygenated blood from the lungs, via the pulmonary vein, and the more muscular **left ventricle** pumps the blood under great pressure around the body, via the **aorta**, the thick-walled main artery. **Valves** in the heart force the blood to flow in the right direction.

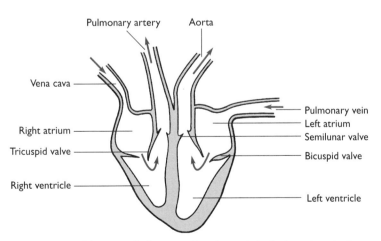

Fig. 3.7 The heart is a powerful pump which pumps blood round the body and to the lungs

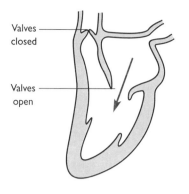

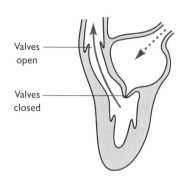

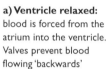

a) Ventricle relaxed:
blood is forced from the
atrium into the ventricle.
Valves prevent blood
flowing 'backwards'

b) Ventricle contracted:
blood is forced from the
ventricle and out of the heart.
The atrium meanwhile
re-fills with more blood

Fig. 3.8 The heart in action

The beating of the heart is controlled automatically so that it beats in a continuous series of rhythmic muscular contractions. Each cycle of contractions is called the **cardiac cycle** and the average adult rate of this cycle is about 72 beats per minute. To control the heart beat artificially, a small electrical device known as a **pacemaker** can be implanted into the chest of a person whose own natural pacemaker fails to work properly.

Composition and functions of blood

Blood consists of:

► **Red blood cells**: These cells carry **oxygen** from the capillaries in the lungs to the body cells. The oxygen readily combines with **haemoglobin**, a blood pigment in the cell, to make oxyhaemoglobin. The shape of the red blood cell, a biconcave disc, provides a *large surface area* to absorb as much oxygen as possible and has no nucleus, so allowing more space in the cell.

► **White blood cells**: These cells **protect** the body against disease by producing antibodies to kill bacteria.

► **Plasma**: This is a liquid which carries the blood cells, platelets, dissolved food substances, mineral salts, urea, carbon dioxide, hormones, antibodies and antitoxins.

► **Platelets**: These help in the **clotting** of the blood.

How oxygen and food reach the cells

1. Oxygen and food molecules diffuse out of the blood into the tissue fluid which surrounds every cell.
2. These substances then diffuse into the cell.
3. Waste products diffuse out of the cell into the tissue fluid and into the blood through the walls of the capillaries, to be carried away from the cells to the excretory organs.

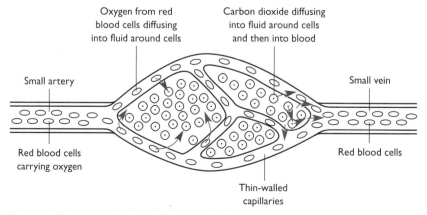

Fig. 3.9 Oxygen diffuses into the tissue fluid around cells

How skin and blood act as defence mechanisms
'the defence mechanisms of the body, including the role of skin and blood' [2.2q]

The body defends itself in a number of ways against infection:

▶ **Stomach acid** kills microbes in food (see above).
▶ The **skin** forms a barrier against bacteria entering the body. If the skin is broken, a blood clot is formed to act as a barrier against bacteria.
▶ **White blood cells** produce **antitoxins** to neutralise the toxins (poisons) which are released by infective bacteria. **Antibodies** are also produced which destroy bacteria. The antibodies stay in the blood for a long time to give built-in resistance (immunity) to a particular disease. The Human Immune Deficiency Virus (HIV) infects and destroys the white blood cells which produce antibodies so the body is unable to protect itself against disease. This condition is known as AIDS (Acquired Immune Deficiency Syndrome). White blood cells also engulf and destroy bacteria, as shown in Fig. 3.10.

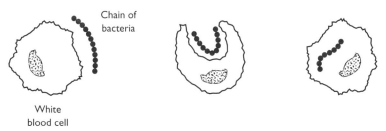

Fig. 3.10 White blood cells engulf and destroy bacteria in your body

▶ **Respiration**   *'respiration may be either aerobic or anaerobic depending on the availability of oxygen'* [2.2f]

'an "oxygen debt" may occur in muscles during vigorous exercise' [2.2g]

Aerobic respiration

Aerobic respiration means **using oxygen** to break down carbohydrates and fats to release energy. The word equation for this process is as follows:

food and oxygen → carbon dioxide and water and energy

The chemical equation for this process using glucose as food is:

$$C_6H_{12}O_6 + 6O_2 \rightarrow 6CO_2 + 6H_2O + 2830kJ$$

Aerobic respiration takes place in the cells of your body, for example, muscle cells.

Your blood carries food and oxygen to the cells and transports waste products, carbon dioxide and water from the cells. These waste products are removed by the lungs when you breathe out.

One way of investigating aerobic respiration in living organisms is to identify the carbon dioxide produced. For example, the gas produced by a mouse can be bubbled through limewater. If the limewater turns cloudy, then the gas is carbon dioxide.

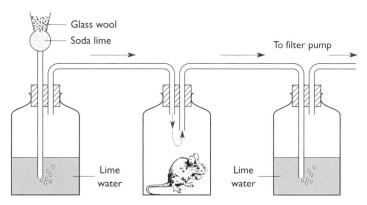

Fig. 3.11 Testing for aerobic respiration

Anaerobic respiration

Anaerobic respiration is the breakdown of carbohydrates and fats to release energy, *without using oxygen*. The food is broken down to substances such as lactic acid and alcohol. Less energy is released compared with aerobic respiration, which uses oxygen.

$$\text{glucose} \rightarrow \text{lactic acid} + \text{energy}$$

An example of anaerobic respiration occurs in your muscles when you are doing vigorous exercise. There is not enough oxygen supplied to your muscles to break down the food quickly enough and release the energy needed by the body. Some energy is released from the food anaerobically and lactic acid is produced as a waste product. When you stop the exercise, your rapid breathing provides extra oxygen to remove the lactic acid, repaying the 'oxygen debt'.

Athletes in sprint races usually use only anaerobic respiration to release energy quickly when they run a 100 metres race.

Micro-organisms can also use anaerobic respiration in the process known as **fermentation**. For example, yeast (a micro-organism) digests sugars in the absence of air and produces alcohol and carbon dioxide. Wine, beer and bread are all produced as a result of fermentation by yeast.

The diagram (Figure 3.12) shows an investigation to show that carbon dioxide is produced by yeast during anaerobic respiration.

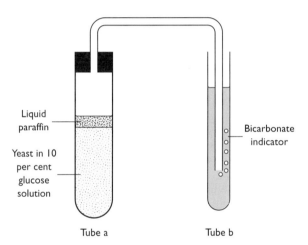

Liquid paraffin

Yeast in 10 per cent glucose solution

Bicarbonate indicator

Tube a   Tube b

Fig. 3.12 Anaerobic respiration in yeast

Remember:

▶   **aerobic** respiration is the release of energy from food *using oxygen*;
▶   **anaerobic** respiration is the release of energy from food *without using oxygen*;
▶   **anaerobic respiration** takes place in the body when there is insufficient oxygen to support aerobic respiration; this leads to an 'oxygen debt'.

▶ Breathing

'the structure of the thorax' [2.2d]

'how breathing, including ventilation of the lungs, takes place' [2.2e]

At rest you are breathing about 15 times a minute. If you put your hands over your ribs and take a deep breath you can feel your chest cavity getting larger as you breathe in. The **intercostal** muscles, between your ribs, contract to pull your ribs up and out and the **diaphragm** muscle at the base of your chest flattens the diaphragm so that your chest cavity is made larger. Air outside your chest cavity is at greater pressure than air inside your chest; this difference in pressure causes air to rush into your lungs.

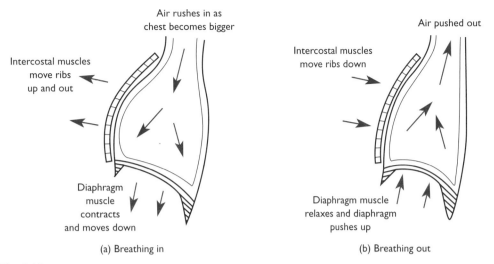

(a) Breathing in

(b) Breathing out

Fig. 3.13

Your lungs are basically two sponge-like structures in your chest which fill up with air. Oxygen from the air diffuses over the moist surface of the air sacs or **alveoli**, into the blood in the capillaries (Fig. 3.13a), where it combines with haemoglobin in the red blood cells, to make a new substance called **oxyhaemoglobin**. The blood is pumped by the heart muscle to the rest of the body through arteries and eventually capillaries. The oxygen diffuses into your cells, and carbon dioxide from the cells diffuses into your blood and is carried back to the lungs (Fig. 3.15b). The intercostal muscles and diaphragm make your chest cavity smaller, therefore increasing the pressure in the lungs, so that the air is pushed out.

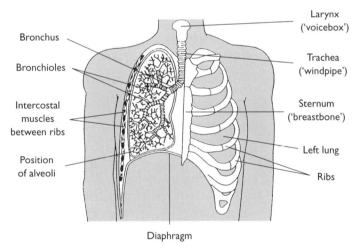

Fig. 3.14 The human chest cavity

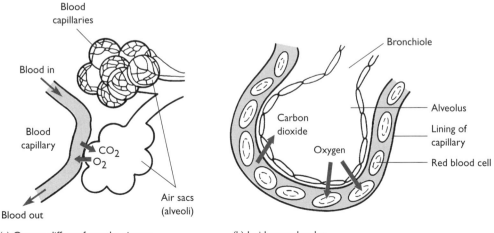

(a) Oxygen diffuses from the air sacs into the blood stream

(b) Inside one alveolus

Fig. 3.15

Inhaled and Exhaled air

Table 3.5 shows the difference in composition between inhaled (atmospheric) and exhaled air.

Table 3.5 Composition of inhaled and exhaled air

Component	Inhaled air	Exhaled air
oxygen	21%	16%
carbon	0.04%	4%
water vapour	variable: average = 1.3%	saturated = 6.2%
temperature	ambient	38°C

The effect of exercise

When your muscles are working harder during rigorous exercise they need more energy. Your heart rate increases to pump blood carrying glucose more quickly to your cells, and your rate of breathing increases so that more oxygen is taken in to release the energy from glucose. More carbon dioxide is produced which is removed by the increased rate of breathing.

'Your heart muscle gets stronger with more exercise'

People who are fit generally have a lower heart rate and therefore a lower pulse rate than people who are unfit, because exercise develops the heart muscle, just like any other muscle. Fit people and non-smokers get back to their resting pulse rate more quickly than unfit people and smokers. Regular exercise, eating a good, well-balanced diet without too much fat, and not smoking, can reduce the risk of heart disease.

▶ Nervous system

'the pathway taken by impulses in response to a variety of stimuli including touch, taste, smell, light, sound and balance' [2.2h]

'how the reflex arc, which involves a nerve impulse carried via neurones and across synapses, makes possible rapid response to a stimulus' [2.2i]

'the structure of the eye and how it functions in response to light' [2.2j]

The reflex arc

The **reflex arc** is a direct pathway from a **receptor** to an **effector** via the **central nervous system** (CNS). **Sensory** and **motor** neurones may connect directly or through an intermediate neurone across a **synapse** (a similar idea to complex road junctions). Synapses allow connections between many neurones so that impulses can be carried to different parts of the body.

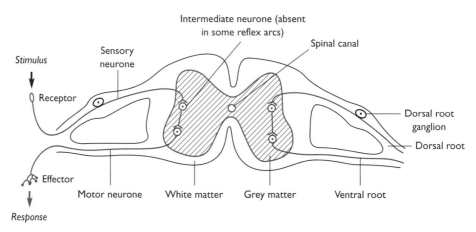

Fig. 3.16 The reflex arc

Reflex responses provide a fast, automatic response to a stimulus. The responses are instinctive and usually increase an animal's chances of survival. Examples are coughing, blinking and eye-focusing and withdrawing a limb from a source of pain. The pathway taken by an impulse from a receptor in the knee jerk reflex is shown in Fig. 3.17.

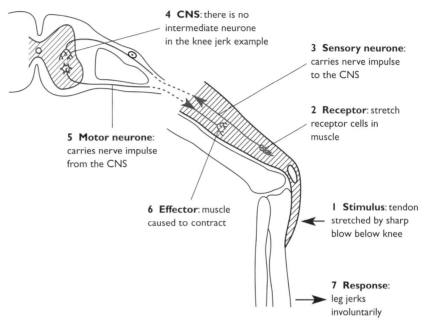

Fig. 3.17 A simple reflex: the knee jerk

1. **Stimulus**: tendon stretched by sharp blow to knee.
2. **Receptor**: stretch receptor in muscle.
3. **Sensory neurone** carries nerve impulse to CNS.
4. Nerve impulse passed across a **synapse** (a tiny space between two neurones) by chemical secretion to motor neurone.
5. **Motor neurone** carries nerve impulse from CNS.
6. **Effector**: muscle contracts.

Sense organs

Sense organs detect the following stimuli:

▶ **eye** – light;
▶ **ear** – sound and 'balance';
▶ **tongue** – chemicals – taste: sweet, sour, bitter, salt;
▶ **nose** – chemicals – smell;
▶ **skin** – touch, pressure and temperature change.

The eye

'See Chapter 15, Waves, p. 283, Refraction'

Light is refracted or bent as it enters the eye through the transparent **cornea**. It is then refracted even more by the convex lens of the eye, and focused on the **retina** at the back of the eye. The retina consists of light sensitive cells called rods and cones which are connected to the brain by nerve fibres. The **cones** are concerned with colour vision and vision in bright light. They are sensitive to red, green or blue light. The **rods** are concerned with non-colour vision and vision in dim light. When these cells are stimulated by light, an impulse is sent to the brain via the optic nerve. The brain then forms images as a result of the impulses it receives. Fig. 3.18 (overleaf) shows the structure of the main parts of the eye.

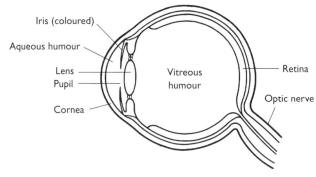

Fig. 3.18 The structure of the eye

The chart shows a summary of the main parts of the eye:

'The main parts of the eye
and their function'

▶	cornea	refracts (bends) the light entering the eye
▶	aqueous humour	supplies nutrient to the lens and cornea
▶	iris	controls the amount of light entering the eye by adjusting the size of the pupil
▶	pupil	the aperture which allows light into the eye
▶	lens	refracts the light rays and changes shape to allow for fine focusing
▶	ciliary muscle	controls the shape of the lens
▶	suspensory ligaments	attach lens to ciliary muscle
▶	vitreous humour	maintains the shape of the eye
▶	retina	contains light sensitive cells which convert light energy into a nerve impulse
▶	fovea	very sensitive region of retina where most light is focused
▶	optic nerve	carries impulses to the brain where they are interpreted

Accommodation

The ciliary muscles control the shape of the lens so that the eye can see objects which are near or far away. This is known as **accommodation**. To focus light from distant objects on the retina the lens needs to be thin and this is brought about by the contraction of the radial ciliary muscles. To focus light from near objects on the retina the lens becomes thicker due to contraction of the circular ciliary muscles. This action is a reflex action and some of the ability of the lens to change shape is lost with age.

Sometimes the lens is unable to accommodate, so that objects which are close to or far away from the eye appear blurred. This gives rise to the medical conditions:

'See Chapter 15, Waves,
p. 285, about lenses'

▶   **Short sight** A short-sighted person is unable to see distant objects clearly and the light rays are focused in front of the retina usually due to the eyeball being too long. To correct this defect a concave lens is used which diverges (spreads out) the rays before they enter the eye, as shown in Fig. 3.19

Eye defect	Cause	Correction
Short sight (myopia)	Long eyeball: distant objects cannot be focused 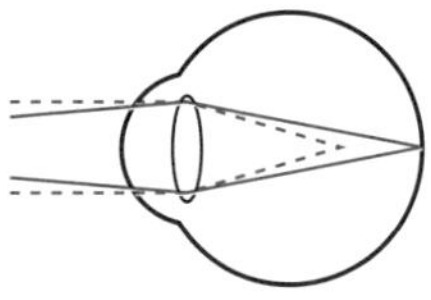	Diverging lens (concave) 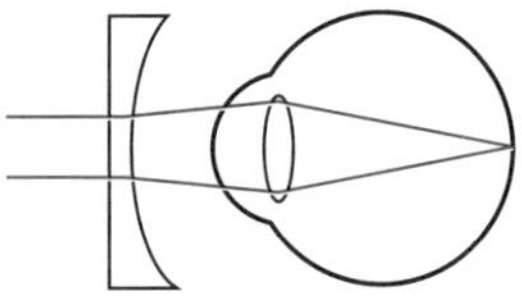

Fig. 3.19 (a) Short sight

▶ **Long sight** A long-sighted person is unable to see objects close to their eye as their lens is too short. A convex lens helps to converge (bend inwards) the light rays before they enter the eye.

Eye defect	Cause	Correction
Long sight (hypermetropia)	Short eyeball: near objects cannot be focused	Converging lens (convex)

Fig. 3.19 (b) Long sight

▶ **Hormones** *'the way in which hormonal control occurs, including the effects of insulin and sex hormones'* [2.2k]

Hormones are chemical substances produced in very small amounts by special glands in the body called **endocrine glands**. Hormones are carried from the gland where they are produced via the blood stream to the target organ where they have their effect. The diagram (Fig. 3.20) shows the position of the main endocrine organs in the body.

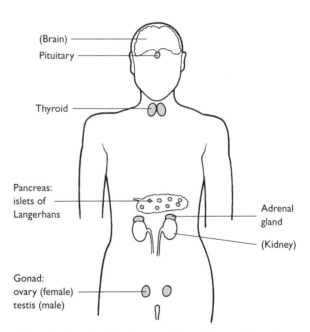

Fig. 3.20 Position of the main endocrine glands in humans (the relative position of some other organs is also shown)

Table 3.6 shows the names of the major hormones and the effects in the body.

Table 3.6 Summary of some of the main hormones in humans

Gland	Hormone	Effects
Pituitary	Trophic hormones	Cause other endocrine glands, e.g. thyroid, adrenal and gonads, to release their hormones.
	ADH	Increases water reabsorption in **nephrons** of the **kidney**.
	Oxytocin	Causes contraction of the **uterus** during birth.
	Prolactin	Stimulates milk production from breasts.
Thyroid	Thyroxine	Increases the general rate of **metabolism** (chemical reactions in the body) and stimulates **growth**.

Table 3.6 continued

Gland	Hormone	Effects
Adrenal gland	Adrenalin	Sometimes called the **fight, flight** or **fright hormones**; prepares the body for potentially difficult or dangerous situations, for instance by increasing **heart rate**, efficiency of **muscles** and **breathing rate**. Adrenalin also raises the *blood glucose* level.
Pancreas (islets of Langerhans)	Insulin	Causes the conversion of glucose to glycogen.
	Glucagon	Causes the conversion of glycogen to glucose.
Ovary	Oestrogen	Promotes the development of female secondary sexual characteristics.
	Progesterone	Maintains the uterus during pregnancy.
Testis	Testosterone	Promotes the development of male secondary sexual characteristics.

H ·· *Control of blood sugar*

In humans the concentration of glucose in the blood is controlled within narrow limits and maintained at around 90 mg of glucose per 100 cm^3 of blood. Two hormones produced by the pancreas, namely **insulin** and **glucagon**, are involved. **Insulin** is released when the concentration of glucose is increased, for example after a meal. The effect of insulin is to *decrease* glucose concentration by converting it to glycogen. **Glucagon** is released when the concentration of blood glucose is decreased, for example during exercise. Its effect is to *increase* glucose concentration by converting glycogen, stored in the liver, to glucose.

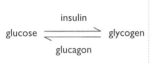

Fig. 3.21

The following table presents a comparison of the nervous and hormonal control systems.

Table 3.7 The nervous and hormonal control systems

Aspect of comparison	Nervous control	Hormonal control
message	nerve impluse	hormone
route	nervous system	blood system
transmission	rapid	slow
origin of message	receptor	endocrine gland
destination of message	effector	target organ(s)
speed and duration of effect	immediate, brief	delayed, prolonged

Medical uses of hormones

'*some medical uses of hormones, including the control and promotion of fertility and the treatment of diabetes*' [2.21]

Diabetes

Diabetes is caused by lack of sufficient **insulin** and this results in an increase in the glucose concentration in the blood. The kidneys are then unable to reabsorb all the glucose and some appears in the urine. Diabetics can control the condition through low-sugar diets and by regular injections of insulin.

Hormones such as **oestrogen** are used to increase fertility in women who are unable to produce sufficient eggs from their ovaries. The hormone stimulates **ovulation** and increases the number of **eggs** released. If the woman's oviducts are blocked then the eggs can be fertilised outside the woman's body '*in vitro*'. This means that sperm fertilise the eggs in a glass dish and the zygotes are taken from the dish and placed in the woman's uterus so that the embryos develop as normal. The use of '**fertility drugs**', however, can lead to multiple births if several embryos develop at the same time.

▶ **Excretion**   *'how waste products of the body functions are removed by the lung and kidney'* [2.2n]

The kidneys

The kidneys are organs of **excretion** and **osmoregulation**. Remember excretion is the removal of waste metabolic products from the body.

The diagram (Fig. 3.22) shows the structure of the kidney.

'The kidneys remove waste and maintain correct fluid balance'

The **medulla** is the region where water, salts and urea are passed from the blood into the urine (see Fig. 3.23).

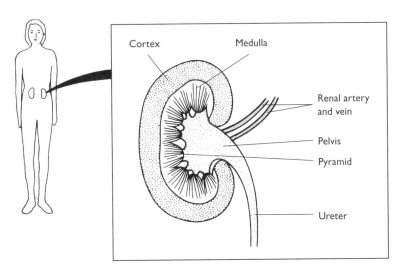

Fig. 3.22 Kidney structure

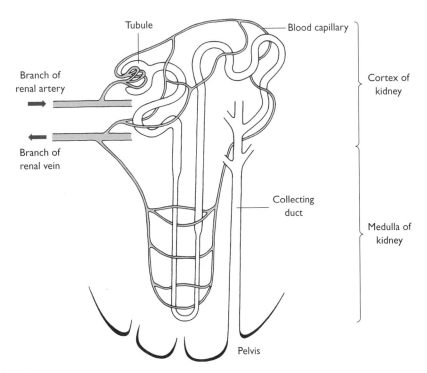

Fig. 3.23 Kidney function

H   The **renal artery** carries blood containing urea, water and salts to the kidney. Molecules such as glucose, water, salts, amino acids and urea are small enough to be forced under pressure into the **tubule**. About 99% of this fluid is reabsorbed into the blood, i.e. most of the water, all of the glucose and some of the salts are replaced into the blood supply. The **renal vein** transports the blood from which the urea has now been removed away from the kidney. The urine is carried by the ureter to the bladder, and then to outside the body by the urethra.

Kidney failure

▶ **Artificial kidney** A person who suffers from kidney failure due to disease can some-times receive treatment on a kidney machine (dialysis machine). This machine, also known as the artificial kidney, carries out some of the functions of a normal kidney and needs to be used for several hours every 2–3 days. Blood from an artery in the patient's arm is diverted through a dialyser where the small molecules of urea and salts are removed from the blood by diffusing through a partially permeable mem-brane. Useful substances such as glucose, amino acids, some salts and water are retained in the blood, which is returned to a vein in the arm.

▶ **Kidney transplant** An alternative to an artificial kidney may be a kidney transplant, providing that a suitable donor can be found, such as a road accident victim or some-one related to the patient who can continue living with one kidney. The tissues of the patient and donor must match to avoid rejection of the new kidney by the body's immune system. There are usually insufficient people able to donate kidneys to meet the demand for transplants.

▶ Homeostasis

'the importance of maintaining a constant internal environment' [2.2m]

'how the kidneys regulate the water content of the body' [2.2o]

Homeostasis can be defined as the **maintenance of a constant internal environment**. There are three homeostatic mechanisms you need to know:

▶ regulation of **water content** by the kidney;
▶ control of **body temperature**;
▶ control of **blood sugar** (see page 48).

Control of water content – osmoregulation

'how humans maintain a constant body temperature' [2.2p]

The average adult human body is some 58% water, and it is vital that the amount remains constant. If we drink too much our body fluids become **dilute**; if we lose too much water they become too **concentrated**. Either way, cells would cease to function properly. **Osmoregulation** is the term we use to describe the process of maintaining the correct fluid balance in our bodies.

H   The organ that controls the amount of water leaving the body is the kidney, which works with the **hypothalamus** and **anti-diuretic hormone** (ADH) to achieve homeostasis, as shown in Fig. 3.24

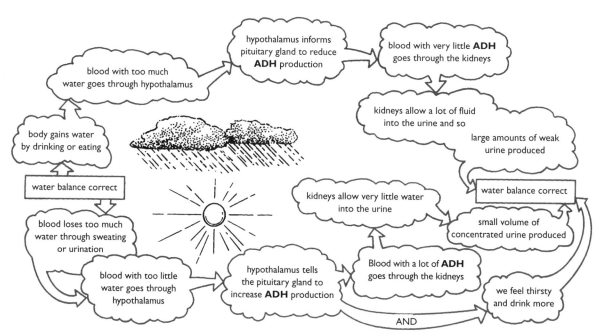

Fig. 3.24 How fluid level is controlled in mammals

Control of body temperature

H In mammals, a part of the brain, the **hypothalamus**, responds to temperature changes both inside and outside the body. The temperature of the blood flowing through the brain is monitored by the hypothalamus. Information about external temperature comes from special **thermoreceptors** in the skin which are connected by nerves to the hypothalamus. The brain initiates responses appropriate to the information received. If the temperature is *too high*:

1. the body is cooled by sweating;
2. the hair lies flat against the skin;
3. blood is pumped to capillaries just below the skin surface;
4. there is a general lowering of the body's metabolic rate.

A *fall* in temperature would cause the *opposite* responses plus shivering to raise the temperature by producing heat in the muscles. Mammals are very sensitive to temperature change and humans soon die if the body core temperature is too high or too low. Human body temperature is maintained at about 37°C.

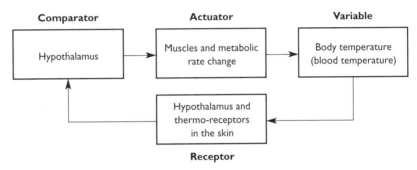

Fig. 3.25 Temperature control in a mammal

The skin

The skin is basically composed of two layers:

1. **outer epidermis,** consisting mostly of dead cells;
2. **inner dermis,** a living layer of cells including sensory cells.

The sensory cells can detect touch, pressure, pain and temperature.
The diagram (Fig. 3.26) shows the position of the sensory receptors in the human skin.

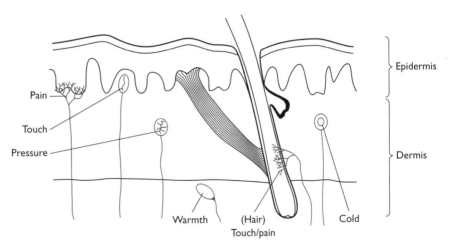

Fig. 3.26 Receptors in the human skin

The skin has an important role in temperature regulation. When the temperature either inside or outside the body is too high, then the capillaries just under the skin dilate or widen. The person looks flushed or red and heat is lost from the blood, with the result that the person cools down. This is known as **vasodilation** (see Fig. 3.27).

'The skin helps with temperature regulation'

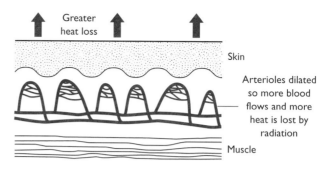

Fig. 3.27 Vasodilation

If the person is too cool then **vasoconstriction** occurs and the blood vessels become narrower, with the result that heat is retained in the body (see Fig. 3.28).

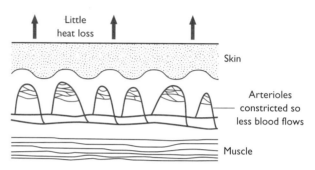

Fig. 3.28 Vasoconstriction

▶ **Health**   *'defence mechanisms of the body including the role of skin, blood and mucous membranes of the respiratory tract'* [2.2q]

'the effects of solvents, alcohol, tobacco and other drugs on body functions' [2.2r]

Tobacco and alcohol

Cigarette smoking
Cigarette smoking can affect the body in many ways:

1. Chemicals in the tobacco smoke can cause cancer in the lungs, and as a result the lungs are destroyed.
2. Carbon monoxide, a gas in cigarette smoke, mixes with haemoglobin in the red blood cells and makes the blood less efficient at carrying oxygen. As a result, the blood vessels around the heart become weak and this may cause a heart attack.
3. The tiny hairs in the lungs which remove dust and mucus from the lungs become paralysed, so sticky **phlegm** collects in the lungs, causing infection. Smokers try to move the phlegm by heavy coughing, which damages the lining of the lungs and reduces the number of air sacs in the lungs. There is less surface area for oxygen to diffuse into the blood stream so the smokers become out of breath and may suffer from bronchitis.
4. Pregnant women who smoke can give birth to babies which are undersized and sometimes born prematurely.

Research has shown that smoking is related to death caused by lung cancer (See Fig. 3.29).

The effect of alcohol on the body
Alcohol is a chemical found in beers, wines and spirits. It affects the nervous system and slows down a person's reaction time, causing a lack of co-ordination of the muscles. It can also lead to a lack of self-control, unconsciousness or even a coma. Drinking excessive amounts of alcohol over a number of years can result in a diseased liver, an ulcerated stomach, weak heart muscles, high blood pressure and depression.

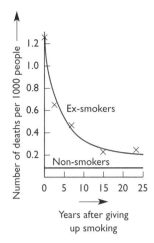

Fig. 3.29 You reduce the risk of dying from lung cancer if you are a non-smoker

Alcohol and its effects on the body can be a serious problem for motorists and is a major cause of many road accidents. One in three drivers who are killed in road accidents have drunk alcohol just prior to the accident. In Britain there are strict controls about the amount of alcohol a person can drink when they are driving. Anyone found driving a car or motorcycle with more than 80 milligrams of alcohol in their blood would be prosecuted. The legal limit for drinking and driving is three units of alcohol which is about three standard drinks as shown in the diagram (Fig. 3.30).

Fig. 3.30 The legal limit for driving is three units of alcohol

Solvents and addictive drugs

Solvent abuse
Many glues and other household products contain a chemical **solvent** to stop them solidifying. Solvent abuse is sometimes referred to as **glue sniffing** because people breathe in the fumes given off by the solvent. The fumes affect the brain and produce a temporary pleasant sensation which may lead to delirium and unconsciousness. As a result of glue sniffing many people have died, often from choking on their own vomit. Glue sniffers are often irritable and moody and usually develop a cough, sore eyes and sores around the mouth. It is a very dangerous habit and can become addictive.

Addictive drugs
There are many dangers associated with using illegal drugs, such as cannabis and heroin, especially those which are injected into the blood. There is no control over the quality of the drug which may be mixed with impurities; these can cause serious side effects. The strength of the drug is unknown so it can be difficult to control the amount of drug being injected. Injecting with unsterilised needles can cause other diseases such as blood poisoning, hepatitis and HIV. People who are addicted to illegal drugs are often unable to keep a regular job and so do not earn the money to pay for the drugs they need, which often results in their stealing money from others. Over a period of time the drugs can affect behaviour and may cause damage to the brain, liver and kidneys.

▶ **The skeleton**   *'the role of the skeleton, joints and muscles in movement'* [KS3]
'the principle of antagonistic muscle pairs, e.g. biceps and triceps' [KS3]

The function of the skeleton is to support the body and give the muscles a firm attachment when they contract to move bones.

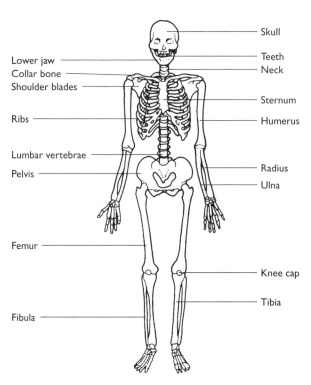

Fig. 3.31 The skeleton

The backbone or vertebral column is made up of many vertebrae which allow attachment for other bones and muscles. The main function of the backbone is to protect the spinal cord. Other parts of the skeleton also have a protective function, for example: the cranium protects the brain; the rib cage and sternum protect the heart and lungs.

Movement and joints

Movement is possible due to **joints** between the bones. For example, at the **shoulder** is a ball and socket joint which allows the arm to swivel around in any direction. At the **elbow** is a hinge joint which allows the lower arm to move backwards and forwards.

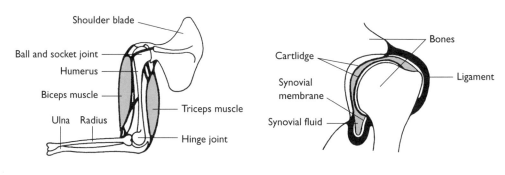

(a) The bones and muscles of the upper arm showing the elbow and shoulder joints

(b) Typical synovial joint (shoulder)

Fig. 3.32

In order to move the lower arm up, the biceps muscle contracts to pull up the radius. The triceps muscle then contracts to pull the lower arm down. These muscles work as a pair of **antagonistic muscles** working against each other. The muscles are attached to bones by **tendons** which transmit the pulling force from the muscle to the bone. The bones are held together by **ligaments**. Inside the joint the **synovial fluid** acts as a cushion and shock absorber to prevent the bones rubbing on each other.

▶ EXAMINATION QUESTIONS

Multiple choice

Fig. 3.33

Fig. 3.33 shows a section though the heart.

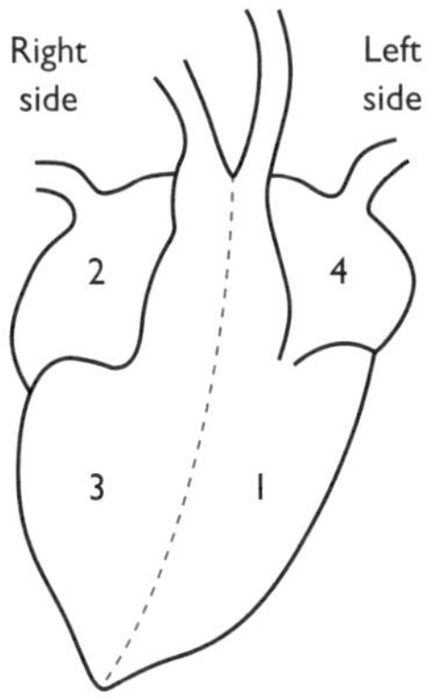

Q1 What is the correct order of blood flow from the vena cava to the aorta?

A 1, 4, 2, 3
B 2, 3, 1, 4
C 2, 3, 4, 1

D 3, 2, 4, 1
E 4, 1, 3, 2

Q2 What is the function of white blood cells?

A to carry nerve impulses to the brain
B to produce hormones to clot the blood
C to help clot the blood
D to transport oxygen to the cells
E to destroy bacteria in the body

Q3 Fig. 3.34 shows the human gut.

What is the part labelled X?

A the duodenum
B the ileum
C the large intestine
D the stomach
E the pancreas

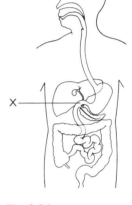

Fig. 3.34

Q4 In which part of the gut does the digestion of protein start?

A the mouth
B the food tube
C the stomach

D the small intestine
E the large intestine

Q5 What is the function of the excretory system?

A to break down food which you eat
B to get rid of undigested food from your body
C to remove harmful waste produced by your body
D to control all the organs in your body
E to take in oxygen and transport it to the cells

Q6 Which of the following is used for growth and repair of cells?

A starch
B fats
C minerals

D proteins
E roughage

Q7 The diagram below shows the chest cavity.

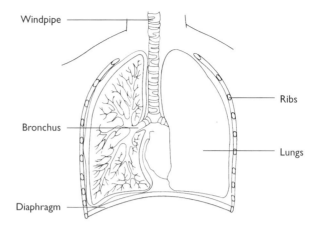

Windpipe

Ribs

Bronchus

Lungs

Diaphragm

Fig. 3.35

Which one of the following contracts when you breathe in?

A   bronchus   D   ribs
B   diaphragm   E   windpipe
C   lungs

Structured questions

Q8 The table below shows the composition of a well-known breakfast cereal. Study the label and answer the questions which follow.

Table 3.8

	Per 100g		Per 100g
Energy	1400kJ	Dietary Fibre	12.9g
Protein	10.5g	Vitamins:	
Fat	2.0g	Niacin	10.0mg
Available		Riboflavin (B$_2$)	1.0mg
Carbohydrate	66.8g	Thiamin (B$_1$)	0.7mg
		Iron	0.6mg

(2)

(a) Which two food groups are carbohydrates?

(i) _____

(ii) _____

(b) What use does the body make of   *(2)*

(i) carbohydrates _____

(ii) proteins? _____

(c) The cereal supplies 1400 kJ of energy per 100 g; what does kJ stand for?   *(1)*

_____

(d) What is the total mass of vitamins the cereal contains per 100 g?   *(1)*

_____ mg

(e) To which food group does iron belong?   *(1)*

_____

(f) Which food group supplies dietary fibre?   *(1)*

_____

(NICCEA)

Q9   The illustration opposite shows a child suffering from malnutrition.

(a)   What do you understand by malnutrition? (2 lines)   *(2)*

(b)   Which food group would be of most benefit to the child shown in the picture?   *(1)*

The histogram shows the consumption of different types of food in three areas of the world.

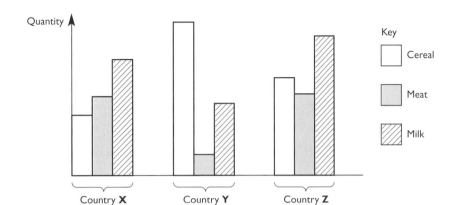

Fig. 3.36

Fig. 3.37

(c)   From the data given, from which country do you think it is likely that the child comes?

_____   *(2)*

(NICCEA)

Q10   (a)   *Scurvy*, *rickets* and *anaemia* are illnesses which can affect different parts of the body. Match these illnesses to the part of the body they most affect:

   Part of body   *Illness it can be affected by*

   (i)   Skin   _____

   (ii) Bones   _____

   (iii) Blood   _____

   (3)

(b)   Each illness listed in (a) is caused by a particular substance missing from the diet. Name the substance and state **one** food which contains the substance.

Table 3.9

Illness	Substance missing from diet	**One** food which contains missing substance
(i) scurvy (ii) rickets (iii) anaemia		

(3)
(WJEC)

Q11   A pupil was provided with samples of the following foods: starch, fat, sugar and protein.
   The pupil selected one of these foods and placed equal amounts of it in each of three test tubes containing an enzyme in solution.
   One test tube was kept at 10°C, one at 37°C and the third was heated until the contents boiled.
   A sample was removed from each test tube at intervals and tested for the presence of sugar. The results are shown in the table overleaf.

Table 3.10

Test tube	Amount of sugar present			
	at 0 min	after 5 min	after 10 min	after 20 min
1	none	a little	a lot	a lot
2	none	none	a little	a lot
3	none	none	none	none

(a) Which one of the following foods was placed in each of the three test tubes: starch, fat, sugar, protein?

_____

(b) Name the enzyme which was present. _____

(c) Which test tube was kept at 10°C? _____

(d) In which test tube had the enzyme been boiled?

_____

(e) Which test tube was kept at 37°C? Give a reason for your answer

_____

_____

(6)

(London)

Q12 The table below gives information about the food values of 100 grams (g) of a number of foods.

Table 3.11

Food	Energy measured in kilojoules (kJ)	Fat measured in grams (g)	Protein measured in grams (g)	Carbohydrate measured in grams (g)	Calcium measured in milligrams (mg)	Iron measured in milligrams (mg)
potato	370	0.0	2.0	21.0	7.0	0.7
fish	300	0.7	16.0	0.0	32.0	1.1
butter	3340	85.0	0.4	0.0	14.0	0.0
rice	1500	1.0	6.0	86.0	4.0	0.4
sugar	1620	0.0	0.0	100.0	0.0	0.0
soya	1810	24.0	40.0	13.0	210.0	7.0
orange	150	0.0	0.7	8.0	42.0	4.0
meat	1600	20.0	15.0	6.0	40.0	0.6

(a) (i) Which food listed in the table has the most fat? *(1)*

_____

(ii) Which food listed in the table only gives energy? *(1)*

_____

(iii) Suggest **one** food in the table which nearly gives a balanced diet. Explain your answer.

Food _____ *(1)*

Explanation (3 lines) _____ *(2)*

(iv) Name one other important group of substances needed for a healthy diet which has been left out of the table.

_____ *(1)*

(b) (i) What pattern can you see between the fat content and the energy given by butter, rice, soya and meat? (3 lines)   *(3)*

(ii) Suggest **one** other food listed in the table which does not fit your pattern.   *(1)*

_____

(c) Choose the **two** foods from the table which are most unsuitable for slimmers. Explain your answers.

Food 1 _____ *(1)*

Explanation (2 lines) _____ *(1)*

Food 2 _____ *(1)*

Explanation (2 lines) _____ *(1)*

(d) Suggest **two** reasons why soya is now replacing meat.

Reason 1 (2 lines) _____ *(1)*

Reason 2 (2 lines) _____ *(1)*

(e) Various forms of single-cell protein (SCP) are now being made and used instead of more usual food materials. *Mycoprotein* is an example. It is made from a fungus which is grown on glucose solution. The fungus grows as fibres that smell faintly of mushrooms. The length and texture of the fibres depend on their growing time. Mycoprotein can be dried to a powder or made to look and taste like chicken, fish or beef. It contains all the nutrients in beef but more fibre.

(i) Suggest **two** reasons why foods such as these are being made.

Reason 1 (2 lines) _____ *(2)*

Reason 2 (2 lines) _____ *(2)*

(ii) Suggest **two** problems which the makers will have to overcome if such food substitutes are to be accepted.

Problem 1 (2 lines) _____ *(1)*

Problem 2 (2 lines) _____ *(1)*

(London)

Q13 (a) What is the main job of the circulatory system? (2 lines)

_____ *(1)*

(b) The diagram below (Fig. 3.38) shows a section through a human heart.

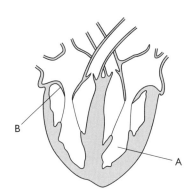

Fig. 3.38

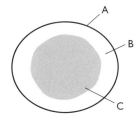

Fig. 3.39

(i) Name the parts labelled A and B. *(2)*

(ii) On the diagram, draw arrows to indicate the direction of blood flow into, through and out of the left side of the heart. *(3)*

(iii) Explain, as fully as you can, how blood is forced to flow in this direction. (4 lines) *(3)*

(c) The diagram left (Fig. 3.39) shows a white blood cell.

Name the parts labelled A, B and C, on the diagram. (3 lines) *(3)*

(d) (i) Give **two** ways in which white blood cells protect us from disease. (2 lines) *(2)*

(ii) Explain, as fully as you can, how immunisation protects us from disease. (8 lines) *(3)*

(Co-ordinated Science, NEAB)

Q14 The graph (Fig. 3.40) shows a person's breathing rate and volume of breathing at the start of a race, during the race and after the race. The following questions relate to this graph.

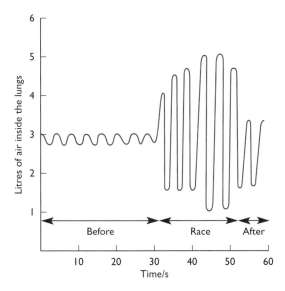

Fig. 3.40

(a) (i) What was the maximum amount of air inside the athlete's lungs during the race? *(1)*

(ii) What was the athlete's breathing rate per minute before the race started? *(2)*

Study the graph below (Fig. 3.41) showing the pulse rates of a trained athlete, and of a person before and after starting to take regular exercise, and answer the questions that follow.

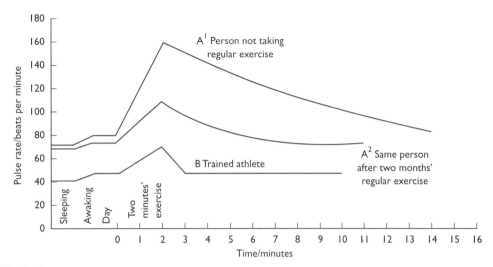

Fig. 3.41

Fig. 3.42

(b) (i) What is the difference between the sleeping pulse rates of A^1 and B? *(1)*

(ii) What is the difference between the recovery times of A^1 and A^2? *(2)*

(c) The illustration left shows two people who are very much overweight. They are said to be suffering from obesity.

(i) Give two dangers to health that might follow from obesity. (4 lines) *(2)*

(ii) State one precaution other than exercise which might be taken to avoid obesity. (2 lines) *(1)*

(NICCEA)

Q15 This is an example of a question requiring extended writing.

Explain how attention to diet, exercise and hygiene can keep your body healthy. Marks will be given both for showing knowledge and understanding and for the way in which your account is organised and expressed. (20 lines) *(8)*

(Co-ordinated Science, London, NEAB, WJEC)

Q16 The diagram below shows some of the major organs in the human body.

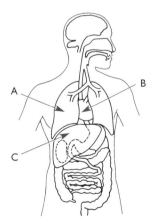

Fig. 3.43

Use the information in the diagram to complete the table below

Table 3.12

Letter	Name of organ	The main function of the organ
A		
B		
C		

(Science Double Award, SEG)

Q17 This question is common to Foundation and Higher Tier with the exception of part (c) which is for Higher Tier only.

Graph 1 shows the glucose and insulin content and Graph 2 shows the glucose and glucagon content of a person's blood.

The person's blood was tested over a period of one hour on two separate occasions.

On one occasion the person ate glucose tablets at the start of the test. On the other occasion the person was injected with insulin at the start of the test.

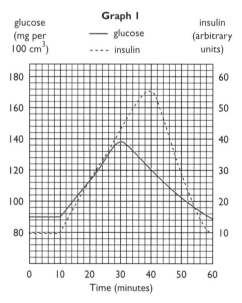 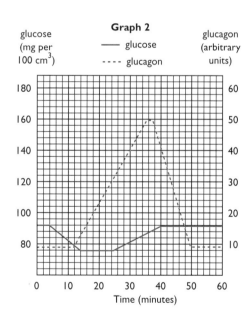

Fig. 3.44

Use the information in the graphs and your own knowledge to answer the following questions.

(a) Which graph shows the effects of the insulin injection?
     Give a reason for your answer.

(1)

(b) (i) What evidence is there that glucose stimulates the production of insulin?   *(1)*

(ii) Which organ produces insulin?   *(1)*

(iii) At which times was the insulin level 30 arbitrary units?   *(1)*

(iv) Describe the effects of insulin in the body. (4 lines)   *(3)*

(c) Explain how a fall in the level of glucagon in graph 2 is an example of homeostasis and negative feedback. (4 lines)   *(3)*

(London Combined Science, Foundation and Higher Tier)

► EXAMINATION ANSWERS

Multiple choice

A1 Key C. The vena cava brings blood from the body to the right atrium (2), and the blood is pumped to the lungs from the right venticle (3), returning from the lungs via the left atrium (4) and then to the left ventricle (1).

A2 Key E. Option D is a function of red blood cells. Option C, platelets, help to clot the blood.

A3 Key A, the duodenum, the first part of the small intestine.

A4 Key C, the stomach. The digestion of *starch* starts in the mouth, option A.

A5 Key C. Be careful of option B, which is a function of the digestive system. Excretion is about removing waste produced by your body.

A6 Key D, proteins. Option A, starch, and option B, fats, are used for energy.

A7 Key B, diaphragm. Lungs have no muscle and do not contract, and ribs are moved by intercostal muscles.

Structured questions

A8 (a) (i) sugar,   (ii) starch
(b) (i) to provide energy,   (ii) to build new cells for growth and repair
(c) kilojoules
(d) 11.7 mg
(e) minerals
(f) carbohydrate

A9 (a) lack of a balanced diet; all seven types of food must be eaten
(b) protein
(c) country Y

A10 (a) (i) scurvy   (b) (i) vitamin C, citrus fruit
(ii) rickets   (ii) vitamin D, green vegetables
(iii) anaemia   (iii) iron, liver

A11 (a) starch
(b) amylase
(c) tube 2
(d) tube 3
(e) tube 1. Reason – the enzyme converted the starch to sugar after 10 minutes. Digestive enzymes work best at body temperature, 37°C.

A12 (a) (i) butter

(ii) sugar

(iii) food – soya. Explanation – contains a proportion of all food types and is a good source of fat, protein, calcium and iron.

(iv) roughage

(b) (i) There is a general pattern which links the fat content and energy value of three of the four foods. The higher the fat, the greater the energy value. Butter has the highest amount of fat, and the highest energy value. Meat and soya have less than half the energy value of butter and only a quarter of the fat. Rice has less than half the energy value of butter and little fat.

(ii) Sugar has half the energy value of butter and contains no fat.

(c) Food 1 – sugar. Explanation – contains a lot of carbohydrate, which produces a lot of energy which has to be used up.

Food 2 – butter. Explanation – contains a lot of fat, which is stored in the body if not used up.

(d) Reason 1 – soya is a plant, and it is more efficient to obtain food at the beginning of the food chain, as less energy has been lost.

Reason 2 – soya is a better source of protein and calcium than meat, and many people are concerned about killing animals for meat.

(e) (i) Reason 1 – to provide a good source of protein and fibre for many more people than could be supplied with meat.

Reason 2 – the food can be stored more easily than meat, as it can be dried and made into different types of meat as necessary.

(ii) Problem 1 – people will need to be convinced that the food substitute contains all the nutrients that are in meat.

Problem 2 – the food will have to look and taste just like the meat it is replacing for it to be acceptable to meat eaters.

A13 (a) to transport substances round the body to all the cells.

(b) (i) A left ventricle

B tricuspid valve

(ii) see Fig. 3.7, page 39 for correct arrows

(iii) the bicuspid valve (1) prevents blood flowing back (1) into the atrium when the ventricle contracts (1)

reference to semilunar valves at base of aorta also acceptable

(c) A cell membrane

B cytoplasm

C nucleus

(d) (i) produce antibodies which kill disease-causing bacteria (pathogens) (1); engulf/ take in/digest disease-causing bacteria (pathogens) (1)

Note: 'give two ways' is asking you for a description; you are given two lines per answer so try to write as much as possible in the space allowed.

(ii) a vaccine made from dead bacteria (or viruses) is injected into the blood (1); antibodies are produced (1) which give immunity against the disease (1); a booster injection can be given to increase the number of antibodies (1)

A14 (a) (i) 5 litres

(ii) 16 times per minute

(b) (i) 30

(ii) 6 minutes

(c) (i) 1 high blood pressure; 2 shorter life expectancy

(ii) balanced diet

A15 In this question you are told that marks are awarded for your knowledge and understanding, and for how you organise and express your answer. For example a maximum of 3 marks would be awarded for a coherent account using scientific language, showing a logical sequence. Only 1 mark would be awarded for an account using everyday language, showing little or no sequence.

You are asked to explain about how attention to diet, exercise and hygiene keep your body healthy, so try to include some facts about each of these in turn.

Some of the points you might include to gain the maximum 5 marks are:

Diet　　　eating a balanced diet (1) with plenty of fibre (1) not too much fat (1)

Exercise　regular exercise maintains a good circulation to the heart (1) fitness increases resistance to disease (1)

Hygiene　regular brushing of teeth removes food and reduces tooth decay (1)

A16　A . . .　lung(s) (1)
　　　　　used for breathing/exchanging gases/taking in oxygen/air/getting rid of water (vapour)/carbon dioxide (1)

　　　　B . . .　heart (1)
　　　　　acts as a pump (for blood) (1)

　　　　C . . .　liver (1)
　　　　　stores some vitamins/produces heat/makes red blood cells (in a baby)/breaks down old red blood cells/makes bile/stores some minerals/makes chemicals which make blood clot/destroys poisons/bacteria/alcohol/deals with amino acids/deamination/keeps glucose level steady (1)

A17　(a)　graph 2 because the glucose level (shown by the solid line) falls after a few minutes (1)
　　　(b)　(i)　in graph 1 the insulin level (dotted line) rises after the glucose level rises (1)
　　　　　(ii)　pancreas (1)
　　　　　(iii)　take care here to read the insulin level of 30 units from the right-hand vertical axis of graph 1; two readings are required 22 and 50 minutes (1)
　　　　　(iv)　reduces glucose concentration in blood (1)
　　　　　　　converts glucose to glycogen (1)
　　　　　　　in liver (1) and muscle (1)
　　　　　　　more glucose can be absorbed by cells (1)
　　　　　　　cell membranes are more permeable to glucose (1)
　　　(c)　(Higher Tier only)
　　　　　the fall in the level of glucagon (dotted line) is an example of homeostasis because the glucose level has returned to normal (1); it also shows negative feedback because, when the level of blood glucose is decreased (1) more glucagon is secreted (1) which increases level of glucose (1)

▶ **STUDENTS' ANSWERS WITH EXAMINER'S COMMENTS**

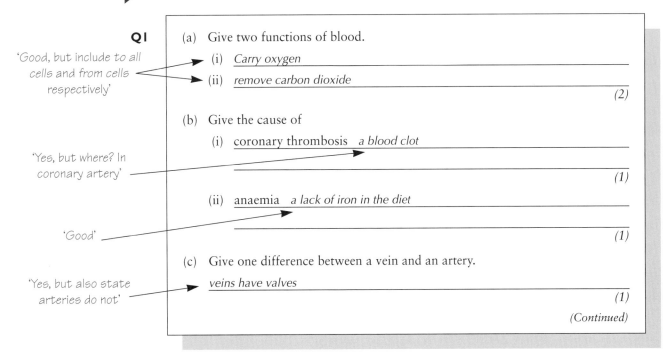

Q1　(a)　Give two functions of blood.

'Good, but include to all cells and from cells respectively'

　　　(i)　*Carry oxygen*
　　　(ii)　*remove carbon dioxide*
　　　　　　　　　　　　　　　　　　　　　　(2)

　　　(b)　Give the cause of

'Yes, but where? In coronary artery'

　　　　(i)　coronary thrombosis　*a blood clot*
　　　　　　　　　　　　　　　　　　　　　　(1)

'Good'

　　　　(ii)　anaemia　*a lack of iron in the diet*
　　　　　　　　　　　　　　　　　　　　　　(1)

　　　(c)　Give one difference between a vein and an artery.

'Yes, but also state arteries do not'

　　　　veins have valves
　　　　　　　　　　　　　　　　　　　　　　(1)

　　　　　　　　　　　　　　　　　(Continued)

The following results were obtained in an investigation to find the relationship between heartbeat and exercise.

Table 3.13

Time in minutes	0	1	2	3	4	5	6	7	8
Number of beats per minute	60	60	80	100	100	88	76	65	60

'Good. This second graph is a line graph and you have followed the pattern of the first'

'Good'

'Error here. 73 should be 76'

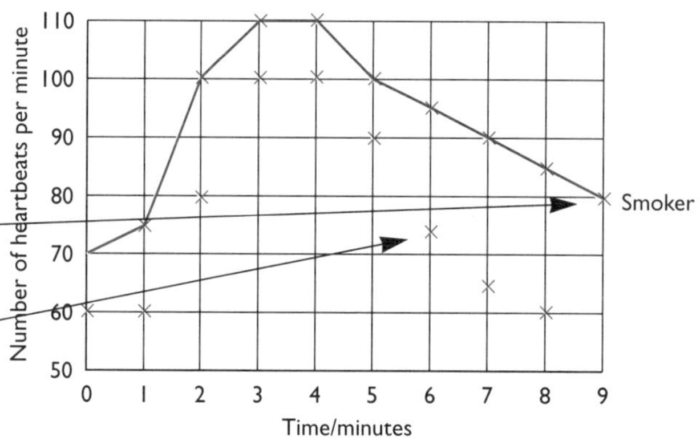

Fig. 3.45

(d) On the graph paper above draw a *line graph* of the number of heartbeats per minute, plotted against time.   *(2)*

'Join points to show line'

(e) Use your graph to answer the following questions.

'Good answers'

   (i) Approximately when did the exercise start?   *between 1 and 2 minutes*

   (ii) Approximately when did the exercise stop?   *between 4 to 5 minutes*

   (iii) What was the heartbeat rate after $2\frac{1}{2}$ minutes?   *90 beats per minute*   *($1\frac{1}{2}$)*

(f) (i) Draw a second graph using the same axes to show the results that you would expect from a person 50 years of age who had been a heavy smoker through life.   *(1)*

   (ii) Explain the graph you have drawn.

   The pulse rate is higher as the heart works harder.

'Well done'

   The pulse takes longer to get back to normal.   *(2)*

(g) Explain why regular exercise is considered to be good for the heart.

'A bit vague; exercise develops the heart muscle'

To keep the person fit.   *(1)*

(h) Quite often people with breathing difficulties as a result of a heart attack are given pure oxygen. Give **one** reason for this.

'Yes, the right idea here'

To get more oxygen into the blood.   *(1)*

(WJEC)

Q2   Fig. 3.46 is a diagram of a kidney tubule (nephron) and surrounding blood vessels.

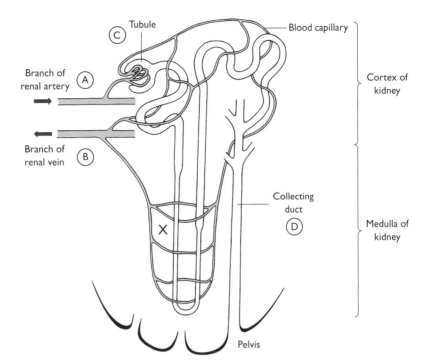

Fig. 3.46

Adapted from Biology – A course to 16+ by G. Jones and M. Jones (1984), by kind permission of Cambridge University Press.

'Anti-diuretic hormone (ADH) affects the kidney tubule'

(a)   Samples of fluids were taken from A, B, C and D shown in the diagram above. Table 3.14 shows the relative amounts of protein, glucose, salt, water, oxygen and carbon found in each sample.

Table 3.14

Sample No.	Water	Protein	Glucose	Salt	Oxygen	Carbon dioxide
1	70%	High	High	High	High	Low
2	95%	None	None	Medium	Very low	Very low
3	70%	High	High	High	Low	High
4	98%	None	High	High	Very low	Very low

(i)   Identify which sample came from each of the points A, B, C and D.

Sample 1 came from point   _A_ ✔

Sample 2 came from point   _D_ ✔

Sample 3 came from point   _B_ ✔

Sample 4 came from point   _C_ ✔   (4)

'Good. High oxygen in artery. No glucose in urine'

(ii)   On the diagram, label a point X where the hormone ADH acts to control water balance.   (1)

(Continued)

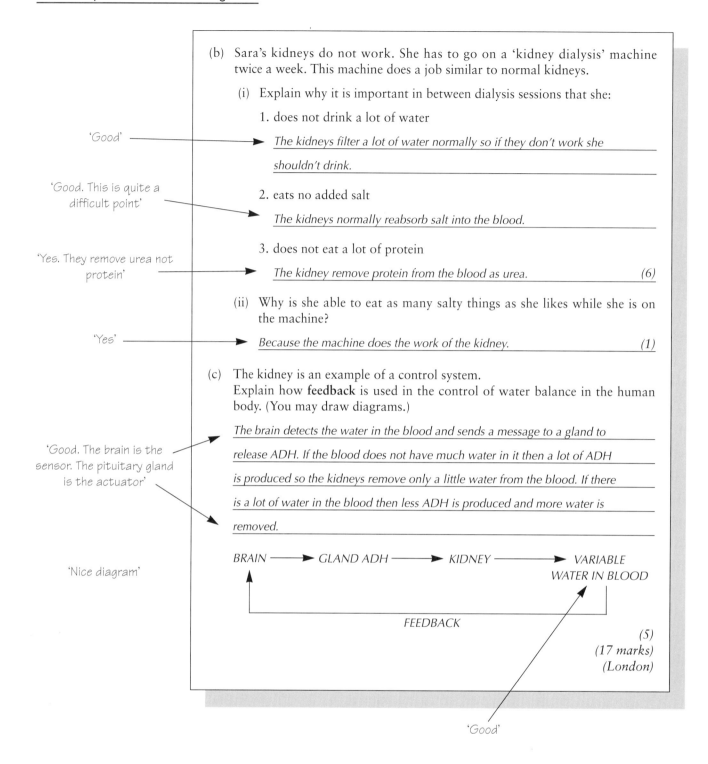

(b) Sara's kidneys do not work. She has to go on a 'kidney dialysis' machine twice a week. This machine does a job similar to normal kidneys.

(i) Explain why it is important in between dialysis sessions that she:

1. does not drink a lot of water

'Good' ——→

The kidneys filter a lot of water normally so if they don't work she shouldn't drink.

2. eats no added salt

'Good. This is quite a difficult point' ——→

The kidneys normally reabsorb salt into the blood.

3. does not eat a lot of protein

'Yes. They remove urea not protein' ——→

The kidney remove protein from the blood as urea.　　(6)

(ii) Why is she able to eat as many salty things as she likes while she is on the machine?

'Yes' ——→

Because the machine does the work of the kidney.　　(1)

(c) The kidney is an example of a control system.
Explain how **feedback** is used in the control of water balance in the human body. (You may draw diagrams.)

'Good. The brain is the sensor. The pituitary gland is the actuator'

The brain detects the water in the blood and sends a message to a gland to release ADH. If the blood does not have much water in it then a lot of ADH is produced so the kidneys remove only a little water from the blood. If there is a lot of water in the blood then less ADH is produced and more water is removed.

'Nice diagram'

BRAIN ——→ GLAND ADH ——→ KIDNEY ——→ VARIABLE
　　　　　　　　　　　　　　　　　　　　　　　WATER IN BLOOD

FEEDBACK

(5)
(17 marks)
(London)

'Good'

SUMMARY

At the end of this chapter you should know:

▷ the **seven life processes** common to animals and plants;

▷ that **organ systems** are adapted for their role in these processes;

▷ the structural similarities between **animal** and **plant cells**;

▷ how substances enter and leave cells by **diffusion**, **osmosis** and **active transport**;

▷ the functions of the **cell membrane**, **cytoplasm** and **nucleus**;

▷ that the nucleus contains **chromosomes** which carry **genes**;

▷ the structure of the **digestive system**, processes involved in **digestion** and the role of **enzymes**, **stomach acid** and **bile**;

▷ the main **food sources** of the components of a **balanced diet**: **carbohydrates, proteins, fats, minerals, vitamins, fibre** and **water**;

▷ the structure of the human **circulatory system**, composition and functions of **blood**;

▷ the structure of the **thorax** and how **breathing** and **gaseous exchange** take place;

▷ the **release of energy** through **aerobic** and **anaerobic respiration** and details of **oxygen debt**;

▷ the pathway taken by **impulses** in response to a **stimulus** such as light, and how the **reflex arc** enables a rapid response to a stimulus;

▷ the structure and function of the **eye**;

▷ the way in which **hormonal control** occurs, **insulin**, **oestrogen**, **progesterone** and **testosterone**, and medical uses of hormones in the treatment of **diabetes** and control of **fertility**;

▷ the importance of maintaining a **constant internal environment**;

▷ how the **kidneys** remove **waste products** and **regulate water content**;

▷ how a constant body **temperature** is maintained;

▷ the role of **skin**, **blood** and **mucous membranes** in the **defence mechanisms** of the body;

▷ the effects of **solvents**, **alcohol**, **tobacco** and other **drugs** on body functions and how **smoking** affects lung structure and gaseous exchange;

▷ the role of the **skeleton**, joints and muscles in movement;

▷ the principle of **antagonistic muscle pairs** e.g. biceps and triceps.

4 Green plants as organisms

This topic is for Double Science only.

▶ **GETTING STARTED**

The process of photosynthesis, by which plants use energy from the Sun to make food, is essential to all other living things. Plants synthesise (make) carbohydrates from carbon dioxide and water, and these carbohydrates are converted into proteins and fats. Animals are dependent on plants to supply a never-ending source of food.

Plants also use up large amounts of carbon dioxide from the atmosphere and release oxygen as a waste gas from the process of photosynthesis. People are sometimes confused about what happens with oxygen and carbon dioxide in plants. Plants **respire** (breathe) all the time, 24 hours a day, taking in oxygen and releasing carbon dioxide. During the daylight hours plants also **photosynthesise** taking in carbon dioxide and releasing oxygen. The amount of carbon dioxide taken in is much greater than the amount produced during respiration, so the net effect is that plants reduce the amount of CO_2 in the atmosphere.

The destruction by burning of large areas of forest produces large amounts of CO_2, the trees are no longer able to remove CO_2 from the atmosphere, so the concentration increases, giving rise to the 'greenhouse effect'. CO_2 in the atmosphere traps heat energy from the Sun which should normally be reflected back into space. The temperature of the Earth then increases, leading to 'global warming', and a subsequent melting of ice caps in the polar regions causing a rise in sea level and possible flooding of coastal areas.

TOPIC	STUDY	REVISION 1	REVISION 2
Photosynthesis			
Limiting factors			
Adaptation of the leaf			
Mineral nutrition			
Uses of the products of photosynthesis			
Respiration and photosynthesis			
Transport of materials			
Transpiration			
Osmosis			
Mineral salts			
Plant hormones			
Sexual reproduction in plants			

▶ **WHAT YOU NEED TO KNOW**

▶ **Photosynthesis**   *'the reactants in, and products of, photosynthesis'* [2.3a]

Green plants use energy from sunlight to convert **carbon dioxide** and **water** into **carbohydrates** (e.g. **glucose**) and **oxygen**. This process is called **photosynthesis**. The **light energy** is absorbed by **chlorophyll**, the green pigment in plant leaves, which is contained in **chloroplasts** in some plant cells.

The equation for **photosynthesis** is:

H

$$\text{carbon dioxide and water} \rightarrow \text{carbohydrates and oxygen}$$
$$6CO_2 + 6H_2O \qquad\qquad C_6H_{12}O_6 + 6O_2$$

The glucose is converted into other sugars and stored as **starch**.
Oxygen is released as a waste product and used by animals and plants for **respiration**.

Practical activities

You may have carried out a series of **investigations** to show that **light, carbon dioxide** and **water** are necessary for photosynthesis.

Remember that to show that photosynthesis has occurred, a plant must be **destarched** by placing it in the dark for two days to use up any starch which has been stored. The plant can then be used in investigations and a **starch test** carried out on a leaf to see if starch has been formed (Fig. 4.1).

The starch test

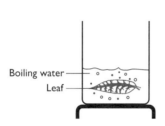

(a) Leaf is boiled in water (about 2 mins). (Purpose: to break down cell walls and to stop the action of enzymes within the leaf.)

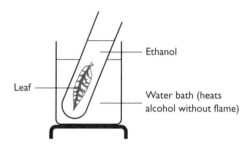

(b) Leaf is warmed in ethanol (until leaf is colourless) CAUTION: ETHANOL IS INFLAMMABLE; NO FLAMES SHOULD BE USED AT THIS STAGE. (Purpose: to extract the chlorophyll, which would obstruct observations later. Chlorophyll dissolves in ethanol but not in water.)

'Testing for starch as evidence of photosynthesis'

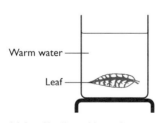

(c) Leaf is dipped into the warm water (briefly). (Purpose: to soften the now brittle leaf.)

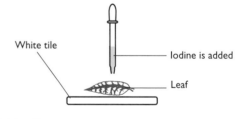

(d) Leaf is placed on white tile and iodine added (Purpose: iodine shows the presence (blue–black) or absence (orange–brown) of starch; colours are shown against the white tile.)

Fig. 4.1 Testing a leaf for starch

Investigations on photosynthesis
To show that **chlorophyll** is necessary for photosynthesis, use a variegated leaf which has areas of green and white. Starch should be present in the green areas only (Fig. 4.2).

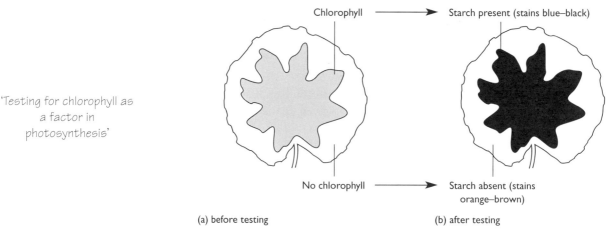

'Testing for chlorophyll as
a factor in
photosynthesis'

Fig. 4.2 A variegated leaf before and after testing for starch

To show that **light** is necessary, a piece of foil is wrapped around part of the leaf to exclude the light. Starch should be present only in the areas exposed to light (Fig. 4.3).

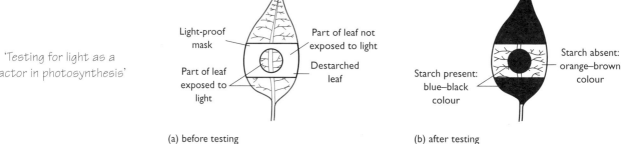

'Testing for light as a
factor in photosynthesis'

Fig. 4.3 A partially covered leaf before and after testing for starch

To show that **carbon dioxide** is necessary, enclose part of the plant in a flask containing **potassium hydroxide** which absorbs the carbon dioxide. Starch should be present only in the leaves where carbon dioxide was available (Fig. 4.4).

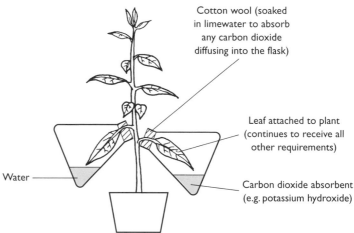

'Testing for carbon dioxide
as a factor in
photosynthesis'

Fig. 4.4 Apparatus to show that carbon dioxide is needed for photosynthesis

To show that **oxygen** is released during photosynthesis a plant can be trapped under a funnel, as shown in the diagram (Fig. 4.5). The gas released can be tested with a **glowing splint**. The splint should **relight** showing the gas is oxygen. This experiment can also be used to study the **rate** of photosynthesis by measuring how many bubbles are produced per minute, given different **intensities of light**. The outcome is likely to be as shown in Figure 4.6.

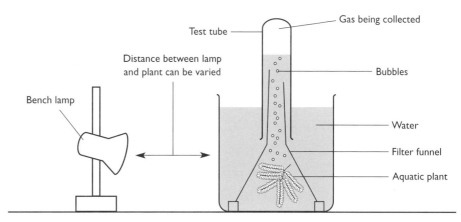

Fig. 4.5 Experiment to demonstrate the effect of light intensity on the rate of photosynthesis

H ···· *Limiting factors*
'that the rate of photosynthesis may be limited by light intensity, carbon dioxide concentration or temperature' [2.3b]

The **rate** of photosynthesis can be affected by factors such as:

▶ light intensity and duration;
▶ carbon dioxide concentration;
▶ temperature.

If any of these factors is in short supply it limits the rate of photosynthesis and is described as a **limiting factor**. For example if the intensity of light is too low at dawn and dusk then light becomes a limiting factor on the rate of photosynthesis. (See the experiment in Fig. 4.5 above and Fig. 4.6.)

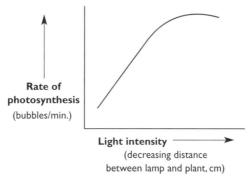

Fig. 4.6 Graph to show the effect of light intensity on the rate of photosynthesis

▶ **Adaptation of the leaf**

The leaves of plants are well adapted for photosynthesis (Fig. 4.7) in the following ways:

▶ leaves are thin and flat and so have a **large surface area**;
▶ chlorophyll is concentrated in the chloroplasts of the **palisade cells,** which are near the upper surface of the leaf to obtain maximum light;
▶ guard cells control the movement of gases through the **stomata.**

▶ **Mineral nutrition**

'the importance to healthy plant growth of the uptake and utilisation of mineral salts' [2.3d]

Plants require **mineral salts** to help them manufacture **proteins** and other substances (see Table 4.1). Elements such as oxygen, hydrogen and carbon are also necessary.

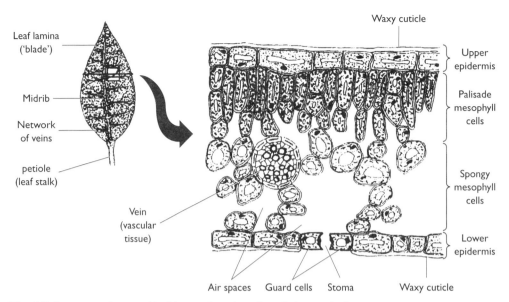

Fig. 4.7 Structure of a typical leaf (vertical section; dicotyledonous leaf)

Table 4.1 Minerals required by plants

Mineral	Needed for	Symptom due to lack of mineral
nitrogen	to make amino acids, proteins and DNA	small leaves, thin weak stems
phosphorus	to make DNA and cell membranes, and for enzyme systems	poor root growth, small leaves
magnesium	to make chlorophyll	yellow leaves

An understanding of the need for **mineral salts** has important implications for the agricultural industry. The yield of a particular crop can be **limited** if an essential mineral is **lacking** from the soil.

Monoculture is practised by some agriculturists where the same crop is planted over a large area. In these areas, fertilisers, either organic or inorganic, must be added to the soil to provide essential mineral salts and hence produce maximum yields.

▶ Uses of the products of photosynthesis

'how the products of photosynthesis are used by the plant' [2.3c]

Green plants convert the **glucose** formed during photosynthesis to other **sugars, insoluble starch, oils** and **amino acids**.

▶ Insoluble starch is stored in roots, stems and leaves. For example, (1) the potato is a **stem tuber** which stores starch; when these tubers are planted, the 'eyes' produce new shoots using the stored starch; (2) maize grains store starch in the **endosperm** so that when germination takes place there is a plentiful supply of energy for the growth of the shoot and roots.

▶ **Sucrose** is stored in fruits, for example apples, pears.

▶ **Oils (lipids)** are stored in seeds as an energy supply for germination.

▶ **Amino acids** are used for making new proteins for growth.

▶ Respiration and photosynthesis

Respiration is a continuous process in green plants whereas **photosynthesis** only occurs when there is sufficient light. The two processes can be thought of as **opposite** to each other as shown in the word equation below.

$$\text{glucose} + \text{oxygen} \underset{\text{photosynthesis}}{\overset{\text{respiration}}{\rightleftarrows}} \text{carbon dioxide} + \text{water} + \text{energy}$$

In bright light the rate of photosynthesis is **greater** than the rate of respiration, so there is a gain in materials required for growth.

Photosynthesis and respiration in action

Respiration in animals (and in green plants at night) releases **carbon dioxide** into the air. Most of this carbon dioxide is converted back into sugars and carbohydrates by green plants, which in turn release **oxygen** into the atmosphere. As a result, the balance of 20% oxygen to <0.05% carbon dioxide is maintained. This balance is being upset by man. For example, by burning **fossil fuels** (increasing carbon dioxide levels) and by cutting down large areas of **rain forest** (reducing oxygen levels) humans have created a slight **increase** in the levels of carbon dioxide in the atmosphere recently. This in turn has given rise to concern that the Earth will warm up slightly, owing to the **greenhouse effect** (see Chapter 16, p. 329–30).

Experiment to investigate the relative rates of photosynthesis and respiration

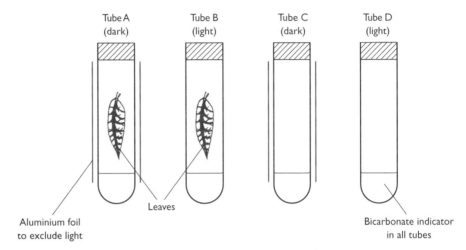

Fig. 4.8 Experiment to investigate respiration and photosynthesis in leaves

Four test tubes can be set up as shown in the diagram (Fig. 4.8) with tubes C and D acting as controls without any leaves present. The bicarbonate indicator should appear red at the start of the experiment.

Table 4.2 Results of experiment

Tube	Colour of indicator at end of experiment	Conclusion
A	Yellow	Carbon dioxide concentration is high; produced by respiration.
B	Purple	Carbon dioxide concentration is low; used in photosynthesis.
C	Red	Carbon dioxide concentration remains constant; no respiration
D	Red	or photosynthesis is occurring because no living tissue is present.

Carbon dioxide is produced as a result of **respiration** in tubes A and B, but in tube B **photosynthesis** is also occurring. As this process is more rapid than respiration in bright light, the concentration of carbon dioxide is **lowered**.

▶ **Transport of materials**

'*how plants take up water and transpire*' [2.3f]
'*the importance of water in the support of plant tissues*' [2.3g]
'*substances required for growth and reproduction are transported within plants*' [2.3h]

The root cells have fine **root hairs** which **increase the surface area** of the root for absorption of water. Water moves through the root hairs into cell cytoplasm by **osmosis** because the solution inside the cell is more concentrated than the solution of soil water. The root hair cells become swollen and turgid and are more dilute than those near the central part of the root, so a **concentration gradient** is set up to draw water into the xylem (see Fig. 4.9).

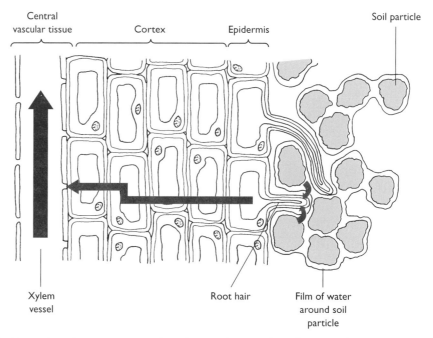

Fig. 4.9 Absorption of water and minerals in the root (arrows show direction of water movement)

H⟶ The vascular tissues in plant stems, leaves and roots transport materials around the plant. There are two types of tissue: **xylem** and **phloem** (see Fig. 4.10).

▶ The **xylem** tubes are dead cells which carry water and mineral salts from the roots to the leaves. This can be observed by cutting a stem and placing it in a red dye. After a few hours the red dye appears in the xylem tissue of the stem.

▶ The **phloem** tubes carry food such as dissolved sugars from one part of the plant to another.

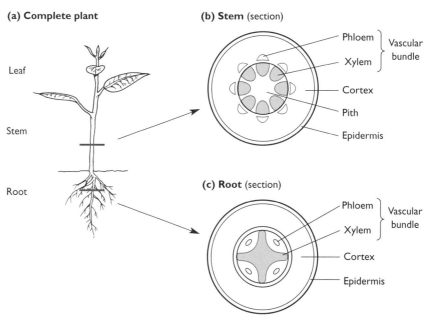

Fig. 4.10 Distribution of vascular tissues in a dicotyledonous plant (vertical and transverse sections)

▶ Transspiration

H

Transpiration is the **loss of water by evaporation** from the leaves of plants. Water vapour moves out of the leaf through the **stomata** (tiny holes), which are usually found on the underside of the leaf where there is less air movement. The stoma opens and closes by changing the shape of **guard cells** either side of the hole (see Fig. 4.11). When these guard cells **take in water** they become swollen and **turgid** and the stoma's opening becomes **larger**. When the guard cells **lose water** they become **flaccid** and the stoma's opening becomes **smaller**. The closure of the stomata prevents excessive water loss by the plant, which can cause **wilting**. However, the stoma need to open from time to time to allow oxygen and carbon dioxide to enter or leave the leaf during photosynthesis and respiration. (Check back to Fig. 4.7 Structure of leaf.)

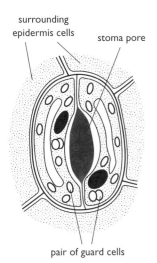

surrounding epidermis cells   stoma pore

pair of guard cells

Fig. 4.11 A stoma showing two guard cells

Transpiration rates

The following factors **increase** the rate of transpiration:

- ▶ light intensity;
- ▶ increase in temperature;
- ▶ increase in air movement;
- ▶ decrease in humidity.

You may have investigated the **rate** of water loss from a plant by using a **potometer** (Fig. 4.12). The potometer has a fine capillary tube containing water which has an air bubble. The rate of movement of the air bubble indicates the rate of **transpiration** from the leaves.

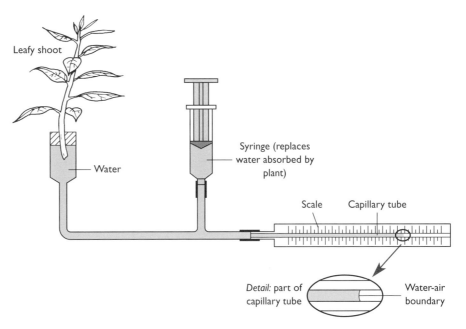

Leafy shoot

Water

Syringe (replaces water absorbed by plant)

Scale   Capillary tube

Detail: part of capillary tube

Water-air boundary

Fig. 4.12 The potometer

Practical points to remember are to cut the plant and assemble the apparatus under water to prevent air bubbles entering the stem. The apparatus can be used to compare the rate of transpiration under **different conditions**. For example, by placing the potometer in the dark, or in the wind.

▶ Osmosis

Osmosis is the diffusion of water molecules from a region of **higher** water concentration to a region of **lower** water concentration through a partially permeable membrane. See Figs 4.13 and 4.14.

One feature of particles is their size; for example, water particles are much smaller than sugar molecules. This difference in size can have some interesting effects.

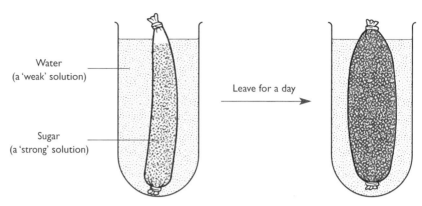

Fig. 4.13 An experiment to show asmosis

Partially permeable membrane

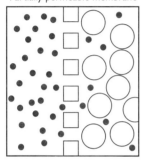

The small molecules of water pass through the membrane

The large molecules of sugar cannot pass through

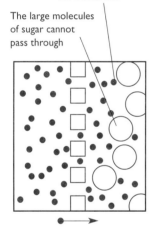

Fig. 4.14 Osmosis

A concentrated **sugar solution** is placed in a bag made of **visking tubing** (a material like cellophane). The bag and its contents are then placed in a beaker of **water**. After a short time the bag will be seen to be much **bigger**. Why?

The effect is due to the visking tubing acting as a sort of **particle sieve**. The tubing material contains **tiny holes** or pores, just big enough to let the **small water particles** pass **into** the bag, but **not** to let the **large sugar particles out**. As a result, the volume of the bag increases.

The movement of water from a dilute to a concentrated solution is called **osmosis**. Materials such as visking tubing are called **partially permeable membranes**. If the process were allowed to continue, water would pass through the tubing walls until the concentration of the solutions inside and out were the same. Using a differentially permeable membrane to separate the substances is called **dialysis**.

Partially permeable membranes in action

1   Cell membranes are partially permeable membranes, allowing water to enter cells. Water passes into **root hairs** (special cells on the tips of roots) by **osmosis**. The cells contain a solution of sugars, salts and other solutes; water can enter through the cell membrane because the solution inside the cell is **more** concentrated than outside.

2   **Kidney** machines, which can take over when some people's kidneys fail because of disease, also use partially permeable membranes (flat tubes of cellophane). Harmful substances are **removed** from the blood by osmosis.

3   Some methods of **food preservation** work with help from DPMs and osmosis. All the bacteria (which cause food to decay) are single-celled organisms. Fruit can be preserved by placing it in a concentrated sugar solution. As the solution outside the cell is more concentrated than the solution inside, water moves out of the cell and the bacteria are dehydrated and killed. Food preservation by 'salting' can be explained in the same way.

▶ Mineral salts

H···· *'how substances enter and leave cells through active transport'* [2.1d]

Mineral ions move from the soil into the root hair cells by **active transport**, which allows the plant to accumulate minerals above the concentration found in the soil.

▶   **Active transport**: the movement of molecules by chemical activity into and out of cells, across a membrane from a region where they are in a **low** concentration to one of a **high** concentration. This process requires the expenditure of **energy** in metabolism and occurs where diffusion is too slow to meet the demands of the cells.

▶ Plant hormones

'the hormonal control of plant growth and development, including commercial applications' [2.3e]

Auxins

Plant shoots grow towards the stimulus of light and plant roots grow towards the stimulus of gravity. These responses are known as **tropic responses**; shoots are **positively** phototropic and roots are **positively geotropic**. These responses are brought about by the action of **hormones**. The growth hormones in plants are **auxins** which stimulate or inhibit growth in plants. These hormones are released in the shoot tip and root tip and move through the plant by **diffusion**. They affect the zone of elongation just behind the shoot tip (plumule) and behind the root tip (radicle).

Phototropism – response to light

Auxins accumulate on the side of the shoot away from the light. The auxins **stimulate** the growth of the shoot so that the side **away** from the light, which has more auxins, grows more rapidly. This has the effect of bending the shoot **towards** the light so that more photosynthesis can take place. This is the positive phototropic response (see Fig. 4.15).

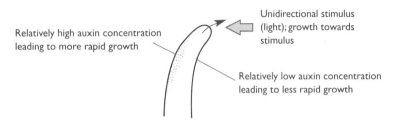

Fig. 4.15 Positive phototropism in a shoot tip

The shoot tip produces substances that inhibit the growth of the side shoots so if the shoot tip is removed, as in the pruning of a hedge, the side shoots grow outwards and the hedge becomes bushier.

Geotropism – response to gravity

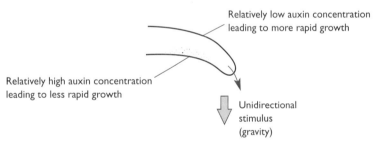

Fig. 4.16 Positive geotropism in a root tip

If the **root tip** is emerging from the seed horizontally, auxin hormones **accumulate** on the lower side of the root. Auxins in the root have the effect of **inhibiting** growth so that the side on top grows more rapidly. This has the effect of bending the root downwards **towards** water and minerals salts – a **positive geotropic** response (towards gravity), as in Fig. 4.16.

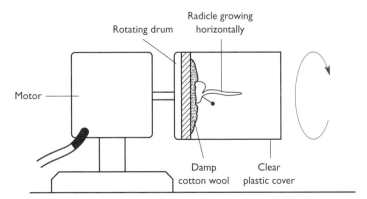

Fig. 4.17 The clinostat

If the **shoot tip** is emerging from the seed horizontally, the auxin has the opposite effect and stimulates growth of the lower side of the shoot so that it curves upwards towards the light. This is described as a **negative geotropic** response (away from gravity).

The diagram (Fig. 4.17) shows a **clinostat** used to investigate geotropism.

Commercial uses of growth hormones

Artificially synthesised hormones are used to control growth and reproduction in plants in many ways, for example:

▶ To stimulate the **formation of fruit** without the need for fertilisation; for example, growth substances can be applied to unpollinated flowers to produce 'seedless' fruits such as citrus fruits and grapes.

▶ In **stimulating root growth** in cuttings; for example, horticulturists using rooting hormone powder to promote the growth of roots in cuttings.

▶ Hormone **weed killers** can be applied to lawns to disrupt the growth patterns of certain weeds.

▶ Sexual reproduction in plants

'*how sexual reproduction occurs in flowering plants, including pollination, fertilisation, seed formation, seed dispersal and germination*' [KS2/3]

The diagram shows a section through an insect-pollinated flower (Fig. 4.18).

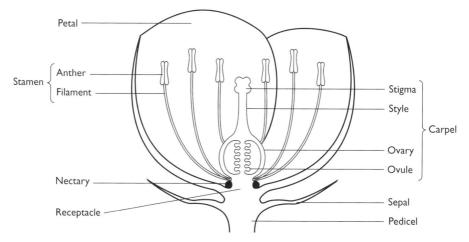

Fig. 4.18 Structure of a generalised flower (vertical section)

Table 4.3 Reproductive parts of a flowering plant

Part			Function
petal			to attract insects
nectary			to produce nectar to attract insect
sepal			to protect the petals
stamen	–	anther	to produce pollen
	–	filament	to support the anther
carpel	–	stigma	to receive pollen
	–	style	to hold up the stigma
	–	ovary	contains the ovules
	–	ovules	to form the seeds

Wind-pollinated flowers have much **smaller** flowers and the reproductive parts usually hang **outside** the flower so that the very light pollen can be blown by the **wind** on to the stigma.

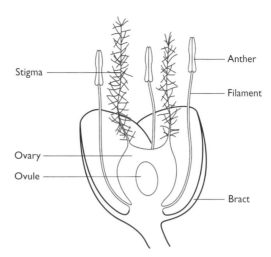

Fig. 4.19 Wind-pollinated flower: meadow grass (Poa spp.) (half flower)

Pollination

Pollen is **transferred** either by insects or wind **from** the anthers (the male part of the flower) **to** the stigma (the female part of the flower).

Fertilisation

The pollen grains on the stigma grow a long tube through the style so that the **nucleus** of the pollen cell can travel down the tube and **fuse** with the nucleus of the ovum inside the ovule.

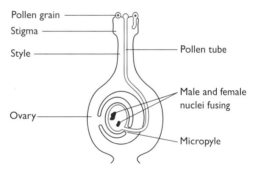

Fig. 4.20 Fertilisation in a generalised carpel

Development of fruit and seeds

The fertilised **ovule** develops into the **seed**. The **ovary** develops into the **fruit** which encloses the seeds and helps to disperse the seeds.

Fruit and seed dispersal

Dispersal is important so that seeds do not **compete** with the parent plant for resources such as light, space and mineral salts. New areas can be **colonised** as seeds may be carried over long distances by animals, wind or water.

Germination of seeds

At the beginning of seed germination **water** is absorbed, which activates **enzymes** to break down **starch** into smaller **soluble** molecules, which release **energy**.

The following are essential conditions for germination:

▶   **oxygen** for respiration;
▶   a suitable **temperature**, about 25°C;
▶   **water** for enzyme activity.

Germination experiments to show that each of these conditions are necessary can be set up as follows.

Oxygen

To show whether **oxygen** is necessary for germination, use the apparatus shown in the diagram (Fig. 4.21).

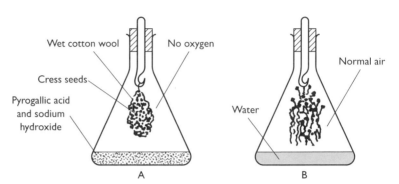

Fig. 4.21 To find out if oxygen is needed for germination

The pyrogallic acid and sodium hydroxide absorb oxygen from the air in the flask, so no germination takes place. The seeds in flask B will germinate because oxygen is present.

Temperature

To investigate the effect of **temperature** on germination you can put three dishes of soaked seeds at different temperatures, e.g. in a refrigerator at 4°C, in an incubator at 30°C and at room temperature at 20°C. Seeds usually have an optimum temperature for growth and the seeds at room temperature will usually germinate best.

Water

To show whether **water** is necessary for germination use the apparatus shown in the diagram (Fig. 4.22).

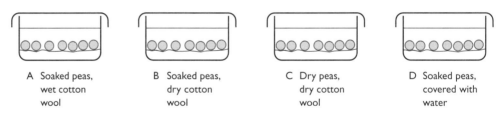

| A Soaked peas, wet cotton wool | B Soaked peas, dry cotton wool | C Dry peas, dry cotton wool | D Soaked peas, covered with water |

Fig. 4.22 Soaked peas covered with water

Results

A   germinate properly
B   seeds shrivel up and die
C   no germination
D   seeds go mouldy and rot

Asexual reproduction

This is covered in Chapter 5 on page 97.

▶ EXAMINATION QUESTIONS

Structured questions

Q1 (a) The diagram below shows the movement of substances into and out of a green leaf during photosynthesis.

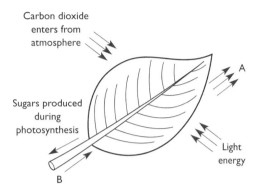

Fig. 4.23

    (i) What gas is passed out into the atmosphere at A? (1 line) *(1)*
    (ii) What raw material, required for photosynthesis, enters the leaf at B? (1 line) *(1)*
    (iii) State **one** way in which the plant uses the sugars produced during photosynthesis (2 lines) *(2)*
    (iv) Some plants have leaves which are green in parts and white in other parts. Why does photosynthesis not take place in the white parts? (2 lines) *(2)*

(b) Two sets of apparatus (A and B below) are used to investigate the process of photosynthesis. Before the apparatus was set up, both plants were kept in the dark for 48 hours.

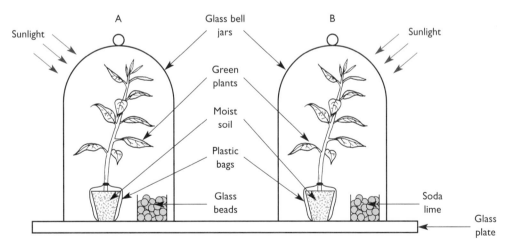

Fig. 4.24

    (i) Why were the plants kept in the dark for 48 hours before starting the investigation? (2 lines) *(1)*
    (ii) Which environment factor necessary for photosynthesis was missing from one of the bell jars? (1 line) *(1)*
    (iii) Why were **two** sets of apparatus used in the investigation? (1 line) *(1)*
    (iv) What chemical substance in the leaves do you usually test for to show that photosynthesis has taken place? (1 line) *(1)*
    (v) How would the result of this test show the importance of the missing environment factor to the process of photosynthesis? (3 lines) *(2)*

(c) Using only the information in the diagram below, describe how the energy used during a hockey match on a cold winter morning comes from the energy of sunlight. (8 lines)

(2)

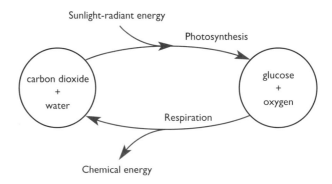

Fig. 4.25

(d) In some countries, farmers have cleared large areas of land for farming by cutting down trees and burning them. Concern has been expressed at this action as it is feared that it will upset the balance of the gases in the atmosphere.

How is the balance likely to be upset by the farmers' actions? (4 lines)   *(2)*

(NICCEA, Non-modular Double Award)

Q2 The diagram below shows a section through a flower.

(a) On the diagram:
  (i)   label with the letter P a structure which produces pollen.
  (ii) label with the letter E a structure which produces egg cells.   *(2)*

(b) Explain what is meant by pollination. (2 lines)   *(2)*

(c) Give **three** conditions that seeds need in order to germinate. (3 lines)   *(3)*

(NEAB, Co-ordinated Science)

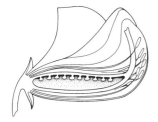

Fig. 4.26

Q3 The amount of water lost from the leaves of a sycamore shoot was measured at hourly intervals throughout a warm, dry, windless day. The results obtained are shown in the graph (Fig. 4.27).

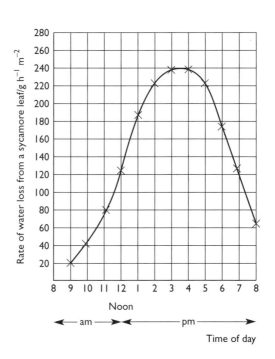

Fig. 4.27

(a) Over which part of the day does the rate of water loss
    (i) increase from 40 to 188 g h^{-1} m^{-2}
    (ii) decrease from 240 to 68 g h^{-1} m^{-2}?   *(4)*

(b) (i) At what time of day is the rate of water loss at a maximum?
    (ii) Suggest **two** reasons for this.   *(3)*

(c) At what other time of day is the rate of water loss the same as it is at 12 noon?   *(1)*

(d) Would you expect the maximum rate of water loss to increase, decrease or stay the same if the measurements had been made on
    (i) a warm, humid, windless day
    (ii) a warm, dry, windy day?
    Give reasons for your choice of answer.   *(6)*

(e) Describe an experiment designed to show which surface of a leaf loses more water vapour.   *(6)*

(f) Give **two** reasons why transpiration is important to a plant.   *(2)*

(g) Explain how a high light intensity increases the transpiration rate.   *(2)*

Q4 (Foundation Tier)   The diagram shows a flowering plant.

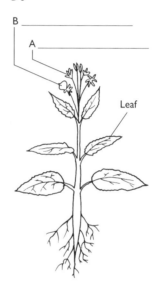

Fig. 4.28

(a) Label organs A and B on the diagram.   *(2)*

(b) Describe the functions of the root system. (3 lines)   *(3)*

(c) The diagram below shows a cell taken from the root of a plant.

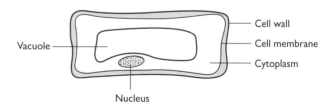

Fig. 4.29

    (i) Give **one** difference between a typical leaf cell and this root cell. Explain the reason for this difference. (4 lines)   *(3)*
    (ii) Give **one** difference between this root cell and a typical animal cell. (2 lines)   *(1)*
                                       (*London, SEG Modular Science*)

Q5 (Foundation Tier)   The picture below shows a plant known as the giant hogweed. It is an annual plant, which means that it grows from a seed each year. Its seeds germinate at the beginning of April and by the end of July the plants could have reached heights of over 2 metres.

Fig. 4.30

(a) Giant hogweed normally grows very quickly. Suggest **two** environmental conditions which would cause it to grow more slowly. *(2)*

Condition 1 _____

Condition 2 _____

(b) In order to grow, green plants need to carry out photosynthesis. Give the name of a carbon compound which is made by a plant during photosynthesis. *(1)*

(c) (i) From the diagram, suggest and explain **two** ways in which the giant hogweed is well adapted for photosynthesis. *(4)*

Suggestion 1 _____

Explanation 1 _____

_____

Suggestion 2 _____

Explanation 2 _____

_____

(ii) Suggest and explain **one** reason why this plant has to photosynthesise at a rapid rate. *(2)*

Suggestion _____

Explanation _____

_____

(d) A single giant hogweed produces many millions of seeds. Each seed is very light and feathery. Explain the advantage to the plant of the seeds being **light** and **feathery**. (4 lines) *(3)*

(Science Double Award, SEG)

▶ **EXAMINATION ANSWERS**

A1 *Structured questions*

(a) (i) oxygen (1)
(ii) water (1)
(iii) for respiration (to release energy) (1)
for amino acids for growth (1)
(iv) there is no chlorophyll present (1), chlorophyll is needed to absorb light during photosynthesis (1)

(b) (i) to use up all the starch (to destarch the plant) (1)
(ii) carbon dioxide is missing (absorbed by the soda lime) (1)
(iii) one set is the control with all factors present (1)
(iv) starch (1)
(v) the leaf from flask B would show no starch present (1)
due to the lack of carbon dioxide (1)

(c) Note: only 2 marks are allocated here but there are 8 lines of space; try to make two clear scientific statements based on the diagram but not just repeating what is in the diagram:

during photosynthesis energy from the sun is absorbed into plants and converted into starch/fats/protein (1);
when plants are eaten (as food/breakfast cereal) the chemical energy is released (1)

(d) trees remove some carbon dioxide from the atmosphere (1) and give out oxygen (1); this maintains the balance of gases, also burning trees adds quantities of carbon dioxide to the atmosphere (1)

A2 (a) (i) and (ii) diagram of flower required from question

(b) the transfer of pollen (1)
from the anthers (male) to the stigma (female) (1)

(c) 1. water/moisture (1)
2. oxygen (1)
3. suitable temperature/warmth (1)

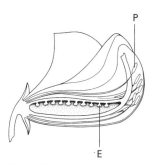

Fig. 4.31

A3 (a) (i) from 10 a.m. to 1 p.m.
(ii) from 4 p.m. to 8 p.m. (4)

(b) (i) between 3 p.m. and 4 p.m.
(ii) hottest part of the day, increased transpiration takes place (3)

(c) 7 p.m. (1)

(d) (i) decrease – transpiration reduced if humid and no wind;
(ii) increase – transpiration increased by dry, moving air. (6)

(e) fix small squares of cobalt chloride paper to each surface of leaf and compare time taken for paper to change from blue (when dry) to pink (when moist) (6)

(f) allows water and mineral salts to be drawn up to leaves;
possible cooling effect of evaporation of water (2)

(g) the stomata open to allow more rapid evaporation. (2)

A4 (a) On the diagram, A is the flower (1), B is the fruit (1)

(b) the root system holds/anchors the plant in the ground (1) obtains water (1) and minerals (1) for the plant stores food (1).

(c) (i) make it clear to which cell you are referring.
Note you are asked to explain the reason for the difference:

a typical leaf cell contains chlorophyll/choroplasts (1),
which are needed to absorb light (1),
to enable the leaf to carry out photosynthesis (1).

(ii) the root cell has a cell wall and a vacuole (1),
whereas the animal cell does not.

A5 (a) Any **two** from:

lack of water/drought (1)
lack of food/fertiliser/minerals (1)
lack of sun (shine) (1)
lack of heat (1)
poor soil (1)

NOTE: each condition **must** be qualified. (2)

(b) carbohydrate/glucose/sugar/starch or any other correct carbohydrate (1)

(c) (i) leaves flat/large (surface area)/not under one another (1)
pick up max/lots sunlight (1)

tall stems (1)
hold leaves above competitors (1)

(ii) needs to get tall/large/quickly (1)
needs a lot of energy/protein for this (1)

(d) Light:
easily carried by the wind (1)

Feathery:
large surface area (1)

Consequence:
get carried a long way (1)

▶ **A STUDENT'S ANSWER WITH EXAMINER'S COMMENTS**

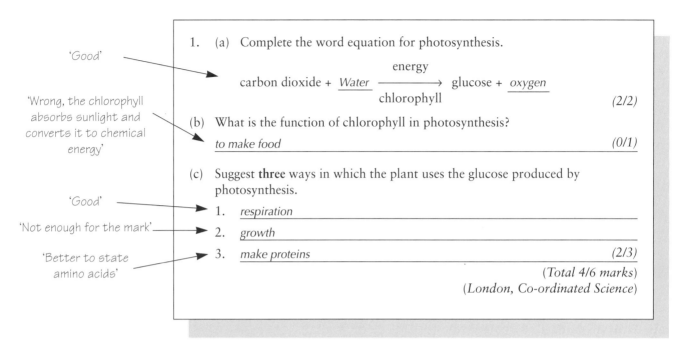

'Good'

1. (a) Complete the word equation for photosynthesis.

$$\text{carbon dioxide} + \underline{Water} \xrightarrow[\text{chlorophyll}]{\text{energy}} \text{glucose} + \underline{oxygen}$$

(2/2)

'Wrong, the chlorophyll absorbs sunlight and converts it to chemical energy'

(b) What is the function of chlorophyll in photosynthesis?

to make food   (0/1)

(c) Suggest **three** ways in which the plant uses the glucose produced by photosynthesis.

'Good'

1. _respiration_

'Not enough for the mark'

2. _growth_

'Better to state amino acids'

3. _make proteins_   (2/3)

(Total 4/6 marks)
(London, Co-ordinated Science)

SUMMARY

At the end of the chapter you should know:

▷ the **reactants** (carbon dioxide and water) and **products** (oxygen and carbohydrates) of **photosynthesis**, and the word equation;

▷ that the **rate** of photosynthesis may be limited by **limiting factors**: **light intensity**, **carbon dioxide concentration** or **temperature**;

▷ how the **products** of **photosynthesis** are used by the plant;

▷ that green plants carry out **aerobic respiration** to release energy;

▷ the importance to healthy **plant growth** of the uptake and utilisation of **mineral salts**, e.g. nitrogen, phosphorus and magnesium;

▷ how plants take up **water** by **osmosis** and lose it through **transpiration**;

▷ the importance of **water** in the **support** of plant tissues;

▷ that substances required for growth and reproduction are **transported** within plants;

▷ the **hormonal control** of plant growth and development including **commercial applications**;

▷ how **sexual reproduction** occurs in flowering plants including **pollination**, **fertilisation**, **seed formation**, **dispersal** and **germination**.

Variation, Inheritance and Evolution

▶ **GETTING STARTED**

This chapter is all about 'changes' – and in today's world change is something we must all come to terms with; *new* models of familiar things appear every day! New cars, personal stereo players, compact discs and cameras keep appearing in the shops, all different in some way to those we have already, and tempting us to part with our money. It is now quite possible to imagine a machine which would behave much like a human, taking in energy, moving about and having enough artificial intelligence to make simple decisions and react appropriately to stimuli. What this machine, and the others listed above, would *not* be able to do is to *reproduce* – this is a unique characteristic of living things and so sets them apart from the machines we make.

Even more amazing is the way in which each generation of living things may be *different* from its parent generation. As we begin to understand the mechanisms of inheritance, this is no longer such a mystery, as we recognise that differences may simply be due to the reshuffling of *existing* genes and the creation of *new* ones by mutation. We think we can now explain how some 200 million different species of plants and animals have come into being on the Earth; according to the *theory of evolution*, organisms changed gradually from one generation to the next and, over many generations, new species have formed. To understand the *processes* that bring about evolution, it is essential to have an understanding of how living things *reproduce*, since this is the key to change.

TOPIC	STUDY	REVISION 1	REVISION 2
Sexual reproduction			
The human reproductive system			
Meiosis and mitosis			
Fertilisation			
Development of the fetus			
Twins			
The menstrual cycle			
Contraception			
Chromosomes and genes			
The mechanism of monohybrid inheritance			
Sex determination			
Sex linkage			
Mutations			
Inherited diseases			
Variation			
Asexual reproduction			
Selective breeding			
Evolution and the fossil record			
Natural selection			

WHAT YOU NEED TO KNOW

▶ **Sexual reproduction**

'sexual reproduction is a source of genetic variation, while asexual reproduction produces clones' [2.46]

Reproduction is a characteristic of all living things. It may occur once, or many times, in an organism's lifetime. All life exists because previous generations have reproduced and the new individuals that survived have also reproduced. Because living things **vary**, they are not all equally well adapted to **survive**, so not all organisms which are born live long enough to reproduce. There seem to be many different *ways* of reproducing, but if we remove the details there are only two basic methods: **asexual** and **sexual**.

'The offspring all differ from each other'

Sexual reproduction usually involves **two** parents and always involves the fusion of two **gametes** – one **male** sex cell (sperm) and one **female** sex cell (egg). The new cell produced, the **zygote**, divides many times to form an **embryo** and eventually grows to become the young organism.

The **first** problem to be solved by organisms reproducing in this way is how to find a member of the opposite sex, and the **second** is how to get the sperm and egg together – both have been solved in many ways. In humans, fertilisation is **internal**, so the egg and sperm fuse inside the female's body. In frogs, fertilisation is **external**, with the sperm being shed over the eggs, which are laid in water. Usually offspring which are produced by **internal** fertilisation are **better protected**, as they develop either in an egg with a tough shell, or inside the mother, as in humans. The main advantage of sexual reproduction, as compared with asexual reproduction, is that the offspring will **vary** from each other and from the parents – variety can mean the difference between success or extinction for the species in a constantly changing environment.

▶ **The human reproductive system**

'the human reproductive system, including the menstrual cycle and fertilisation' [KS3]

'how the foetus develops in the uterus, including the role of the placenta' [KS3]

The male reproductive system

'Learn the names, positions and functions of the parts of the male and female reproductive systems'

▶ The **testes**: a mass of coiled tubes where the sperm (male gametes) are made.
▶ **Sperm tubes**: carry sperm from the testes to the urethra in the penis.
▶ **Urethra**: a dual-purpose tube which carries (1) **urine** from the bladder to the outside, and (2) **semen** containing sperm from the sperm tubes to the outside.
▶ **Penis**: the urethra passes through the penis. The penis has a dual function (1) to pass **urine** out of the body, (2) to pass **sperm** out of the body during ejaculation. The penis is placed in the female's vagina during intercourse.
▶ **Scrotum**: a bag of skin which holds the testes outside the body.

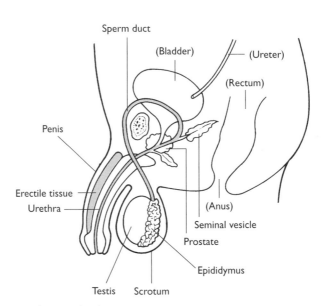

Fig. 5.1 The human male reproductive system

The female reproductive system

- ▶ **Ovaries**: where the eggs (female gametes) are made.
- ▶ **Oviducts**: fine tubes which carry the eggs from the ovaries to the uterus (womb).
- ▶ **Uterus**: a muscular organ with an inner layer of spongy tissue where the fertilised egg develops into a foetus.
- ▶ **Cervix**: a ring of muscle at the neck of the uterus.
- ▶ **Vagina**: a muscular tube which leads to the outside of the body. The penis is placed in the vagina during intercourse.

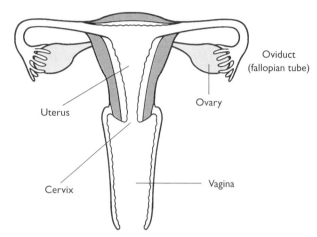

Fig. 5.2 The human female reproductive system

▶ **Meiosis and mitosis**   *'how cells divide by mitosis so that growth takes place, and by meiosis to produce gametes'* [2.1f]

H   Meiosis and **mitosis** are two types of cell division.

Meiosis

- ▶ **Gametes** are produced by **meiosis** (reduction division), which takes place in the sex organs.
- H ▶ The gametes have **half** the chromosome number of the parent cell and only half of the genetic information: male gametes, **sperm**, are produced in the testis; female gametes, the **ova**, are produced in the ovary.
- ▶ One male gamete and one female gamete fuse at **fertilisation** to form the **zygote** which has the full chromosome number.
- H ▶ There is **genetic variation** among the gametes due to the behaviour of the chromosomes during meiosis.

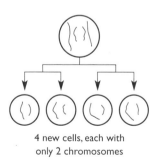

4 new cells, each with only 2 chromosomes

Fig. 5.3 Meiosis in a cell with four chromosomes

Mitosis

H

▶ **Mitosis** is the type of cell division used during **growth** to increase the number of body cells.

▶ Cells produced by mitosis are **identical** to each other and to the parent cell, having exactly the same chromosomes. Each species has a characteristic number of chromosomes; for example, in humans there are 23 pairs of chromosomes in the nucleus of every body cell and the zygote.

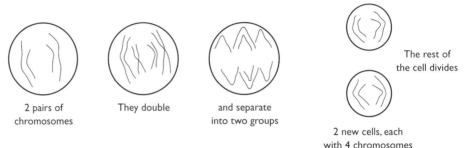

2 pairs of chromosomes   They double   and separate into two groups   The rest of the cell divides   2 new cells, each with 4 chromosomes

Fig. 5.4 Mitosis in a cell with four chromosomes

▶ **Fertilisation**

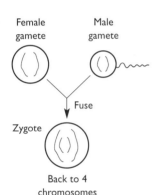

Female gamete   Male gamete

Fuse

Zygote

Back to 4 chromosomes

Fig. 5.5 Fertilisation

Fertilisation occurs when the male and female gamete (sperm and egg) fuse to form a single cell called a **zygote**. During sexual intercourse, the male penis is pushed inside the female vagina so that the sperm (male gametes) are released as close to the cervix as possible. The sperm swim to the uterus and along the oviducts towards the ovaries. If there is an egg in the oviduct then **fertilisation** may occur and a zygote is formed.

▶ Development of the foetus

'how the foetus develops in the uterus, including the role of the placenta' [KS3]

The zygote travels to the **uterus**, embeds itself in the spongy lining of the uterus and starts dividing by **mitosis** into a ball of cells which then becomes known as an **embryo**. The embryo continues to develop and after about 8 weeks, when it begins to look recognisably human, it is called a **foetus**. If no egg is present, the spongy lining of the uterus breaks down and is released from the body during menstruation.

The foetus is joined to the mother by the **placenta**, which allows substances to diffuse from the mother's blood to the baby's blood and vice versa. The blood supply never mixes and this protects the foetus from the higher pressure of the mother's blood. The foetus is connected to the placenta by an **umbilical cord** and supported by **amniotic fluid** which acts as a shock absorber. See Fig. 5.6.

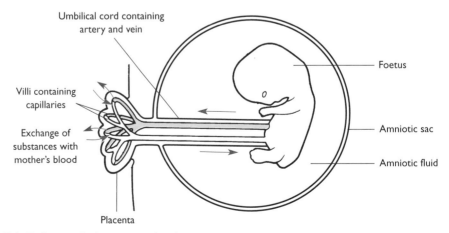

Umbilical cord containing artery and vein

Villi containing capillaries

Exchange of substances with mother's blood

Placenta

Foetus

Amniotic sac

Amniotic fluid

Fig. 5.6 Exchange of substances at the placenta

After about 40 weeks the baby's head is normally positioned above the **cervix** and is pushed out of the **uterus** by rhythmic contractions of the uterus muscles during 'labour'. The **placenta** is also pushed out of the uterus after the baby is born. The sudden drop in temperature causes a reflex response which makes the baby breathe.

Soon after birth, the mammary glands of the mother begin to produce **milk** which contains all the necessary **nutrients** for the baby until the baby is weaned on to solid food.

▶ Twins

Twins can be either identical or non-identical:

▶ **Identical twins** are formed when a **fertilised egg** divides by mitosis into **two separate embryos** which have identical sets of chromosomes. The twins are of the same sex and look exactly alike.

▶ **Non-identical twins** are formed when two different sperm each fertilise an egg at the same time. The zygotes have different combinations of genes and the twins are no more alike than a brother and sister, two brothers or two sisters.

▶ The menstrual cycle

This is a periodic change which occurs in a woman's body about every 28 days. During the first few days of the cycle the **extra lining** of the **uterus** breaks down and is released from the body. During the next 10 days an egg ripens in the **ovary** and the uterus lining thickens again. On about the 14th day the egg is **released** from the ovary during **ovulation**, and this is when **fertilisation** can occur. If there is no fertilisation then the uterus lining breaks down and is released on about the 28th day.

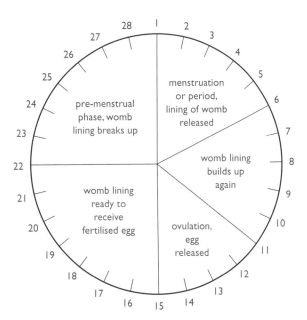

Fig. 5.7 The menstrual cycle

Puberty

Puberty (adolescence) is a time when a person's reproductive organs mature as summarised in the table.

Table 5.1 Changes that occur at puberty

Girls	Boys
ovaries release eggs in monthly (menstrual) cycle	testes produce sperm
breasts (mammary glands) develop	penis grows bigger
hips broaden	voice deepens
under-arm and pubic hair grows	under-arm, pubic and facial hair grows

▶ **Contraception**   The table below provides a useful review of the various methods of **contraception**.

Table 5.2 Methods of contraception

Method	How it works	Advantages	Disadvantages
Contraceptive pill	Contains hormones which prevent ovulation.	Very effective.	Possible side effects, possible to forget.
Cap (diaphragm)	Blocks path of sperm at cervix.	Simple, effective if used with spermicidal cream.	May be incorrectly fitted.
Intra-uterine device (IUD) (coil)	Fitted in uterus; prevents implantation.	Once fitted, does not require frequent attention.	May cause pain or heavy bleeding.
Condom (sheath)	Made of thin rubber, fits over erect penis; retains semen.	Simple, effective; may prevent sexually transmitted diseases e.g. AIDS.	May be damaged; may not be carefully removed.
Withdrawal	Penis withdrawn from vagina before ejaculation.	Does not require any preparation.	Semen may be released before ejaculation and pregnancy may occur.

▶ **Chromosomes and genes**   '*that the nucleus contains the chromosomes that carry the genes*' [2.1e]

'*the gene is a section of DNA*' [2.4g]

The nucleus of the human body cells contains **23 pairs of chromosomes** which contain instructions for many chemical reactions in the body. Chromosomes are long, complex molecules of **DNA** (deoxyribonucleic acid) composed of two strands coiled to form a **double helix**.

H⋯   **Genes** are sections of DNA responsible for a particular protein and therefore for a particular characteristic or trait. The strands are linked by paired bases (adenine with thymine and cytosine with guanine). It is the **sequence** of these four bases within a gene that directs the sequence in which **amino acids** are made to form particular **proteins: one gene – one protein**.

There are genes for all our characteristics, such as eye colour, hair colour and blood type. Each chromosome carries many genes, each a certain length of DNA. We have two copies of each gene in every normal human body cell, one in each of a pair of chromosomes because we inherit one gene of each type – one from our father and one from our mother.

Alleles are components of genes. If a gene determines a particular inherited characteristic (e.g. eye colour), the alleles that form that praticular gene may exit in two forms:

1   A **dominant allele** (e.g. brown) will always be expressed in the individual if it is present in the cell.
2   A **recessive allele** (e.g. blue) will only be expressed in the individual if no dominant allele is present.

The **genotype** is the genetic composition of an individual, and can be one involving three possible combinations of alleles.

▶   Heterozygous A pair of different alleles, one dominant and one recessive.
▶   Homozygous **dominant** A pair of identical dominant alleles.
▶   Homozygous **recessive** A pair of identical recessive alleles.

The **phenotype** is the outward appearance of the individual (e.g. brown or blue eyes) that follows from the genotype.

▶ **The mechanism of monohybrid inheritance**   '*the mechanism of monohybrid inheritance where there are dominant and recessive alleles*' [2.4e]

A monohybrid genetic cross involves one pair of **alleles** and two parents. For example, in a genetic cross involving the alleles for *eye colour* where brown is dominant to blue, if both parents are *brown* eyed but are **heterozygous** for eye colour, they have the **dominant** allele for *brown* eye colour and the **recessive** allele for *blue* eye colour.

Write out your genetic cross using a checkerboard diagram as shown below (stating the letters you are going to use). Let *B* be the symbol for *brown* and *b* be the symbol for *blue*

parent's genotype   Bb × Bb
gametes   B b × B b

offspring (F₁) genotypes are shown in the checkerboard diagram (Fig. 5.8) below.

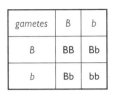

gametes	B	b
B	BB	Bb
b	Bb	bb

Fig. 5.8

Therefore, the resulting **offspring (F₁) phenotypes** are:

BB brown eyes (homozygous dominant);
Bb brown eyes (heterozygous);
bb blue eyes (homozygous recessive)

There is a **3:1 ratio** of brown to blue eyes, which means a **25% probability** of a child inheriting blue eyes from these parents.

▶ **Sex determination**

'*how gender is determined in humans*' [2.4d]

In humans, the sex of an individual is determined by a small pair of chromosomes called the **sex chromosomes**. In a human **female** these chromosomes are **homologous** (identical) and are described as **X** chromosomes. In the **male**, one of the pair is **smaller** and is called the **Y** chromosome, with the larger being the **X** chromosome.

A **female** individual results from having **two X** chromosomes and a **male** from having an **X** and a **Y** chromosome. At **meiosis** all the female gametes carry an **X** chromosome whereas **half** of the male gametes carry an **X** chromosome and **half** carry a **Y** chromosome. If an **X** bearing sperm fertilises the ovum then the zygote is **XX** and develops into a girl. If a **Y** bearing sperm fertilises the ovum the zygote is **XY** and develops into a **boy**. The expected ratio of female to male is therefore 1:1, as shown in Fig. 5.9.

Remember:

X egg with X sperm = **female XX** (gametes are all X)

X egg with Y sperm = **male XY** = (50% of gametes are X, 50% are Y)

'XY = boy; XX = girl'

gametes	X
X	XX
Y	XY

Fig. 5.9

▶ **Sex linkage**H

Certain conditions such as **colour blindness** and **haemophilia** are linked to the **X chromosome** and are more likely to affect a male than a female as only a small part of the Y chromosome is homologous with the X chromosome. For example, the non-homologous part of the X chromosome carries either the dominant gene for normal vision or the recessive gene for colour blindness. If a male inherits an X chromosome bearing the recessive gene then he will be colour blind.

The diagram below (Fig. 5.10) shows the inheritance of colour blindness.

gametes	Xn
XN	XNXn
Y	XnY

N: normal colour vision
n: colour blindness

XNXn: normal daughter
XnY: colour-blind son

Fig. 5.10 Inheritance of colour blindness

▶ **Mutations**

'*mutation is a source of genetic variation and has a number of causes*' [2.4c]

Mutations are caused by errors in copying **genes** and **chromosomes** during mitosis and meiosis. These mistakes can affect whole chromosomes or single genes. Mutations can be increased by exposure to **radiation** such as gamma-rays, X-rays and ultra-violet-rays and to some chemicals such as mustard gas. Mutations in body cells may result in cancer. Some mutations are *harmful*, some *neutral* and some *beneficial*. Gene mutations are usually harmful and may cause genetic diseases. For example, the **albino gene** prevents the formation of

'See Chapter 15, Waves, pp. 281–2 and Chapter 18, Radioactivity, p. 343'

Normal red
blood cells

'Sickle' cells

Fig. 5.11 Sickle cells
compared with normal red
blood cells

dark skin pigment melanin which protects against the Sun's ultra-violet rays. Some mutant genes are helpful, for example the **sickle cell gene** which causes sickle shaped red blood cells. These give some immunity to the person from malaria although the person is anaemic.

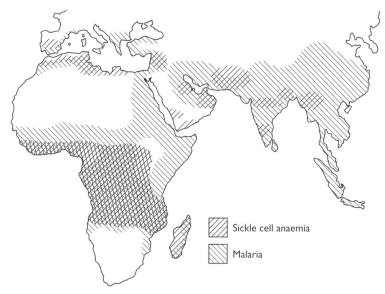

Sickle cell anaemia

Malaria

Fig. 5.12 Distribution of sickle cell anaemia and malaria

Chromosome mutations can also occur when chromosomes are altered during **meiosis**. Bits may be broken off or added to chromosomes, and sometimes whole chromosomes may be lost or gained. The faulty gametes which are produced may be fertilised and produce zygotes with **damaged** chromosomes, or too few or too many chromosomes. An extra number 21 chromosome in humans produces a Down's Syndrome child with a low mental age and very characteristic facial features which led to the previous name for this genetic disorder – **mongolism**. You may know of a Down's person who has developed useful skills through special training and is a happy member of a family. Such diseases can now be detected in the early stages of pregnancy by taking a sample of fluid from the **amniotic fluid** in the womb and by examining some of the embryo's cells.

▶ **Inherited diseases**

'some diseases can be inherited' [Sc 2.4]

The sickle-cell gene can be harmful if a child inherits it from *both* parents. Other genetic diseases, such as **cystic fibrosis**, **muscular dystrophy** and **haemophilia**, can also be inherited from one or both parents. These are some of the 3,000 known genetic diseases. There are now genetic counsellors who help potential parents to assess the risk involved of producing a child with an inherited genetic disease. About 5% of all children admitted to hospitals in the UK are suffering from genetic diseases.

▶ **Variation**

'how variation may arise from both genetic and environmental causes' [2.4a]

Organisms vary even within the same family. The variations are the result of new genes (mutations) and new mixtures of genes (sexual reproduction). There are **two** types of variation between individuals of the same species:

1. **Discontinuous variation.** This enables us to separate individuals into distinct **groups**; one of the most used examples is blood grouping. We all belong to one of the **four** main groups. The groups are A, B, AB and O; there are no in-between groupings such as AO. The information in the **genes** accounts for most of this form of variation, and the environment affects it very little.
2. **Continuous variation.** This refers to characteristics that do not allow us to separate individuals into distinct groups. **Height** and **weight** are good examples of this sort of characteristic. Many genes may influence height and weight, but the **environment** can be important also. In any large population there would be a whole range of heights and weights.

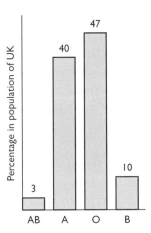

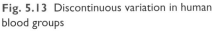

Fig. 5.13 Discontinuous variation in human blood groups

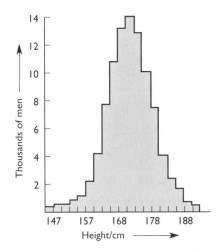

Fig. 5.14 Continuous variation in humans: height

Variation such as differences in height can be caused by the interaction of genetic factors with **environmental factors** such as availability of food in animals, availability of light, minerals, etc. in plants.

▶ **Asexual reproduction**

'asexual reproduction produces clones' [2.46]

Asexual reproduction:

▶ involves cell division by **mitosis** to produce **identical copies** of the parent; if the parent plant is successful in coping with its environment, then it is important that the parent's characteristics are passed on exactly; plants which are genetically identical are called **clones**.

▶ involves only **one parent** and means that an isolated individual can reproduce on its own.

▶ is used by some plants to form bulbs, stem tubers and runners.

▶ is used by gardeners to grow new plants (propagate) and to make sure that the new plants are exactly like the parent. This has important commercial implications; for example, growing exact copies (clones) of disease-resistant plants.

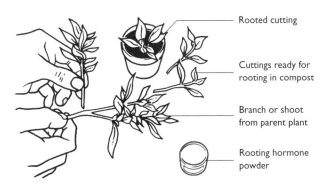

Rooted cutting

Cuttings ready for rooting in compost

Branch or shoot from parent plant

Rooting hormone powder

Fig. 5.15 Cuttings being taken

▶ **Selective breeding** [H]

'the basic principles of cloning, selective breeding and genetic engineering' [2.4h]

Genetic engineering

This is selective breeding, and humans have taken many species from the wild and controlled their evolution, with amazing results. All the different varieties of dog have been produced by artificial selection of the wolf, a single wild species. Our domesticated cattle breeds, poultry, sheep and cereal crops have all been bred from wild species by generations of farmers. Plant and animal breeding is now big business, and so breeders are always on the look-out for wild varieties that could be useful.

[H]   Genetic engineering involves the **transfer** of a section of **DNA** from one organism to the DNA of another organism of a different species. For example the gene determining production of the hormone **insulin** can be inserted into the DNA of **bacteria** or yeast cells. The transferred gene continues to produce insulin which can be used in the treatment of **diabetes**. This process is now carried out on an industrial scale to manufacture large quantities of the hormone.

Genes can also be transferred into the cells of animals or plants at an early stage so that they develop certain beneficial characteristics such as **resistance to disease**. It is also possible to produce **genetically identical** organisms by a process known as tissue culture, using small groups of cells from a part of a plant to grow a new plant, genetically identical to the parent. There are obvious benefits in agricultural terms to being able to produce many **identical** plants, say with high resistance to drought or high yields of fruit. However, all the plants produced in this way from one parent could be affected by the same disease or insect pest as they are all the same. In animals, cells from a developing embryo can be split apart and each can develop into a new, genetically identical organism.

Genetic engineering raises many **social** and **ethical** issues; for example how far should it be used to produce genetically identical human beings?; should research be carried out using potentially viable human embryos which may later have to be destroyed? Guidance on these issues is being developed in the medical profession.

On **medical** grounds, genetic engineering could be used to help treat diseases such as cystic fibrosis and muscular dystrophy. It could therefore help people who have a defect in their immune system and are unable to make a particular protein. The missing gene could be inserted into some white blood cells and the person would then be able to lead a normal life.

Remember: genetic engineering is the insertion of new genes into the DNA of bacteria, using enzymes, to make genetically altered cells which produce useful substances, e.g. human insulin.

▶ **Evolution and the fossil record**

'the fossil record as evidence for evolution' [2.4i]

Evolution is a series of changes in the appearance of animals and plants over millions of years, as observed in the (incomplete) **fossil record** of some organisms, such as the horse. Bones from early ancestors of the horse have become fossilised in sedimentary rocks which can be dated. Over millions of years, layers of **sediments**, which built up from mineral particles, were compressed to form **sedimentary rocks** such as sandstone and limestone. Remains of **animals** and **plants** which accumulated at the bottom of lakes and oceans therefore became preserved as **fossils** in these sedimentary rocks. When these sedimentary rocks were raised above the water level the fossils became exposed. Two factors are evident from the fossil record:

▶   there are many fossilised remains of animals and plants which no longer exist, for example armour-plated fish which are now extinct;

▶   many species of animals and plants which exist today are not present in the fossil record, for example no fossilised remains have been found of mammals in rocks over 300 million years old.

Fossils provide **evidence** for evolution; for example, it is thought from fossil evidence that the horse evolved from a small dog-sized ancestor into the large, strong, modern-day horse (Fig. 5.16).

One of the changes to observe in the illustration is that the teeth have become larger. This may be a result of a change in the food supply which favoured individuals with larger teeth. Another change is in the number of toes, which may have enabled the horse to run faster and escape predators.

▶ **Natural selection** H

'how variation and selection may lead to evolution or extinction' [2.4j]

Natural selection is the theory used to explain **evolution**. It is based on the following factors:

▶   individual organisms within a species show a wide range of **variation** because of **genetic** differences;

▶   **competition, predation** and **disease** cause large numbers of individuals to die;

▶   individuals with characteristics most suited to the environment are more likely to **survive** and **reproduce**;

▶   the **genes** which have enabled those individuals to survive are passed on to the **next generation**.

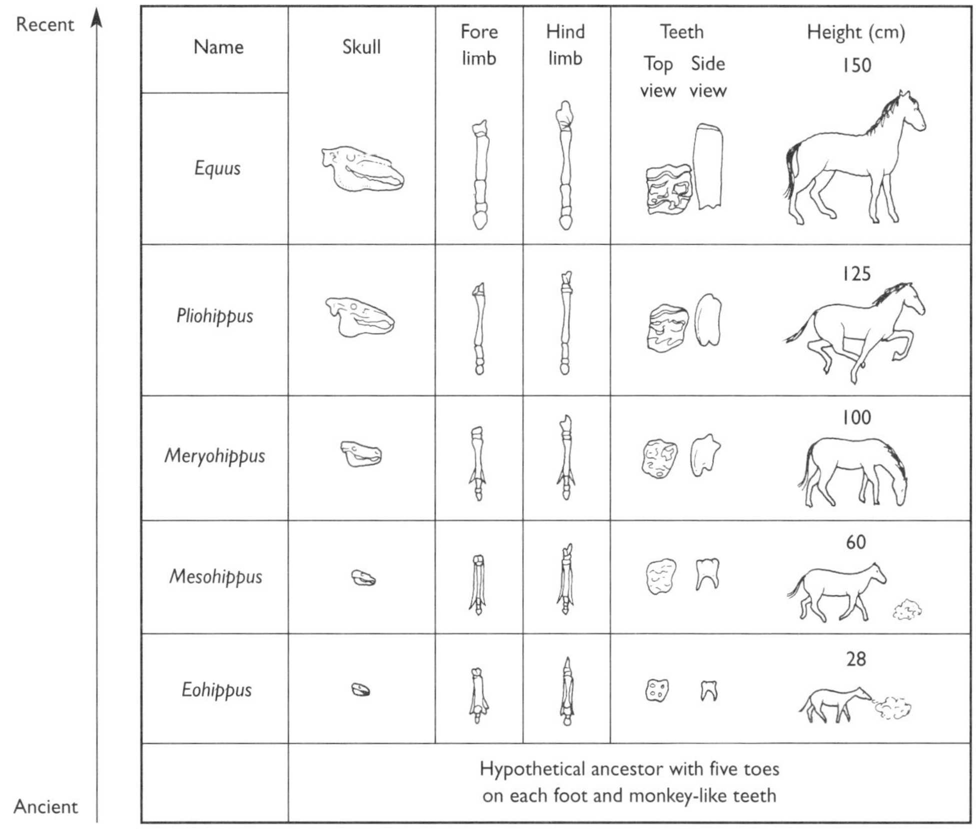

Name	Skull	Fore limb	Hind limb	Teeth Top view Side view	Height (cm)
Equus					150
Pliohippus					125
Meryohippus					100
Mesohippus					60
Eohippus					28
	Hypothetical ancestor with five toes on each foot and monkey-like teeth				

Recent ↑

Ancient

Fig. 5.16 The evolution of the modern-day horse

Natural selection leads to certain **alleles** becoming more or less common and means that those organisms which have **favourable variations** may survive to breed and pass on their favourable traits to the next generation and so on; these organisms are usually better able to adapt to any environmental changes. The organisms with **less favourable traits** may be less able to adapt to any changes in the environment and are often weaker and many die due to predators, disease or lack of food.

Darwin described this as a **struggle for survival** against a harsh environment. Scientists today term the difficulties 'selection pressures'. It is these pressures that determine which individuals survive. Those best adapted survive to pass their genes on to the next generation. Hares that can run fastest will escape the fox, and so genes for powerful leg muscles will be 'selected' and over many generations the performance of the species will be enhanced.

If the environment changes, the process of natural selection allows the species to adapt to the new situation, the most advantageous variations surviving to breed. Without variation, a species is very likely to become extinct. The Peppered Moth is a good example in that the colour of the moths has changed in recent times, the darker mutant ones becoming more common in industrial areas as the Industrial Revolution blackened the environment (see Fig. 5.17). However, they were still rare in the countryside where the lighter form was dominant. Camouflage is the key to understanding this; predators could easily find light-coloured moths in sooty cities, and so selection favoured the dark genes. In the countryside the reverse was true. Now that industrial pollution is less severe the situation should change again.

'The struggle for existence'

H

Table 5.3 Increase in relative numbers of the dark form of the Peppered Moth in an industrial area

	Percentage of each form	
Year	Dark	Pale
1848	1	99
1894	99	1

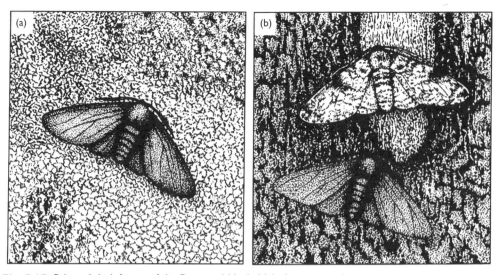

Fig. 5.17 Pale and dark forms of the Peppered Moth (a) Lichen-covered tree in unpolluted area (b) blackened tree in polluted area

► EXAMINATION QUESTIONS

Multiple choice

Q1 In a species of pea plant, red flowers were dominant to white flowers.

Pure-breeding, red-flowered pea plants are crossed with pure-breeding, white-flowered pea plants. What proportion of red- and white-coloured plants will be produced in the F_1 generation?

A   all white-flowered plants
B   equal numbers of white-flowered plants and red-flowered plants
C   a 3:1 ratio of red-flowered plants to white-flowered plants
D   a 3:1 ratio of white-flowered plants to red-flowered plants
E   all red-flowered plants

Q2 Which one of the following organs in the body forms gametes?

A   the brain   D   the uterus
B   the penis   E   the vagina
C   the testes

Q3 How many sperm are needed to fertilise a human egg cell?

A 1; B 10; C 100; D 1000; E 1000 000

Q4 Which one of the following is an example of discontinuous variation?

A   blood group   D   shoe size
B   headsize   E   weight
C   height

Q5 Which one of the following processes takes place when the sperm fuses with an egg?

A fertilisation   D   menstruation
B intercourse   E   selection
C ovulation

Structured questions

Q6 (a) In sexual reproduction, new offspring are formed after fusion (fertilisation) of eggs and sperm.
  (i) In the space below, draw diagrams of an egg and sperm and then show what happens during fertilisation:

                    egg   *sperm*   *fertilisation*

(3)

  (ii) Explain, in words or diagrams, how
    1. non-identical twins are formed   *(2)*
    2. identical twins are formed   *(2)*

(b) A boy had two rabbits. The male was grey and the female was white. He allowed them to mate so that he could make some money from selling baby rabbits. **All** the baby rabbits were grey.

When the baby grey rabbits had grown he let two of them mate several times. One-quarter of their babies turned out to be white.

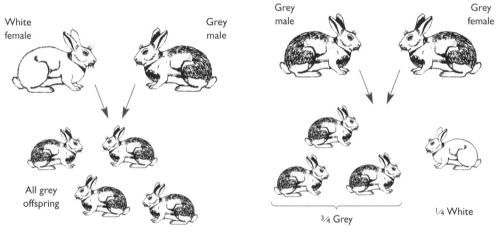

Fig. 5.18   **Fig. 5.19**

  (i) Which coat colour was dominant?
  (ii) Explain why:
    1. the first two rabbits (shown in Fig. 5.18) did not have any white babies; *(2)*
    2. the grey offspring were able to have white babies (see Fig. 5.19). *(2)*
  (iii) White rabbits are easier to sell, and fetch a higher price than grey rabbits. Suggest how the boy could arrange mating so that only white babies were produced. (4 lines) *(2)*

(c) (i) In vegetative (asexual) reproduction, new plants can be made from just one parent. Choose from the examples in Fig. 5.20 (or any other examples you may know about) and describe how you could produce **two** identical plants from one parent.

  Your choice of plant _____

  Method (4 lines available *and* space for optional diagram) *(2)*

  (ii) Plant growers use methods based on **asexual** reproduction to produce many beautiful plants for sale to the public. Give two reasons why they prefer to use these methods rather than the normal sexual reproduction (pollination – seeds – growth).

    1. _____

    2. _____ *(2)*

(London)

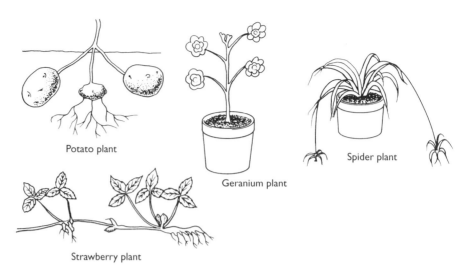

Potato plant

Geranium plant

Spider plant

Strawberry plant

Fig. 5.20

Q7 (a) It is believed, from fossil evidence, that the horse evolved from a small, dog-sized organism into a large, strong organism.

Examine Fig. 5.21 showing the evolution of the horse and then answer the questions which follow.

Explain the environmental factors that may have led to the changes in the horse in Fig. 5.21. (6 lines)   *(4)*

Recent ↑

Name	Skull	Fore limb	Hind limb	Teeth Top view / Side view	Height (cm)
Equus					150
Pliohippus					125
Meryohippus					100
Mesohippus					60
Eohippus					28
	Hypothetical ancestor with five toes on each foot and monkey-like teeth				

Ancient

Fig. 5.21

(b) Table 5.4 below shows some external characteristics of two organisms which look very similar

Table 5.4

	Honey Bee	Hoverfly
Body	3 segments	3 segments
Legs	3 pairs	3 pairs
Wings	2 pairs	I pair
Colour	yellow and black stripes	yellow and black stripes
Length	I.5 cm	2 cm
Sting	present	absent

A predator of insects will not eat either of these organisms, even though the hoverfly is harmless.

   (i) Explain the reason for the predator's behaviour.   (3)
  (ii) What is the meaning of the term 'genetic mutation'?   (1)
 (iii) Explain how genetic mutations in the ancestors of the hoverfly account for the similarities between it and the bee. (3 lines)   (2)
 (iv) Mutations in disease-causing bacteria are a serious medical problem. Suggest a reason for this.   (1)

(c) In 1884, in the Manchester area, a very dark variety of the Peppered Moth was found. Usually this moth is greyish-white in colour with black dots. By 1895 about 95% of the Peppered Moths in the same area were of the very dark form.

  (i) Explain very carefully how it is possible to have had only one very dark Peppered Moth in 1884, but for 95% of the population to be very dark in 1895. (5 lines)
                                                           (3)
  (ii) Nowadays, pollution is being removed from the environment. Explain very carefully what effect the removal of pollution would have on the population of Peppered Moths in Manchester.   (4)

(London)

Q8 This question is common to both Tiers with the exception of (a) (iv) which is for Higher Tier only.
    Fig. 5.22 is a diagram of a sweetcorn plant, which has both male and female flowers. The plant is pollinated by the wind. Once the female flowers have been fertilised, they grow into corn cobs which are made up of fruits.

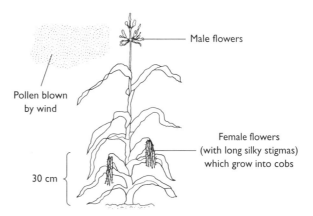

Fig. 5.22

(a) (i) Explain the advantage to the plant in having the male flowers at the top of the stem. (3 lines) *(2)*

(ii) Explain the advantage to the plant in having long, silky stigmas. (3 lines) *(2)*

(iii) When growing sweetcorn plants, many gardeners group them together in a rectangle pattern rather than in a long, single row. Explain the advantage of this. (3 lines) *(3)*

(iv) Describe what happens inside the female flower after pollination has taken place. (3 lines) *(3)*

(b) A pure-breeding sweetcorn plant with starchy fruits was crossed with a pure-breeding sweetcorn plant with non-starchy fruits. Their offspring (F_1 generation) produced cobs containing only starchy fruits. One of the F_1 plants was then self-pollinated. Its cobs (F_2 generation) were found to have both starchy and non-starchy fruits. These crosses are shown in the Fig 5.23.

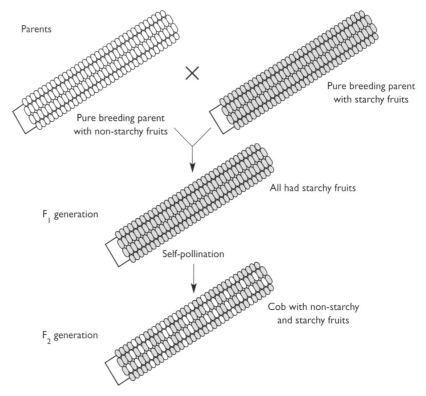

Parents

Pure breeding parent with non-starchy fruits

Pure breeding parent with starchy fruits

F_1 generation

All had starchy fruits

Self-pollination

F_2 generation

Cob with non-starchy and starchy fruits

Fig. 5.23

(i) Count the number of sweet fruits (non-starchy) which can be seen on the self-pollinated (F_2 generation) cob.

Number of sweet fruits _____ *(1)*

(ii) 120 starchy fruits can be seen on the self-pollinated cob. What is the ratio of starchy fruits to non-starchy fruits? Show your working. (3 lines) *(2)*

(c) Two alleles 'starchy' and 'non-starchy' determine the type of fruit produced by sweet corn. Which of the two alleles is dominant? Give a reason for your answer. (3 lines) *(2)*

(d) Using suitable symbols, show in the box below the cross between the two pure breeding parents that produced the F_1 generation.

Symbol for dominant allele = _____

Symbol for recessive allele = _____

gametes		

(Modular Science, London, SEG)

Q9 (Foundation Tier) Cystic fibrosis is a serious disease of humans in which the lungs clog with mucous. The disease is inherited and involves a single gene. This gene exists as two alleles.

Two healthy parents had three children. The third child was found to have cystic fibrosis although the other two children were normal.

(a) Is the allele that causes cystic fibrosis dominant or recessive?

_____

Explain the reason for your answer.

_____

_____ *(1)*

(b) What is the genotype of the parents?

_____ *(1)*

(c) (i) What is the chance of a fourth child having the disease?

_____ *(1)*

    (ii) By means of a genetic diagram explain your answer. *(3)*

(Co-ordinated Science, London, WJEC, NEAB Higher Tier)

Q10 (Higher Tier) This question gives you some stimulus information in a table to help you think about your answers. Part (b) is an example of extended writing where you may find it helpful to draft some key points before writing your answer.

Genetic engineering has recently played an important part in farming, and some applications are listed below.

Table 5.5

Properties of product	Examples
Improved yields	More corn on each cob
Improved nutrient value	Leaner meat
Improved physical properties	Shorter stems in winter wheat
Improved disease resistance	Less black spot in potatoes

(i) Which part of the living cell is changed in genetic engineering? Give reasons for your answer. (3 lines) *(2)*

(ii) Discuss **three** of the concerns that people have about the widespread use of genetic engineering. (40 lines) *(8)*

(Co-ordinated Science, London, WJEC)

 EXAMINATION ANSWERS

Multiple choice

A1 Key E, all red-flowered plants. The red colour is dominant to white, so option A is wrong. The parents are both pure-breeding, so the recessive gene is not present in the red-flowered parent; this invalidates options B, C and D.

A2 Key C, the testes. The uterus and vagina are involved in reproduction but not in formation of sex cells.

A3 Key A, one sperm. Although millions are produced, only one fertilises the egg.

A4 Key A, blood groups. All the others show a gradual change and are therefore continuous variation.

A5 Key A, fertilisation. Option C, ovulation, is when an egg is released, and option D, menstruation, is the release of the extra lining of the womb.

Structured questions

A6   (a)   (i)

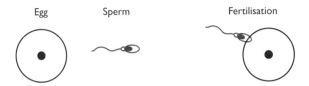

Fig. 5.24

      (ii)   1.   Two different sperm fertilise two ova at the same time to produce non-identical twins.
             2.   When a sperm has fertilised the ovum or egg, the fertilised egg then divides and forms two zygotes. A new individual is formed from each zygote, each having identical chromosomes, so the twins are identical.

   (b)   (i)   grey
         (ii)   1.   The grey gene was dominant over the white gene. The male carried two dominant grey genes and was homozygous, or pure-bred.
                2.   Each offspring carried one dominant grey gene and one recessive white gene, so when they mated the recessive white genes combined to produce a white offspring.
         (iii)   He could only breed from white rabbits.

   (c)   (i)   Geranium
             Take two or more small cuttings from part of the geranium stem where there are side shoots, and put them into some soil.
         (ii)   1.   Plants are produced which are identical to the parent.
                2.   The process is quicker than using seeds.

A7   (a)   There may have been a change in availability of food, so that the horses with better-adapted teeth would survive.
             A change in the type of predator may have favoured larger horses which could run more quickly.

   (b)   (i)   The hoverfly mimics the bee, which has a sting. The predators have learned that the bee has a sting and therefore avoid another insect with the same warning colours.
         (ii)   A genetic mutation occurs when there is a mistake in the way in which the genes are copied in the nucleus, so the number or type of genes is different to the parent.
         (iii)   The hoverflies which may have been produced as mutations with the yellow and black stripes of the bee survived, and those which did not look like the bee were eaten. The genes from the successful hoverflies would be passed on to the next generation.
         (iv)   Bacteria can become resistant to antibiotics and other drugs used to kill bacteria. Mutations are produced at a rapid rate and pass on their resistance to the next generation.

   (c)   (i)   The dark-coloured moth survived against the dark-coloured bark of the polluted trees. This moth passed on its chromosomes to the next generation, so more dark-coloured moths were produced. The light-coloured moths were eaten as they showed up on the bark.
         (ii)   As the bark of the trees becomes lighter, the dark moths will show up and be eaten. Any light-coloured moths will have an advantage and will survive, so the population may change back to that of 1884.

A8   Note the use of the word of instruction 'explain' in many of these questions.

   (a)   (i)   the male flowers produce pollen (1)
             it is easier for the wind to release the pollen from the male flowers at the top of the stem (1)

(ii) the long silky stigmas have a large surface area (1)
so it is easier to collect the pollen (1)

(iii) there is more chance of the pollen being blown across a female flower (1)
in a single row the pollen would be wasted (1) more cobs will be produced (1)

(iv) Higher Tier only
a pollen tube grows from the pollen grain (1)
from the stigma to the ovary/ovule (1)
the male nucleus fuses with/fertilises the female nucleus (1)
a seed/zygote is formed (1)

(b) (i) 'sweet' in the question refers to non-starchy.
count the number of unshaded fruits on the F2 diagram = 40

(ii) the ratio is 120:40 (1) = 3:1 (1)

(c) the starchy allele is dominant (1)
as all the F_1 generation have starchy fruit (1)

(d) choose an appropriate letter for which it is easy to see the difference between the capital and small letter, e.g. B, b; note the parents are pure breeding so the gametes will be identical for one parent (homozygous)
all the F_1 will be identical Bb (heterozygous)

Symbol for dominant allele B (1)
Symbol for recessive allele b (1)

gametes	B	B	
b	Bb	Bb	(1)
b	Bb	Bb	(1)

(1)

A9 (a) the allele is recessive
both parents were healthy but one child had the disease (1)

(b) choose an appropriate letter here to represent the heterozygous parents, e.g. Ff (1)

(c) (i) 1 in 4 chance (1)

(d) (ii) think about setting out your answer as a genetic diagram so that you show the genotypes of the parents, gametes (1) and children (1) and state the phenotypes of the children (1)

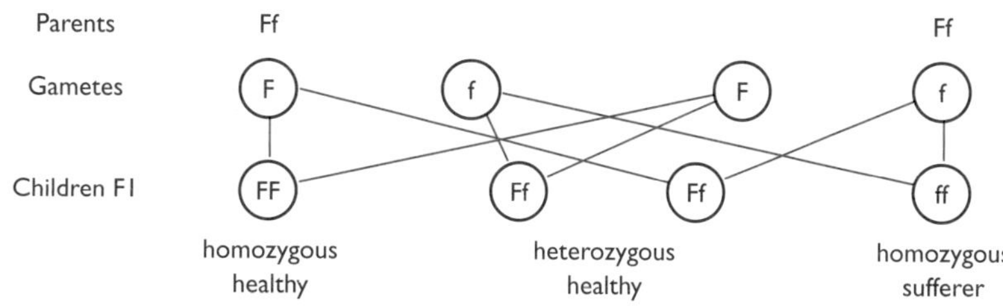

Fig. 5.25

A10 (i) a gene or section of DNA on a chromosome in the nucleus (1)
a new section of DNA is transferred from one organism to another of a different species during genetic engineering (1)

(ii) the 8 marks here are allocated for a well-argued account; some of the points you could make should include reference to medical, ethical and social concerns:

the uses of genetic engineering in treating people who have a defective immune system (1)
and are unable to make a particular protein (1)
and suffer from diseases such as cystic fibrosis and muscular dystrophy (1)
these people could be helped to live a normal life (1)
human individuals need to act as 'guinea pigs' while these techniques are developed (1)

the ethical concerns about using human embryos which are later destroyed (1)
these embryos could have developed into normal individuals (1)

the social concerns that genes could be inserted into reproductive cells (1)
to improve on characteristics such as eye colour or height (1)

A STUDENT'S ANSWER WITH EXAMINER'S COMMENTS

(a) Use has been made of knowledge of genetics and inheritance to breed plants and animals suited to our needs.

(i) What do we call this process?

artificial selection *(1)*

(ii) Explain how a farmer could use this knowledge to breed cows which produce a lot of milk.

'Good, correct answers'

The farmer only breeds from the cows which produce the most milk. *(2)*

(b) Genes are units of inheritance found on chromosomes in cells.

(i) How many chromosomes are found in a human embryo cell?

46 *(1)*

(ii) How many chromosomes are found in a human egg or sperm cell?

23 *(1)*

(iii) Using diagrams, show what happens to these numbers of these chromosomes:

1. At the formation of sperm cells in the testes *(2)*

'Yes, good. Label these: egg/ovum and sperm'

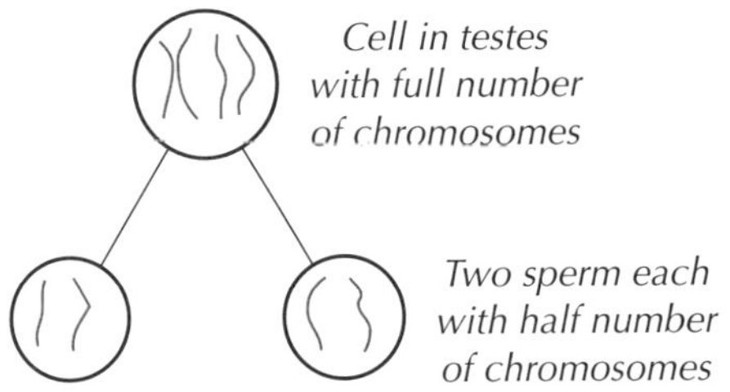
Cell in testes with full number of chromosomes
Two sperm each with half number of chromosomes

Fig. 5.26

2. At fertilisation *(2)*

'Fertilised egg or zygote'

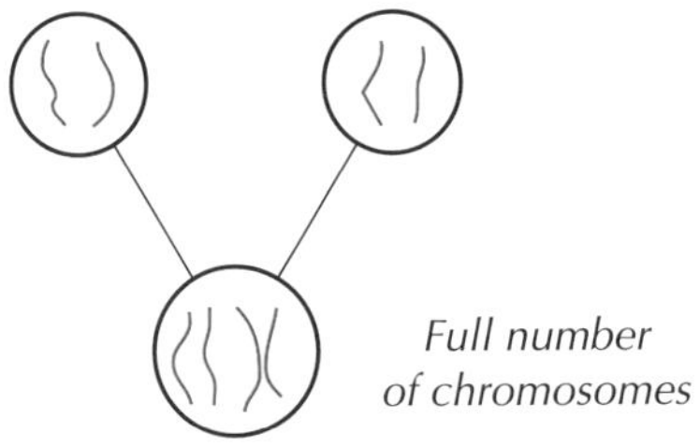
Full number of chromosomes

Fig. 5.27

(c) An experiment was carried out to investigate the inheritance of coat colour in mice.

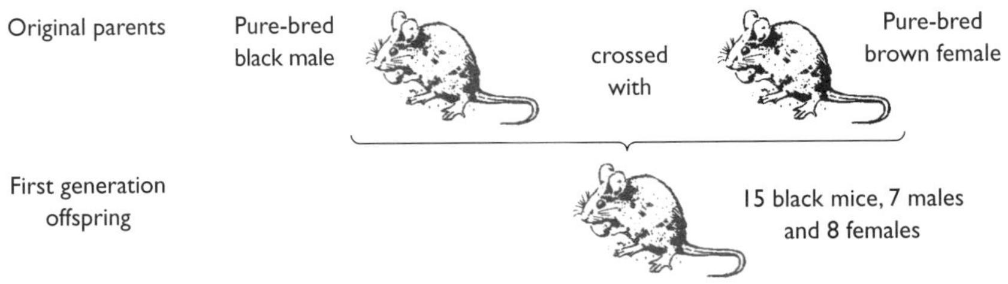
Original parents
Pure-bred black male
crossed with
Pure-bred brown female
First generation offspring
15 black mice, 7 males and 8 females

Fig. 5.28

(Continued)

The male and females of the first-generation offspring were then mated. They produced 33 litters altogether.

The numbers and coat colours of the offspring are given below.

Second generation offspring: 204 black mice

68 brown mice

(i) Which characeresitic for coat colour was *dominant*?

<u>*Black*</u>   *(1)*

(ii) Choose a symbol to represent the gene for

Brown   Black

Symbol <u>*b*</u>   Symbol <u>*B*</u>

Using the symbols you have chosen, write down what genes for coat colour were present in:

'No, she is brown and therefore needs bb'

1. the original female <u>*bB*</u>

'Good'

2. the original male <u>*BB*</u>

3. the first generation offspring <u>*Bb*</u>   *(3)*

(iii) Using the symbols you have chosen, draw a diagram to explain what happened to the passing on (inheritance) of the genes in the *second* breeding.   *(2)*

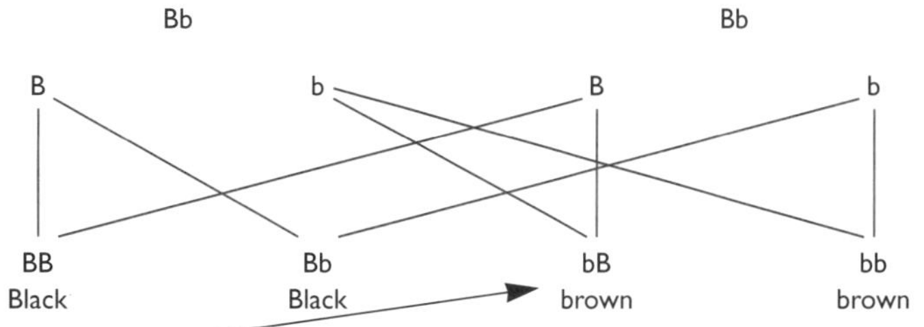

'Good. But label Parents Gametes F₁'

Fig. 5.29

'No. Bb = Black'

(iv) Why do experimenters use such large numbers of mice in such inheritance experiments?

'Yes. The proportions are not exact'

<u>*To get an average result.*</u>   *(1)*

(d) Colour blindness is an inherited characteristic in humans. However, the condition affects *many* more males than females – indeed females with colour blindness are very rare. Explain these observations.

'The gene is carried on the part of the X chromosome not matched by the Y chromosome'

The gene for colour blindness is carried on the sex chromosomes.   *(2)*

SUMMARY

At the end of this chapter you should know:

▷   the structure and function of the **male** and **female reproductive systems**, including **fertilisation**, the **menstrual cycle** and **contraception**;

▷   how the **foetus** develops in the uterus, including the role of the **placenta**;

▷   the physical and emotional changes that take place at **puberty** (adolescence);

▷   how cells divide by **mitosis** so that **growth** takes place and by **meiosis** to produce **gametes**;

▷   that the **nucleus** contains **chromosomes** that carry the **genes**;

▷   the mechanism of **monohybrid inheritance** where there are **dominant** and **recessive alleles**;

▷   how **gender** (sex) is determined in humans;

▷   that some diseases can be **inherited** e.g. sickle-cell anaemia;

▷   that there is **variation** within species and between species and that variation can arise from **environmental** and **genetic** (inherited) causes;

▷   that **sexual reproduction** is a source of **genetic variation** while **asexual reproduction** produces **clones**;

▷   that **mutation** is a source of **genetic variation** and has a number of causes;

▷   that the **gene** is a section of **DNA**;

▷   the basic principles of **cloning**, **selective breeding** and **genetic engineering**, and that selective breeding can lead to new **varieties**;

▷   the **fossil record** as evidence for **evolution**;

▷   how **variation** and **selection** may lead to **evolution** or extinction.

Living things and their environment

Chapter

6

GETTING STARTED

Ecology is the study of the relationships between the *living* and *non-living* factors in the environment. The living factors, the plants and animals, are sometimes called the **biotic** factors; the non-living factors, such as climate, soil and the circulation of carbon, nitrogen and water, are the **abiotic** factors. These living and non-living factors make up the basic unit in ecology, the **ecosystem**.

You may have started this topic by studying the feeding relationships between plants and animals in a habitat near your school, and then used the information you obtained to draw a **food chain**, or a more complex **food web**, to show what was feeding on what.

You may have identified the **producers** or **green plants**, which obtain energy from the Sun by **photosynthesis**. Feeding on the producers will be the **herbivores** or **primary consumers**, and feeding on those will be the **carnivores** or **secondary consumers**. In this way energy flows from the producers to the consumers at the top of the food chain or web. Some energy is lost at each link in the chain, and this means that there are always fewer carnivores than herbivores.

Chemical pesticides, used to control insect pests, may affect other animals in the ecosystem because the chemicals may become more concentrated in animals which are higher up the food web.

TOPIC	STUDY	REVISION 1	REVISION 2
Populations			
Adaptation			
Growth of populations			
Sampling populations			
Food chains and food webs			
Pyramids of numbers and mass			
Energy transfer			
Nutrient cycles			
Food production			
Pest control			
Human influence on the environment			
Deforestation			
Desertification			

111

WHAT YOU NEED TO KNOW

▶ **Populations**

'how the distribution and relative abundance of organisms in a habitat can be explained in terms of adaptation, competition and predation' [2.5a]

Population size is the number of individuals of a species in a particular area. The size of the population can be controlled by several factors:

1. **Competition:** for food, water and space between animals of the same species and animals of different species; this affects the abundance and distribution of a population.
2. **Predation:** an increase in the numbers of predators reduces the number of prey; predators are usually well adapted to catch their prey but the prey animals are well adapted to escape!
3. **Migration:** animals migrating into or out of an area increase or decrease the size of the population of that species.

Predator–prey relationship

Figure 6.1 shows how the population of a **predator** increases and decreases as the population of the **prey** goes up and down. As the population of **prey** increases, more food is available for predators and so their population **increases**. However, as the population of the predators increases, more food is needed and the population of the prey therefore decreases, and so on.

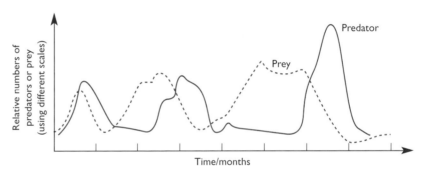

Fig. 6.1 The population of the prey affects the numbers of the predator

▶ **Adaptation**

Adaptation means an animal or plant having special features which enable it to survive in a particular environment.

For example, animals in **desert** and **arctic** regions need to adapt to extremes of climate in the following ways:

▶ their body size and surface area;
▶ the thickness of hair (fur);
▶ amount of body fat;
▶ camouflage.

[H] A good example of adaptation is the **polar bear** which is adapted to live in a very cold climate in the arctic. The bear

▶ is large and has a relatively small surface area to mass ratio;
▶ has a thick layer of fur which traps air and gives insulation;
▶ has large deposits of body fat for insulation and energy;
▶ has white fur to camouflage it against the snow and ice.

In **desert regions** animals such as **camels** are adapted to withstand extremes of temperature and shortage of available water.

The camel has:

▶ a long, thin body shape which increases its surface area to mass ratio to allow heat to escape;
▶ the ability to drink large amounts of water when available and to store water in fat deposits in its hump;
▶ large feet which spread out to prevent it sinking in the sand.

Predators such a lions and cheetahs are adapted for **hunting** prey by having powerful muscles to enable them to chase their prey, eyes at the front of their head to give good distance vision, and good camouflage to help them blend in with their surroundings and not be visible to their prey. The **prey** such as zebra and springbok have eyes at the side of their head to give good all-round vision when they are feeding. They are also camouflaged and able to run very fast for long periods.

Plant adaptations

Plants adapt to survive arid conditions. One example is the **thorn tree** which has very small leaves to reduce water loss by transpiration. The thorns prevent herbivores from eating the leaves and the seed pods have a very thick coat to withstand long periods of drought.

▶ **Growth of populations**

Simple ecological methods can be used to study how populations change in size. Figure 6.2 shows a typical growth curve for a population.

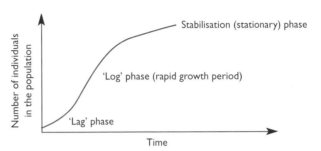

Fig. 6.2 The graph shows a typical growth curve for a population

As you can see, a new population starts with very **low** numbers in the 'lag' phase, and then shows a very **rapid increase** in number in the 'log' phase. When resources limit growth, then a **stabilisation** phase is reached and the population remains fairly constant. This continues until there is **a change** in one of the limiting factors, such as availability of food, space or disease. Remember that a population is **all** the members of the **same species** in an area.

Human populations may also be affected by the following factors:

▶   the extent to which the number of births is controlled;
▶   how well diseases are prevented and cured;
▶   natural disasters such as flooding, drought and earthquakes.

Colonisation

Part of your own study about ecology may have involved finding out how a community of plants and animals becomes established within a particular habitat by the process of **succession**. Succession happens when different species move into a new area and begin to be established. For example, dandelion seeds are sometimes blown on to an area of bare soil, where they become established very quickly. Each plant or animal which settles in a new area helps to **stabilise** the soil and release **nutrients** and may help to provide a **habitat** for other species. Gradually the numbers of different plants and animals which occupy the area increase, until a stable and balanced **community** of animals and plants is reached. This is known as a **climax community**. Figure 6.3 shows how the numbers of species increase with time.

'A mature woodland is a "climax" community'

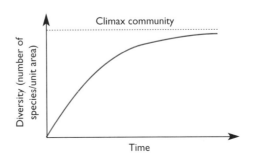

Fig. 6.3 The number of species increases over a period of time

▶ Sampling populations

Your own studies of the **abundance** and **distribution** of species in a particular habitat or locality should indicate to you that the numbers and types of animals and plants vary from place to place. Different species live and grow where, and when, conditions are most suitable for them. The following **physical** factors, which vary from place to place and at the time of the year, will affect organisms:

- ▶ temperature,
- ▶ light,
- ▶ water,
- ▶ availability of oxygen,
- ▶ concentration of carbon dioxide,
- ▶ nutrients.

When you studied an ecosystem you may have been involved in estimating the **population** of a particular species of animal or plant. One of the techniques which you may have used is **random sampling**, as outlined below.

Random sampling

1. Measure the whole area of study.
2. Use a quadrat of known size, e.g. $\frac{1}{4}m \times \frac{1}{4}m = \frac{1}{16}m^2$.
3. Place the quadrat at random.
4. Count the numbers of a particular species of animal, or assess the proportion of the quadrat which is covered by a particular plant.
5. Record your result.
6. Repeat stages 3, 4 and 5 until data has been collected.
7. Find the average numbers of the species, or average percentage cover of a plant per square metre.
8. Multiply by the total number of square metres to find the total population of the area.

Mark–release–recapture

Another commonly used method of counting a population is mark–release–recapture. This method could be used to count a population of snails, for example, and would involve using a special non-toxic paint or marker pen.

1. Capture, count and mark a representative sample of a population.
2. Release the animals in the same area.
3. At a later stage, when the marked animals have mixed with the rest of the population, recapture and count the numbers of animals, and record how many of the marked animals are in the second sample.
4. Use the formula below to estimate the total population:

$$\frac{\text{number in first sample} \times \text{number in second sample}}{\text{number of marked animals recaptured}}$$

'Refer to your own field work here'

Quadrat

Species A   Species B

Fig. 6.4 Using a quadrat to estimate percentage cover

▶ Food chains and food webs

'how food chains may be described quantitatively using pyramids of numbers and pyramids of biomass' [2.5c]

When you studied an ecosystem, you were probably able to identify the main species of plants and animals, and to find out what was feeding on what. A **food chain** simply shows how an animal obtains its food directly from another animal or plant. The arrows show the **direction** of transfer of **energy**.

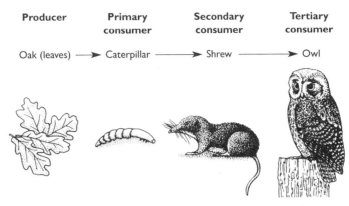

Fig. 6.5 A simple food chain. The arrow shows the direction of energy transfer

Food webs are more complicated, as they show how one animal may be feeding on **several** others to obtain food, or how one plant may have several different animals feeding on it.

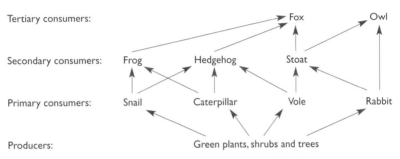

Fig. 6.6 In a food web one animal feeds on more than one source of food

Producers

At the start of all food chains and webs are the green plants, called the **producers**. Green plants make their own food by using solar energy from the sun in the process of **photosynthesis**. Plants convert carbon dioxide and water into carbohydrates, which are then converted into plant protein, oils and fats.

Consumers

These are all the animals in the food chain, and can be divided into herbivores and carnivores. The **herbivores** are the **primary consumers**, which feed directly on the plants or producers. The **carnivores**, which obtain their energy by feeding on the herbivores, are the **secondary consumers**. Some carnivores obtain their energy from **other carnivores**, and these are described as **tertiary** or **third level consumers**; for example, a hawk or fox which feeds on other carnivores in the food chain. Some animals feed on a **mixed diet** of plants and animals, and these are described as **omnivores**. They feed at more than one level in the food chain.

Decomposers

When plants and animals die, all the nutrients which are stored in their bodies are recycled by **decomposers** such as **bacteria** and **fungi**. These organisms break down the bodies of dead animals and plants and release **nutrients** such as nitrogen into the soil.

▶ Pyramids of numbers and mass

Pyramid of numbers

Figure 6.7 shows how energy is **lost** at each stage of the food chain. This means that there is a **decrease** in the number of organisms at each stage of the food chain, as there is **less energy** available. The **pyramid of numbers** in Figure 6.7 indicates how the number of producers supports fewer herbivores, which in turn support fewer carnivores, supporting still fewer tertiary consumers. However, the pyramid of numbers can also look like Fig. 6.8.

This (Fig. 6.8) shows how **one organism**, an oak tree, provides energy for many caterpillars, which provide energy for a few shrews, which in turn provide energy for just one owl.

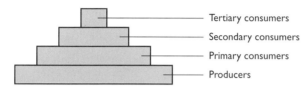

Fig. 6.7 Pyramid of numbers

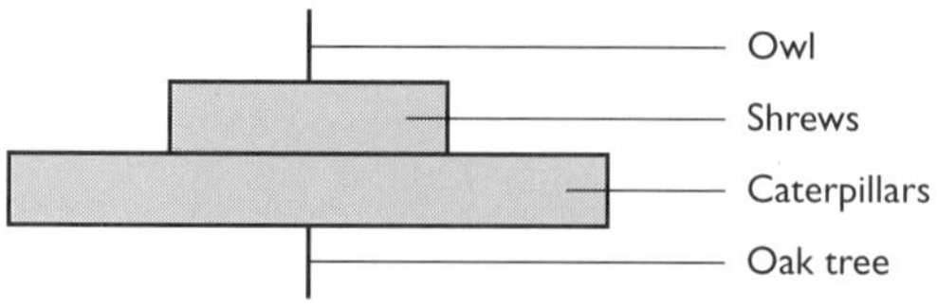

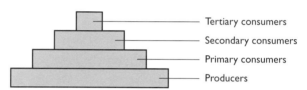

Fig. 6.8 A pyramid of numbers based on one oak tree

Pyramid of mass

The total mass or biomass of organisms in a population decreases along the food chain, because **less energy** is available at each stage. The **pyramid of biomass** may look like Figure 6.9.

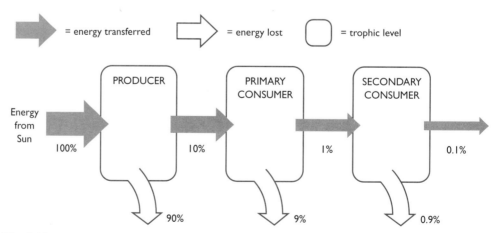

Fig. 6.9 Pyramid of biomass.

▶ Energy transfer

H

'how energy is transferred through an ecosystem' [2.5d]

Energy is **transferred** at each stage of the food chain, from the plant producer to the herbivores and then to the carnivores. Only about **10%** of the available energy is transferred at each stage of a food chain (Fig. 6.10). The other 90% is **lost** by life processes such as **respiration**, **excretion** and **movement**. The amount of living material or **biomass** is therefore reduced at each stage of the food chain.

▶ = energy transferred   ▷ = energy lost   ☐ = trophic level

Energy from Sun

PRODUCER   100%   10%   PRIMARY CONSUMER   1%   SECONDARY CONSUMER   0.1%

90%   9%   0.9%

Fig. 6.10 Energy is lost at each stage of the food chain

'Long food chains are inefficient!'

For example, when a cow eats grass, the cow excretes about **60%** of the energy taken in from the grass. Another **30%** is used up by the cow in respiration, growth and movement. When the cow is eaten by man, only about **10%** of the energy originally taken in by the cow is available for food.

Figure 6.11 shows how one hectare of land can produce either enough food for cows to feed **10 people**, or enough grain to feed **100 people**. It is evidently much more efficient for man to obtain food from **producers** instead of from **consumers** who have wasted so much energy.

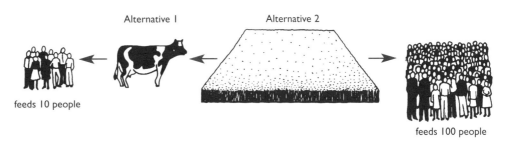

Fig. 6.11 The alternative ways in which the corn produced by one hectare of land could be used

'Use information from your own field studies where possible'

You may have been out of school on a 'field trip' as part of your science course, in order to study an **ecosystem** such as a woodland, a rocky shore or a pond. You may have just done some field work in the immediate area around your school, and looked at a rotting log, or a hedgerow. During your studies you will probably have noted the living (biotic) and non-living (abiotic) factors that made up the ecosystem which you were studying (Fig. 6.12).

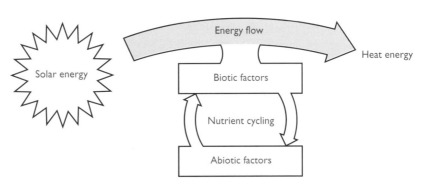

Fig. 6.12 How the biotic and abiotic factors interact in an ecosystem

For any ecosystem the non-living (abiotic) factors will include rainfall, temperature, wind and light intensity, as well as factors which affect the soil, such as the presence of minerals, air and humus.

The living (biotic) factors will include the community of animals and plants which are found in the ecosystem. You may have counted the numbers in a population of just one species of animal or plant. You may also have noticed how different populations are not always competing for food, space, light, etc., and are therefore able to live together in the same ecosystem.

▶ **Nutrient cycles**

'the role of microbes and other organisms in the decomposition of organic materials and in the cycling of carbon and nitrogen' [2.5e]

'how the carbon cycle helps to maintain atmospheric composition' [3.2w]

Many natural substances such as animal and plant waste are described as biodegradable as they are broken down by the action of **bacteria** and **fungi**. Many of the nutrients contained in the waste are returned to the soil and **recycled**. The recycling of nitrogen, carbon and water forms an essential link between the **living** and **non-living** factors in the ecosystem.

H *The nitrogen cycle*

Plants such as peas, beans and clover are able to absorb nitrogen gas from the air through special lumps on their roots called **nodules**. These nodules contain **nitrogen-fixing** bacteria

'Trace the cyclical path taken by each substance in the three cycles'

which take in or 'fix' the nitrogen as **nitrates**. The nitrates are then used by plants to make **proteins**. The proteins are taken in by animals when they eat the plants, and are returned to the soil when animals and plants are **decomposed** by **bacteria** and **fungi** which live in the soil. The decomposers form ammonium compounds, which are converted into **nitrates** by **nitrifying bacteria**.

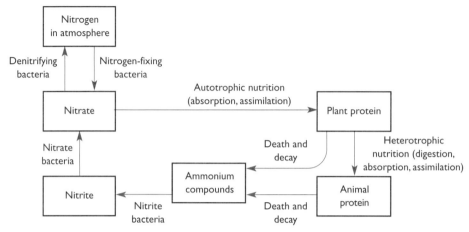

Fig. 6.13 The nitrogen cycle

'Beans and clover add nitrogen to soil'

Farmers often plant peas, beans or clover to help increase the amount of nitrates in the soil, instead of adding nitrogen in the form of nitrate fertilisers. The peas, beans and clover can then be ploughed back into the soil, and the nitrates can be used by other plants to make proteins.

Some nitrates are **lost** from the soil when **denitrifying bacteria** convert the **nitrates** into **nitrogen gas**, which is released into the air. However some nitrates are added to the soil when lightning converts nitrogen, oxygen and water in the air to acids in rain.

Plant nutrients can be lost from the soil when animals or plants are removed for food, for example, during **harvesting**. This means that fertilisers or compost must be added to the soil to replace the lost nutrients

The carbon cycle

'See also Chapter 16, p. 311'

Carbon is breathed out, as **carbon dioxide**, by all animals and plants. Whenever **fossil fuels** such as coal, oil or gas, are burned, carbon dioxide is also released into the atmosphere.

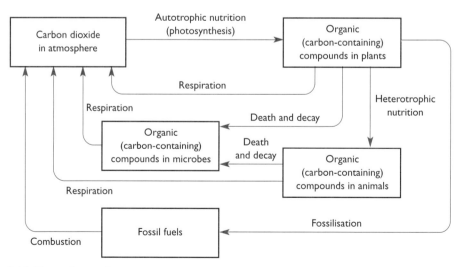

Fig. 6.14 The carbon cycle

'The level of CO_2 in the atmosphere is about 0.04%'

Green plants take in carbon dioxide during the daytime, and combine the carbon dioxide with water to make carbohydrates. This process is known as **photosynthesis**, and it releases oxygen as a waste product.

The plants are eaten by animals, and the carbon, in the form of carbohydrates, proteins and fats, is used to make the cells of the animals. As the animals **respire**, the carbohydrates are broken down to form **carbon dioxide** and water. The carbon is released as carbon dioxide into the atmosphere.

▶ Food production ⒣

'*how food production can be managed to improve the efficiency of energy transfer*' [2.5f]

It is estimated that about 30% of the world's land area can be cultivated; the rest is either too dry, too steep or otherwise unsuitable. Of the land being cultivated about half is used for **growing crops**, the rest is used for **pasture** or **forest**. Due to the **increasing world population**, yields of food from the land and sea have to be **increased**.

In the developed world, agricultural yields are improved by use of:

'Ways of increasing food yields'

- ▶ **fertilisers** to increase grain yields;
- ▶ **pesticides** to control predators and disease;
- ▶ **herbicides** to reduce competition from weeds;
- ▶ **selective breeding and genetic engineering** to produce disease-resistant high-yielding strains;
- ▶ **irrigation** to increase yields.

These techniques are usually **expensive** and usually not available to farmers in developing countries.

In the harvesting of **animals** it is essential that quotas are agreed as to how many organisms are removed each year to allow a **breeding population** to remain to build up numbers for the following year. The oceans offer vast **food resources**, especially fish which are an excellent form of protein, but in large-scale fishing in the sea, a minimum mesh size for fishing nets allows smaller fish to escape. If too many organisms are removed at the same time the population **declines** rapidly and consequently fewer organisms are available for another year.

▶ Pest control ⒣

Chemical pesticides

'Chemical pesticides can build up in the food chain'

Gardeners and farmers often use chemical **pesticides** to control insects which are damaging crops and other plants. The advantage of using chemical pesticides is that they are very **effective** and **fast-working**. Herbicides are also used to kill unwanted plants which otherwise affect the yield of crops. Although these chemicals may be used only in very small quantities, the **concentration** of chemical may **build up** at each stage of the food chain, and **accumulate** in the **top carnivore**: for example, a bird of prey such as an owl or hawk. The chemicals would affect each organism in the food chain, but the top carnivore, which receives the **highest** concentration, would be affected the most, and may even be killed or have very low rates of reproduction.

Biological control

'Biological methods of control are safer but slower'

An alternative method of controlling pests without the use of chemicals is to introduce **another animal** into the food chain which will feed on the pest. This method avoids pollution, but is much **slower** in its effects than using chemical pesticides. Also the new species which has been introduced can itself become a **pest** if it starts to feed on another animal or plant in the chain.

A common insect pest in greenhouses is a tiny red spider which damages plants. Instead of spraying with insecticide, gardeners can introduce another insect which is a predator on the red spider and which eats about 20 red spiders a day! An advantage of using such **biological control** is that no dangerous chemicals have to be used and strains of insects that are resistant to chemicals do not develop.

▶ Human influence on the environment

'Types of pollution'

'how the impact of human activity on the environment is related to population size, economic factors and industrial requirements' [2.5b]

In the year 2000 it is estimated that there will be more than **6 billion people** on Earth. Since 1900 the world population has roughly **doubled** in number. This rapid increase in world population has increased the demand for **raw materials**, including non-renewable energy resources, and has increased the amount of **waste** produced. One of the main effects of human activity on the environment has been the increase in **pollution** of **water**, **land** and **air** as described below.

Pollution of water by sewage

This can cause **rapid growth** of water plants; when these plants die they are broken down by microbes which use up the **dissolved oxygen** in the water and lead to **suffocation of fish** and other animals.

Pollution of water by chemical waste

This pollution can come from factories, farms, waste dumps and oil spills. Chemical wastes are usually **poisonous** (toxic) and are discharged into rivers and lakes, often ending up in the ocean where they affect the food chains and can be harmful to marine life. The chemicals are not broken down by the cells of living organisms and become **concentrated** within the food chain.

Pollution of land by fertilisers, pesticides and rubbish dumps

An example of this is when pesticides **accumulate** in predators which have eaten prey treated with pesticides.

Pollution of air by waste gases

These are produced by power stations, factories and vehicle exhausts; for example, lead from car exhaust fumes can cause **brain damage** in children. See also: Acid Rain, Chapter 11; the Greenhouse Effect, Chapter 17; the Ozone Layer, Chapter 16.

▶ Deforestation

Deforestation is the **large-scale removal** and **destruction** of **natural forests**. For example, one of the reasons for deforestation is to **clear land** in order to grow crops and to **raise cattle**. These activities generate more **income** for a farmer than maintaining large areas of impenetrable forest. The effects of deforestation are:

▶ the **extinction** of many plant and animal species;
▶ a reduction in the rate at which **carbon dioxide** is removed from the atmosphere during photosynthesis;
▶ an **increase** in the level of **carbon dioxide** due to the burning of large areas of forests;
▶ **erosion** of topsoil by wind and water due to the removal of the tree cover and, as a result, very little vegetation is able to grow.

▶ Desertification

Desertification occurs when the land gradually changes into a **desert** as a result of the over-exploitation of land by clearing of vegetation, overcultivation and overgrazing. Desertification threatens **35%** of the Earth's land surface and **20%** of the **world population**. It is almost impossible to reverse the process of desertification and to create good agricultural land from the desert.

As a result of desertification, the land:

▶ produces less food and so feeds fewer people;
▶ sustains fewer livestock.

▶ **EXAMINATION QUESTIONS**

Multiple choice

Q1   The diagram below shows a food web.

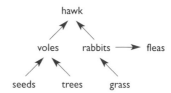

Fig. 6.15

Which of the following is a primary consumer?

A   fleas   D   seeds
B   grass   E   voles
C   hawks

Q2   Look at the following simple food chain.

oak tree → caterpillars → small birds → buzzard

Which of the following diagrams shows the pyramid of mass for this food chain?

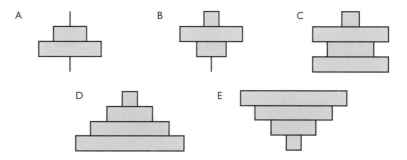

Fig. 6.16

Q3   What are the organisms called which first occupy a newly formed sand dune?

A   colonisers   D   herbivores
B   consumers   E   predators
C   decomposers

Structured questions

Q4   Below is drawn part of the carbon cycle.

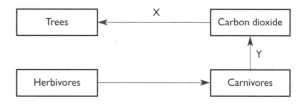

Fig. 6.17

(a)   Name the processes represented by X and Y.

X is _____   Y is _____   *(2)*

(b)   Could fungi be used instead of trees? Give one reason for your answer. (2 lines)   *(1)*
(WJEC)

Q5   (a)   The curves below show how the populations of rabbits and foxes change over a two-year cycle. Use the curves to answer the questions which follow.

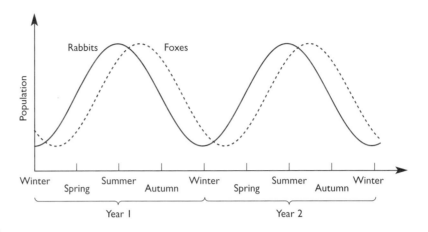

Fig. 6.18

(i)   At what time of year is the rabbit population lowest?

_____   *(1)*

(ii)   At what time of year does the rabbit population rise most rapidly?

_____   *(1)*

(iii)   Why do you think that the fox population falls each year?

_____   *(1)*

(b)   Use the information given in the simple food web below to answer the questions which follow.

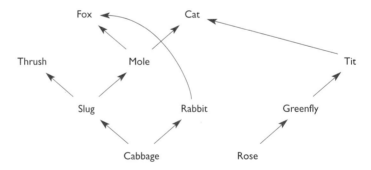

Fig. 6.19

Name:

(i) a major predator _____   *(1)*

(ii) a herbivore _____   *(1)*

(iii) a carnivore _____   *(1)*

(iv) a producer _____   *(1)*

(c)   Complete the following food chain.

cabbage → rabbit →_____   *(1)*

(d) What would be the effects of removing the foxes? (2 lines)   *(3)*

(e) Many rose growers need to protect their crops from greenfly attack. Suggest **two** ways of controlling greenfly.

1. _____   *(1)*

2. _____   *(1)*

Q6 The diagram below shows how different living things depend on others.

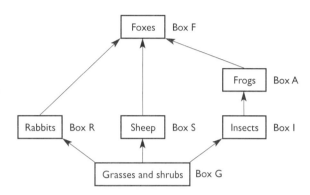

Fig. 6.20

After each group or 'box' there is a code letter. Use this code letter to answer some of the questions where indicated.

(a) What is the name or term given to this type of diagram?   *(1)*

(b) Which group or 'box' would contain
    (i) the *smallest number* of individual living things?
    (ii) the *greatest total weight* of living things?   *(2)*

(c) (i) Which box contains the primary producers?
    (ii) Where do these primary producers get their energy from?   *(2)*

(d) If the rabbit population was cut off by disease, what two effects could this have on sheep-farming in the area?

(i) _____

_____

(ii) _____

_____   *(2)*

(WJEC)

Q7 The diagram shows the energy pathway through a simple food chain.

(a) (i) In the diagram, **X** and **Y** represent energy losses from living organisms. Suggest **one** process for each which could illustrate the loss.   *(2)*
    (ii) Calculate the percentage of the Sun's energy absorbed by plants.   *(2)*

(b) (i) What happens to most of the Sun's energy falling on grassland?   *(1)*
    (ii) Explain why it is more efficient for man to obtain his energy from grassland (e.g. wheat) rather than meat (e.g. cow).   *(2)*

(c) In the arctic, human communities have difficulty in growing food crops.
    (i) Suggest **two** factors that are mainly responsible for this.   *(2)*
    (ii) What would be the probable effect of lack of food on the size of the human communities?   *(1)*

(MEG)

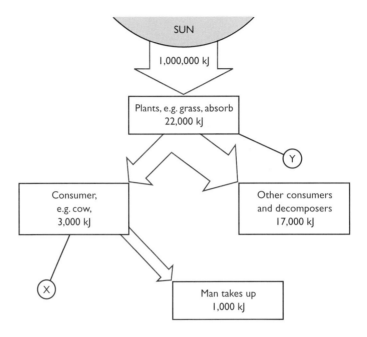

Fig. 6.21

Q8 The diagram below shows the position of a sewage outflow pipe at a local beach.

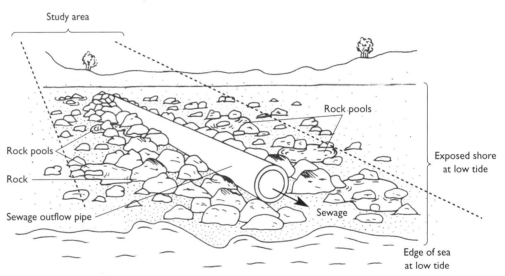

Fig. 6.22

The whole beach is covered in different types of seaweeds, growing on rocks and in rock pools. The main species of animals are snails, crabs, mussels, barnacles, limpets and fish. The animals live in the rock pools.

There is concern that the animals and plants are being affected by the sewage from the pipe.

You and a group of friends decide to investigate the situation by collecting some information about the different types of animals and plants.

(a) Describe how you would measure the size of the population of **one** of the types of animals found in the study area on the beach.   (4)

(b) Describe how you would compare the seaweeds growing in the study area on this beach with those growing on a beach where there was no sewage pipe.   (4)

(c) Suggest three factors, other than the presence of the sewage pipe, which could affect the types of plants and animals found on the two beaches.   (3)

Q9   Beans are important in the diet of many people in the world. In addition, growing bean crops helps improve the soil fertility. This can be very important in parts of the world where farmers cannot afford expensive fertilisers.

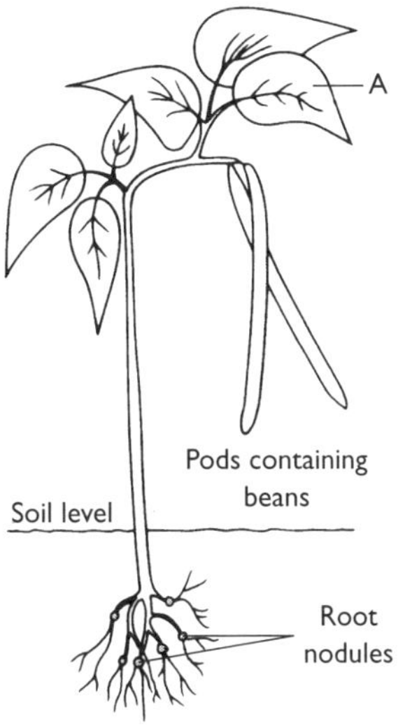

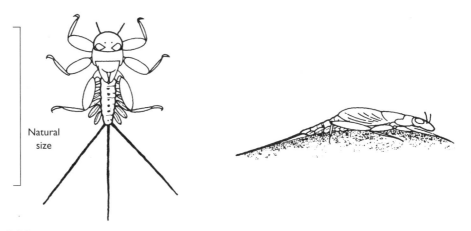

Fig. 6.23

(a)   (i)   Name the structures at **A** through which the plants lose water to the atmosphere.

_____ *(1)*

(ii)   Name the process by which plants lose water to the atmosphere.

_____ *(1)*

(b)   (i)   What kind of organism lives inside the bean root nodules?

_____ *(1)*

(ii)   What important element is obtained for the plant through the root nodules?

_____ *(1)*

(iii)   Explain how the organisms in the root nodules help the plant to obtain this element. (2 lines)   *(1)*

(iv)   After harvesting the beans, farmers dig in the roots of beans. They do not remove them. Explain why they do this. (2 lines)   *(1)*

(v)   Explain how growing beans can help to improve soil fertility. (2 lines)   *(2)*

(c)   Write a paragraph to explain why in some underdeveloped countries beans may be an important part of the diet of the people. (4 lines)   *(3)*

(London)

Q10 (Foundation Tier)   This is typical of a question which presents you with unusual or novel information and asks you to use your scientific knowledge. In this question you are given diagrams of an animal you may never have seen. Look carefully at the diagrams and think about the habitat this animal lives in, namely a fast-flowing stream.

The diagrams below (Fig. 6.24) show an animal which lives in fast-flowing streams.

Natural size

Fig. 6.24

Using **only** the information shown in the diagrams, explain **three** ways in which the animal is adapted for life in running water.

1.   _____
_____ *(2)*

2.   _____
_____ *(2)*

3.   _____
_____ *(2)*

(Co-ordinated Science, NEAB, London, WJEC)

Q11 (Higher Tier)   This question presents you with data in the form of a table.

The table below (Table 6.1) shows a number of features of the population of six countries in 1980.

Table 6.1

Country	Population (millions)	Birth rate (per 1000)	Death rate (per 1000)	Infant mortality rate (per 1000)	Life expectancy (years)	Population under 15 years (%)	Estimated population by year 2000 (millions)
Canada	24.1	16	6	16	74	30	32.6
France	54.1	16	9	12	73	25	62.9
Egypt	40.2	41	17	100	54	43	65.6
Angola	7.2	51	28	203	41	42	12.9
Turkey	42.3	40	14	119	57	44	73.0
Japan	115.4	20	7	11	75	26	134.7

(a) The world mean life expectancy in 1980 was 61 years.

How many of these countries had a life expectancy greater than this? _____ *(1)*

(b) (i) Which country is estimated to have the largest increase in population by the year
2000? _____ *(1)*

(ii) Suggest **two** reasons why the population of this country is estimated to rise so much.

1. _____

_____

2. _____

_____ *(2)*

(c) Suggest **two** possible reasons for the high infant mortality rate in Angola.

1. _____

_____

2. _____

_____ *(2)*

(Co-ordinated Science, NEAB, London, WJEC)

Q12   The diagram shows pyramids of numbers and biomass for the same community.

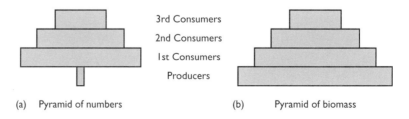

| 3rd Consumers |
| 2nd Consumers |
| 1st Consumers |
| Producers |

(a) Pyramid of numbers   (b) Pyramid of biomass

Fig. 6.25

(a) What does a pyramid of biomass show? (3 lines) *(2)*

(b) (i) Why is there a decrease in the amount of biomass in each level of the pyramid
compared to the level below? (2 lines) *(1)*

(ii) Suggest a reason for the difference in the shape of these pyramids for the same community. (3 lines) *(2)*

(Co-ordinated Science, London)

▶ EXAMINATION ANSWERS

Multiple choice

A1 Key E, voles; remember primary consumers are herbivores which feed from the green plants or producers in the food chain. The hawks and fleas are secondary consumers.

A2 Key D; remember pyramid of mass means the amount of biomass in a food chain, not the number of organisms. Option A shows a pyramid of numbers for this food chain, one oak tree and one buzzard, represented by a single line, with many caterpillars and fewer small birds.

A3 Key A, colonisers; the other options are all organisms involved in food chains but not in colonisation of a new area.

Structured questions

A4 (a) X is photosynthesis, Y is respiration.
(b) No, because green plants are needed in the carbon cycle to carry out photosynthesis and to make carbohydrates. Fungi are not green plants as they do not have chlorophyll. They obtain their energy from decaying animals and plants.

A5 (a) (i) in the winter (note the rabbit population is the solid line).
(ii) in the spring
(iii) The foxes feed on the rabbits. When there are fewer rabbits the number of foxes declines.

(b) (i) fox (or cat)
(ii) slug, rabbit or greenfly (all acceptable)
(iii) mole, tit, thrush, fox, cat (all acceptable)
(iv) cabbage (or rose)

(c) cabbage → rabbit → *fox*

(d) The numbers of rabbits and moles would increase, the numbers of cabbages and slugs may decrease.

(e) 1. putting more ladybirds on the rose bush to eat the greenfly
2. adding chemical pesticide to the rose bush to kill the greenfly.

A6 (a) food web

(b) (i) box F
(ii) box G

(c) (i) box G
(ii) the Sun

(d) (i) more grasses and shrubs available for the sheep, so the numbers of sheep could increase
(ii) the foxes may eat more sheep as they cannot feed on rabbits, so the numbers of sheep may decrease.

A7 (a) (i) Energy loss X could be excretion and respiration.
Energy loss Y could be reflection and transpiration.
(ii) 2.2%

(b) (i) Most of the energy is reflected, some is used to evaporate water, some goes into the soil.
(ii) Energy is wasted at each level of the food chain, so it is more efficient for man to obtain energy as close to the start of the food chain as possible.

(c) (i) low temperatures, short growing season, poor soil
(ii) population size may be reduced in number.

A8 (a) 1. Measure the total area of the beach to be studied.
2. Using a $\frac{1}{4}$m² quadrat, place the quadrat at random and count the numbers of individuals in that small area.
3. Record results and repeat until ten quadrats have been sampled.
4. Add all results together; divide by ten to find average result.
5. Multiply by total area of beach to find total population.

(b) Using random quadrats, sample the proportion of a particular species of seaweed on the two different areas of beach. Repeat for different species. Observe differences in colour, size, etc., of seaweeds of the same species on the two different beaches.

(c) 1. exposure of the beach to strong waves and wind.
2. amount of human interference on the beach, e.g. tourism, boating, etc.
3. different types of pollution such as oil and other chemicals in the seawater.

A9 (a) (i) stomata
(ii) transpiration

(b) (i) bacteria
(ii) nitrogen (as nitrates)
(iii) bacteria in the nodules absorb the nitrogen from the air in the soil, and combine it with other elements.
(iv) the bacteria can live freely in the soil to fix nitrogen.
(v) beans increase the nitrogen content of the soil. Nitrogen is required by plants to make plant protein.

(c) Beans provide a good source of proteins, minerals and vitamins. They are at the beginning of the food chain, so it is a more efficient use of the total energy which is available, rather than having cattle grazing on the land and converting the plants into meat.

A10 Remember to only use information shown in the diagrams, and to explain rather than just describe three ways the animal is adapted for life in running water. You would probably obtain only 3 marks for description instead of the 6 available.
Your answers could include:

the shape of the animal is very flat (1)
which offers little resistance to the flow of water (1)

the animal has strong, well-developed legs (1)
to enable it to swim against the current (1)

the animal has hooks at the end of its legs (1)
so that it can cling to rocks (1)

A11 (a) Look for the countries where life expectancy is above 61 years
Answer = 3

(b) (i) Look for the country where the figures for estimated population and actual population show the greatest difference. You can roughly work out that the biggest differences are for Turkey and Egypt, and then work out the accurate increase. Turkey has an increase of 30.7 millions whereas Egypt has only 25.4 millions.

Answer = Turkey

(ii) The word of instruction asks you to 'suggest' so any reasonable scientific answer will obtain the mark. For example: immunisations have reduced infant mortality (1), birth control may not be widely used (1).

(c) Again you are only asked to suggest reasons, you do not have to know the correct answer, and there may not be one correct answer. Possible answers include: lack of immunisation/lack of basic health care facilities (1), poor nutrition (1).

A12 (a) The pyramid of biomass shows the mass/weight of living material/animals and plants/ organisms (1), at each (trophic) level (1).

Note: take care to answer the question. (a) asks about the pyramid of *biomass* although the diagram shows pyramid of numbers *and* that of biomass; so no marks would be gained for stating that the pyramid of biomass shows the number of organisms.

(b) (i) some is lost through excretion/respiration
or not all biomass is eaten at each level (1)

(ii) the pyramid of numbers shows a few individuals (1), for example, a few oak trees which have a large biomass (1) as shown on the pyramid of biomass.

▶ A STUDENT'S ANSWER WITH EXAMINER'S COMMENT

1. The diagram below shows part of a food web.

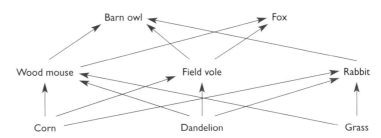

Fig. 6.26

Suppose all the field voles were suddenly killed by disease.

(a) Why would the number of dandelions be likely to increase?

not being eaten by voles (2)

'Good'

(b) Why would the number of foxes be likely to decrease?

less voles to eat

owls may eat more mice so less for fox (2)

The label below shows the chemical composition of a rose fertiliser.

Analysis	
COMPOUND FERTILISER	10.5-7.5-10.5
NITROGEN (N) Total	10.5%
PHOSPHORUS PENTOXIDE (P_2O_5) Total	7.5%
of which Soluble in water	4.5%
Insoluble in water	3.0%
POTASSIUM OXIDE (K_2O) Total	10.5% (K8.7%)
MAGNESIUM (Mg)	2.7%

'Yes, but state how plants use up nitrogen to make proteins'

(c) Why is it necessary to put substances such as nitrogen back into the soil?

it is lost from the soil (2)

'Good. Also fish die from lack of oxygen when algae are decomposed'

(d) Explain briefly the dangers to the environment of fertilisers which are readily soluble in water.

they are washed into lakes and cause algae to grow. (3)

(NICCEA)

SUMMARY

At the end of this chapter you should know:

▷   how some organisms are **adapted** to survive changes in their habitat;

▷   how the **population size** and the **distribution** of organisms in a habitat can be explained in terms of **adaptation, predation** and **competition** for resources;

▷   that in **food webs** there may be several overlapping **food chains**;

▷   how toxic material can **accumulate** in a food chain;

▷   how food chains can be described quantitatively using **pyramids of numbers** and **pyramids of biomass**;

▷   how **energy** is **transferred** through an ecosystem;

▷   the role of **microbes** and other organisms in the **decomposition** of materials and in the cycling of **carbon** and **nitrogen**;

▷   how **food production** can be managed to improve the efficiency of energy transfer;

▷   that the impact of **human activity** on the **environment** is related to **population size, economic factors** and **industrial requirements**.

Atomic structure and bonding

 GETTING STARTED

Chapters 7 to 11 of this book will take you through the main topics and points needed to cover Attainment Target 3: Materials and their properties.

Materials can be grouped in a variety of ways for different purposes:

► solid/liquid/gas;
► metals/non-metals;
► element/compound/mixture;
► ionic/covalent.

Each form of classification has its uses. However, if we want to understand why materials are placed in one group or another and why materials have the properties they do, then we need to understand something about the internal structure of matter.

The **kinetic theory** is a model (an idea) that takes the view that:

► all substances are made of particles;
► these particles have energy and are constantly moving – they have **kinetic energy**.

This idea can help us understand and explain many properties, such as expansion, melting, evaporation, diffusion, osmosis.

Atomic structure. Another useful idea is to imagine that atoms are themselves made of particles, which are found in the nucleus (centre) and as electrons orbiting the nucleus.

► A knowledge of the nucleus helps us understand radioactivity.
► A knowledge of the electrons and how they fit into an atom helps us understand how and why chemical reactions take place.

TOPIC	STUDY	REVISION 1	REVISION 2
Solids, liquids and gases			
Diffusion			
Expansion			
Atoms, molecules and ions			
Elements, compounds and mixtures			
Fractional distillation			
Atomic structure			
Ionic and covalent bonding			
Giant structures			
Macromolecules			

WHAT YOU NEED TO KNOW

▶ **Solids, liquids and gases**

'that solids, liquids and gases are composed of particles' [3.1a]

All matter can be classified as **solid**, **liquid** or **gas**. These are called the three **states of matter**. The idea that matter (solid, liquid or gas) is made up of particles which are in constant motion is called the **kinetic theory**. This idea can help us explain several properties of solids, liquids and gases.

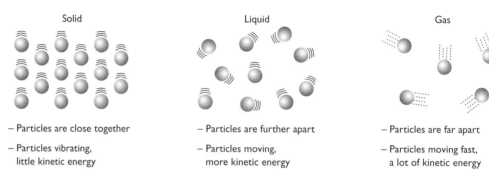

Solid	Liquid	Gas
– Particles are close together	– Particles are further apart	– Particles are far apart
– Particles vibrating, little kinetic energy	– Particles moving, more kinetic energy	– Particles moving fast, a lot of kinetic energy

Fig. 7.1 Relationships between the particles in solids, liquids and gases

'Make sure you read this carefully and try to understand these ideas'

▶ In a **solid** the particles are very close together and are 'vibrating' rather than moving freely.
▶ The particles in a **liquid** are moving more **slowly** and are **closer** together.
▶ The particles in a **gas** are moving very **fast** (they have a lot of kinetic energy) and are a great distance apart.

This idea is often shown by a piece of equipment similar to that in Fig. 7.2. The motor, turning very **fast** (providing a lot of energy), makes the metal spheres imitate a **gas** but when it is moving more **slowly** (providing less energy) the spheres imitate a **liquid**.

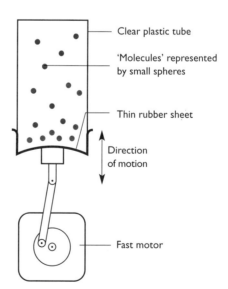

Clear plastic tube

'Molecules' represented by small spheres

Thin rubber sheet

Direction of motion

Fast motor

Fig. 7.2 This equipment imitates the movement of particles

Brownian motion

Brownian motion was first seen by a scientist called Robert Brown. He noticed that when he looked at pollen grains in water through a microscope they were 'jiggling' around in a **random** way. This was explained in later years by another scientist, who said that the strange movement was due to the very much smaller **water particles** (water molecules) hitting the **pollen grains** and making them **move**. This can also be seen in a 'smoke cell', where the particles of smoke are being moved by the air molecules striking them. The water or air molecules cannot be seen, even with the most powerful microscope; they are far too small, but the **effect** they have on the much, much larger pollen grains or smoke particles is very obvious.

This odd movement could be explained only by assuming that air (gas) and water (liquid) were made of **particles** and that these particles were **moving**.

By adding more energy to the system by *heating*, we can change a **solid** to a **liquid** to a **gas**. Similarly, by taking energy away from the system by *cooling*, we can change a **gas** to a **liquid** to a **solid**.

▶ **Diffusion**   Diffusion means **mixing**; gases, liquids and even solids can mix together or **diffuse** if left alone (even without anyone stirring them!). Diffusion provides **evidence** for the kinetic theory.

Diffusion in gases

'Ammonia molecules are moving faster than hydrogen chloride'

▶ When the top is removed from a bottle containing ammonia solution, you can smell the ammonia (which is a **gas**), even if you are some distance away. The ammonia has mixed with the air and spread out.

▶ When the equipment in Fig. 7.3 is set up and left for a short time, a white ring appears in the tube. This white substance is ammonium chloride, which is formed when the gas ammonia meets the gas hydrogen chloride. This could only happen if the gas particles had **kinetic energy** land were able to spread out and mix. Notice the white ring where the gases meet is **not** in the centre. Which gas spreads out the faster? Does this tell you which has the lighter particles?

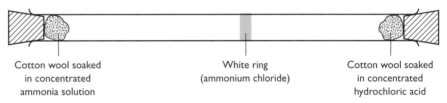

Cotton wool soaked in concentrated ammonia solution

White ring (ammonium chloride)

Cotton wool soaked in concentrated hydrochloric acid

Fig. 7.3 Diffusion in gases

Diffusion in liquids

Diffusion can also occur in **liquids** e.g. between ink and water. This can be shown by leaving a layer of water in contact with a layer of ink (see Fig. 7.4). The diffusion takes place more slowly than between gases because the particles have less energy. They are moving more slowly and are closer together.

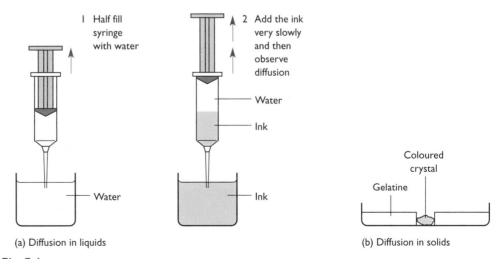

1 Half fill syringe with water

2 Add the ink very slowly and then observe diffusion

Water

Ink

Water

Ink

Coloured crystal

Gelatine

(a) Diffusion in liquids

(b) Diffusion in solids

Fig. 7.4

Diffusion between solids

'Molecules move more
slowly in solids'

Diffusion can take place between **solids**, although this takes place even more slowly. In Fig. 7.4b a coloured crystal is placed in some gelatine; after a day or two the colour has spread throughout the gelatine.

The only way to explain these results is to assume that substances are made of **particles** and that these particles have **kinetic energy** (are moving).

Diffusion in action

Gas exchange in the alveoli of the lungs takes place by **diffusion** (see Table 7.1). Diffusion of particles takes place from where there is a **higher** concentration to where there is a **lower** concentration. Particles will diffuse until they are evenly distributed.

Table 7.1 Concentration of gases in the lung

	Concentration of gas in blood flowing to alveoli	Concentration of gas in air in alveoli
oxygen	low	high
carbon dioxide	high	low

Diffusion can also be a nuisance; it is because of diffusion that **pollutant gases** e.g. from car exhausts, power stations and aerosols, can spread throughout the atmosphere.

▶ Expansion

In general, when matter is heated it **expands**, although some substances expand more than others. Again, this can be understood if we imagine all substances to be made of particles. In Fig. 7.5 we see that heating transfers energy to the substance, increasing the kinetic energy of its particles.

A common mistake is to say that the particles themselves get bigger; this is not so, it is the **gaps** between the particles that increase.

Expansion can be seen in action in many ways. For example:

1. **Bimetallic strip**: this consists of two metals with different expansion rates stuck together. When heated, the strip bends. Bimetallic strips are often used in **thermostats** as a switching device, as well as for flashing light bulbs.
2. **Gaps** are left between the end joints of rails on railways to allow for expansion.

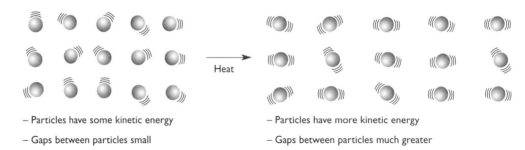

    – Particles have some kinetic energy   – Particles have more kinetic energy

    – Gaps between particles small   – Gaps between particles much greater

Fig. 7.5 Expansion is caused by increased kinetic energy of particles

▶ Atoms, molecules and ions

The **particle** is the building block of all matter. There are **three** types: atom, molecule and ion.

The atom

This is the simplest particle; there are just over 100 different atoms. It is from these atoms, and combinations of these atoms, that the other two types of particles can be made. Each atom has its own **name** and **symbol** to represent it.

Atom	Symbol
Hydrogen	H
Oxygen	O
Carbon	C
Copper	Cu
Chlorine	Cl
Sodium	Na

Each chemical symbol is either a single **capital letter** (e.g. H) or a **capital letter** followed by a **small letter** (e.g. Cl). Atoms are not generally found on their own.

The molecule

This is a particle that contains **two or more atoms chemically joined** together. Molecules can contain the **same** type of atom or **different** atoms chemically joined (bonded). Each molecule has a name and a chemical formula to represent which atoms are joined together.

Molecule	Name	Formula
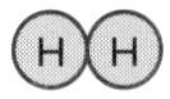 H H	hydrogen	H_2
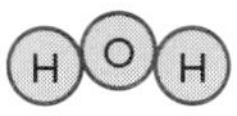 H O H	water	H_2O

Fig. 7.6 Each molecule can be represented by a formula

The numbers show the **proportions** of atoms present in the molecule. They refer to the atoms immediately before the number, and are always written below the line (subscript).

For example, glucose (a sugar), $C_6H_{12}O_6$ contains 6 atoms of carbon, 12 atoms of hydrogen and 6 atoms of oxygen.

The ion

'Ions have either lost or gained electrons'

This is a particle that carries an **electrical charge**, which may be **positive** or **negative**. Each ion has a name and formula. Ions can be derived from single atoms or from combinations. The **charge** on the ion is shown as a + or − above the symbols (superscript). The **size** of the charge is indicated as a **number**, for example, 1+, 2+, 3+, or 1−, 2−, 3−.

Ion	Formula
oxide	O^{2-}
chloride	Cl^-
copper	Cu^{2+}
carbonate	CO_3^{2-}

Not all possible combinations of atoms produce molecules and ions. There are rules governing their formation.

▶ Elements, compounds and mixtures

'that elements consist of atoms and that all atoms of the same element contain the same number of protons' [KS3]

'that compounds have definite composition and to represent compounds by formulae' [KS3]

'that mixtures, e.g. air, contain constituents that are not combined' [KS3]

'learn about methods, including filtration, distillation and chromatography, that can be used to separate mixtures into their constituents' [KS3]

All substances can be classified according to the **type of particles** they contain and how these particles are joined (chemically bound or not). Substances can be classified as:

▶ elements;
▶ compounds;
▶ mixtures.

Elements

Elements are substances that contain only **one** type of atom. For example, **copper** is an element containing copper atoms as shown in Fig. 7.8. Hydrogen is also an element. **Hydrogen** gas contains hydrogen molecules as shown in Fig. 7.7. Elements cannot be broken down into simpler chemical substances.

Compounds

Compounds are substances which contain **more than one** type of atom chemically joined. The particles in a compound may be molecules or ions. A compound can be chemically split into simpler substances.

Water is a compound. It consists of water molecules. Each water molecule contains **two** atoms of **hydrogen** and **one** atom of **oxygen**, shown in Fig. 7.9. Water can be split by electrolysis into hydrogen and oxygen. **Sodium chloride** is also a compound. It consists of sodium ions and chloride ions, shown in Fig. 7.10. There is one sodium ion for every chloride ion. It can be split by **electrolysis** into sodium atoms and chlorine molecules.

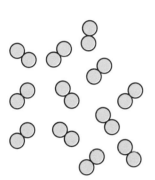

Fig. 7.7 Hydrogen molecules

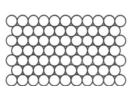

Fig. 7.8 Copper atoms

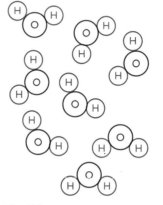

Fig. 7.9 Water molecules

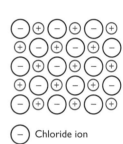

Fig. 7.10 Sodium chloride

Mixtures

Mixtures are substances which can contain various amounts of elements and/or compounds **mixed together**. They can easily be **physically separated**. For example, a mixture of iron and sulphur can easily be separated with a magnet.

Other methods of separating mixtures include **filtration**, **distillation** and **chromatography**.

Filtration

This is the technique for separating solid particles from a liquid (or gas). This is done by passing the liquid (or gas) through a sieve such as filter paper which has very tiny gaps between the fibres to allow the molecules of liquid to pass through but not any solid particles. For example, to separate muddy water by filtering, the sand and grit particles stay on the filter paper while the water that passes through is clear (see Fig. 7.11).

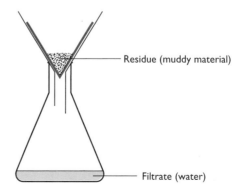

Fig. 7.11 Filtration

Other examples of filtration include filters in air-conditioning units to remove dust particles from the air, filters in cooker hoods to remove grease and dust from the air; air and oil filters in cars.

Distillation

'Methods for separating mixtures'

This is the process in which a solution is heated to produce a vapour which is then condensed by cooling to become liquid again. The vapour is usually condensed in a Liebig Condenser, a tube around which cold water flows, which is shown in Fig. 7.12. Distillation is used to separate a single, pure liquid from one or more liquids in a solution, e.g. to obtain pure water from sea water; to obtain alcohol from a mixture of alcohol and water.

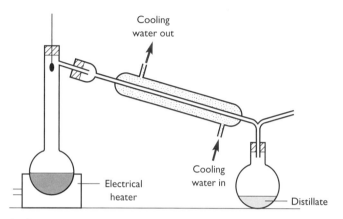

Fig. 7.12 Simple distillation

Chromatography

This is a technique for detecting the parts of a mixture by separating them. Paper chromatography involves placing a drop of the mixture to be separated on a type of blotting paper called chromatography paper which is then dipped into a **solvent**. As the solvent soaks through the paper it carries the mixture with it. As different substances dissolve at **different rates** the solvent carries some parts of the mixture further than others, so separating them. For example, in Fig. 7.13 you can see the number of different coloured dyes in ink food colouring.

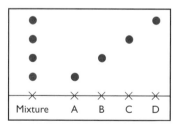

Fig. 7.13 Chromatagram showing four different components in a mixture

▶ Fractional distillation

'A technical application'

Fractional distillation is a process used in industry to separate liquids of **different boiling points**. It is used in the chemical industry to separate **crude oil** into 'fractions', i.e. mixtures of liquids with similar boiling points. The liquids with **high** boiling points have **large, heavy particles**, whereas those with **low** boiling points have **small, light** particles. The **heavier** particles need **more energy** to help them escape the surface of the liquid. The **forces** which attract the **heavier** particles to each other are **greater** than the forces between the lighter particles, as shown in Fig. 7.14.

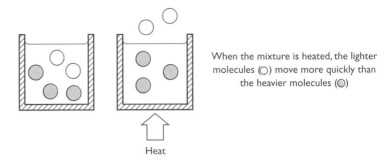

When the mixture is heated, the lighter molecules (○) move more quickly than the heavier molecules (◉)

Heat

Fig. 7.14

Fractional distillation in action

1. Fractional distillation can also be used to separate other liquids of differing boiling points, such as alcohol from wine.
2. It can also be used to purify zinc. When zinc is extracted from zinc ore it often contains a small amount of lead. Zinc and lead can be separated by fractional distillation, because the boiling point of zinc (908°C) is much lower than that of lead (1651°C).

▶ Atomic structure

'atoms consist of nuclei and electrons' [3.1b]

'the charges and relative masses of protons, neutrons and electrons' [3.1c]

'mass number, atomic number and isotopes' [3.1d]

'a model of the way electrons are arranged in atoms' [3.1e]

'the reactions of elements depend upon the arrangement of electrons in their atoms' [3.1f]

Structure of atoms

Atoms have a central **nucleus** containing **positively charged protons** and **neutral neutrons**, surrounded by cloud of **negatively charged electrons** arranged in shells as shown in Fig. 7.15.

▶ protons
▶ neutrons } found in the nucleus
▶ electrons   found orbiting the nucleus

The differences in these particles are shown in the table:

Table 7.2

Sub-atomic particle	Mass (*u*)*	Charge
proton	1	+1
neutron	1	0
electron	very small (1/2000)	−1

* (*u* = atomic mass unit)

Patterns for atoms

▶ The number of **protons** in an atom is called the **atomic number**. Atoms have atomic numbers of 1 to 107.
▶ There are **always** the **same number** of electrons and protons, so every atom is electrically neutral. Charges on the electrons and protons 'cancel out'.
▶ Electrons are arranged in a series of **shells** around the nucleus. Each shell can only contain a limited number of electrons. For elements with an atomic number up to eighteen the **maximum** numbers in the first three shells are shown; thereafter the arrangement becomes more complex.

1st shell   maximum 2 electrons
2nd shell   maximum 8 electrons
3rd shell   maximum 8 electrons

For example, in the sodium atom, which has 11 electrons, the arrangement is: 2 (in 1st shell); 8 (in 2nd shell); 1 (in 3rd shell).

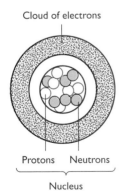

Cloud of electrons

Protons   Neutrons

Nucleus

Fig. 7.15 Particles which make up the atom

The total number of **protons** and **neutrons** in the nucleus is called the **mass number** (each proton and neutron has a mass of $1u$). There are usually about the same number of protons as of neutrons in a nucleus. You can work out the structure of an atom from the atomic number and the mass number:

▶ **mass number (A)** (nucleon number): number of protons + number of neutrons in the atomic nucleus;

▶ **atomic number (Z)**: number of protons in the nucleus (= number of electrons).

These numbers can be added to the chemical symbol for the atom as follows:

Mass number A $\mathbf{X}$ ← chemical symbol

Atomic number Z

For example, in the **sodium atom**, $^{23}_{11}$Na:

the atomic number   = 11, therefore there are 11 protons and 11 electrons;
the mass number   = 23 = number of protons + number of neutrons;
the number of neutrons = mass number – atomic number
                       = 23 – 11 = 12

Therefore, sodium has 11 protons, 12 neutrons and 11 electrons. We can show the electron configuration (arrangement of electrons in their shells) for sodium as Na:2,8,1, as seen in Fig. 7.16. The table shows the patterns for the atoms of some common elements.

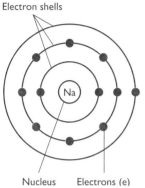

Electron shells

Nucleus   Electrons (e)

Fig. 7.16 The sodium atom

Table 7.3

Element	Number of protons in the nucleus (atomic number)	Number of protons and neutrons (mass number)	Number of electrons in each shell			
			Shell 1	Shell 2	Shell 3	Shell 4
Hydrogen	1	1	1			
Helium	2	4	2			
Lithium	3	7	2	1		
Beryllium	4	9	2	2		
Boron	5	11	2	3		
Carbon	6	12	2	4		
Nitrogen	7	14	2	5		
Oxygen	8	16	2	6		
Fluorine	9	19	2	7		
Neon	10	20	2	8		
Sodium	11	23	2	8	1	
Magnesium	12	24	2	8	2	
Aluminium	13	27	2	8	3	
Silicon	14	28	2	8	4	
Phosphorus	15	31	2	8	5	
Sulphur	16	32	2	8	6	
Chlorine	17	35.5	2	8	7	
Argon	18	40	2	8	8	
Potassium	19	39	2	8	8	1
Calcium	20	40	2	8	8	2

Remember: if you draw the arrangement of **electrons** they are **arranged in shells** around the nucleus: 1st shell maximum 2 electrons; 2nd and subsequent shells maximum 8 electrons.

Isotopes

Isotopes are **atoms of the same element** which contain **different numbers of neutrons** (but same number of protons) and have **different mass numbers**.

The type of atom is determined by its atomic number (number of protons). Carbon is carbon because it has 6 protons. Chlorine is chlorine because it has 17 protons. It is possible, however, for atoms such as these to have **different** mass numbers. This means that they contain different numbers of **neutrons** in their nuclei. Such atoms, which are chemically the same, but differ in their mass numbers, are called **isotopes**.

Chlorine has two isotopes: chlorine 35 (with a mass number of 35), and chlorine 37 (with a mass number of 37). Both these atoms behave in identical ways in chemical reactions (they have the same number of protons and electrons), but they have different numbers of **neutrons** in their nuclei. This is shown in Fig. 7.17. In chlorine gas the proportion of these isotopes is always the same. There are 3 chlorine-35 atoms for every 1 chlorine-37 atom. The average number of protons and neutrons in a chlorine nucleus is therefore

$$\frac{35u + 35u + 35u + 37u}{4} = 35.5u \text{ (where } u = 1 \text{ atomic mass unit)}$$

'Isotopes have the same number of protons and different numbers of neutrons. Chlorine 35 has 18 newtrons. Chlorine 37 has 20 neutrons'

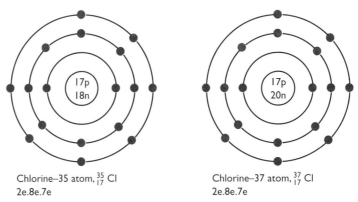

Chlorine–35 atom, $^{35}_{17}$ Cl
2e.8e.7e

Chlorine–37 atom, $^{37}_{17}$ Cl
2e.8e.7e

Fig. 7.17 Isotopes of chlorine

Relative atomic mass

Different elements have different proportions of isotopes (some of which may be radioactive. The **relative atomic mass** of an element is based on the average **mass** of all the atoms in the element (taking the isotope carbon 12 as the standard) and will not be a whole number. This is the number that is usually quoted in a list of atomic masses or given in the periodic table.

Detecting atoms – flame tests

It is not always easy to know which atoms are present in a compound. Some, although not **all**, give distinct colours to flames, a fact used widely in making fireworks. In the laboratory, substances can be tested by placing a small amount on a clean wire in a 'blue' bunsen flame. The colour of the flame indicates the atom present.

Colour of flame	Atom present
apple green	barium
orange (brick red)	calcium
green	copper
blue flashes	lead
lilac	potassium
yellow	sodium
red	strontium

▶ Ionic and covalent bonding

'new substances are formed when atoms combine' [3.1g]
'chemical bonding can be explained in terms of transfer or sharing of electrons' [3.1h]
'ions are formed when atoms gain or lose electrons' [3.1i]
'ionic lattices are held together by the attraction between oppositely charged ions' [3.1j]

'The Periodic Table is discussed in Chapter 9'

There is a stable arrangement for electrons in atoms. This occurs when an atom has a **filled outer shell**. All the atoms in group 0 of the Periodic Table have filled outer shells. These atoms do not react with other substances except for a very few special cases.

All other atoms react in order to fill their outer electron shells. They can do this in two ways: either ionic bonding or covalent bonding.

Ionic bonding

In the reaction between sodium and chlorine atoms, **electron transfer** has occurred to form ions:

$$Na + Cl \rightarrow Na^+ + Cl^-$$

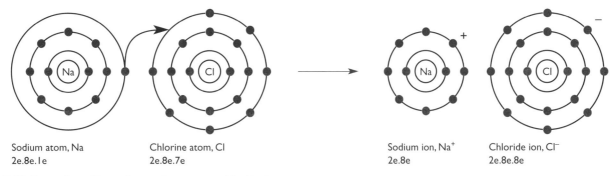

| Sodium atom, Na | Chlorine atom, Cl | Sodium ion, Na⁺ | Chloride ion, Cl⁻ |
| 2e.8e.1e | 2e.8e.7e | 2e.8e | 2e.8e.8e |

Fig. 7.18 Formation of ions when sodium reacts with chlorine

The sodium atom has **lost** an electron to become a sodium ion: we show this as Na^+. The chlorine atom has **gained** an electron to become a chloride ion: we show this as Cl^-. Both the ions that are formed have filled outer shells, as shown in Fig. 7.18.

Once these two ions have been formed, they will attract each other because of the **opposite charges** of the ions. (Like charges **repel**; unlike charges **attract**.) The reason the electron transfer takes place in this direction is that any transfer of electrons takes energy. It is easier to take 1 electron from sodium than 7 electrons from chlorine. This results in the general rule:

▶   Metals form **positive ions**.
▶   Non-metals form **negative ions**.

A positive ion is called a **cation**; a negative ion is called an **anion**.

Table 7.4 Some atoms and their ions

Metal atoms	Group	Electrons lost	Ion formed
lithium	1	1	Li^+
sodium	1	1	Na^+
potassium	1	1	K^+
magnesium	2	2	Mg^{2+}
calcium	2	2	Ca^{3+}
aluminium	3	3	Al^{3+}

Non-metal atoms	Group	Electrons gained	Ion formed
oxygen	6	2	O^{2-}
sulphur	6	2	S^{2-}
chlorine	7	1	Cl^-
bromine	7	1	Br^-
iodine	7	1	I^-

Also, as a general rule:

▶ Group 1 elements form ions with **one positive** charge (they have one electron to lose).
▶ Group 2 elements form ions with **two positive** charges (they have two electrons to lose).
▶ Group 3 elements form ions with **three positive** charges (they have three electrons to lose).
▶ Group 7 elements form ions with **one negative** charge (they have one space to fill).
▶ Group 6 elements form ions with **two negative** charges (they have two spaces to fill).

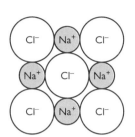

Fig. 7.19 The sodium chloride lattice

'Try to understand the differences between ionic and covalent bonding'

H⋯ *Properties of ionic compounds*

The formation of ions in this way (from the reaction between metal and non-metal atoms) results in positively and negatively charged particles which have a strong attraction for each other. These ions form a **giant ionic lattice**, in which each ion is surrounded by as many ions of the opposite charge as possible, similar to that in Fig. 7.19.

These strong forces of attraction mean that ionic substances have **high melting points** and **high boiling points** and are **solids** at room temperature. Ionic substances will also usually **dissolve in water**. Since ionic compounds contain charged particles they will conduct **electricity**, but only if the ions are free to move. This can happen if:

▶ the compound is heated until it is molten;
▶ the compound is dissolved in water.

Electrolysis

The process of ionic substances conducting electricity is called **electrolysis**. During this process the ions are turned back into atoms. This is illustrated by the electrolysis of molten sodium chloride as shown in Fig. 7.20.

'See also Chapter 8'

The two rods that extend into the liquid are called the **electrodes**. The positive electrode is called the **anode** and attracts the negative ions (**anions**). The negative electrode is called the **cathode** and attracts the positive ions (**cations**).

At the **anode** the chloride ions **lose** electrons and turns back into atoms. The atoms join in pairs to form **chlorine molecules**. At the **cathode** the sodium ions **gain** electrons and turn back into **sodium atoms**. This reaction can be summarised as follows:

H⋯ cathode reaction   anode reaction

$2Na^+(l) + 2e^- \rightarrow 2Na(l)$ $2Cl^-(l) - 2e^- \rightarrow Cl_2(g)$

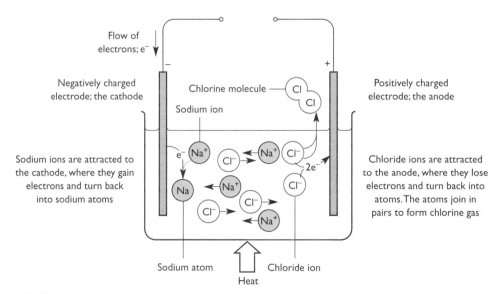

Fig. 7.20 Electrolysis of molten sodium chloride

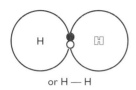

or H — H

Fig. 7.21 The hydrogen molecule

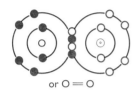

or O = O

Fig. 7.22 The oxygen molecule

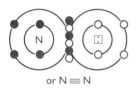

or N ≡ N

Fig. 7.23 The nitrogen molecule

H   **Covalent bonding**

'*covalent bonds are formed when atoms share electrons*' [3.1k]

'*substances with covalent bonds may form simple molecular structures or giant structures*' [3.1l]

'*the physical properties of some substances with giant structures and some with simple molecular structures*' [3.1m]

Atoms have stable arrangements if their **outer** electron shells are **filled**. This can happen by the **sharing** of electrons. **Non-metal** atoms combine to form **molecules** by sharing electrons in their outer shells. The exception to this is the atoms in Group 0, which have stable electron arrangements already.

▶ Two **hydrogen** atoms will join together to form a hydrogen molecule, by sharing their electrons. Each atom can then be considered to have a filled electron shell (two electrons), as shown in Fig. 7.21. The shared pair of electrons is called a **covalent bond** and can be shown as a line between the two atoms H-H. The molecule is represented as H_2.

▶ An **oxygen** molecule is formed in a similar way, but because each oxygen molecule has six electrons in its outer shell (electron configuration 2,6) it has two 'spaces' to be filled. It does this by each atom sharing **two** of its electrons; this forms a **double covalent bond**. The molecule is represented as O_2 (Fig. 7.22).

▶ Similarly, **nitrogen** atoms will pair up to form nitrogen molecules, but this time by forming a **triple covalent bond**. Each covalent bond is a shared pair of electrons, shown in Fig. 7.23. The nitrogen molecule is represented as N_2.

    Non-metal atoms exist in the free state as molecules (see Fig. 7.24) because in this way they can have **stable electron arrangements**.

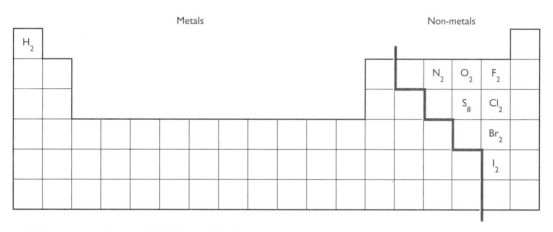

Fig. 7.24 It is only the non-metal atoms which form molecules

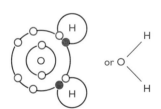

Fig. 7.25 Water molecule

Some common covalent compounds

Non-metal atoms will combine with other non-metal atoms to form covalent compounds: for example, water (H_2O) (shown in Fig. 7.25).

    Remember: each line represents a shared pair of electrons or, in other words, a covalent bond.

Properties of covalent compounds

Although the covalent bonds holding together the **atoms** in a molecule are **strong**, the forces holding the **molecules** themselves are **weak**. This means that covalently bonded substances are often gases or liquids, or solids with relatively **low melting points** and **low boiling points**. They **do not conduct electricity** and **do not usually dissolve** in water.

Name	Formula	Structure
carbon dioxide	CO_2	O = C = O
ammonia	NH_3	H—N(—H)(—H)
methane	CH_4	H—C(—H)(—H)—H
ethane	C_2H_6	H—C(—H)(—H)—C(—H)(—H)—H
ethene	C_2H_4	H₂C = CH₂
ethyl alcohol	C_2H_5OH	H—C(—H)(—H)—C(—H)(—H)—O—H

Fig. 7.26 Some common covalent compounds

Comparing covalent and ionic compounds

Table 7.5

	Ionic compounds	Covalent compounds
relation to periodic table	formed between metal atoms and non-metal atoms	formed between non-metal atoms
melting point	high>250°C	low<250°C
boiling point	high>500°C	low<500°C
electrical conductivity	good conductor when molten or in solution	non-conductors
solubility in water	usually soluble	usually insoluble

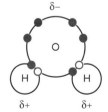

Fig. 7.27 The polar water molecule

Water as a solvent

Water dissolves ionic substances. The reason is that the water molecule is **polar** – it has a slight negative charge (δ–) at one end and a slight positive charge (δ+) at the other, as shown in Fig. 7.27. This is a result of the oxygen atoms attracting the electron pairs of the bonds with the hydrogen atoms more strongly. Water can therefore dissolve ionic substances. Water is not the only polar molecule (although it is more polar than most). Water will also dissolve other molecular compounds which are themselves slightly polar, e.g. ethanol.

▶ Giant structures   ### Metals as giant structures

H   **Metals** are **giant structures**. The metal atoms are 'bonded' together in an unusual way. The metal atoms lose some of their outer electrons and so become, in effect, positive ions. These electrons then move around the atoms freely. The metal atoms/ions are in a sea of

Fig. 7.28 Metals are giant structures

electrons, as shown in Fig. 7.28. The electrons are free to move and are shared by all the atoms. This idea helps to explain many of the properties of metals.

▶ **High boiling points and melting points**: the attraction between the 'ions' and electrons is strong, so usually the metals will have high melting points and boiling points and will be strong and hard.

▶ **Conduction of electricity**: the ease of movement of electrons will mean that metals will easily conduct electricity when a potential difference is applied across the metal.

▶ Macro- H molecules

Some covalently bonded molecules do not have the properties indicated above, because their molecules are **very large**. They have a large number of **covalent bonds** and form **giant molecules** or **macromolecules**.

Elements

Carbon is an example of an element which forms large numbers of covalent bonds between its atoms. It can do this in two ways, to form **diamond** or **graphite**. These two forms of carbon are called **allotropes**, as shown in Fig. 7.29. Some other elements have different allotropic forms, but not necessarily forming giant molecules (e.g. sulphur).

Diamond is very strong because **each carbon atom** is linked to **four** other carbon atoms. A diamond crystal is one giant molecule. Graphite is very strongly bonded, but in layers; each **layer** is a **giant molecule**. However, the forces holding the layers together are **weak**, so they slide over each other. This property is made use of in pencils; the pencil 'lead' is really graphite.

Silicon is in the same group as carbon; it too has similar abilities to form **giant structures**. The structure of silicon is the same as that of diamond. Silicon dioxide, a compound of silicon, has a giant structure, the atoms being bonded by covalent bonds. We come across this substance quite often; it appears as sand and as quartz in rocks and it can be made into glass. Silicon is in fact the second most common element found in the Earth's crust (28%), the first being oxygen.

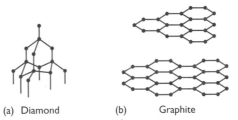

(a) Diamond (b) Graphite

Fig. 7.29 Allotropes of carbon

H Compounds of carbon

'A definition of polymers'

There are many **compounds** of carbon that form very large molecules. They exist because of carbon's ability to form **long chains** (as well as rings) of **covalently bonded carbon atoms**. These macromolecules are called **polymers**: some exist naturally, and some are man-made. Examples of these are starch, wool, polythene and nylon. These compounds contain atoms other than carbon, but it is the carbon atoms that provide the ability to form large molecules.

Although the polymers have large molecules which contain many thousand atoms, the giant molecules of carbon and silicon contain many **billion** atoms.

H Properties of maromeolecules

The **giant** molecules, such as carbon, have very high melting points and boiling points, will not dissolve in water and generally will not conduct electricity. Graphite, one form of carbon, is an exception. Silicon will also weakly conduct electricity, and is regarded as a 'semi-conductor'; it is this property that makes silicon valuable for use as 'microchips' in computer technology.

The **large** molecules (polymers), such as starch, have higher melting points and boiling points than ordinary molecules, but not as high as giant molecules or ionic compounds (which are also giant structures). They are not very soluble in water (most are insoluble) and will not conduct electricity.

Remember:

▶ **Ions** are formed when atoms gain or lose electrons.
▶ **Metals** form positive ions (cations) by *losing* electrons.
▶ **Non-metals** form negative ions (anions) by *gaining* electrons.
▶ Ionic lattices are held together by attraction between oppositely charged ions.
▶ **Ionic bonding**: atoms *lose* or *gain* electrons (transfer of electrons); for example sodium chloride – the sodium atom *loses* an electron to become a **positively charged sodium ion** (Na^+); the chlorine atom *gains* an electron to become a **negatively charged chloride ion** (Cl^-). The ions have both filled their outer shells and **attract** each other electrostatically owing to opposite charges.
▶ **Covalent bonding**: formed when atoms **share pairs of electrons in their outer shells**; for example, non-metal atoms, such as hydrogen, form molecules by sharing electrons.

 EXAMINATON QUESTIONS

Multiple choice

Q1   If fine pollen grains on the surface of water are examined under a microscope, it will be seen that the pollen grains are in random motion, frequently changing direction. The movement is most likely to be due to:

A   movement of air across the water
B   chemical reaction between the pollen and the water
C   attraction and repulsion between charged particles
D   collisions between water molecules and pollen grains
E   electrolysis of pollen grains

Q2   When ice is changing from a solid to a liquid at its melting point:

A   heat is given out
B   its particles become more ordered
C   its particles gain energy
D   its temperature increases

Q3   When water changes into steam, the molecules become:

A   much larger   D   separate atoms
B   more widely spaced   E   much smaller
C   less in mass

Q4   The separation of a liquid into different substances with similar boiling points is called:

A   chromatography   D   filtration
B   distillation   E   heating
C   evaporation

Q5   When copper forms an ion it loses two electrons. This can be shown by:

A   Cu;   B Cu^-;   C Cu^{2-};   D Cu^+;   E Cu^{2+}

Q6   Phosphorous has an atomic number of 15 and a mass number of 31. How many protons does it have?

A   3;   B   15;   C   16;   D   31;   E   46

Q7 Chlorine has two isotopes. What is different about the atomic structure of the isotopes?

A   the number of electrons
B   the number of protons
C   the number of neutrons
D   the number of protons plus electrons

Structured questions

'A question on particles aimed at Foundation Tier'

Q8 The diagrams below show the arrangement of molecules of water when it is a solid (ice), a liquid (water) and a gas (steam/vapour).

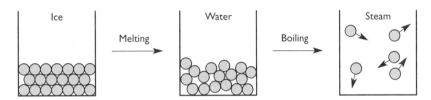

Fig. 7.30

Complete the table below (Table 7.6) by putting ticks into the appropriate boxes.

Table 7.6

State	Molecules have most energy	Molecules change places randomly	Molecules have least energy
ice water steam			

(Co-ordinated Science, NEAB, London, WJEC)

Q9 The table below refers to the radius of some common atoms and their ions.

Table 7.7

Element	Radius of atom	Radius of ion
Lithium	1.3	0.7
Sodium	1.5	1.0
Calcium	1.4	1.0
Tin	1.4	0.9
Oxygen	0.7	1.3
Sulphur	1.0	1.8
Bromine	1.1	2.0
Iodine	1.3	X

(a) What pattern do you observe about the relative sizes of an atom and its ion when comparing metals and non-metals?   *(2)*
(b) Predict the size of the radius of the iodine ion, X.   *(1)*
(c) Name **two** elements from the above list which form negative ions.   *(2)*

Look at the periodic table in Chapter 9, and identify the position of sodium and lithium.

(d) What is the size of the charge on these ions?   *(1)*
(e) Sodium chloride has the following properties: high melting point, solid, dissolves in water to become an electrolyte.

    (i) State the type of bonding which holds together the sodium and chloride ions. *(1)*

    (ii) Describe, with the help of diagrams, how the bonding between sodium and chloride ions differs from the bonding between two chlorine atoms. *(3)*

(MEG)

Q10 (Foundation Tier) This question gives you some information in the form of two diagrams. Read the heading to the diagrams and study them carefully before you answer the question.

(a) This apparatus is used to make a chromatogram to show the composition of three inks to find out what dyes they contain (Fig. 7.31).

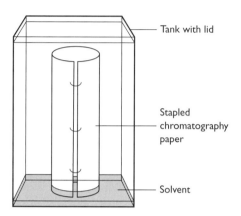

Fig. 7.31

Here is the resulting chromatogram (Fig. 7.32).

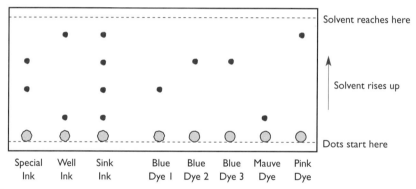

Fig. 7.32

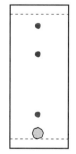

Fig. 7.33

    (i) Which ink(s) could contain blue dye 1? *(2)*

    (ii) Explain why you cannot say for certain that Special Ink must contain blue dye 2. (3 lines) *(3)*

    (iii) Mr Smith is accused of forging Mrs Brown's name on a cheque. Mrs Brown always uses Well ink. The ink on the cheque is tested in the same way. Here is the result (Fig. 7.33).

       Explain why this is evidence that the document might have been forged. *(2)*

(b) You are given a solution of sugar in water.

    (i) Describe, using a diagram if you wish, how you would obtain a sample of pure water. (5 lines) *(4)*

    (ii) Why is it not possible to separate the sugar from the water by filtering the solution? (2 lines) *(2)*

(Integrated Science, NEAB, London)

Q11   (a)   Table 7.8 compares the number of protons and electrons in sodium and chlorine atoms and gives the arrangement of electrons in each atom.

Table 7.8

	Sodium Na	Chlorine Cl
Number of protons	–	17
Number of electrons	11	–
Arrangements of electrons	2, 8, 1	2, 8, 7

(i)   Complete the table above.   *(2)*
(ii)   Which particles, apart from protons, are found in the nucleus of a sodium or chlorine atom?   *(1)*
(iii)   In which group of the periodic table are the elements sodium and chlorine placed?

Sodium _____   Chlorine_____   *(2)*

(b)   Table 7.9 compares the number of protons and electrons in sodium and chloride **ions**.

Table 7.9

	Sodium Na⁺	Chlorine Cl⁻
Number of protons	11	17
Number of electrons	10	18
Arrangements of electrons	2, 8	2, 8, 8

(i)   What change takes place when a sodium ion is formed from a sodium atom?   *(1)*
(ii)   What change takes place when a chloride ion is formed from a chlorine atom?   *(1)*

(c)   Figure 7.34 below shows the arrangement of sodium and chloride ions in a crystal of sodium chloride.

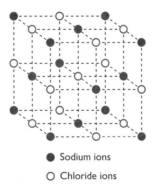

● Sodium ions
○ Chloride ions

Fig. 7.34

(i)   State **two** changes which take place in the crystal when melting occurs.

1.   _____

2.   _____   *(2)*

(ii)   Why does sodium chloride have a high melting point?

_____   *(1)*

(London)

Q12

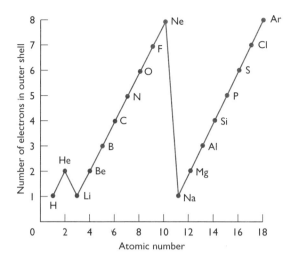

Fig. 7.35

(a) The graph shows the relationship between the number of electrons in the outer shell of the first 18 elements in the periodic table and their atomic numbers.
     Use the graph to help you answer the following questions.

 (i) Name **two metals** having two electrons on their outer shells.   (2)
 (ii) Name **two non-metals** having seven electrons on their outer shells.   (2)

(b) Name the kind of bond formed between elements when
 (i) the outer electrons are donated and received

_____

 (ii) the outer electrons are shared

_____   (2)

 (iii) Considering (i) and (ii) above, write down the formula of the compounds formed between

   1. aluminium (Al) and chlorine (Cl) _____

   2. boron (B) and fluorine (F) _____

   3. carbon (C) and fluorine (F) _____   (3)

 (iv) What kind of bonds are formed between carbon and fluorine?   (1)
                                                                                                     (WJEC)

Q13   The following table shows the properties of five substances.

Table 7.10

Substance	Melting point (°C)	Boiling point (°C)	Electrical conductivity when solid	liquid	Effect of heating in air
A	800	1470	poor	good	no reaction
B	650	1110	good	good	burns to form a white solid
C	19	287	poor	poor	burns to form carbon dioxide and water
D	114	444	poor	poor	burns to form an acidic gas only
E	1700	2200	poor	poor	no reaction

Each substance can be used once, more than once or not at all to answer the following.
Choose from A to E a substance which is:

(a) a metal _____ *(1)*

(b) a non-metallic element _____ *(1)*

(c) a molecular covalent compound _____ *(1)*

(d) an ionic compound _____ *(1)*

(e) a giant covalent structure _____ *(1)*

(Co-ordinated Science, London)

 ## EXAMINATION ANSWERS

Multiple choice

A1 Key D. It is the water molecules moving about which make the pollen grains appear to be moving on their own.

A2 Key C, the particles gain energy Option B is incorrect because the particles are gaining energy and moving about more quickly. Option D, temperature rise, does not occur when ice is changing state from a solid into a liquid.

A3 Key B, more widely spaced. Option A and E are wrong because the molecules do not change in size, they just have more space.

A4 Key B, distillation. Option A is separating different coloured substances using paper.

A5 Key E, Cu^{2+}. Electrons are negatively charged, so the ion has a positive charge as it has lost the electrons.

A6 Key B, 15 protons: the atomic number ($31 - 16 = 15$).

A7 Key C. In isotopes the number of neutrons varies, the protons and electrons stay the same.

Structured questions

A8 The table should look like this:

Table 7.11

State	Molecules have most energy	Molecules change places randomly	Molecules have least energy
ice			✓ (1)
water		✓ (1)	
steam	✓ (1)	✓ (1)	

A9 (a) The diameter of the metal atoms is larger than the diameter of the metal ions. The diameter of the non-metal atoms is smaller than the diameter of the non-metal ions.

(b) Larger than 2.0

(c) Any two non-metals, e.g. oxygen and sulphur

(d) 1

(e) (i) Ionic bonding

(ii) In the bonding between sodium and chloride ions, an electron has moved from the outer shell of the sodium atom, so forming a positively charged sodium ion. The electron has joined the outer shell of the chlorine atom, so forming a negatively charged chloride ion. The two ions are attracted to each other.

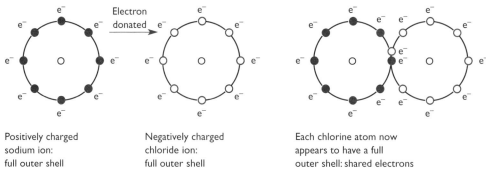

Fig. 7.36

In the bonding between two chlorine atoms, one electron from each atom is shared between the two atoms.

A10 (a) (i) Look at the dot for blue dye 2. It is on the same level as dots in 2 of the inks
Answer Special ink (1)   Sink ink (1)

(ii) The chromatogram dots for blue dye 2 and 3 and Special ink are on the same level (1), so Special ink could contain blue dye 2 (1) or 3 (1).

(iii) the pattern for Well ink shows only 2 dots but this ink pattern from the ink used on the cheque shows three dots (1), so it must be a different ink (1).

(b) (i) Try to include as much experimental detail here as possible. An accurate, well-labelled diagram is also acceptable but may take too much time to draw.
boil the water in a flask (1)
use a condenser (1)
to condense the vapour (1)
and collect the pure water in a beaker (1)

(ii) The sugar is dissolved in the water and forms a solution (1)
filtering would only separate solid particles from a mixture (1)

A11 (a) (i) Sodium has 11 protons. Chlorine has 17 electrons.
(ii) neutrons
(iii) Sodium is in group 1. Chlorine is in group 7.

(b) (i) An electron is lost from the sodium atom.
(ii) An electron is gained by the chlorine atom.

(c) (i) 1. The atoms vibrate more quickly.
2. The bonds between the sodium ions and chloride ions are broken.
(ii) A lot of energy is needed to break the bonds.

A12 (a) (i) magnesium, beryllium
(ii) fluorine, chlorine

'Use the Periodic Table to look up the names of elements'

(b) (i) ionic bonding
(ii) covalent bonding
(iii) 1. $AlCl_3$
2. BF_3
3. CF_4

(c) covalent

A13 (a) B – metals have good conductivity; B is the only substance with good conductivity.
(b) D – non-metals have low melting points and boiling points and D is the only substance which burns to form an acidic gas only.
(c) C – molecular covalent compounds have low melting points and boiling points.
(d) A – ionic compounds have good conductivity when molten or in solution; A is the only liquid with good conductivity.
(e) E – giant covalent structures have high melting points and high boiling points.

A STUDENT'S ANSWER WITH EXAMINER'S COMMENTS

'Read all this information'

1. **Three** pieces of information are given below.
   1. Substances can be elements, compounds or mixtures.
   2. Elements can be metals or non-metals.
   3. A group in the periodic table contains elements having similar properties.

   Using only this information, say which **one** of the substances in **each** of the following lists is different from the other three.
       For **each** list give the reason for your choice.

'Good – this is linked to statement 2'

   (a) Carbon, iron, copper, magnesium.

   Carbon is a non-metal, the others are all metals

   (1/1)

'Yes but you are asked for a reason in the question; the others are all non-reactive inert gases' linked to statement 3'

   (b) Neon, hydrogen, argon, helium.

   hydrogen

   (0/1)

   (c) Sulphur dioxide, zinc oxide, copper (II) sulphate, air.

   air is different as it's a mixture of elements not chemically combined

   (1/1)

'Good, this is linked to statement 1'

   (Total 2/3 marks)
   (WJEC)

SUMMARY

At the end of this chapter you should know:

▷ that **solids**, **liquids** and **gases** are composed of **particles**;

▷ that **elements** consist of **atoms** and that all atoms of the same element contain the **same number of protons**;

▷ that **compounds** have a definite composition and how to represent compounds by **formulae**;

▷ that **mixtures**, e.g. air, contain constituents that are not combined;

▷ about **methods** that can be used to **separate mixtures** into their constituents, e.g. **filtration**, **distillation** and **chromatography**;

▷ that **atoms** consist of **nuclei** and **electrons**;

▷ the charges and relative masses of **protons**, **neutrons** and **electrons**;

▷ about **mass number**, **atomic number** and **isotopes**;

▷ about a model of the way **electrons** are arranged in **atoms**;

▷ that new substances are formed when **atoms combine**;

▷ that chemical **bonding** can be explained in terms of **transfer** or **sharing** of **electrons**;

▷ how **ions** are formed when **atoms gain** or **lose electrons**;

▷ that **ionic lattices** are held together by the **attraction** between **positively charged ions**;

▷ that **covalent bonds** are formed when atoms **share** electrons;

▷ that substances with covalent bonds may form simple **molecular** structures or **giant structures**;

▷ the **physical properties** of some substances with **giant** structures and some with simple **molecular** structures.

Chapter

8 Useful products from oil and metal ores

▶ **GETTING STARTED**

In this chapter we will look at how oil deposits were formed millions of years ago. This knowledge is essential to our understanding of the problems of using up renewable resources. When oil undergoes distillation, it separates into different hydrocarbons, for example, petrol and diesel which are used as fuels. When those fuels are burnt carbon dioxide and other gases are released which can cause pollution.

There are different groups of hydrocarbons depending on whether a single or double bond is present between the carbon atoms. The alkanes are saturated hydrocarbons and have single bonds whereas the alkenes are unsaturated hydrocarbons which have a double bond.

Polymers, such as plastics, can be formed from these carbon-based compounds during a process known as cracking. Scientists can synthesise (make) polymers to have special properties, for example polythene is a long carbon chain which has hydrogen atoms attached to it. By replacing these with fluorine atoms a different polymer (PTFE) can be made, which is used on non-stick frying pans.

Metals exist as compounds in rocks; those rocks which contain large enough quantities of metals to be mined are called ores. Metals can be extracted from their ores by techniques such as smelting (reduction using carbon) or electrolysis.

Why should one of the most abundant metals in the earth's surface, aluminium, have been discovered last of all? In this chapter we will look at the reason for this when we consider the two methods of extraction of metals.

TOPIC	STUDY	REVISION I	REVISION 2
Useful products from oil			
Combustion			
Alkanes and alkenes			
Addition polymers			
Extraction of metals			
Useful substances from rocks			

▶ **WHAT YOU NEED TO KNOW**

▶ **Useful products from oil**

'*how oil deposits are formed*' [3.2a]

'*crude oil is a mixture of substances, most of which are hydrocarbons, which can be separated by fractional distillation*' [3.2b]

'*some products from the distillation of crude oil are used as fuels*' [3.2c]

▶ Crude oil (petroleum) and **natural gas** (methane) are formed by the effects of heat and pressure on organic matter trapped in sediments.

▶ Crude oil is a mixture of **hydrocarbons**, which are compounds of **carbon** and **hydrogen** only.

▶ **Fractional distillation** is used to separate crude oil into different **fractions**, which are mixtures of hydrocarbons with **similar boiling points**; products such as petrol, paraffin and diesel oil are used as **fuels**.

The table shows the different fractions produced by the fractional distillation of petroleum.

Table 8.1 Fractions produced by fractional distillation of petroleum

Boiling range (°C)	Fraction	Use
<30	liquefied gases	Calor gas, butane
20–200	petrol	petrol for cars, solvents
175–250	paraffin (kerosene)	oil stoves, aircraft fuel
200–350	diesel oil	diesel engine fuel in trains, lorries, tractors, etc.
300–400	lubricating oil	lubricant
350–450	fuel oil	fuel for power stations and ships
350–500	wax, grease	candles, wax paper, lubricant
>500 (solid)	bitumen	road making, roofing material

The hydrocarbon molecules in petroleum vary in size. As the molecules in a hydrocarbon get larger:

▶ the boiling point increases;
▶ it flows less easily (becomes more viscous);
▶ it ignites less easily (less flammable);
▶ it is less volatile.

Smaller hydrocarbon molecules (liquid gas, petrol, paraffin) have **lower** boiling points, and are very flammable and very volatile. **Larger** hydrocarbon molecules (fuel oil, grease, bitumen) have **higher** boiling points, burn with smoky flames and are less volatile.

▶ **Combustion**

'*the products of burning hydrocarbons*' [3.2d]

Combustion of fuels

Fuels are substances that give out a lot of energy when they burn; their reactions are strongly **exothermic**. The fuels react with the oxygen in the air. The **fossil fuels** we use (coal, gas and oil) contain carbon and hydrogen and are referred to as **hydrocarbons**. The products of **complete combustion** are carbon dioxide and water.

Coal is mainly carbon:

carbon + oxygen → carbon dioxide
$$C + O_2 \rightarrow CO_2$$

Natural gas is methane:

methane + oxygen → carbon dioxide + water
$$CH_4 + 2O_2 \rightarrow CO_2 + 2H_2O$$

Combustion in action

Natural gas is often considered to be a very suitable fuel for greenhouses as it produces not only heat, but also carbon dioxide, which the plants can use, as well as water to keep the atmosphere humid. However, if natural gas is burned in a limited amount of air, then combustion is **incomplete** and carbon monoxide (CO) will also be produced. The gas is poisonous because it combines strongly with haemoglobin in the blood, forming **carboxyhaemoglobin**, preventing it from carrying oxygen around the body. For this reason it is important to keep a room well ventilated when coal or gas is being burned.

Remember:
▶   **complete combustion**: an exothermic reaction, when there is a plentiful supply of oxygen;
▶   **incomplete combustion** occurs when fuel burns in a **limited** amount of oxygen – poisonous **carbon monoxide** is formed;
▶   **pollutants** such as carbon, carbon monoxide, sulphur dioxide and oxides of nitrogen can also be formed during combustion.

▶ Alkanes and alkenes

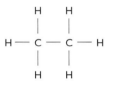

Fig. 8.1 Structural formula of ethane C_2H_6

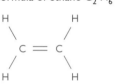

Fig. 8.2 Structural formula of ethene C_2H_4

'there are different groups of hydrocarbons' [3.2e]

'alkanes are saturated hydrocarbons containing a single covalent bond, and alkenes are unsaturated hydrocarbons containing one double covalent bond between carbon atoms' [3.2f]

'hydrocarbon molecules can be cracked to form smaller molecules including alkenes' [3.2g]

Alkanes are **saturated** hydrocarbon molecules with **single covalent** bonds between two carbon atoms C—C, e.g. methane CH_4, ethane C_2H_6, propane C_3H_8, butane C_4H_{10}.

Cracking is a process which breaks down long hydrocarbon molecules into shorter more useful chains; for example, **alkanes** are cracked to form **alkenes**, such as ethene.

Alkenes are **unsaturated** hydrocarbon molecules with **double covalent** bonds between two carbon atoms, C = C, e.g. ethene C_2H_4, propene C_3H_6.

Remember: one test to distinguish between alkanes and alkenes is that a colourless solution is formed when an **alkene** is shaken with **bromine water**; alkanes only decolourise bromine water very slowly.

▶ Addition polymers

'addition polymers can be made from alkenes formed during cracking' [3.2h]

'some uses of addition polymers' [3.2i]

Polymers are large molecules which can be formed by combining many small molecules; for example, unsaturated monomers (alkenes such as ethene) formed during cracking are made into **addition polymers** (such as poly(ethene), which is used for plastic bags and bottles).

Polymer molecules are very long chains consisting of repeating **monomer** units. There can be between 1,000 and 50,000 monomers in a chain. The chemical reaction in which monomers combine is called **polymerisation**.

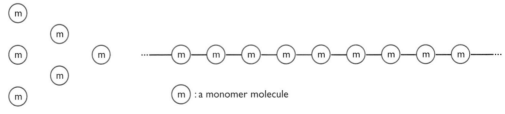

Fig. 8.3 A polymer molecule: polymers are made by joining together many small molecules called monomers

There are two ways in which monomers can react to form polymers:

▶   addition polymerisation;
▶   condensation polymerisation.

H *Addition polymerisation*

Unsaturated monomers which have a **double** carbon–carbon bond join together to form a polymer as shown in Fig. 8.4 (the formation of an addition polymer). For example, ethene, an **unsaturated** hydrocarbon, forms **poly(ethene)**, i.e. polythene, a saturated hydrocarbon.

$$n\left(\begin{matrix} | & | \\ C = C \\ | & | \end{matrix}\right) \longrightarrow \left(\begin{matrix} | & | \\ -C-C- \\ | & | \end{matrix}\right)_n$$

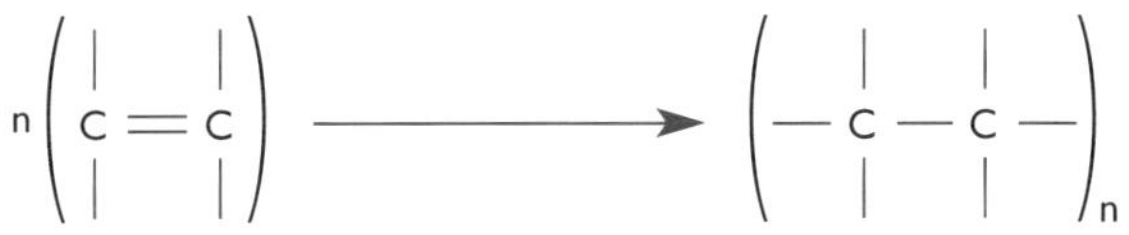

Fig. 8.4

Condensation polymerisation

Condensation polymers are formed when small molecules are lost when the monomers react together. These small molecules are usually water or hydrogen chloride. For example, nylon – a polyamide; terylene – a polyester.

Table 8.2 Uses of plastics

Plastic	Uses
Polyethene (Polythene)	bags, films for packaging toys, household goods, insulation for electrical wiring
Polypropylene	tableware, chair seats, toilet seats, heels for shoes, filaments for brushes
PVC	water pipes, drain pipes, packaging gramophone records, coating fabrics, rainwear, floor tiles
Polystyrene	household containers, toys, expanded foam insulating material, packaging
Polyester	clothes, sheets, ropes, tents, sails, safety belts

Advantages of plastics

▶ They are cheap and easy to mould into shapes.
▶ They are not corroded and can resist chemical attack.
▶ They are waterproof.
▶ They can easily be coloured.
▶ They are lightweight.

Disadvantages of plastics

▶ Their manufacture uses raw material derived from oil (a non-renewable resource).
▶ They are flammable and give off toxic fumes when they burn.
▶ They cannot easily be disposed of; plastics waste in land-fill sites will not break down in the soil.

▶ Extraction of metals

'*metal ores are found in the Earth*' [3.2j]
'*the way in which a metal is extracted from its ores is related to its reactivity*' [3.2k]

The history of metals

The most abundant metal in the Earth's crust is aluminium, yet it was one of the last to be discovered. Why should this be so? Yet again, reference to the reactivity series can help us answer this question.

Table 8.3

Metal	Approximate date of first use
Gold, silver, copper	5,000 BC
Tin	2,500 BC
Iron	1,200 BC
Zinc	BC/AD
Aluminium	AD 1825

If we compare this list with the reactivity series, we can see that it shows the **reverse** pattern. In other words, the metals that were **discovered first** were those that showed the **least** tendency to form ions. In fact, the metals gold and silver and small amounts of copper can be found on the ground in their **native state**, i.e. as the metals themselves. The other metals, however, only exist in the Earth's crust as compounds, i.e. the metals are present as metal ions chemically locked with other substances. The **more reactive** a metal (the higher in the reactivity series), the **more stable** it becomes as a **compound**. This means that it will be **difficult** to extract it from its ore (to change the ion into an atom).

Extraction methods

Many metals exist in the Earth's crust as metal ores. Some of the most common are shown in the table below.

Table 8.4

Metal ore	Compound	Formula	Metal
Limestone	calcium carbonate	$CaCO_3$	calcium
Bauxite	aluminium oxide	Al_2O_3	aluminium
Haematite	iron oxide	Fe_2O_3	iron
Pyrites	iron sulphide	FeS_2	iron
Galena	lead sulphide	PbS	lead
Chalcopyrite	copper iron sulphide	$CuFeS_2$	copper

'Techniques for extracting metals from their ores'

There are two basic techniques for extracting the metal from the ore; either **reduction**, using heat energy and carbon as the reducing agent, or **electrolysis**, using electrical energy. In either case, the problem is the same – to reduce the metal **ion** to a metal **atom**. The technique that is chosen depends on cost and the reactivity of the metal.

Metals exist in ores in an oxidised state. In order to extract the metal, the ores all have to be reduced; this requires adding **electrons** to the metal **ion** and so requires **energy**:

$$\text{metal ion} + \text{electrons} \xrightarrow{\text{reduction}} \text{metal atom}$$

The choice of the extraction method for a metal depends largely on two things:

1. the **activity** of the metal;
2. the cost of **energy** to perform the reduction.

Carbon can act as a **reducing** agent for all the less reactive metals (those below aluminium in the series). Carbon in the form of coke is plentiful and its combustion provides a relatively **cheap** form of energy (in the form of heat). **Electrolysis** is normally much more **expensive**, so is used if there is no alternative. However, an electrolysis metal extraction plant is often sited to take advantage of **cheap electrical power**, e.g. hydro-electric power. There is also an advantage in a metal extraction plant being sited near the mine, as the transport of crude ore would cost more than the transport of the metal.

Remember: there are **two** basic techniques for the extraction of a metal from its ore:

1. electrolysis;
2. reduction by carbon or carbon monoxide.

Electrolysis

'an example of how a reactive metal can be extracted by electrolysis e.g. aluminium' [3.21]

'A topic often tested in the exam'

Extraction by **electrolysis** is used for **more reactive** metals such as **aluminium** and **copper** but can be expensive as large amounts of energy are required.

Metals are present in metal ores as **positive ions**. If electricity is passed into a solution of the ore, or into the molten ore (both states where the ions are free to move), then the **positive** metal ions will be attracted to the **negative** electrodes. All the metals can be extracted from their ores by electrolysis.

An electrolysis cell always contains a positive electrode (**anode**), a negative electrode (**cathode**) and an **electrolyte** – a liquid containing ions (an aqueous solution of an ionic substance or a molten ionic substance).

'Try to understand this process'

The anode and cathode are connected to an electrical power source. The electricity is conducted through the liquid electrolyte by the ions themselves moving.

The **positive** metal ions are attracted to the **cathode**.
The **negative** ions are attracted to the **anode**.

Let's examine the reactions occurring.

At the cathode: the positive metal ions gain an electron and become **atoms**:

$$M^+ + e^- \rightarrow M$$

The metal is deposited as a layer on the cathode.

At the anode: the negative ions lose electrons and become **atoms**:

$$X^- - e^- \rightarrow X$$

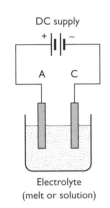

DC supply

A   C

Electrolyte
(melt or solution)

Fig. 8.5 An electrolysis cell

An example of electrolysis is the extraction of **aluminium** from its ore. The ore **bauxite** (mainly aluminium oxide) is first concentrated by removing the impurities. The concentrate (alumina) is then dissolved in **molten cryolite** at about 1,000°C to give a solution which provides free-moving aluminium **ions**. Aluminium oxide has a melting point above 2,000°C, so melting the oxide to provide free-moving aluminium ions is not practical. The anodes and cathodes are made of carbon. Aluminium, when it is formed, is molten, so it is tapped off from the bottom of the cell (see Fig. 8.6).
Let's examine the reactions occurring.

$$\text{At the cathode: } Al^{3+} + 3e^- \rightarrow Al$$
$$\text{At the anode: } 2O^{2-} - 4e^- \rightarrow O_2$$

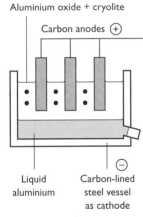

Aluminium oxide + cryolite

Carbon anodes ⊕

Liquid   Carbon-lined
aluminium   steel vessel
                 as cathode

Fig. 8.6 The electrolysis of alumina to extract aluminium

All metals **above** aluminium in the reactivity series are normally extracted by **electrolysis**, because they are **too reactive** to be reduced by carbon. Sometimes metals lower down, such as zinc, are extracted by electrolysis.

Purification of copper

'an example of how a metal can be purified by electrolysis e.g. copper' [3.2n]

One use of electrolysis is to purify **copper**. The positive electrode (**anode**) is made of the **impure** copper and the negative electrode (**cathode**) is made of a thin plate of **pure** copper, which is greased to allow the deposits of pure copper to be peeled off. The electrolyte is an aqueous solution of copper (II) sulphate. During electrolysis the copper present in the **impure copper anode** dissolves into the electrolyte and is then plated on to the **pure copper cathode**. When all the copper from the anode has been deposited on the cathode, the deposit of pure copper is peeled off the cathode which is reused.

Remember: Aluminium is extracted from bauxite; it has a very high melting point (2,000°C) so the ore is dissolved in **molten cryolite** at 1,000°C; the solution formed has free aluminium ions which change into atoms at the cathode and metal is run off.

Reduction by carbon

'an example of how a less reactive metal can be extracted by reduction with carbon or carbon monoxide e.g. iron' [3.2m]

Reduction using **carbon** is used for **less reactive** metals. **Coke** is used as a cheap source of carbon, e.g. reduction of iron ore to iron. The raw materials are **coke, haematite, limestone** and **air**.

Carbon is a suitable reducing agent for obtaining many metals from their oxides, e.g.

lead oxide + carbon → lead + carbon dioxide
$$2PbO \quad + \quad C \quad \to 2Pb + \quad CO_2$$

Coke is a relatively **cheap** and **abundant** source of carbon, which is capable of reducing oxides of all the metals below aluminium in the reactivity series. Coke is therefore suitable for large-scale metal extraction.

Iron extraction

▶ Iron is extracted from its ore **haematite** (which contains iron oxide) by smelting in a **blast furnace**. Once the furnace is started it operates as a continuous process, the raw materials being added at the top and the molten iron and molten waste being run off at the bottom.

▶ The **raw materials** include **iron oxide ore**, which will be reduced to iron; **coke**, which provides the reducing agent; and **limestone**, which is added to remove the waste material from the iron ore.

▶ During the process, at the **bottom** of the furnace a **blast of hot air** is forced up into the hot, raw materials. The air provides **oxygen**, which reacts with the carbon to produce **carbon monoxide**:

$$2C(s) + O_2(g) \to 2CO(g)$$

▶ **Carbon monoxide** is a powerful reducing agent, and **reduces** the **iron oxide** to **iron**, which is molten at the temperature of the furnace:

carbon monoxide + iron oxide → iron + carbon dioxide
$$3CO(g) \quad + \quad Fe_2O_3(s) \quad \to 2Fe(l) + \quad 3CO_2(g)$$

▶ Iron ore contains a lot of rocky material as **impurity** (mainly silica). This would soon clog the furnace and have to be removed, requiring the furnace to be shut down and allowed to cool – a very costly process. The **limestone** (calcium carbonate) reacts with the **silica** at high temperature to produce a molten glassy material (calcium silicate). This is less dense than the molten iron and floats to the top of the molten iron; where it is tapped off as **slag**.

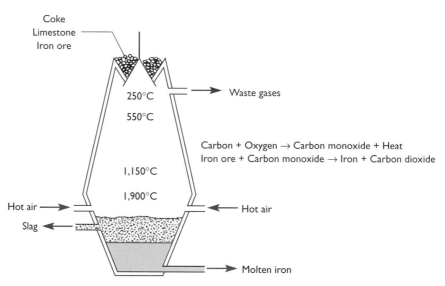

Fig. 8.7 The blast furnace used to extract iron from iron ore

'Producing slag and pig iron'

▶ The molten **iron** is very **dense** and travels down through the furnace. It is tapped off at the bottom hole into large moulds called **pigs**. The iron that is produced is called **pig iron**.

▶ The hot waste **gases** including **carbon monoxide** and **carbon dioxide** are removed through the top of the furnace.

Other metals, such as lead, zinc and copper, can also be extracted in this way. Sulphide ores (e.g. galena, PbS) first have to be roasted in air to convert the compound to a metal oxide:

$$\text{lead sulphide} + \text{oxygen} \rightarrow \text{lead oxide} + \text{sulphur dioxide}$$
$$2PbS(s) + 3O_2(g) \rightarrow 2PbO(s) + SO_2(g)$$

▶ **Useful substances from rocks**

'a variety of useful substances can be made from rocks and minerals' [3.2o]

The Earth's crust, as well as the sea and the atmosphere, are the source of all the **raw materials** used in manufacturing processes. Rocks in the Earth's crust contain mixtures of **minerals** from which useful substances can be made. For example, **limestone** (calcium carbonate) is extracted from the Earth by quarrying. Blocks of limestone are used for **buildings** and powdered limestone can be added to lakes and soils to **neutralise acidity**. **Cement** is also made from limestone and, when mixed with water, sand and rock, it forms another useful building material, namely **concrete**.

The constant demand for **raw materials** can produce problems:

▶ **social**: creation of jobs and towns based on a particular raw material, e.g. coal, gold, which may run out;

▶ **environmental**: pollution from waste materials (slag heaps), destruction of the environment, e.g. mining and quarrying;

▶ **economic problems**: a country's economy may be based on the fluctuating price of one raw material such as copper or uranium.

▶ **EXAMINATION QUESTIONS**

Structured questions

Crude oil produces many simple molecules, some of which are monomers. A glue can be made, using a monomer which polymerises as the glue sets.

Q1 (a) Explain what a polymer is. (2 lines) *(1)*

(b) The polymerisation must not happen while the glue monomer is stored in a tube.
Suggest **two** ways in which the polymerisation reaction can be **started** when the glue is used.

1. (2 lines)
2. (2 lines) *(2)*

(c) Solvent glues have a solid dissolved in a solvent. The solvent evaporates easily but leaves tiny gaps in the solid.
Explain which type of glue – a polymerisation glue or a solvent glue – you consider to be better. (3 lines) *(2)*

(Modular Double Award, London)

Q2 The first humans used stones to make their tools. Our history has been influenced by metals and their discovery. The dates are shown in Table 8.5 below.

Table 8.5

Metals	Dates of Discovery
Gold	Before 6,500 BC
Bronze	6,500 BC
Iron	1,750 BC
Aluminium	⎫
Sodium	⎬ After AD 1800
Magnesium	⎭

(a) Gold was discovered very early. Why was this? (4 lines)   *(1)*

(b) Bronze, a mixture of copper and tin, was used early in human history. The copper and tin were extracted by heating their ores (oxides) with carbon.

Complete the word equation for the extraction of copper and tin (bronze)

Copper oxide + tin oxide	+		→		+	

(3)

(c) The next metal to be extracted from its ore (oxide) by heating with carbon was iron. Figure 8.8 shows the furnace that is now used.

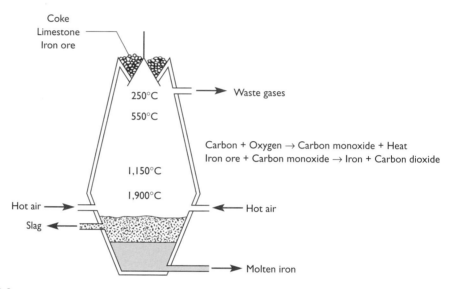

Coke
Limestone
Iron ore

250°C

550°C

Carbon + Oxygen → Carbon monoxide + Heat
Iron ore + Carbon monoxide → Iron + Carbon dioxide

1,150°C

1,900°C

Waste gases

Hot air

Hot air

Slag

Molten iron

Fig. 8.8

Use the diagram to find **two** reasons why this discovery took place so long after the discovery of bronze.

Reason 1 (3 lines)
Reason 2 (3 lines)   *(4)*

(d) Aluminium, sodium and magnesium could be extracted from their ores only after we began to use electricity. Why was this? (4 lines)   *(2)*

(London)

Q3 There are more atoms of aluminium in the Earth's crust than of any other metal. Until about 100 years ago it was rare and expensive, but now it has many uses. It is the lightest of the common metals and is easily shaped.

(a) (i) Aluminium can be made easily from bauxite (aluminium oxide) by heating it with a more reactive metal. Give **one** example of a metal which might be used.

_____   *(1)*

(ii) Suggest **one** reason why this method is not widely used.

_____   *(1)*

(iii) Bauxite is found in the Earth's crust. What name do we give to compounds such as this?

_____   *(1)*

Aluminium is usually extracted by passing electricity through a cell containing molten **alumina** mixed with molten **cryolite**. The diagram (Fig. 8.9) below shows the main parts of the cell used.

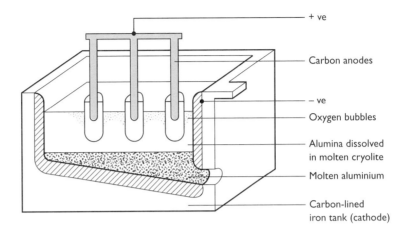

Fig. 8.9

(b) What is the name of this type of extraction process?

(1)

(c) The temperature in the cell stays at about 1,000 degrees Celsius (°C) but it is not heated from outside at all.

Suggest how this temperature is maintained. (3 lines) *(2)*

(d) Suggest and explain why aluminium was so expensive one hundred years ago.

Suggestion _____ *(1)*

Explanation (2 lines) _____ *(1)*

(e) Aluminium appears to be unreactive. This is because a coating of aluminium oxide quickly forms on the outside of the metal. Without its oxide layer, aluminium is reactive and burns easily.

Aluminium has replaced other metals in a number of uses. It is used for overhead power cables instead of copper, and because it is a good reflector of heat it can be used to trap heat inside an area or keep it out.

 (i) Suggest **one** property which aluminium **must** have if it is used for overhead power cables.

(1)

 (ii) Suggest and explain **one** reason, apart from cost, for the use of aluminium instead of copper for these cables.

Reason _____ *(1)*

Explanation (2 lines) _____ *(1)*

 (iii) Tiny babies are sometimes wrapped in a blanket made from polyester fabric coated with a thin film of aluminium. Suggest and explain one reason why this is done.

Reason _____ *(1)*

Explanation (2 lines) _____ *(1)*

 (iv) Many cars are now partly made of aluminium, but the main frame is still made of steel. Apart from cost, suggest why they are made this way. (4 lines) *(3)*

(SEG)

Q4 (a) Crude oil is a mixture of hydrocarbons. Crude oil is first separated into fractions by fractional distillation. Some of the fractions are used as fuels. The heavier fractions can be split up into smaller molecules by catalytic cracking.

One molecule of decane can be cracked to produce one molecule of ethene and one molecule of octane. This is done by passing decane over powdered aluminium oxide catalyst at 500 °C.

(i) Balance the equation:

Decane $\longrightarrow$ ethene + octane

$C_{10}H_{22} \longrightarrow C_2H_4$ + ...   *(1)*

(ii) What is a catalyst? (2 lines)   *(1)*

(iii) Why is the catalyst used in the form of a powder? (2 lines)   *(2)*

(iv) Explain, in terms of particles, why an increase in temperature increases the rate of this reaction. (2 lines)   *(2)*

(b) The ethene is used in the manufacture of the plastic poly(ethene). Ethene is heated under high pressure in the presence of a catalyst. Many ethene molecules join together to form a giant molecule of poly(ethene). The diagram below shows what happens in the reaction:

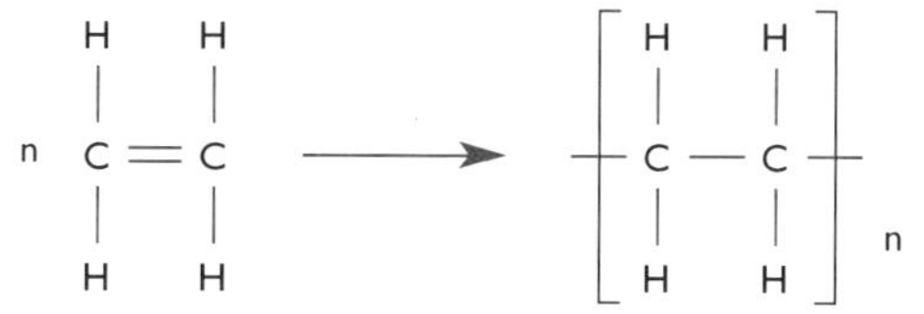

Fig. 8.10

(i) What is the name of this type of reaction? (1 line)   *(1)*

(ii) Describe how the ethene molecules join together to form poly(ethene). (4 lines)   *(3)*

(c) Chemists have found ways of converting natural gas (methane) into methanol and then into petrol. The process used is shown in the diagram (Fig. 8.11) below.

(i) Catalysts can be classified as

either homogeneous – catalyst is in the same state of matter as the reactants;

or heterogeneous – catalyst is in a different state of matter to the reactants.

In the process shown in Fig. 8.11, are the catalysts homogeneous or heterogeneous? Give an example from the process to support your answer. (3 lines)   *(2)*

(ii) Explain why using a solid catalyst makes it easier to obtain pure products in this process. (2 lines)   *(1)*

(iii) In the conversion of methanol to petrol, heat is released. What type of reaction is this? (2 lines)   *(1)*

(d) Cars have been developed which can run on methanol (CH_3OH). There are a number of problems with using methanol. It is difficult to start the engine when it is cold because methanol does not vaporise as easily as petrol. Methanol is corrosive, conducts electricity and has a lower energy content than petrol.

(i) Write a balanced symbol equation for the complete combustion of methanol.

.... + ... $\rightarrow$ .... + ...   *(2)*

(ii) Explain why methanol is difficult to vaporise. (2 lines)   *(1)*

(iii) Suggest and explain why the fuel tank in a methanol-powered car has to be made of stainless steel rather than ordinary steel. (3 lines)

Suggestion

Explanation   *(2)*

(Co-ordinated Science, London)

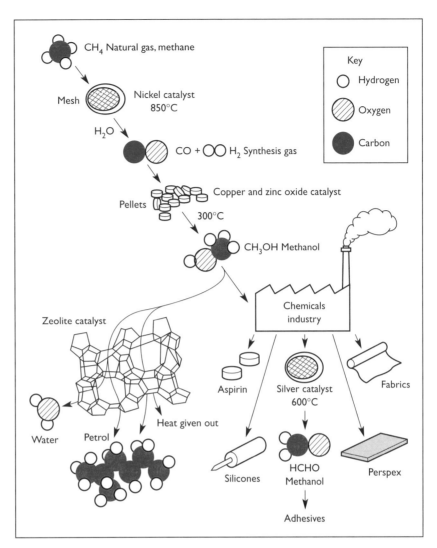

Fig. 8.11

EXAMINATION ANSWERS

Structured questions

A1 (a) a polymer is a long chain of monomers/molecules
(b) the polymerisation reaction can happen when the glue is opened and exposed to air

the glue can be mixed with a hardener/fixer stored in a separate tube

(c) the solvent in the solvent glue could be toxic

the gaps in the solid could be an area of weakness in the glue

Note: there is no 'right' answer here; a reasoned explanation would gain the marks for whichever glue you selected.

A2 (a) Gold is not combined with other elements in the Earth's surface.

(b)

(c) Reason 1 – very high temperatures are required to extract the iron from iron ore.
Reason 2 – a way of making carbon monoxide had to be found which would remove the oxygen from the iron ore.
(d) Very large amounts of energy are required to separate the metals from their ores.

A3 (a) (i) magnesium (or sodium)
   (ii) magnesium is very reactive and expensive
   (iii) ores

(b) electrolysis

(c) heat generated by electric current passing through the cell during electrolysis, which balances heat loss to surroundings.

(d) Because the method of extraction was being developed and large amounts of electricity were required.

(e) (i) conduct electricity
   (ii) Reason – they are much lighter.
       Explanation – the metal is less dense.
   (iii) Reason – babies lose a lot of body heat.
        Explanation – aluminium reflects heat.
   (iv) Aluminium is very lightweight but may dent easily. Steel is used for the main body of the car, as it is stronger.

A4 (a) (i) C_8H_{18}
   (ii) changes the rate of a chemical reaction
       (or) speeds up/slows down a chemical reaction
   (iii) to increase the surface area
        which increases the chance that the reacting molecules will come into contact
   (iv) particles have more kinetic energy/move faster
       more collisions per second

(b) (i) (addition) polymerisation
   (ii) (Note: reading the information given in the question will help you to gain marks here.)
       the double bond breaks due to heating under pressure,
       the bond then joins with another molecule of ethene,
       a long chain of ethene molecules is formed

(c) look carefully at the diagram to see where a nickel catalyst has been used for the reaction between methane gas and the synthesised gas; so the catalyst (solid) is in a different state of matter to the reactants (gases)
   (i) heterogeneous
       catalyst is a solid; the reactants are gases/liquids
   (ii) the solid catalyst makes it easier to separate the products
   (iii) exothermic

(d) Note you are given the formula for methanol in the question.
   (i) $2CH_3OH + 3O_2 \rightarrow 2CO_2 + 4H_2O$
       only one mark would be awarded for the correct formula if the equation was not balanced; however, just writing a word equation would probably gain you one mark so it is worth trying;
   (ii) methanol has strong bonds between the molecules/it has a higher boiling point than petrol
   (iii) suggestion: stainless steel will not rust
        explanation: methanol is very corrosive

▶ **STUDENT'S ANSWER WITH EXAMINER'S COMMENTS**

1. In an oil refinery, crude oil is split into the following fractions inside a distillation column:

    Table 8.6

Fraction	Boiling point range (°C)
Kerosene	174–275
Residue	above 400
Refinery gas	below 25
Diesel	200–400
Gasoline	20–200

    'Tick each one off when you have used it'

    (a) In Table 8.7 below,

    (i) in column 1, arrange the fractions in the order that they are collected from the column and show their boiling point ranges in column 2. *(1/1)*
    (ii) in column 3, for each fraction, show the correct lengths of carbon chains, chosen from the following:

    'Look at the sequence of numbers. They increase as boiling point increases'

         C_1–C_4

    (2/2)

    Table 8.7

Fraction	Boiling point range (°C)	Length of carbon chain
refinery gas	below 25	C_1–C_4
gasoline	20–200	C_4–C_{11}
kerosene	174–275	C_{11}–C_{15}
diesel	200–400	C_{15}–C_{19}
residue	over 400	C_{30} and over

    'Excellent. You have used the data in a logical way'

    'All correct'

    (b) At the refinery, the residue is further broken down into more gasoline and kerosene. Explain why this is done.

    to make two useful products which can be sold to make money   *(2/2)*

    'Good, the residue is not much use as it has a high boiling point'

    (Total 5/5 marks)
    (London)

SUMMARY

At the end of this chapter you should know:

▷ how **oil deposits** are formed;

▷ that **crude oil** is a **mixture** of substances, most of which are **hydrocarbons**, which can be separated by **fractional distillation**;

▷ that some of the products from **crude oil distillation** are used as **fuels**;

▷ the **products** of burning **hydrocarbons**;

▷ that there are different **groups** of **hydrocarbons**;

▷ that **alkanes** are **saturated hydrocarbons** containing a **single covalent bond**, and **alkenes** are **unsaturated hydrocar-**
▷ **bons** containing one **double covalent bond** between carbon atoms;

▷ that **hydrocarbon molecules** can be **cracked** to form smaller molecules including **alkenes**;

▷ that **addition polymers** can be made from **alkenes** formed during cracking;

▷ some uses of **addition polymers**;

▷ that **metal ores** are found in the **Earth**;

▷ that the way in which a metal is **extracted** from its ores is related to **reactivity**;

▷ an example of how a **reactive** metal can be extracted by **electrolysis**, e.g. **aluminium**, **copper**;

▷ an example of how a **less reactive** metal can be extracted by **reduction with carbon** or carbon monoxide, e.g. **iron**;

▷ an example of how a metal can be **purified** by **electrolysis**;

▷ that a variety of **useful substances** can be made from **rocks** and **minerals**.

The Periodic Table

▶ **GETTING STARTED**

The Periodic Table is a useful way of grouping together **different elements** which have **similar properties**: for example, metals and non-metals. The elements are arranged in order of their **atomic number** (proton number) and approximately in order of **relative atomic mass**.

The Periodic Table can be used as a basis for predicting the physical and chemical properties of different elements. The position of an element in the table enables you to predict its melting point, density and reactivity, and the formulae of any compounds which the element may form.

Across the Periodic Table are **periods** or rows, and down the table are the **groups** or columns.

In this chapter we will look at three important groups in more detail, the **alkali metals**, the **halogens** and the **noble gases**. We also consider **metals**, **non-metals** and the **transition elements**.

TOPIC	STUDY	REVISION 1	REVISION 2
The Periodic Table			
Periods			
Groups			
Valency and writing formulae			
Properties and reactions of the alkali metals			
Properties, reactions and uses of the halogens			
Compounds of the alkali metals and the halogens			
Properties and uses of noble gases			
Metals and non-metals			
Transition elements			

WHAT YOU NEED TO KNOW

▶ **The Periodic Table**

'*the Periodic Table shows all elements arranged in order of ascending atomic number*' [3.3a]

'*the connection between the arrangement of the outer electrons and the position of an element in the Periodic Table*' [3.3b]

The **Periodic Table** shows the **elements** arranged in order of **increasing atomic number** and mass. The simplest and lightest atoms are at the top left of the table and the most complex and heaviest are at the bottom right of the table. The elements are arranged in a grid pattern of **rows** and **columns**. Each row is called a **period** and each column is called a **group**.

▶ **Periods**

A period is a **horizontal row of elements** which go across the table. Each period corresponds to an electron shell. As you move across the **first period** you are filling the **first electron shell**:

atom:	H	He
atomic number:	1	2
electron configuration:	1	2

As you move across the **second period** you are filling the **second electron shell**:

'*Properties of the periods*'

atom:	Li	Be	B	C	N	O	F	Ne
atomic number:	3	4	5	6	7	8	9	10
electron configuration:	2, 1	2, 2	2, 3	2, 4	2, 5	2, 6	2, 7	2, 8

In the **third period** you are filling the **third** electron shell:

atom:	Na	Mg	Al	Si	P	S	Cl	Ar
atomic number:	11	12	13	14	15	16	17	18
electron configuration:	2, 8, 1	2, 8, 2	2, 8, 3	2, 8, 4	2, 8, 5	2, 8, 6	2, 8, 7	2, 8, 8

This means that as you go **across** the table the atoms are getting **heavier** (more protons and neutrons). As you go **down** the table the atoms are getting **bigger** (more electron shells which take up more space).

Trends across a period

As you move across a period you are adding **one electron** to the **outer** shell of the atom each time.

▶ elements change from **metals** to **non-metals**;
▶ number of **electrons** in outer shell increases from **1** to **8**;
▶ number of **outer** electrons equals **group** number;
▶ **valency** of elements **increases** from 1 to 4 in groups 1 to 4, then **decreases** from 4 to 1 in groups 4 to 7;
▶ **melting points** and **boiling points** of elements increase to a maximum for group 4 then decrease again to group 0;
▶ the **oxides** of the elements change from basic to acidic;
▶ the **formulae** of compounds of the elements show the change in **valency** or oxidation number.

Table 9.1 Trends across the third period

Metal/non-metal	Na m	Mg m	Al m	Si n/m	P n/m	S n/m	Cl n/m	Ar n/m
Outer shell electrons	1	2	3	4	5	6	7	8
Valency	1	2	3	4	3	2	1	0
Oxidation no.	+1	+2	+3	+4	−3	−2	−1	0
Melting point/°C	98	650	660	1410	44	113	−100	−189
Boiling point/°C	880	1100	2470	2355	280	444	−35	−186
Oxide nature	basic	basic	amphoteric	acidic	acidic	acidic	acidic	−
Formula of oxide	Na_2O	MgO	Al_2O_3	SiO_2	P_2O_3	SO_2	Cl_2O	−
Formula of chloride	NaCl	$MgCl_2$	$AlCl_3$	$SiCl_4$	PCl_3	S_2Cl_2	Cl_2	−

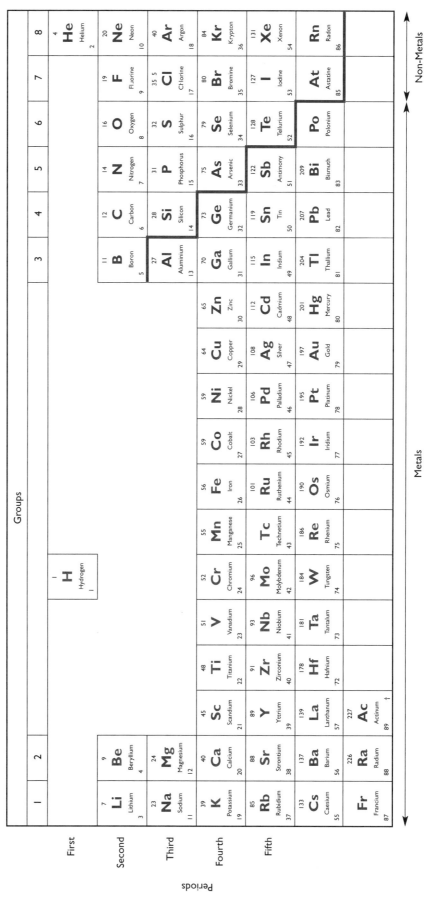

Fig. 9.1 The Periodic Table

Trends across the elements of the **third** period are shown in Table 9.1. Similar trends in properties occur across the second period from lithium to neon.

▶ **Groups**

'elements in the same group of the Periodic Table have similar properties' [3.3c]

'there is a gradual change in the properties of the elements from the top to the bottom of the group' [3.3d]

A **group** is a **vertical** column of elements which go down the table. The groups can be considered to consist of 'families' of elements that behave in similar ways in chemical reactions. You will notice that as you go **down a group**, the atoms have the **same number of electrons in their outer shell**.

For example, in group 1:

atom	electron configuration
H	1
Li	2, 1
Na	2, 8, 1
K	2, 8, 8, 1

'Properties of the groups'

This is important since it is the **arrangement** of electrons in their shells which determines the way in which atoms behave in chemical reactions.

Trends down a group

The groups show general trends (gradual change of properties) from top to bottom of the group with **increasing atomic number**.

▶ the **diameter** of the atom increases so the atom becomes **larger**;
▶ the number of electrons in the **outer shell** is equal to the **group number**, for example, alkali metals, group 1, have 1 electron in their outer shell;
▶ elements with the **same number** of **electrons** in their **outer shell** behave in similar ways in chemical reactions;
▶ the atoms **lose** their **outer electrons** more easily;
▶ the **density** of the element increases.

A summary of general trends in the Periodic Table is shown in Fig. 9.2.

'Remember, these are general trends – there are exceptions'

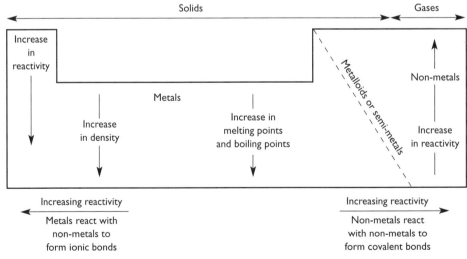

Fig. 9.2 Trends in the Periodic Table

▶ **Valency and writing formulae**

'to represent reactions, including electrolytic reactions, by balanced equations using chemical symbols' [3.2s]

A **formula** for a compound shows the ratio of atoms present in that compound, whether it is ionic or covalent. Each atom has a '**combining power**', which is called the **valency**. The valency of an atom depends on the number of **electrons** in its **outer** shell and hence its position in the Periodic Table. For example, atoms in **group 1** have a **valency of 1**; atoms in **group 2** have a **valency of 2**.

In general as one moves **across** the Periodic Table the valency gradually **increases** to a maximum of 4, then gradually **decreases** to 0. This is not always the case, and there are some important exceptions, but it is a good 'rule of thumb'.

Table 9.2

Atom	Na	Mg	Al	Si	P	S	Cl	Ar
Outer shell electrons	1	2	3	4	5	6	7	8
Group number	1	2	3	4	5	6	7	0
Valency	1	2	3	4	3	2	1	0

The reason for this of course is that if we consider atoms reacting to form **ions**, one atom has to **lose** electrons, whereas the other atom has to **gain** electrons. Those atoms (non-metals), like sulphur, which have **6** electrons in their outer shell can be considered to have **2** spaces (to complete the full set of 8). It is easier to fill **2** spaces than it is to remove **6** electrons. When atoms join up to form ions, the number of electrons **leaving** one atom must match the number of electrons being **gained** by the others. How can this happen? It often helps to imagine the atoms to have **hooks** representing their **valencies** (electrons to be donated or accepted).

Example 1: Sodium will react with **chlorine** to form a compound, **sodium chloride**

Na has a valency of 1

Cl has a valency of 1: we can represent it as

When these atoms combine **all** hooks must be attached:

So the formula is NaCl.

Example 2: Magnesium will react with **chlorine** to form **magnesium chloride**

Magnesium: valency 2:

Chlorine: valency 1: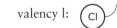

When they join, **all** hooks must be attached, so we need an extra Cl to take care of the otherwise spare hook:

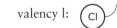

The formula is therefore $MgCl_2$. The 2 as subscript refers to 2 atoms of what is immediately before, in other words 2 Chlorine (Cl) atoms.

Example 3: The formula of **aluminium oxide**

Aluminium: valency 3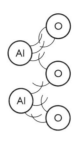

Oxygen: valency 2

When they join, **all** hooks must be attached:

So the formula is Al_2O_3.

Sometimes we can regard a **collection** of atoms, referred to as a radical, as having a valency. For example:

sulphate	SO_4^{2-}	: valency 2
nitrate	NO_3^-	: valency 1
carbonate	CO_3^{2-}	: valency 2
hydroxide	OH^-	: valency 1

Example 4: The formula of **copper nitrate**

Copper: valency 2

Nitrate: valency 1

Formula $Cu(NO_3)_2$

Notice the use of brackets with the 2 as subscript outside. This means 2 of whatever is inside the brackets.

You will not be expected to remember all the valencies for these atoms or radicals, but it is worth remembering how they are related to the position in the Periodic Table.

▶ **Properties and reactions of the alkali metals (group 1)**

'the properties and reactions of the alkali metals' [3.3f]

The alkali metals, group 1, have **one electron** in their outer shell. Their **reactivity increases** down the group as the number of shells increases; the **further away** the outer shell is from the **positive nucleus** the more easily the electron is **lost**. When one electron is removed from the outer shell the atoms form **ions** with a charge of **+1**.

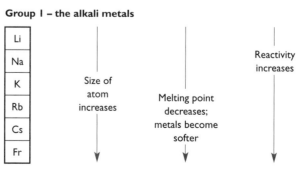

Fig. 9.3 The alkali metals

Reaction with air

Lithium, sodium and potassium react with air to form oxides. When the metal is cut with a knife its surface quickly tarnishes. The speed of **reaction increases** as you move **down the group**. If any of the alkali metals are represented by M, the general reaction is:

$$4M + O_2 \rightarrow 2M_2O$$

Formulae of oxides formed: Li_2O, Na_2O, K_2O. These oxides dissolve in water to produce alkaline solutions.

Reaction with water

'Reactivity increases down the group'

Lithium, sodium and potassium react quickly with water. Lithium when placed on water 'fizzes' and quickly reacts. Sodium will buzz around on the surface of the water giving the odd spark. Potassium reacts more violently, producing a lilac flame. Reactivity **increases** as you move **down** the group. Each produces a strong alkaline solution with water. The general reaction is:

$$2M + 2H_2O \rightarrow 2MOH + H_2$$

Formulae of hydroxides produced: LiOH, NaOH, KOH.

Reaction with halogens

Each will react with halogens to form compounds called **halides**. The reactivity will **increase** as one moves **down** the group. For example, the reaction with chlorine:

$$2M + Cl_2 \rightarrow 2MCl$$

Formulae of halides formed: LiCl, NaCl, KCI.

Reactivity trends

The atoms react to form **ions** which have a charge of **1+**. In forming these ions, e.g. Na^+, an electron has to be removed from the outer shell. Those atoms which have outer shells **further away** from the positive nucleus (the bigger atoms) will require **less energy** to remove that electron, and so will tend to be **more reactive**: hence reactivity **increases** as you move **down** the group: Cs>Rb>K>Na>Li.

Remember: the Group 1 elements, **the alkali metals**:

▶ are metals;
▶ react with non-metals to form **ionic compounds** in which the metal ion carries a **+1 charge**;
▶ react with water releasing **hydrogen**;
▶ form **hydroxides** which dissolve in water to give **alkaline** solutions.

▶ **Properties, reactions and uses of the halogens**

'the properties, reactions and uses of the halogens' [3.3h]

The **halogens**, group 7:

▶ have **7 electrons** in their outer shell;
▶ **reactivity decreases** down the group as the number of shells increases;

H ▶ the closer to the pulling power of the positive nucleus the outer shell is, the more easily an electron is **gained**;
▶ the atoms form **ions** with a charge of **–1**, one electron is added to the outer shell.

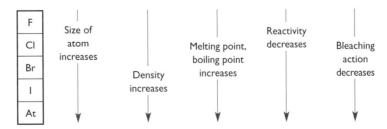

Fig. 9.4 The halogens

Reaction with water

'Reactivity decreases down the group'

The halogens will react with water to form **acidic solutions** which also act as bleaches. The reactivity **decreases** as you move **down the group**, as does the bleaching power of the solutions. The solutions produced from iodine and bromine are weak acids, whereas chlorine and fluorine will produce strong acids. For example:

$$H_2O + Cl_2 \rightarrow HCl + HOCl \text{ (chloric acid – bleach)}$$

Reactivity trends

When halogens react with metals they do so to form ions:

F^-, fluoride ion; Cl^-, chloride ion; Br^-, bromide ion; I^-, iodide ion

The ease with which these atoms form ions depends on the number of electron shells the atom has. In order to form an ion, the atom has to **gain** an electron. The atom with its outer shell **closer** to the positive nucleus will find this easiest, because of the strong pulling power of the positive nucleus. The **larger** the atom, the **further away** the outer electron shell, so the less influence the nucleus will have. Thus we would expect fluorine to be much more reactive than iodine, which is indeed the case.

Reaction with metals

The halogens will react with metals to form **metal halides**. For example, iron with chlorine:

$$2Fe + 3Cl_2 \rightarrow 2FeCl_3$$

The reactivity of the halogens **decreases** as you move down the group.

Remember: the **Group 7** elements, the **halogens**:

▶ are **non-metals**;
▶ have **coloured vapours**;
▶ consist of molecules made of **pairs** of atoms;
▶ form **ionic salts** with metals in which the chloride, bromide or iodide ion (halide ions) carry a **−1 charge**;
▶ form **molecular compounds** with other non-metallic elements.

Remember: chlorine is used as a **bleaching** agent and for **sterilising** water.

▶ Compounds of the alkali metals and the halogens

'the properties, reactions and uses of simple compounds of the alkali metals' [3.3g]
'the properties, reactions and uses of simple compounds of the halogens' [3.3i]

Alkali metal halides are ionic compounds which dissolve in water. **Sodium chloride** (common salt) is a compound of an **alkali metal** and a **halogen**. It is found in large quantities in the sea and in underground deposits.

The **electrolysis of sodium chloride solution** (see page 142 and Fig. 7.20) is an important industrial process. **Chlorine gas** is formed at the **positive** electrode (anode) and **hydrogen gas** at the **negative** electrode (cathode). A solution of **sodium hydroxide** is also formed. Each of these products can be used to make other useful materials.

▶ **chlorine**: used to **kill bacteria** in drinking water and swimming pools; to manufacture disinfectants, **bleach** and the plastic polymer PVC;
▶ **hydrogen**: used to manufacture **margarine** and **ammonia**;
▶ **sodium hydroxide**: used to manufacture **soap**, **paper** and ceramics.

'See also Chapter 7 (Properties of ionic compounds and Electrolysis)'

The **silver halides** – silver chloride, silver bromide and silver iodide – are reduced to **silver** by the action of light, X-rays and radiation from radioactive substances. They are used to make **photographic film** and photographic paper.

Alkali metal hydroxides are ionic compounds which dissolve in water to form alkaline solutions.

Hydrogen halides are gases which dissolve in water to form acidic solutions owing to the formation of H^+ ions.

▶ Properties and uses of noble gases

'the properties and uses of the noble gases' [3.3e]

Group 0, the **noble gases**, show no reactivity (with very few exceptions) because they have **completely filled outer electron shells**, which are very stable. They do not form molecules but exist as separate atoms.

Helium, neon and **argon** are **colourless** and **unreactive** gases at room temperature; helium is used in **airships**; **neon** is used electric discharge tubes used for coloured **advertising signs**; **argon** is used in filament **lamps**.

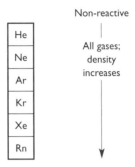

Fig. 9.5 The noble gases

▶ Metals and non-metals

'elements can be classified as metals or non-metals' [KS 3]

'most metallic elements are shiny solids at room temperature and that most are good thermal and electrical conductors, and that a few are magnetic' [KS 3]

'non-metallic elements vary in their physical properties, many are gases at room temperature, most are poor thermal and electrical conductors' [KS 3]

All metals are **elements** and are grouped on the **left-hand** side of the Periodic Table. The common everyday metals are found in the block referred to as the **transition metals**. Metals are **giant structures** in which the metal atoms exist as **positive** ions in a **sea** of **electrons**. This gives rise to their characteristic physical properties of strength, hardness and the ability to **conduct electricity**.

In the majority of their reactions, metal atoms react to form **positive ions**. The charge on the ion depends on the **position** in the Periodic Table (see Table 9.3).

Table 9.3

Group	Charge on ion	Example
1	1+	Na
2	2+	Ca
3	3+	Al

More than three-quarters of all elements are metals whereas a quarter are non-metals. Table 9.4 shows a summary of the properties of metals and non-metals.

Table 9.4 Summary of the properties of metals and non-metals

Metals	Non-metals
usually have high melting points and are all solids at room temperature (except mercury)	usually have low melting points and boiling points (half are gases) (bromine is liquid at room temperature)
are shiny when polished	usually dull in appearance
can be easily bent into shape or hammered	brittle and crumbly when solid
good conductors of heat and electricity	poor conductors of heat and electricity when solid or liquid

▶ **Transition elements**   *'similarities between transition metals and characteristic properties of their compounds'* [3.3j]
'some uses of transition metals' [3.3k]

The **transition elements** are between groups 2 and 3 of the table; for example, iron, manganese, copper, zinc. They are metals which all:

▶ have **high melting points**;
▶ have **high density**;
▶ are used as **catalysts**;
▶ form brightly **coloured compounds** owing to the colour of the transition metal **ion**.

The transition metals can form ions with **different** charges; they are said to have **variable valency**. In compounds, the charge on the metal ion is indicated by roman numerals.

Table 9.5 Some transition metal compounds

Compound	Colour	Formula	Metal ions
Copper (II) sulphate	blue	$CuSO_4$	Cu^{2+}
Iron (II) sulphate	green	$FeSO_4$	Fe^{2+}
Iron (III) oxide	red	Fe_2O_3	Fe^{3+}
Copper (I) oxide	red	Cu_2O	Cu^+
Copper (II) oxide	black	CuO	Cu^{2+}

Uses of transition metals

▶ **Iron**: when mixed with carbon and other elements, iron is used to make steel alloys; such as stainless steel and tungsten steel; it is also used for cast iron gates and railings.
▶ **Copper**: electrical wiring, water pipes; it is also mixed with other metals to make alloys such as brass and bronze.
▶ **Zinc**: used as a coating for galvanised steel; also mixed with other metals to make alloys such as brass.

▶ **EXAMINATION QUESTIONS**

Multiple choice

Questions 1, 2 and 3 refer to the Periodic Table shown below.

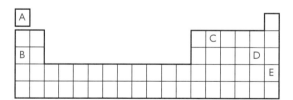

Fig. 9.6

Q1   Which letter represents the lightest element?

Q2   Which letter represents a halogen?

Q3   Which letter represents a very reactive metal?

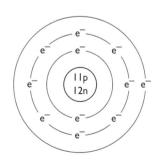

Fig. 9.7

Questions 4 and 5 refer to the diagram above (Fig. 9.7) showing the atomic structure of sodium.

Q4 What is the atomic number of sodium?
A 1; B 7; C 11; D 12; E 23

Q5 What is the valency of sodium?
A 1; B 2; C 3; D 11; E 23

Structured questions

Q6 Fig. 9.8 shows the first three rows of the Periodic Table.

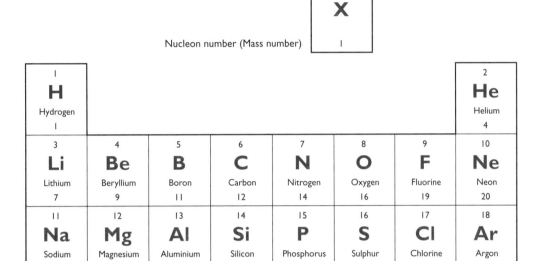

Fig. 9.8

Element	lithium	beryllium	boron	fluorine	neon	hydrogen
State at room temperature	solid	solid	solid	gas	gas	gas
Reaction with oxygen	reacts slowly forms layer of oxide	forms oxide when heated	forms layer of oxide slowly	no reaction	no reaction	burns to form water
Reaction with water	reacts steadily forms hydrogen	no reaction	no reaction	reacts to form oxygen	no reaction	no reaction

Table 9.6 Some physical and chemical properties of elements in the Periodic Table

(a) Use the information in Table 9.6 to predict **three** different properties of sodium. (4 lines) *(3)*

(b) Hydrogen is shown in Fig. 9.8 as a member of group 1. Give reasons for **not** placing it in this position. (3 lines) *(2)*

(c) (i) Look at Fig. 9.8 and describe and explain how the nucleon number (mass number) of the elements changes as the proton number (atomic number) increases. (4 lines) *(3)*

   (ii) Describe and explain the pattern in the electronic structures of the 18 elements shown in Fig. 9.8. A diagram may help your answer. (5 lines and space) *(4)*

(d) Table 9.7 contains some information about two elements not shown in this part of the Periodic Table.

Table 9.7

	Element A	Element Z
Melting point (°C)	840	–7
Boiling point (°C)	1,490	59
Chemical property	Reacts vigorously in water to form hydrogen and an alkaline solution	Reacts with element A to form a salt of formula AZ_2

Element A belongs to group 2 and element Z belongs to group 7.

List the evidence from Table 9.7 that confirms element A and element Z have been put in the correct groups. (4 lines)   *(2)*

(e)   There are two kinds of chlorine atom – one with a nucleon number (mass number) of 35, the other of 37. What are the similarities and differences between these atoms? (4 lines)   *(2)*

(Modular Double Award, London)

Q7   (a)   The element astatine has an atomic (proton) number of 85 and a mass number of 210.

(i)   How many protons are in the nucleus? _____   *(1)*

(ii)   How many neutrons are in the nucleus? _____   *(2)*

(iii)   How many electrons are orbiting the nucleus? _____   *(1)*

(b)   Astatine is at the bottom of the same group of the Periodic Table as chlorine, bromine and iodine. Table 9.8 below gives some information about these elements.
(i)   Use the patterns shown in the table to fill in the spaces for astatine.   *(4)*

Table 9.8

	Chlorine	Bromine	Iodine	Astatine
At room temperature	gas	liquid	solid	1
Reaction with iron	very fast	fast	slow	2
Reaction with potassium iodide solution	reacts	reacts	no reaction	3
Effect on indicator paper	bleaches	bleaches	bleaches	4

(ii)   Which **two** of these elements have their molecules closest together at room temperature?

1   _____

2   _____   *(1)*

(iii)   Which **one** of these elements is most likely to have a smell at room temperature?

_____   *(1)*

(SEG)

Q8   Fluorine (F) is the most reactive element in group 7 of the Periodic Table of elements. Fluorine reacts with all metals and most non-metals. During the past 70 years or so, it has become an important industrial chemical.

(a)   Suggest **one** reason why we do not study fluorine in school laboratories.

_____   *(1)*

(b)   One compound in which fluorine occurs is fluorspar. Fluorspar is heated with concentrated sulphuric acid to make hydrogen fluoride. Hydrogen fluoride is a gas which does not conduct electricity. It reacts with water to produce highly corrosive hydrofluoric acid.

(i) Complete this flow chart for the manufacture of hydrofluoric acid by writing in the names of the correct substances in the boxes.

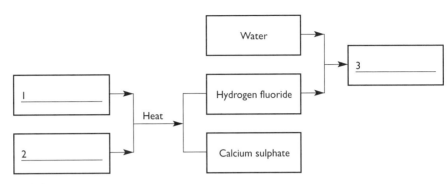

Fig. 9.9

(ii) Briefly explain **two** different pollution problems which might result from manufacture of hydrogen fluoride.

Problem 1 (3 lines) _____ *(2)*

Problem 2 (3 lines) _____ *(2)*

(c) A large chemical company has several chemical plants throughout Europe at which concentrated sulphuric acid is manufactured. However, at only a few of these is hydrogen fluoride also manufactured.

Suggest **two** different reasons why you think hydrogen fluoride is manufactured only at a few of these plants.

Reason 1 (2 lines) _____ *(2)*

Reason 2 (2 lines) _____ *(2)*

(d) A lot of fluorine is used in the manufacture of fluorocarbons and other compounds.

Tetrafluoroethene (C_2F_4) is polymerised into PTFE, which is used as the non-stick coating on cooking utensils.

Difluorodichloromethane (CF_2Cl_2) is used in aerosols and in the cooling coils of refrigerators.

(i) Briefly explain what is meant by the word *polymerised*. (3 lines) *(1)*

(ii) Suggest two properties which PTFE should have if it is to be used as a non-stick coating on cooking utensils.

Property 1 (2 lines) _____ *(1)*

Property 2 (2 lines) _____ *(1)*

(iii) Suggest **one** property of difluorodichloromethane (CF_2Cl_2) which makes it suitable for use in aerosols **and** in the cooling coils of refrigerators.

Property (2 lines) _____ *(2)*

(SEG)

Q9 (Higher Tier) You are given a lot of information at the beginning of the question so spend some time reading it carefully to help you answer the questions which follow.

Chlorine, bromine and iodine are in group 7 of the Periodic Table. At room temperature chlorine is a gas, bromine is a volatile liquid and iodine is a solid which easily vaporises.

Chlorine is manufactured by the electrolysis of sodium chloride. The sodium chloride must be molten or in the form of a concentrated aqueous solution. Chlorine is given off at the positive electrode.

Chlorine can also be produced from hydrogen chloride. The hydrogen chloride is reacted with oxygen from the air at 400°C in the presence of a catalyst. Chlorine is used in the manufacture of both bromine and iodine.

Bromine is found in sea-water as bromide ions. If chlorine is bubbled through sea-water, bromine is displaced and forms a solution in water.

Iodine can be obtained from certain sea-weeds which absorb the element as iodide ions. The sea-weed is dried and burned to an ash. The ash is treated with water and the solution formed is evaporated. On cooling, chlorides and carbonates precipitate out. Iodine is then displaced from the remaining solution by adding chlorine.

(a) Name the substance formed at the negative electrode during the electrolysis of:

   (i) molten sodium chloride _____ *(1)*

   (ii) sodium chloride solution _____ *(1)*

(b) In terms of atomic structure, explain why chlorine can displace both bromine from a solution containing bromide ions, and iodine from a solution containing iodide ions. (9 lines)   *(6)*

(c) In terms of their molecular properties, explain the differences in the physical properties of chlorine, bromine and iodine. (3 lines)   *(3)*

(Co-ordinated Science, NEAB, London, WJEC)

▶ **EXAMINATION ANSWERS**

Multiple choice

A1 Key A. It indicates hydrogen.

A2 Key D. The halogens are group 7 elements, in the last but one column.

A3 Key B. The reactive metals are the group 1 alkali metals.

A4 Key C, 11. The atomic number is the number of protons. Option A is the number of electrons in the outer shell. Option D is the number of neutrons.

A5 Key A, valency of 1. The number of electrons in the outer shell.

Structured questions

A6 (a) Study the Periodic Table supplied with the question to find that sodium (Na) is in the same group as lithium (Li), so the properties will be similar. Information for lithium appears in Table 9.6 under three headings, so follow this pattern. Sodium is likely to:
   be a solid at room temperature (1)
   form an oxide when reacted with oxygen (1)
   react with water to form hydrogen (1)

(b) hydrogen is a gas/it is not a metal (1)
   hydrogen does not react with water (1)
   hydrogen does not form a solid oxide (1)

(c) (i) look at Fig. 9.8, the Periodic Table, to help you; you are asked to state how the nucleon (mass) number changes as the atomic (proton) number increases; a key is provided in Fig. 9.8 to remind you which number represents the nucleon number and which is the atomic number.
   as the atomic (proton) number increases so the nucleon (mass) number increases (1)
   the increase varies/there is no pattern to the increase (1)
   the number of additional neutrons varies each time (1)
   (ii) electrons are arranged in shells (1)
   each period/row corresponds to a new electron shell (1)
   the number in each shell can be worked out from the table (1)
   (e.g. lithium has an atomic number of 3 and its electron configuration is 2, 1, beryllium is 2, 2, boron is 2, 3 , etc.) a diagram could also be used here (e.g. see Fig. 7.16 page 139)

(d) element A should be in group 1 or 2 (metals) because it has a high melting point and boiling point; it has a combining power of 2 so it is in group 2 (1)
element Z should be in group 5, 6 or 7 (non-metals) because it has a low melting point and boiling point; it has a combining power of 1 so it is in group 7 (1)

(e) they have the same atomic number as they have the same number of protons and electrons (1)
they have different numbers of neutrons (1)

A7 (a) (i) 85
(ii) 125 (210 – 85)
(iii) 85 (same as proton number)

(b) (i) 1 solid, 2 no reaction/very slow reaction, 3 no reaction, 4 bleaches
(ii) iodine and astatine
(iii) chlorine

A8 (a) It is very reactive and possibly too dangerous to use.

(b) (i) Use the information in (b) to help you answer this.
1 fluorspar, 2 concentrated sulphuric acid, 3 hydrofluoric acid
(ii) Problem 1 – hydrogen fluoride is a very acidic gas. It can dissolve in water vapour in the atmosphere and cause acid rain, which damages buildings and kills trees and fish.
Problem 2 – hydrogen fluoride gas can dissolve in water vapour in the atmosphere to form a corrosive acid which will cause metals to go rusty very quickly.

(c) Reason 1 – availability of fluorspar
Reason 2 – adequate amounts produced for present use

(d) (i) many small identical monomers joined together to form a long chain polymer
(ii) Property 1 – very high melting point
Property 2 – non-reactive with food
(iii) low boiling point

A9 (a) (i) sodium (1)
(ii) hydrogen (1)

(b) from chlorine to iodine the size of the atom increases (1)
all three atoms have 7 electrons in their outer shell (1)
all three react by gaining electrons (1)
the smallest atom, chlorine, does this most easily (1)
chlorine is more reactive than bromine and iodine (1)
as the outer shell of electrons is closer to the nucleus (1)
the positive nucleus exerts a stronger force of attraction (1)
and attracts electrons readily (1)
and forms compounds more readily than iodine or bromine (1)

(c) down the group from chlorine to iodine (1)
the size of the diatomic molecules increases (1)
the melting point and boiling point increases (1)
the reactivity decreases (1)

A STUDENT'S ANSWER WITH EXAMINER'S COMMENTS

100g of WONDERWHITE toothpaste is made up as follows:

calcium carbonate	50%
glycerol	23%
distilled water	20%
bonding agent	3%
detergent	2%

Peppermint flavouring and the fluorine compound NaF and Na_2FPO_3 are also present in small quantities.

(a) Name the elements found in

'Good. You have used the information given in the question'

    (i) group 1 of the periodic table   _Sodium_ ✔

'Yes'

    (ii) group 7 of the periodic table   _Fluorine_ ✔   (1)

(b) (i) What is the purpose of fluoride in toothpaste?

    to stop decay ✔

'Good'

    (ii) What gas is produced when an acid is added to calcium carbonate?

    carbon dioxide ✔

'And teeth'

    (iii) How does calcium benefit the human body?

    strong bones ✔ $(1\frac{1}{2})$

(c) (i) How many different atoms are there in the compound having the formula Na_2FPO_3?

'Good. Na, F, P, O'

    4 different ✔

    (ii) What is the total number of atoms in one molecule of this compound?

    _7_ ✔

    (iii) Calculate the number of grams of distilled water needed to make 250g of toothpaste.

'Well done. 20% of water is needed in 100g'

    50 grams ✔ $(1\frac{1}{2})$

(d) A summary of the properties of some of the elements in group 7 is given below.

Table 9.9

Name	Symbol	Colour	State at room temperature (20°C)	M. pt °C	B. pt °C
Chlorine	Cl	greenish/yellow	gas	–101	–34
Bromine	Br	dark red	liquid	–7	58
Iodine	I	dark grey		114	183

Study the table and then answer the following questions.

    (i) What is the state of iodine at room temperature?

'Yes. It doesn't melt until 114°C'

    Solid ✔   (1)

    (ii) Astatine (At) is another member of group 7 and comes below iodine in the group.
        Considering the patterns shown in the table, predict

'Good prediction'

    1. the colour of astatine   _very dark grey or black_ ✔

    2. its state at room temperature   _solid_ ✔   (2)

(WJEC)

SUMMARY

At the end of this chapter you should know:

▷   that the **Periodic Table** shows all **elements** arranged in order of **ascending atomic number**;

▷   the connection between the arrangement of the **outer electrons** and the **position** of an element in the Periodic Table;

▷   that elements in the same **group** of the Periodic Table have **similar properties**;

▷   that there is a **gradual change** in the **properties** of the elements from the top to the bottom of the **group**;

▷   the **properties** and **reactions** of the **alkali metals**;

▷   the **properties**, **reactions** and **uses** of the **halogens**;

▷   the **properties**, **reactions** and **uses** of simple **compounds** of the **alkali metals**;

▷   the **properties** and **uses** of the **noble gases**;

▷   the **properties**, **reactions** and **uses** of simple **compounds** of the **halogens**;

▷   that elements can be classified as **metals** or **non-metals**;

▷   that most **metallic** elements are **shiny solids** at room temperature and that most are **good thermal** and **electrical conductors**, and that a few are **magnetic**;

▷   that **non-metallic** elements vary in their physical properties, many are **gases** at room temperature, most are **poor thermal** and **electrical conductors**;

▷   similarities between **transition metals** and characteristic **properties** of their **compounds**;

▷   some **uses** of **transition metals**.

Chemical reactions

![arrow] **GETTING STARTED**

Chemical reactions are described as interactions between particles (atoms, molecules or ions) which involve the 'breaking' and 'making' of chemical bonds. They follow a general pattern:

Reactants ⟶ Products
(starting materials)   (new materials)

In any chemical reaction **new substances** are always formed. These have different sets of either physical or chemical properties to those of the reactants. However, in any chemical reaction the **mass** always stays the same. That is, the *total mass of the products* is always the same as the *total mass of the reactants*. The reason for this is that chemical reactions involve only the *rearrangement* of the particles involved.

$$\left(A\right)\left(B\right) + \left(C\right) \rightarrow \left(A\right)\left(C\right) + \left(B\right)$$

This idea is similar to dismantling a model of a house, and using the same bricks to build a small factory. This allows us to write equations and to make calculations for particle interactions, such as the mass of reactants needed to produce 1 kg of a certain product, an invaluable ability in the chemical industry.

Not all substances will react with each other, but many do. Some combinations of reactants need a push to get them going – usually in the form of heat. This is referred to as the **activation energy**. Reactions with high activation energies are slow. In the chemical industry **catalysts** are often used to **speed up reactions**, because time is money.

Chemical reactions always involve energy. In some reactions, energy is transferred to the surroundings in the form of heat (*heat given out*); these are called **exothermic reactions**. Here the products are **warmer** than the reactants. In other reactions, energy in the form of heat is transferred from the surroundings to the substances (*heat taken in*); these are called **endothermic reactions**. Here the products are **cooler** than the reactants. In the chemical industry, ways are often looked for to save energy, because energy costs money.

TOPIC	STUDY	REVISION 1	REVISION 2
Representing reactions			
Ionic equations			
Rates of reactions			
Catalysts			
Reactions involving enzymes			
Reversible reactions			
Energy changes			
Quantitative chemistry			

WHAT YOU NEED TO KNOW

▶ **Representing reactions**

'how to represent reactions by word equations' [3.2r]

'how to represent reactions, including electrolytic reactions, by balanced equations using chemical symbols' [3.2s]

A chemical reaction always follows the general pattern:

Reactant(s) → Product(s)

'Try and work through this section slowly and logically'

There may be one or more reactants and one or more products, but the mass of the **reactants** at the beginning will be the **same** as the mass of the **products** at the end. In an equation representing the reaction, you will have the same number of **atoms** (represented by their symbols) on the **left** hand side as you will have on the **right** hand side. Bear in mind that all that is happening is a **rearrangement** of these atoms.

Example 1

Sodium reacts with **chlorine** to form **sodium chloride**

Step 1   Write the equation in **words**.

sodium + chlorine → sodium chloride

Step 2   Write each substance as a **formula** (see page 173).

$Na + Cl_2 → NaCl$

Remember: sodium is an **element**, Na; reactive gaseous elements are **diatomic**, Cl_2; the formula for sodium chloride is NaCl (Na^+Cl^-).

Step 3   Imagine the reaction as **particles**.

$Na + Cl_2 → NaCl$

$(Na) + (Cl)(Cl) → (Na)(Cl)$

'Balancing the equation'

Step 4   **Balance** the equation,

There are 2 Cl on the left, so there must be 2 Cl on the right. The only way to obtain this is to have 2 NaCl on the right, as follows:

2 NaCl   (Na)(Cl)
          (Na)(Cl)

$Na + Cl_2 → 2NaCl$

$(Na) + (Cl)(Cl) → \begin{matrix}(Na)(Cl)\\(Na)(Cl)\end{matrix}$

Now, to **balance** the equation, we must have **2 Na** on the left.

$2Na + Cl_2 → 2NaCl$

$\begin{matrix}(Na)\\(Na)\end{matrix} + (Cl)(Cl) → \begin{matrix}(Na)(Cl)\\(Na)(Cl)\end{matrix}$

4 atoms   4 atoms

Remember: when balancing an equation: **never** change the actual formulae.

Example 2

Magnesium reacts with **hydrochloric acid** to produce **magnesium chloride** and **hydrogen**.

Step 1   Write the equation in **words**.

magnesium + hydrochloric acid → magnesium chloride + hydrogen

Step 2   Write each substance as a **formula**.

$Mg + HCl → MgCl_2 + H_2$

Step 3   Imagine the reaction as **particles**.

Step 4   **Balance** the equation.

$Mg + 2HCl → MgCl_2 + H_2$

5 atoms   5 atoms

Example 3

Sulphuric acid neutralises **sodium hydroxide**.

Step 1   Write the equation in **words**.

sodium hydroxide + sulphuric acid → sodium sulphate + water

Step 2   Write each substance as a **formula**.

$NaOH + H_2SO_4 → Na_2SO_4 + H_2O$

Step 3   Imagine the reaction as **particles**.

Step 4   **Balance** the equation.

$2NaOH + H_2SO_4 → Na_2SO_4 + 2H_2O$

This example also shows that we can regard some **groups** of particles as **one unit** which is not usually changed in a chemical reaction, for example the sulphate ion: SO_4^{2-}. Other such examples are the hydroxide ion (OH^-), the nitrate ion (NO_3^-) and sometimes the carbonate ion (CO_3^{2-}) in displacement reactions.

More unusual examples are the hydrogen carbonate ion (HCO_3^-), the sulphite ion (SO_3^{2-}) and the nitrite ion (NO_2^-).

Remember: a **chemical reaction** is a rearrangement of the atoms in the **reactant(s)** to form the atoms of **product(s)**.

reactants(s) → product(s)

An energy change sometimes occurs which is detected by a change in temperature.

State symbols

The equations written above tell us which substances react, but they do not tell us the **state** of the reactants or products. This is important, as some reactants will react only if they are in a particular state. For example, they may need to be in a **gaseous** form, or to be **dissolved in water**. We can show the state of reactants and products by adding **symbols of state**:

'Symbols of state'

► **(g)** represents a state of **gas**;
► **(l)** represents a state of **liquid**;
► **(s)** represents a state of **solid**;
► **(aq)** represents the aqueous state (**dissolved in water**).

For example, in the equation

$$Mg(s) + 2HCl(aq) \rightarrow MgCl_2(aq) + H_2(g)$$

HCl(aq) indicates that **dilute** hydrochloric acid is being used.

Ionic equations

There is another way of showing reactions involving **ions**. These are called **ionic equations**. In these equations, ions that are unaffected in a reaction are ignored and those that are affected in some way are written down. To illustrate this, in Example **3** of the previous section, the sulphate ion (SO_4^{2-}) and the sodium ion (Na^+) are unaffected, so we can ignore them. We can rewrite the equation in ionic terms as:

$$OH^-(aq) + H^+(aq) \rightarrow H_2O(l)$$

This **ionic equation** is also the general pattern for all **neutralisation** reactions.

Patterns of ion interactions

Redox reactions

A **redox reaction** is one in which oxidation and reduction take place. **Oxidation** is the **addition of oxygen** or the **removal of hydrogen**. It is also the **removal of electrons**. **Reduction** is the **removal of oxygen** or the **addition of hydrogen**. It is also the **addition of electrons**.

'Learn this difference'

Substances that are good at oxidising substances are called **oxidising agents**, e.g. oxygen and chlorine. Substances that are good at reducing other substances are called **reducing agents**, e.g. carbon and hydrogen.

As an example, in the reaction between lead oxide and carbon, lead oxide is the oxidising agent and carbon is the reducing agent:

lead oxide	+	carbon	$\rightarrow$	lead	+	carbon dioxide
$2PbO$	+	C	$\rightarrow$	$2Pb$	+	CO_2

The lead oxide has been **reduced** by carbon to lead (the oxygen has been removed), while the carbon has been **oxidised** to carbon dioxide (oxygen has been added).

Another example is the reaction between iron and chlorine gas:

iron	+	chlorine	$\rightarrow$	iron (III) chloride
$2Fe$	+	$3Cl_2$	$\rightarrow$	$2FeCl_3$

The iron has been **oxidised** to iron chloride. Three electrons have been **removed** from the iron atom. Chlorine has been **reduced** to the chloride ion, one electron has been **added** to each of the three chlorine atoms.

Redox reactions in action

Oxidation cannot take place without reduction, so the reactions are called **redox reactions**. Reducing agents are used in the **extraction of metals** from their ores. Carbon (in the form of coke) can be used to extract lead, iron and zinc. In all these cases the metal ore is being reduced to the metal by the removal of oxygen.

'Why metals go rusty'

'See Chapter 11, Reactions
of Metals'

An understanding of oxidation is useful when dealing with the corrosion of metals. **Corrosion** is a process which involves the production of metal ions from their atoms (oxidation – the removal of electrons). For example, iron rusts to form iron oxide in the presence of oxygen and water. The reaction could be represented by:

$$Fe - 3e^- \rightarrow Fe^{3+}$$

Displacement reactions

Displacement reactions are examples of redox reactions which involve an element and a salt solution.

▶   **Metal/salt solutions**   Some metals will displace other metal ions from solutions of their salts. The metal's ability to do this is related to its position in the reactivity series (see Chapter 11). If a metal is **above** the metal ion in solution, then one will **displace** the other. For example:

zinc	+	copper sulphate	$\rightarrow$	zinc sulphate	+	copper
Zn	+	$CuSO_4$	$\rightarrow$	$ZnSO_4$	+	Cu
$Zn(s)$	+	$Cu^{2+}(aq)$	$\rightarrow$	$Zn^{2+}(aq)$	+	$Cu(s)$

▶   **Halogen/halide solutions**   A halogen can also displace a halide from a solution of its salt. Its ability to do this depends on its reactivity, i.e. its position in the Periodic Table.

Remember the order of reactivity F>Cl>Br>I of the halogens:

chlorine	+	potassium iodide	$\rightarrow$	potassium chloride	+	iodine
Cl_2	+	$2KI$	$\rightarrow$	$2KCl$	+	I_2
$Cl_2(g)$	+	$2I^-(aq)$	$\rightarrow$	$2Cl^-(aq)$	+	I_2

Chlorine is **more reactive** than iodine, so it has a **greater attraction** for electrons, and so it displaces the iodine.

Precipitation reactions

Some reactions between solutions of metal salts will take place because there is a possibility of a **solid** being formed. This solid is called a **precipitate**.

potassium iodide	+	lead nitrate	$\rightarrow$	potassium nitrate	+	lead iodide
$2KI(aq)$	+	$Pb(NO_3)_2(aq)$	$\rightarrow$	$2KNO_3(aq)$	+	$PbI_2(s)$

Notice that all that has happened is that the ions have swapped partners. This chemical change occurs because one possible combination, PbI_2, is insoluble in water.

Precipitation in action

'Hard water'

Precipitation reactions can be used to remove the hardness from water. Hardness in water is caused by the presence of calcium or magnesium ions. These ions can be precipitated out of solution (so removing the hardness) by adding sodium carbonate (washing soda). Calcium carbonate and magnesium carbonate, which are both insoluble, are formed.

Neutralisation reactions

In these reactions an acid is **neutralised** by a base. A salt and water are formed. The general pattern of the reaction is as follows:

acid   +   base $\rightarrow$ salt   +   water

'Check with Chapter 11'

In ionic terms, this reaction is expressed as:

$$H^+(aq) + OH^-(aq) \rightarrow H_2O(l)$$

An example is the reaction between hydrochloric acid and sodium hydroxide:

$$HCl + NaOH \rightarrow NaCl + H_2O$$

Remember: ionic equations show the **ions** involved in a reaction (and ignore the ions that are unchanged); for example,

neutralisation: $OH^-(aq) + H^+(aq) \rightarrow H_2O(l)$
electrolysis: $2Cl^- + 2e^- \rightarrow Cl_2$

▶ **Rates of reactions**

'reactions occur when particles collide' [3.3n]

'there is great variation in the rates at which different reactions take place' [3 .3l]

'how the rates of reactions can be altered by varying temperature or concentration, or by changing the surface area of a solid reactant, or by adding a catalyst' [3.3m]

'the rates of many reactions can be increased by increasing the frequency or energy of collisions between the particles' [3.3o]

Reactions **vary in speed**; for example, rusting is a **slow** reaction, an explosion is a **rapid** reaction. The rate of a reaction can be detected by **rate of formation of the product** (often a gas), or the **rate of disappearance of reactant**.

The **speed** at which the reaction takes place depends on a number of factors:

▶ the **surface area** of solid reactants;
▶ the **concentration** of reactants (including pressure in the case of gases);
▶ the **temperature**;
▶ the presence of a **catalyst**.

H In order for a chemical reaction to take place, the particles of the reactants must **collide** (bump into each other). The **more often** the particles collide, the more likely they are to react, and so the **faster** the reaction.

Increasing the speed of a reaction

Increasing the surface area of solid reactants
A greater **surface area** will provide more opportunities for particles to collide. For example, calcium carbonate will react with hydrochloric acid to produce calcium chloride, water and carbon dioxide:

$$CaCO_3 \ + \ 2HCl \ \rightarrow \ CaCl_2 \ + \ H_2O \ + \ CO_2$$

Powdered calcium carbonate will react much faster than **lumps** of calcium carbonate (marble chips), because the **surface area** of the powder is much **greater**. There will be more calcium carbonate in contact with the acid. Stirring the powder in the acid will further increase the speed of reaction for the same reason.

Transporting or storing fine powders which can burn is a problem, as it might only take a spark to cause a very rapid reaction (explosion); e.g. flour, especially in flour mills when powder is in the atmosphere.

Increasing the concentration of the reactants
This will increase the **number of particles** present and so increase the chance of any collision. For example, in the reaction above, if the concentration of the hydrochloric acid is increased, then there is more chance of the particles interacting, and so the reaction will proceed at a **faster** rate.

Increasing the temperature of the reactants
Increasing the **temperature** of reactants provides the particles with **more kinetic energy**, so they will move **faster**. This increases the number of **collisions** per second, and hence increases the **rate** of the reaction. In the reaction above, increasing the temperature of the acid will increase the speed of the hydrochloric acid particles and so the number of collisions per second.

▶ **Catalysts** A **catalyst** is a substance that **changes** the rate of a chemical reaction, but remains unchanged at the end of a reaction and can be re-used. Catalysts are used to **speed up** reactions; for example, manganese (IV) oxide in the decomposition of hydrogen peroxide, iron oxide in the manufacture of ammonia. Substances used to slow down reactions are called **inhibitors**.

Gas reactions and catalysts

One way in which catalysts are thought to work in reactions involving gases is that the surface of the catalyst provides sites where the reacting molecules can meet. The transition metals are often used as catalysts in this way.

Manufacture of ammonia

$$N_2 \;+\; 3H_2 \;\rightleftharpoons\; 2NH_3$$

Iron is used as a catalyst. Nitrogen and hydrogen do not combine in the gas state; when they collide they bounce off each other without reacting. However, they are **adsorbed** on to the catalyst surface, where they come into contact and react.

Manufacture of sulphuric acid
One stage involves the production of sulphur trioxide from sulphur dioxide:

$$2SO_2 \;+\; O_2 \;\rightleftharpoons\; 2SO_3$$

Vanadium (V) oxide is the catalyst and works in a similar way to the iron in the previous example.

Pollution control on cars
Petrol engines in cars burn petrol (a hydrocarbon fuel) and produce carbon dioxide and water as waste products. In addition, however, carbon monoxide and some oxides of nitrogen are produced which pollute the atmosphere. The car exhaust systems in California (where the problem of pollution from cars is a serious one) are fitted with a metal catalyst. As the hot exhaust gases pass over the catalyst, the pollutants are converted into carbon dioxide and nitrogen.

Antioxidants
Certain chemicals can be added to foods which slow up the natural oxidation of foods. These chemicals (antioxidants) are acting as catalysts; they are reducing the rate of a chemical reaction which would otherwise result in loss of flavour and decay.

▶ **Reactions involving enzymes**

'Technological application'

'Check Chapter 3 the Humans as Organisms'

'how the rates of enzyme-catalysed reactions vary in temperature' [3.3p]

'the use of enzymes in the baking, brewing and dairy industries' [3.3q]

Many chemical reactions take place in living things (often in the cells). These reactions are controlled by **biological catalysts** called **enzymes**. Enzymes are **protein** molecules, which consist of long chains that can be folded and coiled into different shapes. Each enzyme has its own special shape; it is this shape which causes the enzyme to act as a catalyst. Figure 10.1 shows how the molecule(s) on which the enzyme acts fits the protein molecule like a key in a lock.

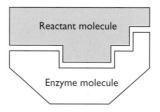

Fig. 10.1 Enzyme action: the lock and key principle

Enzymes have unique properties:

'Properties of enzymes'

▶ They are **specific**: because the way an enzyme works depends on its shape, it will only work for one molecule or reaction.
▶ They will only work within a small **temperature range**, e.g. enzymes in the human body will only work around normal body temperature (37°C).
▶ They are very sensitive to **pH** changes and most only work within small pH ranges, e.g. pH6 → pH7.
▶ They can help **large** molecules break into **smaller** ones, help small molecules join to form larger ones, or help atoms rearrange within a molecule.

Enzymes in action

'Digestion again'

Enzymes take part in every stage of the digestive process, helping to break large molecules into smaller ones. The enzyme in saliva, called **salivary amylase**, breaks down starch into smaller sugar molecules.

Yeasts contain enzymes which help convert sugar into **alcohol** in the process of **brewing**.

Enzymes are becoming increasingly important in **industry**, e.g. for the manufacture of biodegradable dressings for wounds, biological **washing powders**, new food sources – **mycoprotein**.

Remember: enzymes are **biological catalysts** made of proteins; enzymes in yeast convert **sugar** into **alcohol** in brewing; other enzymes are used in making cheese and yogurt.

Enzyme catalysed reactions vary with **pH** and **temperature**; for example, the optimum temperature for fermentation is between 20 and 30°C.

▶ Reversible reactions

'*some reactions are reversible*' [3.3r]

'*how the yield of products from reversible reactions depends on conditions*' [3.3s]

'*some manufacturing processes are based on reversible reactions*' [3.3t]

'*how nitrogen can be converted to ammonia in industry*' [3.2p]

'*how nitrogenous fertilisers are manufactured and their effects on plant growth and the environment*' [3.2q]

Patterns for reversible reactions

Some reactions involving particles are **reversible**, i.e. they can proceed in **both** directions even at the same time. An example occurs in the **Haber process**, where nitrogen and hydrogen are combined to produce **ammonia**, but ammonia simultaneously **decomposes** to produce **nitrogen** and **hydrogen**.

'The Haber process'

$$\text{nitrogen} + \text{hydrogen} \rightleftharpoons \text{ammonia}$$
$$N_2 + 3H_2 \rightleftharpoons 2NH_3$$

The sign $\rightleftharpoons$ indicates that the reaction can go in **both** directions. By changing the conditions, we can determine in which direction the reaction proceeds, and what proportion of ammonia is formed (the yield).

- ▶ High **pressure** favours the production of ammonia.
- ▶ High **temperature** increases the rate of reaction between nitrogen and hydrogen (production of ammonia).
- ▶ However, high **temperature** also favours the **decomposition** of ammonia (production of nitrogen and hydrogen).

A balance has to be made. Optimum conditions are usually about 400°C and 200 atmospheres.

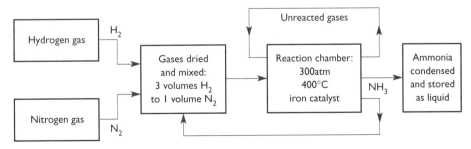

Fig. 10.2 Stages in the production of ammonia

Manufacture of fertiliser

Ammonia can be reacted with **oxygen** in the presence of a hot platinum catalyst to form **nitrogen monoxide** which is then reacted with water to produce **nitric acid**; nitric acid is neutralised by ammonia to produce **ammonium nitrate fertiliser**.

Another example of a reversible reaction is the hydration (water content) of copper sulphate crystals. (This can be used as a test for water.)

$$\text{Copper sulphate crystals } (\textit{blue}) \overset{\text{heat}}{\rightleftharpoons} \text{ anhydrous copper sulphate } (\textit{white}) + \text{ water}$$

▶ Energy changes

'*changes of temperature often accompany reactions*' [3.3u]

'*reactions can be exothermic or endothermic*' [3.3v]

'*making and breaking chemical bonds in chemical reactions involves energy transfers*' [3.3w]

Energy and chemical bonds

In any chemical change, **energy** is either **given out** or **absorbed**. In any reaction between particles, bonds holding particles in the reactants together will need to be **broken**, and **new bonds** will need to be formed when the particles rearrange themselves to form the products.

'Understand the difference between these two'

▶ Energy is needed to **break** bonds.
▶ Energy is released when bonds are **formed**.

If the energy that is released when new bonds are formed in the products is **greater than** the energy required to break the bonds in the reactants, then the reaction is **exothermic** (energy is released to the surroundings). If the reverse is true, then the reaction is **endothermic**. The amount of energy that is absorbed or released in a reaction is referred to as the **heat of reaction** and is measured in kJ/mol. Note that a kJ, or a kilojoule, is a unit of energy; a mol, or mole, is a measure of a quantity of particles.

The heat of reaction is given the symbol ΔH. If a reaction is exothermic, then ΔH is negative, and energy is given out. If a reaction is endothermic, then ΔH is positive, and energy is absorbed.

'An exothermic reaction'

The following is an example of an exothermic reaction:

$$HCl(aq) + NaOH(aq) \rightarrow NaCl(aq) + H_2O(l)$$
$$\Delta H = -55.9 kJ/mol$$

[H]   The amount of energy that is absorbed or released in a reaction can be calculated from **bond energies**. The amount of energy that is required to break different bonds has been calculated. Consider the reaction between hydrogen and chlorine, to produce hydrogen chloride:

$$H_2(g) + Cl_2(g) \rightarrow 2HCl$$

Bonds present H—H   Cl—Cl   →   H—Cl
                                    H—Cl

In the case of the **reactants**

▶ the energy needed to break one H—H bond is +437kJ/mol;
▶ the energy needed to break one Cl—Cl bond is +244kJ/mol.

The total energy required to break all bonds = +437 +244 = +681kJ/mol.

'Find the net energy change'

In the case of the **products**

▶ the energy released when one H—Cl bond is formed is –433kJ/mol;
▶ the total energy released on forming 2 H—Cl bonds = 2 × (–433) = –866kJ/mol.

As a result, the energy change for the reaction is

$$\Delta H = +681 - 866 = -185 kJ/mol: \text{The reaction is } \textbf{exothermic}.$$

These overall energy changes for a reaction can be represented on an energy level diagram (Figure 10.3).

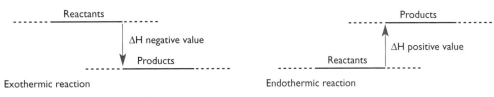

Fig. 10.3 Energy level diagrams

H *Activation energy*

Almost all chemical changes need an amount of energy to get them going. This initial amount of energy can be quite small or sometimes quite large. This initial energy requirement is called the **activation energy** and is often the energy required initially to **break bonds** to allow a reaction to proceed. Fuels need to be supplied with a source of heat to **start** the combustion reaction, e.g. from a match. Activation energy must not be confused with the energy change in exothermic or endothermic reactions, both of which may require an initial input of energy.

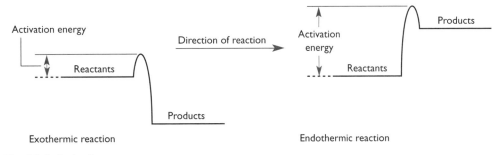

Fig. 10.4 Activation energy

Remember: energy is needed to break and make bonds. The **breaking** of bonds is **endothermic**, heat energy is taken in; for example, dissolving potassium chloride in water. The **making** of bonds is **exothermic**, heat energy is given out; for example, adding a small volume of water to anhydrous copper sulphate.

▶ **Quantitative chemistry**

'to use chemical equations to predict reacting quantities' [3.2t]

'to determine the formula of simple compounds from reacting masses' [3.2u]

H As we saw previously, in any chemical change:

▶ the total **mass** of the **products** = the total **mass** of the **reactants**
▶ the total **number of atoms** in the products = the **total number of atoms** in the reactants

'Check your syllabus requires this topic'

'This number is known as the Avogadro Constant'

These two facts allow us to make **calculations** involving chemical reactions. In order to do this in a satisfactory way, we need some means of counting the number of particles present; for this purpose a unit called the **mole** was invented. It is a measure of the amount of substance; it is equivalent to

6×10^{23} particles (a very large number)

When large amounts of coins are handed into the bank they do not count them individually but instead they **weigh** them. In order to convert the weight of the coins to a number, the bank needs to know certain facts – 'How much do 100 lp coins weigh?' or 'How much do 100 2p coins weigh?'

We can apply the same principle to particles, since each atom has its own distinct mass: the **relative atomic mass**. The number we use has to be very much larger than 100, since the mass of each atom is very small. That number is the **mole**. The conversion of numbers to mass is very simple:

Moles of atoms

The **relative atomic mass** of an atom in grammes contains **one mole** (1 mol) of **atoms**.

Table 10.1

Atom	Atomic mass	Mass of 1 mol of atoms
hydrogen	1	1g
carbon	12	12g
oxygen	16	16g
chlorine	35.5	35.5g
sodium	23	23g

In other words, in **32g** of oxygen we have **2 mol** of atoms; in **8g** of oxygen we have **0.5 mol** of atoms.

Moles of molecules

The **molecular** mass in grammes contains 1 mol of **molecules**.

'Mole is the name; mol is the unit

Table 10.2

Molecule	Molecular Formula	Mass of molecule	Mass of 1 mol of molecules
oxygen	O_2	32	32g
water	H_2O	18	18g
carbon dioxide	CO_2	44	44g
hydrogen	H_2	2	2g

In other words, in 36g of water there are 2 moles; in 9g of water there are 0.5 moles.

Moles of ionic compounds and ions

The same rules apply for formulae representing **ionic compounds** and for **individual ions**.

Table 10.3

Compound or ion	Formula/ion	Formula mass/ mass of ions	Mass of 1 mole
hydrochloric acid	HCl	36.5	36.5g
sodium hydroxide	NaOH	40	40g
sulphuric acid	H_2SO_4	98	98g
sulphate ion	SO_4^{2-}	96	96g
chloride ion	Cl^-	35.5	35.5g

Using the mole idea

What mass of magnesium chloride is produced when **12g** of magnesium reacts with excess hydrochloric acid? (Excess means that you have more acid than you need, so the mass of this compound is not a restriction and can be ignored.)

Write down the **equation** for the reaction:

$$Mg + 2HCl \rightarrow MgCl_2 + H_2$$

This tells us that **one particle of magnesium produces **one** particle of magnesium chloride. Therefore, **one** mole of magnesium produces **one** mole of magnesium chloride. To answer the question:

Step 1:   Convert **masses** to **moles**.

The atomic mass of magnesium is **24**, so the mass of 1 mol of magnesium is **24g**. The number of moles present in **12g** of Mg = **0.5**.

Step 2:   Use the **equation**.

1 mol of **Mg** produces **1 mol** of **MgCl$_2$**, so **0.5 mol** of Mg produces **0.5 mol** of MgCl$_2$.

Step 3:   Convert **moles** to **mass**.

1 mol of MgCl$_2$ has a mass of **95g**, so **0.5 mol** of MgCl$_2$ has a mass of $0.5 \times 95g = 47.5g$

Answer: **47.5g of MgCl$_2$ is produced.**

Molar solutions

'1 cm^3 = $^1/_{1000}$ dm^3'

Often reactions take place in solution, so we need to know **concentrations** of the reactants in **solutions**. Concentrations are given in **mol/dm^3**.

A solution which contains 1 mol/dm^3 contains 1 mol per dm^3 (litre) or, in words, one mole per cubic decimetre, and this is often expressed as a **1 M solution** (1 molar). Thus a 2 M solution contains 2 mol/dm^3.

A 1 M solution of sulphuric acid contains **1 mol** of H$_2$SO$_4$/dm^3, or in other words, 98g of H$_2$SO$_4$/dm^3. We can use this information to work out the **number of moles** present in a solution. For example, how many moles are present in **25cm^3** of a **2 mol/dm^3** solution of NaOH?

$$\text{No. of moles} = \text{concentration} \times \text{volume (in dm}^3) = 2 \times \frac{25}{1,000} = 0.05 \text{ mol.}$$

These principles can be used to calculate the concentration of solutions. For example, if 25cm^3 of a 2 mol/dm^3 solution of sodium hydroxide exactly reacts with 10cm^3 of sulphuric acid, what is the **concentration** of the sulphuric acid?

Use the **equation** for the reaction:

$$2NaOH \quad + \quad H_2SO_4 \quad \rightarrow \quad Na_2SO_4 \quad + \quad 2H_2O$$

Step 1:   From the question, the number of **moles** of NaOH used

= concentration × volume
  2   × 25/1,000
= 0.05 mol

Step 2:   From the equation, **2 mol** of NaOH reacts with 1 mol of H$_2$SO$_4$. Therefore, **0.05 mol** of NaOH reacts with **0.025 mol** of H$_2$SO$_4$.

Step 3:   Since no. of moles = concentration × volume
        0.025   = concentration × 10/1,000
        2.5   = concentration

Therefore, the concentration of H$_2$SO$_4$ = **2.5 mol/dm^3**.

▶ **EXAMINATION QUESTIONS**

Multiple choice

Q1 Which of the following formulae correctly shows the reaction between sodium and chlorine?

A Na $+$ Cl_2 $\rightarrow$ $NaCl_2$
B Na_2 $+$ Cl_2 $\rightarrow$ Na_2Cl_2
C Na $+$ Cl $\rightarrow$ $NaCl$
D $2Na$ $+$ Cl_2 $\rightarrow$ $2NaCl$
E $2Na$ $+$ Cl_2 $\rightarrow$ $2NaCl_2$

Q2 Which pair of substances are pollutants produced by a petrol-burning engine?

A   carbon and sulphur dioxide
B   carbon monoxide and lead compounds
C   carbon monoxide and steam
D   carbon dioxide and steam
E   nitrogen dioxide and steam

Q3 Which one of the following is the main reason for using catalysts in industrial processes?

A   to increase the temperature of the reaction mixtures
B   to increase the yield of the reaction mixtures
C   to increase the rate of formation of the products
D   to remove impurities from the reaction mixtures.   *(SEG)*

Q4 Which of the following reactions is a redox reaction?

A   changing lead oxide to lead, using carbon
B   neutralising sodium hydroxide
C   making carbohydrates during photosynthesis
D   releasing energy during respiration

Q5 A chemical reaction occurs when

A   an electric current is passed through a copper wire
B   salt solution is heated
C   crude oil is distilled
D   dilute hydrochloric acid is added to magnesium ribbon
E   ice melts to form water

Q6 What is the mass of oxygen contained in 36g of pure water?

A   16g;   B   32g;   C   48g;   D   64g;   E   70g

Q7 A metal, M, forms a hydroxide, $M(OH)_3$. The mass of one mole of the hydroxide is 78g. What is the relative atomic mass of M? (H = 1, O = 16)

A   27;   B   30;   C   59;   D   61;   E   78
                                                                            (London)

Q8 What is the concentration in mol/dm^3 (mol/litre) of $250cm^3$ of a solution containing $1.0g^3$ of sodium hydroxide? ($M_r = 40$)

A   0.025;   B   0.1;   C   0.25;   D   1.0;   E   2.0

Structured questions

Q9 In an experiment to find a suitable catalyst for a certain reaction, the following results were obtained.

Table 10.4

Temperature of each experiment (°C)	Substance under test as a catalyst	Time for the reaction to be completed (seconds)
20	cobalt chloride	18
20	sodium nitrate	30
20	cobalt nitrate	12
20	sodium chloride	41

(a) Use the table to answer the following questions.

   (i) Which substance gives the greatest increase in the rate of reaction?

   _____

   (ii) Which substance is the least effective as a catalyst?

   _____

   (iii) Which metal ion is most likely to be the best catalyst?

   _____

   (iv) Which ion is the least effective as a catalyst?

                                                                        (4)
   _____

(b) Give two reasons why catalysts are very important to the efficiency of several industrial processes. Give two processes in which catalysts are used. (3 lines)   (4)
                                                                        (WJEC)

Q10 A student added magnesium ribbon to dilute hydrochloric acid and recorded the volume of hydrogen released every 30 seconds; the results are shown below.

Table 10.5

Time (s)	Volume of hydrogen (cm^3)
0	0
30	25
60	50
90	75
100	100

(a) What is the relationship between the volume of gas released and the time taken? (2 lines)
                                                                        (2)
(b) How would you present the results so that the relationship might be more easily seen? (2 lines)   (1)
(c) If you were doing this experiment, describe two safety precautions you would take. (2)

   (i) _____

   (ii) _____
                                                                        (NICCEA)

Q11 (a) When hydrogen peroxide is left to stand in a clear glass container, it slowly decomposes to produce oxygen and water.

   (i) Write a balanced symbolic equation to show how 2 mol of hydrogen peroxide decomposes.   (2)
   (ii) From your equation calculate how many moles of oxygen would be produced if 10 mol of hydrogen peroxide completely decomposed.   (1)
   (iii) Hydrogen peroxide can be used by hairdressers. Suggest a reason why it is usually stored in brown bottles.   (1)

(b) Adding manganese (IV) oxide to hydrogen peroxide affects the rate at which oxygen is produced, as shown in the graph below (Fig.10.5).

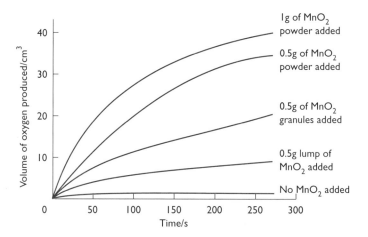

Fig. 10.5

   (i) What volume of oxygen will be produced after 125s by adding 1g of MnO_2 powder? *(1)*
   (ii) From the information on the graphs, state **two** factors which affect the rate of oxygen production and the evidence for your answer. *(4)*
   (iii) Give **one** other factor, not indicated on the graphs, which might affect the rate of reaction. *(1)*

(c) Devise a simple experiment that would enable you to check whether any of the manganese (IV) dioxide had been used up in the reaction. State clearly which procedures you would take and what measurements you would make. You need not include a diagram. *(5)*

(MEG)

Q12 (Higher Tier)   A structured question consisting of four sub-questions (a) to (d) which can be answered independently of each other so if you cannot do one part go on to the next.

Methane burns in the presence of oxygen to form water and carbon dioxide.

$$CH_4 + 2O_2 \rightarrow CO_2 + 2H_2O \qquad \Delta H = -890kJ/mol$$

(a) Describe the bonding of each of the following compounds. Include the names of the types of bond involved. *(4)*

   (i) Methane (3 lines) _____

   (ii) Carbon dioxide (3 lines) _____

(b) (i) Explain why a source of ignition (heat) is needed before methane will start burning in oxygen. (5 lines) *(3)*
    (ii) Explain why this reaction gives out energy. (4 lines) *(3)*

(c) Hydrogen reacts with chlorine.

$$H_2 + Cl_2 \rightarrow 2HCl$$

Approximate bond energies:

   H – H   436kJ/mol
   Cl – Cl   242kJ/mol
   H – Cl   431kJ/mol

Calculate how much energy is released or absorbed by this reaction. (2 lines) *(3)*

(d) Some copper (II) sulphate solution is poured into a beaker and its temperature is recorded every 15 seconds. After a short time some zinc is added to this solution. The temperature is recorded for a total time of two minutes as shown on the graph (Fig. 10.6).

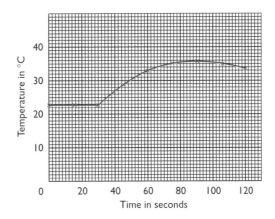

Fig. 10.6

(i) Explain why the graph line is as shown. (6 lines) *(4)*

(ii) The equation for the reaction between copper (II) sulphate and zinc is shown below.

$$CuSO_4 + Zn \rightarrow ZnSO_4 + Cu$$

If 16.25g of zinc are added to excess copper (II) sulphate solution, what mass of copper will be formed? (4 lines) [The relative atomic mass of copper is 64 and of zinc is 65.] *(3)*

(Science Double Award, SEG)

▶ EXAMINATION ANSWERS

Multiple choice

A1 Key D; there must be four atoms on each side to balance.

A2 Key B; steam is not considered to be a pollutant, so the correct answer is carbon monoxide and lead compounds.

A3 Key C; remember catalysts increase the rate of reactions but are not used up by the reactions.

A4 Key A; the redox reaction here involves the removal of oxygen from lead oxide and the addition of oxygen to carbon to form carbon dioxide.

A5 Key D; the other options are physical changes.

A6 Key B; the mass of one mole of water is 18g [$(2 \times 1) + 16 = 18$]. There are 2 moles of water which contain 2 mol of oxygen = $2 \times 16 = 32$g.

A7 Key A; the relative formula mass of the hydroxide OH is 17. There are three hydroxides, so the mass is $3 \times 17 = 51$. Then, $78-51 = 27$, the mass of one mole of M.

A8 Key B; there is 1g in 250cm^3, so there are 4g in 1 litre. The mass of one mole of NaOH is 40, so $4 \div 40$ is 0.1.

Structured questions

A9 (a) (i) cobalt nitrate
        (ii) sodium chloride
        (iii) cobalt
        (iv) sodium

(b) they increase the rate of reaction;
    they lower the amount of energy required to start a reaction;
    manufacture of sulphuric acid;
    manufacture of ammonia.

A10 (a) The volume of gas increases as the time increases, every 30 seconds; 25cm³ of gas is released until the final 10 seconds.

(b) on a graph

(c) (i) wear safety goggles
(ii) make sure no acid is spilled

A11 (a) (i) $2H_2O_2 \rightarrow 2H_2O + O_2$
(ii) 5 mol
(iii) to stop light affecting the substance

(b) (i) 30cm³
(ii) Mass of MnO_2; 1g of powder works faster than 0.5g
powder is faster than granules as there is more surface area
(iii) temperature

(c) Weigh the dry manganese dioxide, then add to hydrogen peroxide. When reaction stops, dry and weigh again. If the two weights are the same, then no manganese dioxide has been used.

A12 You are given information in the form of an equation. Use this information to help you remember the structure of methane and carbon dioxide.

(a) (i) covalent bonding (1)
single bonds between carbon and each hydrogen atom (1)
(ii) covalent bonding (1)
double bond between carbon and each oxygen atom (1)

(b) (i) heat is required to break the bonds (1)
radicals are then formed (1)
which then react (1)
(ii) energy is required to break bonds (1)
energy is released when bonds are made (1)
in this reaction more energy is released than used (1)

(c) breaking bonds H – H = 436
Cl – Cl = 242
= 678 kJ (1)
making bonds H – Cl = 431 × 2
= 862 kJ (1)
energy released = 862 – 678
= 184 kJ (1)

(d) (i) temperature of copper sulphate solution
is room temperature approx. 22°C (1)
as zinc reacts with copper (II) ions the temperature rises (1)
after about 80 seconds the reaction is complete (1)
solution starts to cool towards room temperature (1)
(ii) Note you are given the equation and the relative atomic masses of copper and zinc in the question.

1 mole of zinc produces 1 mole of copper (1)
65g of zinc produces 64g of copper (1)
16.25g of zinc produces $\dfrac{64 \times 16.25}{65}$ = 16g of copper (1)

► A STUDENT'S ANSWER WITH EXAMINER'S COMMENTS

Ammonia and nitric acid are both important chemicals. Nitric acid is made from ammonia.

The charts below show substances made from ammonia and nitric acid.

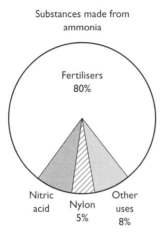

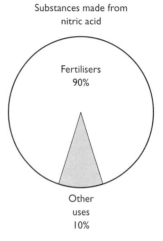

Fig. 10.7

(a) Use the charts to help you answer these questions.

(i) What is the main use of both ammonia and nitric acid?

fertiliser ✓ _____ *(1)*

'The largest section on each pie chart'

(ii) Work out the percentage of ammonia used to make nitric acid.

Percentage = __7__ % ✓ *(1)*

'The rest totals 93%'

(iii) 100 million tonnes of ammonia are made in the world each year. How much of this ammonia is used to make nylon?

__5__ million tonnes ✓ *(1)*

(b) The word equations below show how nitric acid is made.

1. nitrogen + hydrogen → ammonia
2. ammonia + oxygen → nitrogen monoxide + water
3. nitrogen monoxide + oxygen → nitrogen dioxide
4. nitrogen dioxide + water → nitric acid

Use the word equations to help you answer these questions.

(i) From which **two elements** is ammonia made?

__nitrogen__ and __hydrogen__ ✓ *(1)*

'Both answers correct for the mark'

(ii) Name **two** of the raw materials needed to make nitric acid.

__nitrogen__ ✗ and __water__ *(2)*

'Take care, nitrogen dioxide'

(c) A large amount of nitric acid is reacted with ammonia to make a fertiliser.

nitric acid + ammonia → fertiliser

(Continued)

(i) The reaction is a neutralisation reaction.
What type of chemical must ammonia be?

an alkali ✔ (1)

(ii) Complete the chemical name for the fertiliser made from ammonia and nitric acid.

ammonium   *nitrate* ✔ (1)

(iii) The reaction of nitric acid with ammonia is exothermic.
Name the piece of equipment you could put into the solution to prove that the reaction is exothermic.

'To measure temperature change'

a thermometer ✔ (1)

(Co-ordinated Science, NEAB)

SUMMARY

At the end of this chapter you should know:

▷   how to represent **reactions** by **word equations**;

▷   how to represent **reactions**, including **electrolytic** reactions, by **balanced equations** using **chemical symbols**;

▷   to use chemical equations to predict **reacting quantities**;

▷   to determine the **formula** of **simple compounds** from **reacting masses**;

▷   that there is **variation** in the **rates** at which different reactions take place;

▷   how the **rates of reactions** can be altered by varying **temperature** or **concentration**, or by changing the **surface area** of a solid reactant, or by adding a **catalyst**;

▷   that reactions occur when **particles collide**;

▷   that the rates of many reactions can be **increased** by increasing the frequency or energy of **collisions** between the **particles**;

▷   how the rates of **enzyme-catalysed** reactions vary with temperature;

▷   the use of **enzymes** in the **baking, brewing** and **dairy industries**;

▷   that some reactions are **reversible**;

▷   how the **yield of products** from reversible reactions depends on **conditions**;

▷   that some **manufacturing processes** are based on **reversible** reactions;

▷   how nitrogen can be converted to **ammonia** in industry;

▷   how **nitrogenous fertilisers** are manufactured and their effects on plant growth and the environment;

▷   that changes of **temperature** often accompany reactions;

▷   that reactions can be **exothermic** or **endothermic**;

▷   that **making** and **breaking chemical bonds** in chemical reactions involves **energy transfers**.

11

The Reactivity Series and Acidity

▶ **GETTING STARTED**

In this chapter we first look at the reactivity series of metals. This will help us to understand why some metals corrode (rust) and others do not. The reactivity of metals depends
on their atomic structure and position in the periodic table so make sure you understand
Chapter 9 before studying this topic. The more reactive alkali metals have the strongest
tendency to form ions and are able to displace other metals from solution.

Almost all compounds which contain ions can be classified as acid, base or salt.

Acids are substances which have a sharp or sour taste. We can recognise this taste in
fruits or in vinegar. Acids can also be corrosive; they can dissolve many substances such as
metals and some rocks. This can be useful but can also be a nuisance, as with the corrosion
of iron and buildings by acids in the atmosphere, e.g. acid rain.

Bases are substances which can neutralise acids; they react with acids to produce salts.
Bases include the oxides, hydroxides and carbonates of metals. Most bases are insoluble in
water; those which do dissolve are called *alkalis*.

Salts are substances which are formed when acids are neutralised by bases. These salts are
giant ionic structures and often form crystals. The neutralisation of acids by bases can be
explained in terms of the interaction between hydrogen ions (H^+) and hydroxide ions (OH^-).

$$H^+ + OH^- \rightarrow H_2O$$

TOPIC	STUDY	REVISION I	REVISION 2
The reactivity series			
Reactions of metals			
Acids			
Alkalis			
Detecting acids and alkalis			
Neutralisation			
Patterns of acid reactions			
Acids in action			
Salts			

WHAT YOU NEED TO KNOW

Most of this work you will have studied in Key Stage 3 but it forms an important part of the Key Stage 4 Science syllabuses.

▶ **The reactivity series**

'*the reactions of metals with oxygen, water and acid*' [KS3]

'*the displacement reactions that take place between metals and solutions of salts of other metals*' [KS3]

'*how a reactivity series of metals can be determined by considering these reactions*' [KS3]

'*how this reactivity series can be used to make predictions about other reactions*' [KS3]

'*Check with Chapter 9, Periodic Table*'

When metals react they do so to form **positive ions**. Some metals are **more reactive** than others; this means the atoms form ions **more easily**. The metals can be placed in order of their **reactivity**, which depends on the ease with which they can form positive ions. This is referred to as the **reactivity series** for metals. This order of reactivity tends to be about the same no matter with what the metals are reacting.

The **reactivity series** is a list of **metallic elements** in order of their reactivity towards:

▶ **oxygen** when forming metal oxides;
▶ **cold water** when forming metal hydroxides and hydrogen;
▶ **dilute hydrochloric acid** when forming metal chlorides and hydrogen (magnesium, aluminium, zinc and iron will react; copper is below hydrogen in the series and will not react);
▶ **dilute sulphuric acid** when forming metal sulphates and hydrogen.

Reactivity series

'*Spot the pattern*'

potassium	greatest tendency to form ions
sodium	
calcium	
magnesium	
aluminium	
carbon	
zinc	increasing tendency to form ions
iron	
hydrogen	
copper	
gold	least tendency to form ions

The **reactivity series** can help us understand:

'*See Chapter 8, Extraction of metals*'

▶ why some metals **corrode** and not others;
▶ how we can **prevent** corrosion;
▶ why some metals react with **dilute acids** and not others;
▶ why some metals are extracted from their ores by **reduction** with **carbon** and why some can be extracted only by **electrolysis**;
▶ why metals were **discovered** in the order they were.

▶ **Reactions of metals**

Metal and oxygen

When heated in air, metals are **oxidised** to form **metal oxides** which are **bases**. The more reactive metals will burn in air. Gold and silver are metals which are not oxidised by heating in air. For example,

'*There's a pattern here*'

$$2Mg(s) + O_2(g) \rightarrow 2MgO(s)$$

Metals and water

The more reactive metals react with **water** to produce **hydrogen**. Potassium, sodium, lithium and calcium will react with cold water, to produce **hydroxides**:

'And a pattern here'

$$2Na(s) + 2H_2O(l) \rightarrow 2NaOH(aq) + H_2(g)$$

On the other hand, magnesium, zinc and iron will react only with **steam**, to form **oxides**:

$$Zn(s) + H_2O(g) \rightarrow ZnO(s) + H_2(g)$$

Metals and acids

All the metals in the reactivity series above copper will form **hydrogen** by reacting with **hydrochloric acid**. For example,

'Metal plus acids produce hydrogen'

$$Mg(s) + 2HCl(aq) \rightarrow MgCl_2(aq) + H_2(g)$$

Dilute nitric acid, however, does not give hydrogen. The **lower** in the reactivity series the metal, the **slower** the reaction.

Metals and metal salt solutions

'Identify the pattern'

If a metal is placed in a solution of the salt of another metal, a reaction may or may not take place. We can **predict** whether a reaction will occur if we know the **position** of the metals in the **reactivity series**. A metal **high** in the reactivity series, which has the **greater** tendency to form **ions**, will **displace** a metal **low** in the reactivity series from solution. For example:

$$Mg(s) + CuSO_4(aq) \rightarrow MgSO_4(aq) + Cu(s)$$

Mg is **above** Cu in the reactivity series, so electrons are transferred from the magnesium atom to the copper ion. This can be shown as an **ionic equation**, as it does not matter what negative ion is present:

$$Mg(s) + Cu^{2+}(aq) \rightarrow Mg^{2+}(aq) + Cu(s)$$

Metals and cells

The difference in tendency of metals to form ions can be very useful. If two different metals are placed in a solution containing ions and are linked by a wire, then **electrons** will flow through the wire. This means that a **current** is flowing through the wire, and there is a voltage between the two metals. This arrangement is called a **simple cell** (see Fig. 11.1).

'Properties of cells'

All cells contain three things:

▶ a + terminal (the positive electrode or **anode**);
▶ a – terminal (the negative electrode or **cathode**);
▶ a solution containing ions through which electricity can pass – the **electrolyte**.

'Refer back to the reactivity series'

The **voltage** that is produced between the two metals generally depends on their relative positions in the reactivity series. If the metals are **far apart** in the reactivity series then a **large** voltage is produced, whereas if the two metals in the pair are **close together** then a **small** voltage is produced.

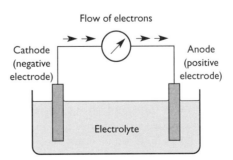

Fig. 11.1 A simple cell

Table 11.1

Metal pair	Voltage produced
magnesium/copper	large voltage
iron/zinc	small voltage

Dry cells (batteries) that you can buy essentially consist of **metal pairs** in an **electrolyte**, except that one of the metals is replaced by **carbon** (in the form of graphite). In normal dry cells the electrolyte is a **weak acid**; **alkaline** batteries have electrolytes which are **alkalis**.

Metals and corrosion

'Corrosion can be costly'

Corrosion is a chemical reaction. Corrosion of a metal will take place only if the metal is in contact with a solution containing **ions**. When the metal corrodes it **loses** electrons to form positive ions:

Metal atom – electron(s) → metal ion
$$M (s) \quad - e^- \quad \rightarrow M^+$$

Metals corrode at different rates, depending on their position in the reactivity series. Magnesium will corrode **more quickly** than copper, because it is **higher** in the reactivity series and has a **greater** tendency to form **ions**. As an example, **iron** will corrode (rust) when it is in contact with **water** and **air**. The water acts as a weak **electrolyte** (a solution containing ions) because it contains dissolved substances. Iron will corrode much more quickly when in contact with **sea water**, because this is a much **stronger** electrolyte (it contains a larger amount of dissolved salts). This is a real problem for ships; also cars that are kept near the sea (in seaside towns) tend to corrode more quickly than their counterparts inland. The reaction occurring in the corrosion of iron is as follows:

$$Fe(s) - 3e^- \rightarrow Fe^{3+}(aq)$$

'Factors affecting the rate of corrosion'

Corrosion can be a greater problem with structures built of more than one metal, e.g. if the steel plates of a ship's hull are riveted together with brass rivets, then the **steel** will corrode much **more quickly** than if the rivets were also made of steel. The **sea water** is acting as the **electrolyte**, so that a simple cell is set up between the iron (steel) and the copper (in the brass). The iron has a greater tendency to form ions than the copper, so will corrode much more rapidly.

The **rate of corrosion** of a metal therefore depends on:

▶ the **position** of the metal in the **reactivity series**;
▶ the concentration of the **electrolyte** with which the metal is in contact;
▶ the nature of any **other metal** with which it is in contact;
▶ the **temperature** of the metal – a higher temperature speeds up chemical reactions (this is why car exhausts corrode quickly).

Preventing corrosion

'A popular exam topic'

1. **Surface coating**: the simplest method of preventing metals from corroding is either to paint the metal or to cover it with a polymer layer which is bonded to the surface. Some oil rigs in the North Sea are protected in this way.

'Technological application'

2. **Sacrificial protection**: in this process one metal is 'sacrificed' to protect another. In **galvanising**, **iron** is coated with a thin layer of **zinc**. As the zinc is **higher** in the reactivity series, it will corrode, leaving the iron metal intact. A similar method is used to protect ships and oil rig platforms in the North Sea. This time, large blocks of zinc are welded to the ship's hull or the legs of the oil rig. These corrode away, protecting the legs, and can be easily replaced with new ones.

3. **Electroplating**: another method of preventing corrosion is to cover the surface of the metal with a thin layer of another metal which does not corrode. This is done by placing the metal to be protected in an **electrolysis cell** connected as the cathode (see Chapter 7, section on Electrolysis). Examples of electroplating are tin cans (steel coated with a thin layer of tin), and chromium-plated bumpers on cars.

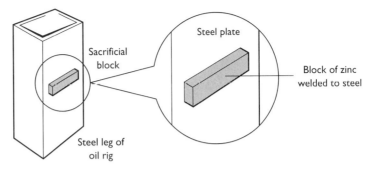

Fig. 11.2 Sacrificial corrosion

Acids in water contain hydrogen ions

Acids only behave as acids when they are **dissolved in water**. So we only really meet them as **solutions** in water. The reason for this is that water is a **polar solvent**. In water the acid produces **hydrogen ions** (H^+). All acids contain **hydrogen ions** in water. The importance of water can be demonstrated by dissolving some citric acid crystals (the acid from fruits such as oranges and lemons) in water and some citric acid crystals in another solvent, such as ethoxyethane (ether).

When the citric acid crystals are dissolved in **ether** the solution will *not* affect the colour of indicators, nor will it react with bases or metals. However, in **water** the citric acid behaves as an acid, changing the colour of the indicator.

In fact, the acid reacts with the water to produce a **hydrated hydrogen ion** called a hydroxonium ion (H_3O^+):

$$H^+ + H_2O \rightarrow H_3O^+$$

'Acids provide hydrogen ions'

It is really this ion that is responsible for acidity; however, in order to keep things simple we can think of acids as just providing **hydrogen ions** in water. These symbols can be regarded as representing the same ions:

$$H^+ \quad H^+(aq) \quad H_3O^+(aq)$$

Strong and weak acids

Those acids which give up all their hydrogen ions in water are called **strong** acids whereas those which only provide some of their hydrogen ions are called **weak** acids.

Table 11.2

Strong acids	Weak acids
sulphuric acid	citric acid (citrus fruits)
nitric acid	ethanoic (acetic) acid (vinegar)
hydrochloric acid	malic acid (apples)

Some common acids

Table 11.3

Acid	Formula	Ions present	
hydrochloric acid	HCl	H^+ Cl^-	(chloride)
sulphuric acid	H_2SO_4	$2H^+$ SO_4^{2-}	(sulphate)
nitric acid	HNO_3	H^+ NO_3^-	(nitrate)
ethanoic acid	CH_3COOH	H^+ CH_3COO^-	(ethanoate)

Notice the names of acids are taken from the ion present. This ion is referred to as the **acid radical**. Ethanoic acid (acetic acid) is a **weak** acid, because not all of the ethanoic acid molecules in solution split up to provide hydrogen ions, but only a proportion of them.

Concentration of acid solutions

'See Chapter 10'

Acid solutions can be **concentrated** or **dilute**, depending upon how much water is present. The concentration of a solution can be measured in mol/dm^3, as we've already seen. For example, a 1 M (1 molar) solution of sulphuric acid contains 98g H_2SO_4 per dm^3. This is calculated from the formula mass of $H_2SO_4 = (2 \times 1) + 32 + (4 \times 16) = 98$.

Strong acids must not be confused with **concentrated** acids. We can have concentrated solutions of strong *and* weak acids as well as dilute solutions of strong *and* weak acids. The acids that are used in a laboratory are dilute acids of concentrations 2 M, 1 M, 0.1 M, etc.

An **acid** is a substance which:

► has a **sour** taste;
► will change the **colour** of plant dyes (**indicators**);
► will **neutralise bases**;
► will react with many **metals** to form **salts**;
► produces **hydrogen ions** when dissolved in water.

► Alkalis

An alkali is a substance which:
► is a soluble **base**;
► will change the **colour** of **indicators**;
► will **neutralise acids**;
► contains **hydroxide ions**.

Some common alkalis

Table 11.4

Name	Formula	Ions presents	
sodium hydroxide	NaOH	Na^+ (sodium)	OH^-
ammonium hydroxide	NH_4OH	NH_4^+ (ammonium)	OH^-
calcium hydroxide	$Ca(OH)_2$	Ca^{2+} (calcium)	$2OH^-$

In the same way as there are strong and weak acids, so there are strong and weak **alkalis**. Aqueous sodium hydroxide is a strong alkali, whereas aqueous ammonia is a weak alkali.

► Detecting acids and alkalis

'that pH is a measure of the acidity of a solution' [KS3]

'to use indicators to classify solutions as acidic, neutral or alkaline' [KS3]

There are two main ways of **detecting** acids and alkalis:

1. using **indicators**: substances whose colours are changed by acids and alkalis;
2. using **pH meters**: instruments whose meter reading is affected by the H^+ and OH^- ions in the solution.

Indicators

'Learn the pH scale'

The most commonly used indicator is **universal indicator**, since it not only tells us if something is acid or alkaline but also if the acid (or alkali) is strong or weak. It can be used as a liquid (usually green) or soaked on to a type of blotting paper and used as a paper. The paper, of course, has to be wet in order to work, since acids only behave as acids in solution. The **colour** of the indicator matches a number which indicates the acidity of the solution.

The strength of an acid or alkali is measured on the **pH scale**. The pH scale has a range of 1 to 14 and is a measure of the hydrogen ion concentration (acidity). Notice that low numbers indicate **high** acidity (and high H^+ ion concentration).

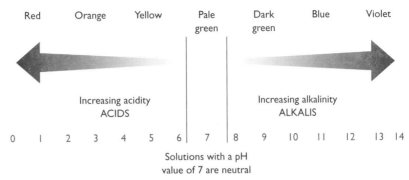

Fig. 11.3 The pH scale

'Water is a neutral
substance'

▶ If a solution turns the indicator **light green**, then it is **neutral** and has a pH of 7.
▶ If a solution turns the indicator **yellow** then it is a **weak** acid and has a pH of 6.

Other indicators

The reactions of other, less common, indicators are as follows:

Table 11.5

Indicator	in acid	in alkali	in water (neutral)
litmus	red	blue	purple
phenolphthalein	colourless	pink	colourless

▶ Neutralisation

'some everyday applications of neutralisation, e.g. the treatment of indigestion, the treatment of acid soil' [KS3]

Following acid/alkali reactions

'Check in your notes to
see if you have done
this at school'

Indicators can also be used to follow the course of a **neutralisation** reaction between an acid and an alkali. If universal indicator is added to a strong alkaline solution, the indicator will turn **violet**. If a **solution of acid is added**, a small amount at a time, then the indicator will change colour **through blue to green**, at which point the solution is **neutral** (the acid has reacted with all the alkali present). If acid **continues** to be added, the indicator will eventually turn **red**, indicating the solution is now **strongly acidic**.

You may have performed an experiment such as this and will have noticed how difficult it is to add just the right amount of acid to produce a neutral solution (green colour with the indicator). If you need to produce a neutral solution, an accurate measuring device (a **burette**) is required and it would also be helpful to use an indicator (such as phenolphthalein) which has a more distinct colour change. The process, shown in Fig. 11.4, is called **titration**. The acid is titrated into the alkali, using an indicator to show when the exact amount of acid has been added.

An example is the reaction between **hydrochloric acid** and **sodium hydroxide**, when **a salt** (sodium chloride) and **water** are produced. We can use the titration method to find exact quantity of hydrochloric acid to neutralise the sodium hydroxide solution exactly.

hydrochloric acid + sodium hydroxide → sodium chloride + water
$HCl(aq)$ + $NaOH(aq)$ → $NaCl(aq)$ + $H_2O(l)$

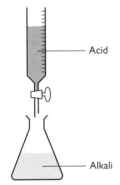

Fig. 11.4 Titration of acid
and alkali

A measured volume of sodium hydroxide is placed in the flask, together with a few drops of indicator. The hydrochloric acid is then added from the burette, a little at a time, and the liquid is swirled in the flask to make sure the solutions are mixed. When the indicator **just changes colour** then the exact amount of acid has been added to neutralise the alkali. The volume of the acid required can be read off the burette. If the same experiment is repeated with the same volumes of acid and alkali but without the indicator, then a **neutral solution** can be produced which contains only sodium chloride and water. This can be shown by **evaporating** the water in the flask, when crystals of **sodium chloride** will be left.

Making acids and alkalis

The **oxides** of **non-metals** when dissolved in water give **acidic solutions**. The **oxides** of **metals** are **bases** and those which dissolve in water produce **alkaline solutions**. Thus acids and alkalis relate to the elements' position in the periodic table (see Fig. 11.5).

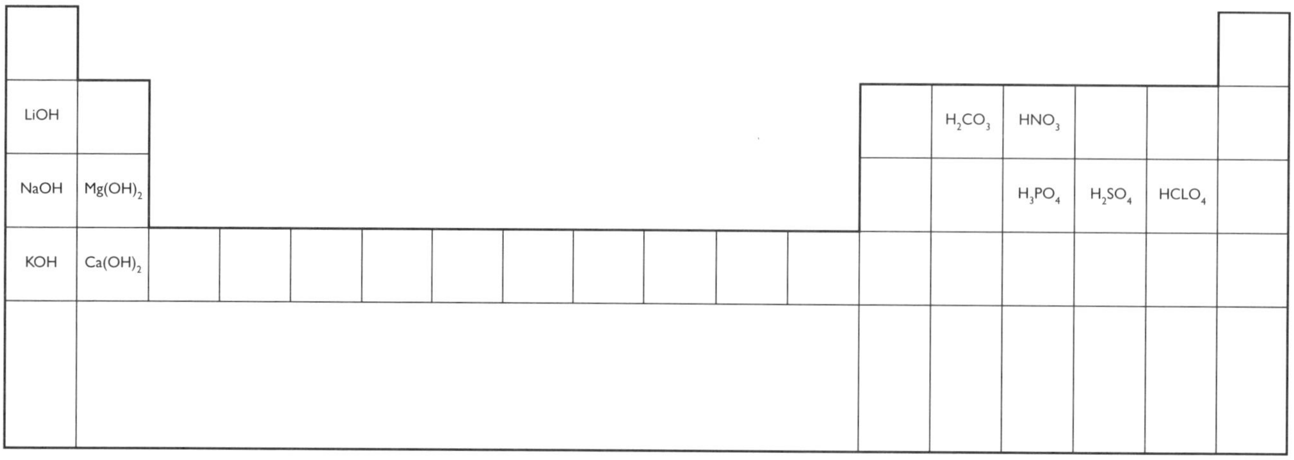

LiOH														H_2CO_3	HNO_3		
NaOH	$Mg(OH)_2$														H_3PO_4	H_2SO_4	$HCLO_4$
KOH	$Ca(OH)_2$																

Fig. 11.5 The change from alkalis on the left to acids on the right when oxides of elements react with water

'A popular topic on exam papers'

Indigestion is often caused by too much **acid** in the stomach and can be relieved by taking 'antacid' tablets. These contain **bases** which **neutralise** the excess acid in the stomach. Examples are Settlers and Rennies, which both contain calcium carbonate and magnesium hydroxide.

Acidity and the soil

Most plants prefer to grow in a soil which is slightly **acidic**, about pH 6–7. There are even some plants which prefer more acidic soils (pH 4.5–6) such as azaleas, rhododendrons and heathers. No plants will grow in strongly alkaline soils, however, although some plants will grow in weakly alkaline soils (up to pH 8). When there is a change from growing one type of plant to another, the acidity of the soil has sometimes to be changed to get the best results. In addition, the soil acidity itself may well change over a period of time because of the plants themselves. Needing to reduce the acidity of the soil is a common problem to farmers; they do this by adding **lime** to the soil. Lime is calcium oxide, but calcium hydroxide (slaked lime) or calcium carbonate (limestone or chalk) is often used:

$$CaO \quad + \quad 2H^+ \quad \rightarrow \quad Ca^{2+} \quad + \quad H_2O$$
(lime or quicklime)
$$Ca(OH)_2 + \quad 2H^+ \quad \rightarrow \quad Ca^{2+} \quad + \quad 2H_2O$$
(slaked lime)
$$CaCO_3 \quad + \quad 2H^+ \quad \rightarrow \quad Ca^{2+} \quad + \quad H_2O \quad + \quad CO_2$$
(limestone)

▶ Patterns of acid reactions

Acids are very useful substances, because they react with a large number of other substances in fairly **predictable** ways. They are used extensively in industry in the manufacture of a large variety of materials.

Reactions with metals

'Hydrogen given off'

The reaction follows a general pattern:

metal	+ acid	→ salt	+ hydrogen
zinc	+ hydrochloric acid	→ zinc chloride	+ hydrogen
Zn	+ 2HCl	→ $ZnCl_2$	+ H^2
magnesium	+ sulphuric acid	→ magnesium sulphate	+ hydrogen
Mg	+ H_2SO_4	→ $MgSO_4$	+ H_2

'Spot the pattern'

The solution that is produced is neutral, and the salt produced depends on the acid. Some metals react with acids faster than others. The metal's reactivity depends on its position in the **reactivity series**.

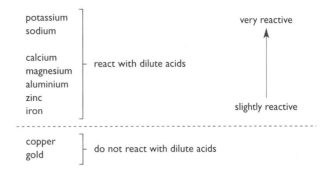

Fig. 11.6

'Test for H$_2$'

When **hydrogen gas** is produced it can be tested for by igniting a test tube of hydrogen with a **lighted splint**; the result is a '**pop**'.

Reactions with metal oxides

Metal **oxides** are **bases** and react with **acids** to produce **salt** and **water**. All metal oxides will react with dilute acids. The reaction follows a general pattern:

metal oxide	+	**acid**	→	**salt**	+	**water**
copper (II) oxide	+	nitric acid	→	copper nitrate	+	water
CuO	+	$2HNO_3$	→	$Cu(NO_3)_2$	+	H_2O
magnesium oxide	+	sulphuric acid	→	magnesium sulphate	+	water
MgO	+	H_2SO_4	→	$MgSO_4$	+	H_2O

Reactions with metal hydroxides

Metal **hydroxides** are **bases** which will react with **acids** to produce **salt** and **water**. Metal hydroxides which are soluble are called **alkalis**. All metal hydroxides react with acids. The reaction follows a general pattern:

metal hydroxide	+	**acid**	→	**salt**	+	**water**
calcium hydroxide	+	hydrochloric acid	→	calcium chloride	+	water
$Ca(OH)_2$	+	$2HCl$	→	$CaCl_2$	+	$2H_2O$
potassium hydroxide	+	sulphuric acid	→	potassium sulphate	+	water
2KOH	+	H_2SO_4	→	K_2SO_4	+	$2H_2O$

Reaction with carbonates

'CO$_2$ given off'

Metal carbonates can be thought of as bases; they too will react with acids to produce salt and water, but they also produce **carbon dioxide**. The reaction follows a general pattern:

acid	+	**carbonate**	→	**salt**	+	**water**	+	**carbon dioxide**
sodium	+	nitric	→	sodium	+	water	+	carbon dioxide
carbonate		acid		nitrate				
Na_2CO_3	+	$2HNO_3$	→	$2NaNO_3$	+	H_2O	+	CO_2
calcium	+	hydrochloric	→	calcium	+	water	+	carbon dioxide
carbonate		acid		chloride				
$CaCO_3$	+	$2HCl$	→	$CaCl_2$	+	H_2O	+	CO_2

'Spot the pattern'

'See Chapter 16, pp. 308–10'

This is a general pattern for all carbonates, and as some **rocks** are **carbonates** it can be used as a test to help **identify rocks**. For example, limestone, marble and chalk are all mainly calcium carbonate and will therefore react with hydrochloric acid. When a small amount of acid is placed on the surface, the rocks fizz and give off carbon dioxide.

There is an exception to this 'rule'; sulphuric acid will not react well with calcium carbonate rock, since during the reaction a layer of calcium sulphate builds up on the surface, preventing any further reaction.

'Test for CO₂'

The **carbon dioxide** produced can be tested for by bubbling the gas through **limewater**, when the limewater turns **cloudy**.

▶ Acids in action

'how acids in the atmosphere can lead to corrosion of metal and chemical weathering of rock' [KS3]

Acid rain

The rain which normally falls is very slightly **acidic** (pH 5). This is due to a small amount of **carbon dioxide** from the atmosphere which dissolves in the rain water to produce a weakly acidic solution:

$$H_2O + CO_2 \rightarrow H_2CO_3$$

'See Chapter 17, Energy Resources, p. 325–6'

Acid rain, however, has a pH of between 5 and about 2.2. The strongest acid rain has an acidity comparable to that of lemon juice. The **causes** of acid rain are not fully understood, but enough is known to realise that the burning of **fossil fuels** (hydrocarbons) and the exhaust emission from cars contribute greatly to acid rain.

Fossil fuels like coal and oil contain impurities of sulphur, so that when they **burn** they produce **sulphur dioxide** in addition to the normal products of combustion (carbon dioxide and water). Sulphur dioxide is an **acidic gas**. The **exhausts** of cars also emit gases other than the normal products of combustion. In the car engine where the petrol (hydrocarbon fuel) is burned, the temperature is so high that **nitrogen** from the air reacts with oxygen to form **oxides of nitrogen** which escape through the exhaust, together with unburned hydrocarbons and car on monoxide.

'Look at Chapter 6, Human Influence on the Environment, p. 120'

This mixture of gases (particularly sulphur dioxide and the oxides of nitrogen) react in the atmosphere with water to produce **rain** which contains **sulphuric** and **nitric** acids. It is this that gives the rain its reactivity. **Acid rain** will obviously be a problem in parts of the world which are **industrialised** (burn fossil fuels in power stations and factories) and have large numbers of cars, e.g. Europe, USA, Canada and Japan.

Effects of acid rain

Acid rain will **corrode** metals and will react with some **building materials** (limestone and marble), gradually eating them away. Perhaps the largest worry, however, is the effect it has, either directly or indirectly, on **living things**.

When acid rain falls on to the **soil** it progressively dissolves away many of the **minerals** (salts) in the soil. **Metal ions** are **leached** (dissolved) out of the soil and washed into **rivers** and **lakes**, which become increasingly **acidic** and increasingly concentrated in metal ions. The first metal ions to be removed from the soil are **magnesium** (Mg^{2+}) and **calcium** (Ca^{2+}), because they dissolve most easily. These are needed by plants to ensure healthy growth, so are no longer available.

The next metal ions to be leached out of the soil are **aluminium** (Al^{3+}) and the heavier metal ions of **lead** (Pb^{2+}), and **copper** (Cu^{2+}). These ions are particularly troublesome, since they are **poisonous**. Dissolved **aluminium** in the water prevents the gills of fish working, as well as being poisonous to other organisms, including ourselves. (**Note:** it is not the acid water that kills the fish, but the **dissolved metal ions**.)

The areas that are affected more than others are those with **thin soil** covering and granite rock, such as Scotland, Dartmoor, the Black Forest in Germany, and Scandinavia. Areas which are lucky enough to have deep soil covering limestone rock are not so badly affected, since the **limestone** rock and its soil can **neutralise** the effects of the acid rain. The degree to which an area is affected also depends on its position, since the acidic gases are carried on prevailing winds.

Combating acid rain

'A very relevant aspect of science'

1. Some **lakes** which are very **acidic** have large amounts of **lime** (calcium hydroxide) added to them to **neutralise** the acidity. This is only a temporary measure, however, since it has to be frequently repeated and costs a large amount of money.

2. **Power stations** which burn coal and oil can be fitted with equipment which will remove the **sulphur dioxide** from the gases before they are released into the atmosphere.
3. **Car exhausts** can be fitted with **catalytic converters** which can convert the harmful gases into harmless ones. These can only be fitted to cars which run on unleaded petrol because the lead in petrol would prevent the catalyst from working.

Acids in industry

Sulphuric acid is one of the most important acids in **industry** and is produced in very large quantities each year. It has a wide variety of uses in the manufacture of other substances. Sulphuric acid is manufactured by the **contact** process. Sulphur is the starting point:

$$S \quad \rightarrow \quad SO_2 \quad \rightarrow \quad SO_3 \quad \rightarrow \quad H_2SO_4$$

| | heated in air | reacts with more oxygen over catalyst | reacts with water | |

Sulphuric acid is needed for the manufacture of agricultural chemicals (**fertilisers**), plastics, paints and pigments, detergents and soaps, fibres, dyestuffs, oil and petrol, as well as other chemicals (including other acids).

Nitric acid is another important industrial chemical, and is manufactured in quantity for use mainly in the manufacture of fertilisers and explosives.

▶ **Salts** These are **ionic** substances which are formed in reactions between **acids** and **bases** or between acids and metals. If solutions of these salts are allowed to **evaporate**, then **crystals** (giant ionic structures) are formed. Solutions of these salts will conduct **electricity**, showing that they contain **ions**.

Naming salts

The name of the salt depends on the ions present. Each salt contains a positive ion, or **cation**, that is derived from the metal, e.g. Na^+, Mg^{2+}. In addition, each salt contains a negative ion, or **anion**, that is derived from the acid, e.g. SO_4^{2-} (sulphate), or CO_3^{2-} (carbonate).

The name of the salt comes from a combination of **both** ions, e.g. magnesium sulphate ($Mg^{2+} SO_4^{2-}$). The **charge** on the metal ion depends on its group in the periodic table (see Chapter 9 and Fig. 11.7). Some metals (those from the **transition metal** block in the periodic table) can have ions with different charges. An example is iron, where the charge on the ion is indicated by roman numerals in the name:

| iron (II) sulphate | $FeSO_4$ | Fe^{2+} ion present |
| iron (III) sulphate | $Fe_2(SO_4)_3$ | Fe^{3+} ion present |

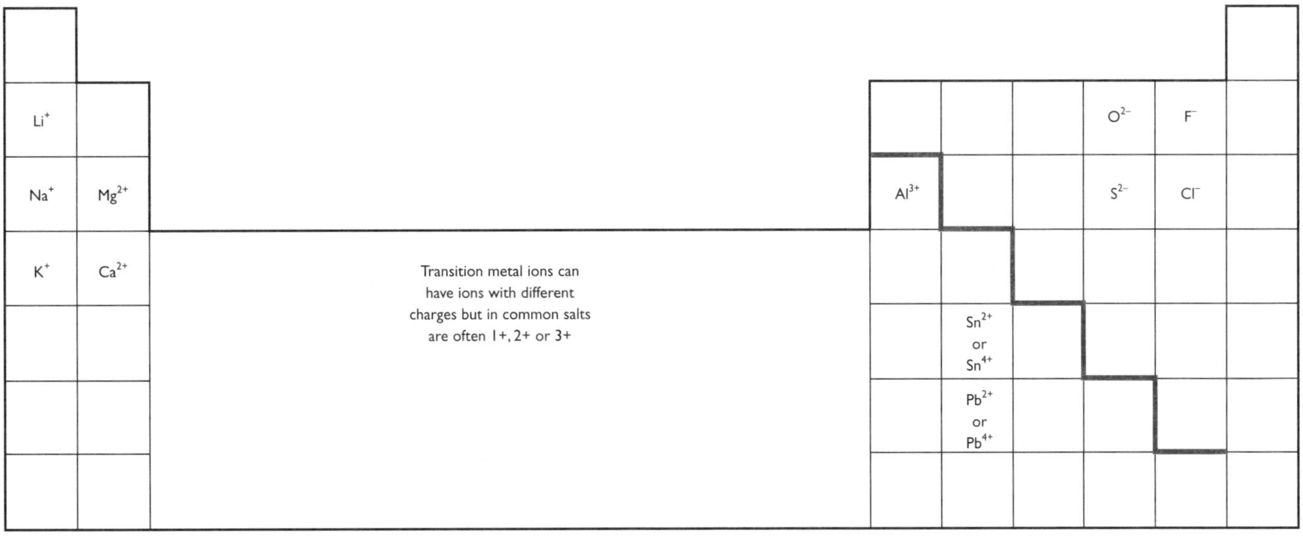

Fig. 11.7 The charge on the ion depends on its group in the periodic table

Patterns for salts

Solubility

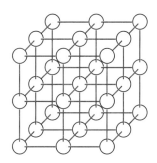

Fig. 11.8 Ionic lattice of a salt

In the case of **cations**, all salts containing sodium, potassium or ammonium ions are **soluble**. Although the ammonium ion (NH_4^+) is not a metal ion, it may be regarded as such in salts.

In the case of **anions**, all **nitrates** (NO_3^-) are soluble; all **chlorides** (Cl^-) are soluble (except silver and lead); all **sulphates** (SO_4^{2-}) are soluble (except barium, calcium and lead); but all **carbonates** (CO_3^{2-}) are **insoluble** (except Na^+, K^+, NH_4^+).

The solubility of a salt often increases with **temperature**, although there are a few exceptions. The reason for this is that in order for the water to dissolve the salt it has to break down the **ionic lattice** (Fig. 11.8). The higher the temperature, the greater the kinetic energy of the particles (water molecules and ions). **Remember:** water is able to **dissolve** ionic substances because it is a polar molecule (see Chapter 7).

Colour of salts

The colour of salts is often due to the **metal ion** present.

Table 11.6

Ion	Colour	Ion	Colour
Na^+	colourless	Fe^{2+}	green
K^+	colourless	Fe^{3+}	red
Cu^{2+}	blue/green		

Salts in action

'Check with nitrogen cycle, Chapter 6 and Chapter 4, Green Plants as Organisms'

Salts are present in the sea and in the soil and provide plants with the elements they need. For example:

▶ **nitrogen** as **nitrates** (NO_3^-) in the soil provides the plant with vital materials to manufacture **amino acids**;
▶ **phosphorus**, as **phosphates** (PO_4^{3-}) is essential for **energy transfer** within the plant cell;
▶ **potassium** (K^+) makes many **enzymes** active;
▶ **calcium** (Ca^{2+}) provides a **raw material** for cell walls;
▶ **magnesium** (Mg^{2+}) is a vital component of **chlorophyll**;
▶ **sulphur**, as **sulphates** (SO_4^{2-}), is a component of some **amino acids**.

Because each of these elements is needed by plants, their salts are manufactured as **fertilisers**. Examples are ammonium nitrate, ammonium phosphate and potassium chloride. Fertilisers containing these three salts are called **N, P, K fertilisers** because they provide **nitrogen (N)**, **phosphorus (P)** and **potassium (K)**.

As well as in agriculture, salts are used in other, industrial or medical, applications. **Calcium sulphate** (gypsum) is used as wall plaster and plaster of Paris. **Silver chloride** is used as photographic film emulsion. **Iron (II) sulphate** is used in iron tablets to treat anaemia.

▶ EXAMINATION QUESTIONS

Multiple choice

Questions 1–3 below refer to the following pH numbers.
A   pH1;   B   pH4;   C   pH7;   D   pH10;   E   pH14

Q1   What is the pH of a strongly alkaline solution?

Q2   What is the pH of a neutral solution?

Q3   What is the pH of a weakly acidic solution?

Q4   How many grams of sulphuric acid H_2SO_4, are present in a 2 M solution of sulphuric acid? (H = 1, S = 32, O = 16)

A   49g;   B   50g;   C   98g;   D   194g;   E   196g

Q5   What gas is released when zinc reacts with hydrochloric acid?

A   carbon dioxide   D   nitrogen
B   chlorine   E   oxygen
C   hydrogen

Q6   What new substance, apart from magnesium sulphate, is formed when magnesium oxide reacts with sulphuric acid?

A   carbon dioxide   D   a salt
B   hydrogen   E   water
C   oxygen

Q7   How would you correctly identify the gas produced when an acid reacts with a carbonate?

A   use a glowing splint   D   use limewater
B   use a lighted splint   E   pass the gas through an acid
C   carefully smell the gas

Structured questions

Q8   (a) A list of pH values is given below:

pH1   pH4   pH7   pH9   pH14

Select from this list the pH value of each of the following substances. Each value may be used once, more than once or not at all.

(i) distilled water _____ *(1)*

(ii) toothpaste _____ *(1)*

(iii) vinegar _____ *(1)*

ATAKA

Contains Formic Acid

Keep out of reach
of children

Do not breathe in vapour

Wash off skin immediately

CORROSIVE POISON

CAUSES BURNS

NOT TO BE TAKEN

Contents 250cm³

Fig. 11.9

(b) A householder bought a bottle of the stain remover called ATAKA shown alongside.
(i) Which piece of laboratory apparatus would you use to confirm that the bottle contains $250 cm^3$?

_____
(1)

(ii) A little of the liquid is accidentally dropped on the carpet. Suggest a household substance which could be used to prevent damage, and explain your choice.

name _____

explanation _____

_____
(3)

(NICCEA)

Q9   In a chemist's shop, two brands of indigestion tablets are on sale, Burney and Rumbley. Sarah did an experiment to try to find out which one would be better.

She crushed the tablets and dissolved 1g of each kind of tablet in $100 cm^3$ of distilled water. Then she did an experiment to find out what volume of the same acid solution was needed to neutralise each tablet solution.

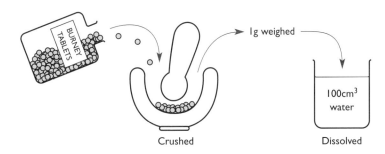

Crushed   Dissolved

Fig. 11.10

(a)   What is the chemical in the stomach that can cause indigestion?

_____   *(1)*

(b)   (i)   What is meant by a **neutral** solution? (2 lines)   *(1)*
      (ii) Give two reasons why Sarah crushed the tablets rather than using whole tablets.

        1.   _____

        2.   _____   *(2)*

The apparatus she used is shown below.

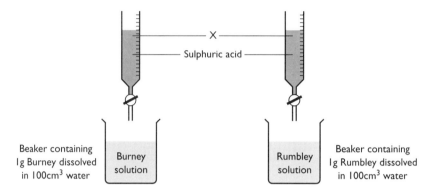

Fig. 11.11

(c)   (i)   What is the name of the apparatus **X** that she used?

_____   *(1)*

      (ii) What indicator might Sarah use to show when neutralisation has taken place?

_____   *(1)*

      (iii) What colour change would have taken place at neutralisation?

Table 11.7

Colour in tablet solution	Colour at neutralisation

      (iv) Name **one** chemical which you might find in an indigestion tablet.

_____   *(1)*

      (v)   Write a word equation for the reaction of sulphuric acid with this chemical.

_____   *(2)*

(d)   The results of the experiment were as follows:

> Volume of sulphuric acid needed to neutralise Burney tablet solution = 25cm³
>
> Volume of sulphuric acid needed to neutralise Rumbley tablet solution = 20cm³

      (i)   Which of the tablets would be better to cure indigestion?

_____

      (ii) Give a reason for your answer. (2 lines)   *(2)*

(e) State and explain **two** safety measures (precautions) that Sarah should take while doing this experiment.

Safety measure	Reason
1 _____ _____ _____	_____ _____ _____
2 _____ _____ _____	_____ _____ _____

(2)
(London)

Q10 (a) The components of washing powders Soapso and Sudso are listed below.

Table 11.8

Washing powder	Soapso	Sudso
Sodium sulphate %	29	35
Sodium carbonate %	20	0
Sodium silicate %	20	26
Sodium soap %	0	6
Detergent %	15	13

Dilute nitric acid was added to each powder in turn. Only one of the powders fizzed. The gas turned limewater milky.

(i) Which powder fizzed? _____ *(1)*

(ii) Which sodium compound was reacting with the acid? _____ *(1)*

(iii) Name the gas given off. _____ *(1)*

(iv) Draw and label apparatus which you would use to add the acid to the soap powder. Your diagram should show how you would pass the gas through limewater. *(4)*

(v) Why is it sensible to wear gloves when using nitric acid? (3 lines) *(1)*

(b)

Fig. 11.12

(i) From the items above (Fig. 11.12) select **one** which is *not* acidic. _____ *(1)*

(ii) Name **one** which would have a pH value below 7. _____ *(1)*

Soothers

NEW IMPROVED SOOTHERS BRING
30% MORE ACID NEUTRALISING POWER

EACH TABLET CONTAINS: Calcium Carbonate B.P. 534mg.
Magnesium Hydroxide B.P. 160mg.
KEEP OUT OF REACH OF CHILDREN.

'MILK OF MAGNESIA' LIQUID

Shake bottle well before using. Please use
'Milk of Magnesia' within six months
of opening. Each 5ml contains 415mg
MAGNESIUM HYDROXIDE B. P.

BENNIES

Each tablet contains: Calcium Carbonate 680mg.
Light Magnesium Carbonate Ph. Fur. 80mg.
If symptoms persist, consult your doctor.

Fig. 11.13

(iii) Soothers, Bennies and Milk of Magnesia all claim to neutralise acid indigestion.

What is meant by 'neutralise'? _____

_____ *(1)*

(iv) Name the **two** substances produced when Milk of Magnesia reacts with hydrochloric acid.

A _____ B _____ *(2)*

(v) Where in the body might this reaction occur? _____ *(1)*

(vi) If each packet of Soothers contains 12 tablets, what is the total mass of magnesium hydroxide in the packet?

_____ *(1)*

(vii) Imagine some powdered Bennies were accidentally mixed with washing soda. Using your knowledge of the chemical properties of the contents of each, describe how you would separate them. (4 lines) *(4)*

(c)   Study the graph below (Fig. 11.14), which shows the variation of pH in the mouth of a child who only eats at meal times.

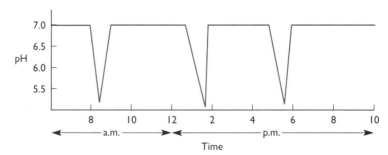

Fig. 11.14

(i)   At what time in the morning does the child start eating?

_____ *(1)*

(ii) Explain what causes the increase in acidity. (3 lines) _____ *(2)*

(iii) What effect will the acid have on the teeth? (2 lines) _____ *(1)*

(iv) For how long after starting each meal does the child's mouth remain acid?

_____ *(1)*

(v) Draw on the graph what would happen if the child ate sweets at 10a.m. *(1)*

(vi) What would be the effect on the acidity in the mouth of continuously eating sweets throughout the day?

(1)

(NICCEA)

Q11 The manufacture of sulphuric acid can be represented by the following flowchart:

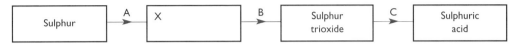

Fig. 11.15

(a) Stage A involves the burning of sulphur.
  (i) Write in the box labelled **X** the name of the main substance formed. *(1)*
  (ii) Write a chemical equation for this reaction.

(1)

(b) Vanadium (V) oxide is a catalyst for the reaction.
  (i) What effect does vanadium (V) oxide have on the reaction?

(1)

  (ii) State **one** other general property of a catalyst.

(1)

  (iii) Sulphur trioxide is not dissolved directly in water at stage C. Describe how stage C is carried out. (3 lines) *(3)*

(c) (i) Sulphur dioxide is produced in most power stations in Britain as part of the waste gases. Explain what effect this gas may have on

  1. living organisms (3lines) _____

  2. buildings (4 lines) _____ *(5)*

  (ii) Suggest a method of removing sulphur dioxide from the waste gases. (3 lines) *(2)*

(London)

Q12 (Foundation Tier) An example of a short, structured question typical of this level. Notice the use of straightforward words of instruction such as 'name' 'what is' 'complete'.

The following news item appeared in the *Daily Mirror* on 16 February 1987.

> TV newsreader Jan Leeming was sprayed with acid when she challenged a gang of muggers in the BBC studios last night.

> The three men sprayed the ammonia-like substance into her face and grabbed her handbag minutes before the 9.10 news bulletin.

There is a mistake in the article because ammonia is not an acid.

(a) Name a suitable indicator which could be used to test if the substance was acid or alkaline.

(1)

(b) What colour would an acid turn this indicator?

(1)

(c) Ammonia is an alkali.
    What colour would ammonia turn this indicator?

(1)

(d) What is the reaction between an acid and an alkali called?

_____   *(1)*

(e) Complete the following equation.

Acid + Alkali = _____ + _____   *(2)*

(Co-ordinated Science, NEAB, WJEC, London)

Q13 Zinc reacts with dilute hydrochloric acid to form a gas which may be collected in the following apparatus.

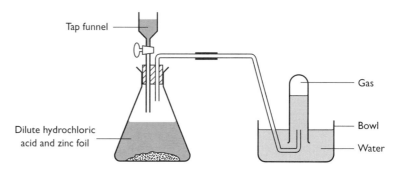

Fig. 11.16

(a) (i) Name the gas formed in the reaction. (1 line)   *(1)*
  (ii) What property of this gas makes it possible for it to be collected by this method? (1 line)   *(1)*
  (iii) How would the first sample of gas collected in the test tube differ from those collected later in the experiment? (2 lines)   *(1)*

(b) Describe and explain how the rate of the reaction will be affected by each of the following changes.
  (i) Using zinc powder instead of zinc foil. (2 lines)   *(2)*
  (ii) Heating the mixture. (2 lines)   *(2)*

(c) After an experiment in which the mixture of zinc and acid had been heated, the apparatus was left set up as shown. As the apparatus cooled, water from the bowl flowed back into the flask.

Explain why this happened. (4 lines)   *(3)*

(d) The experiment was repeated using magnesium instead of zinc.

At the end of the experiment, water again flowed back, even though the flask had not been heated. Suggest why the reaction between magnesium and acid should cause this to occur. (4 lines)   *(3)*

(Combined Science Double Award, London)

EXAMINATION ANSWERS

Multiple choice

A1 Key E, pH14.

A2 Key C, pH7.

A3 Key B, pH4.

A4 Key E, 196g. The solution is 2 M, so it's $2 \times [(2 \times 1) + 32 + (16 \times 4)] = 196$.

A5 Key C, hydrogen. Option A, carbon dioxide, is released when acids react with carbonates.

A6   Key E, water. Option B, hydrogen, is released when acids react with metals, not metal oxides.

A7   Key D, limewater. The gas released by acids and carbonates is carbon dioxide, which turns limewater milky. Option A is the test for oxygen, and option B is the test for hydrogen.

Structured questions

A8   (a)   (i)   pH7;   (ii)   pH9;   (iii)   pH4

(b)   (i)   a measuring cylinder or graduated beaker
(ii)   Most household cleaners are alkaline and would neutralise the acidic Ataka.

A9   (a)   hydrochloric acid

(b)   (i)   a solution that is neither acidic nor alkaline
(ii)   1.   to increase the surface area
2.   to increase the rate of reaction

(c)   (i)   a burette
(ii)   universal indicator
(iii)   purple or blue in solution, green at neutralisation
(iv)   calcium carbonate
(v)   calcium carbonate + sulphuric acid = calcium sulphate + carbon dioxide + water

(d)   (i)   Burney tablets
(ii)   They are a stronger tablet, as more acid is needed to neutralise them.

(e)   1.   to wear safety goggles – to stop any acid entering the eyes
2.   to wear plastic gloves – to stop acid getting on the skin.

A10   (a)   (i)   Soapso
(ii)   sodium carbonate
(iii)   carbon dioxide
(iv)

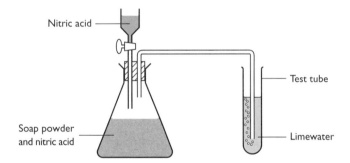

Fig. 11.17

(v)   Nitric acid is corrosive and can burn your skin.

(b)   (i)   bicarbonate of soda (or Milk of Magnesia)
(ii)   lemonade (or vinegar)
(iii)   to remove the acidity
(iv)   A, magnesium chloride; B, water
(v)   in the stomach
(vi)   1,920mg (160 × 12)
(vii)   Calcium carbonate and magnesium carbonate are insoluble, so you could mix with water. The washing soda dissolves but the Bennies contains insoluble substances, so filter and evaporate to dryness.

(c)   (i)   8a.m.
(ii)   drinking an acidic drink, e.g. orange juice
(iii)   attacks the enamel
(iv)   about 1 hour
(v)   The line should dip to pH5.5 after 10a.m., and then rise to pH7.0 by 11a.m.
(vi)   The pH would be about 5.5, slightly acidic all day.

A11 (a) (i)   X is sulphur dioxide

(ii) $S + O_2 \rightarrow SO_2$

(b) (i)   increases the rate of reaction

(ii) it is not used up in the reaction

(iii) sulphur trioxide is dissolved in 98% sulphuric acid, and water is then added.

(c) (i)   1.   can kill leaves on trees, so trees die; can cause breathing problems for humans

2.   causes damages to limestone buildings, as it corrodes the limestone and causes the buildings to crumble.

(ii) to pass the waste gases through an alkali to neutralise the sulphur dioxide.

A12 (a) write the name of any indicator you are familiar with, for example, universal indicator, litmus (1)

(b) these indicators change to red with acid (1)

(c) a blue colour (1)

(d) neutralisation (1)

(e) the rest of the equation should read: salt (1), water (1)

A13 (a) (i)   hydrogen

(ii) it is insoluble in water

(iii) the gas would be mixed with air already in the apparatus

(b) (i)   note here you are asked to 'describe and explain' so one mark will be given for each part of the answer
the rate would speed up/increase
due to increased surface area

(ii) the rate would speed up/increase
as the molecules have more energy and so move faster

(c) as the air/gas inside the apparatus cools it contracts
the pressure is reduced (1)
atmospheric pressure greater (1)
so water is pushed into apparatus (1)

(d) the reaction between magnesium and acid is exothermic/heat is given out (1)
2 more marking points awarded as in (c) (2)

▶ **STUDENTS' ANSWERS WITH EXAMINER'S COMMENTS**

Q1   Judith Harris is an Environmental Health Officer. She took samples of water from the local river. Waste water from the Turbo-Chemical Company flows into the river.

Fig. 11.18

Judith then measured the pH of the water. She found that water from point A had a pH of 7.0 whereas that at point B had a pH of 2.0.

(a)   (i)   What can you state about the river water at A and at B?

The water at B is acidic   *(2)*

'State water at A is neutral'

(ii)   What is likely to have changed the pH value of the water in travelling from A to B?

The outflow pipe   *(1)*

'Yes, but it is the waste water from the pipe which is important'

(b)   The local Environmental Health Regulations state that waste water from factories must have a pH between 7.5 and 9.5. The pH can be increased by adding alkaline substances. Mr Harminder Singh, the works chemist, talked to three of his laboratory technicians about possible substances to be added to the waste water (Fig. 11.19). Some facts about these substances are shown in Table 11.9.

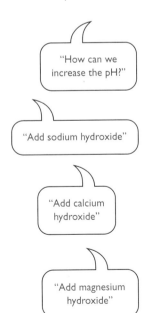

"How can we increase the pH?"

"Add sodium hydroxide"

"Add calcium hydroxide"

"Add magnesium hydroxide"

Fig. 11.19

Table 11.9

Alkaline substance	Solubility at 10°C (g/100g of water)	pH of saturated solution
Calcium hydroxide	0.125	12.0
Magnesium hydroxide	0.070	9.3
Sodium hydroxide	102	14.0

(i)   Which is the most soluble of these alkaline substances, and what is the pH of its saturated solution?

sodium hydroxide ◀   *(2)*

'Yes, and state pH14.0 for the second mark'

(Continued)

(ii) What would be the effect of adding too much calcium hydroxide?

'Good'

The waste water would be too alkaline (1)

(iii) Which saturated solution has the lowest pH?

magnesium hydroxide (1)

'Yes and it has the highest pH'

(iv) Which substance should Mr Singh choose? Why should he choose it?

sodium hydroxide

It is very soluble

(3)

(v) You are provided with several litres of the waste water and the following apparatus and chemicals:

      beakers with a 1 litre mark
      balance
      universal indicator paper
      glass stirring rods
      suitable containers for weighing the chosen substance
      spatula
      chosen substance

Describe how you would find out how much of the chosen substance has to be added to the waste water to increase its pH to about 8.0.

'State: take pH of waste water; use measured volume of waste water e.g. 1 litre; add measured amount of sodium hydroxide; stir to dissolve; record result each time; continue until pH7'

Add some of the substance to the waste water, stir and take the pH.

Add some more until the pH is neutral.

(8)

(London)

Q2

(a) Which **two** of the following substances are needed for iron to corrode (rust) at room temperature?

    A   carbon dioxide
    B   nitrogen
    C   oxygen
    D   sodium chloride (salt)
    E   water

'Good'

C oxygen   E water (2)

(b) The rate at which iron corrodes depends upon the climate and the location. Table 11.10 gives information about the climate and location of cities, and the amount of corrosion that occurs.

(Continued)

Table 11.10

City	Temperature	Amount of moisture in the atmosphere	Location	Rate of corrosion
Birmingham	moderate	moderate	inland	moderate
Bogota	high	high	inland	high
Nairobi	high	low	inland	low
Seattle	moderate	moderate	coastal	high
Singapore	high	high	coastal	very high
Sydney	moderate	high	coastal	high
Vladivostok	low	moderate	coastal	moderate

'Good. You have used the information and selected "low"'

(i)   In which of the above cities is the rate of corrosion the slowest?

Nairobi   (1)

'But in (a) you state water is necessary; so a better answer is that sea coastal air holds more moisture'

(ii) Explain why corrosion is faster at coastal places than inland.

More salt in the air.   (2)

(c)   Figure 11.20 gives more information about different ways of preventing iron corroding.

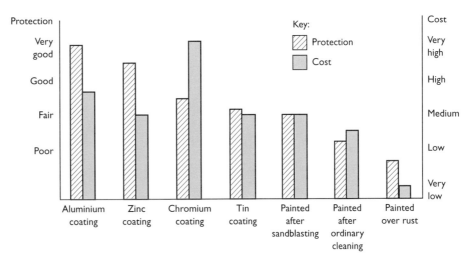

Fig. 11.20

Suggest the most suitable method for protecting an iron bridge in the following cities. Give reasons for your choices.

'Good. You have made 3 points for 3 marks'

(i)   Singapore: *aluminium coating as Singapore has a very high rate of corrosion and this method gives the best protection although expensive.*

'Yes. Include medium cost as well for 3rd mark'

(ii) Birmingham: *tin coating, there is only a moderate rate of corrosion and tin coating is quite good enough.*   (6)

(London)

SUMMARY

At the end of this chapter you should know:

▷ about the **reactions** of metals with **oxygen**, **water** and **acid**;

▷ about the **displacement reactions** that take place between **metals** and **solutions of salts** of other metals;

▷ how a **reactivity series** of metals can be determined by considering these reactions;

▷ how this **reactivity series** can be used to make **predictions** about other reactions;

▷ that **pH** is a measure of the **acidity** of a solution;

▷ about **acidic**, **alkaline** and **neutral solutions**;

▷ about **hydrogen ions**;

▷ how **indicators** are used to classify solutions as acidic, neutral or alkaline;

▷ about **neutralisation**;

▷ some everyday **applications** of neutralisation, e.g. the treatment of indigestion, the treatment of **acid soil**;

▷ how acids in the atmosphere can lead to **corrosion** of metal and **chemical weathering** of rock.

Chapter 12

Electricity

▶ **GETTING STARTED**

Chapters 12 to 18 of this book will take you through the main topics and points needed to cover Attainment Target 4: Physical Processes.

Imagine a day in your life without electricity and you have some idea of how important electricity is to everyone, at home, at school and in offices and factories. Most people come home from school or work in the colder months of the year to a warm, well-lit house, and sit in front of the fire to watch TV, with a cup of tea or coffee. At the same time dinner is being cooked in an electric oven, and an electric washing machine is doing the family wash!

So why do you need to know anything about electricity? Clearly a basic knowledge of how electricity can be used safely and how much it costs and an understanding of electrical circuits can be very important for you in your everyday life, as well as in a Science examination. For example, you may have seen all the decorative lights on the Christmas tree go out, just because of one faulty lamp, but other rows of decorative lights appear to work even though more than one of the lamps may be faulty. You may also have wondered why electricity is transmitted by overhead power cables at very high voltages, when the voltage used at home is only 240V. Is the reason so that every house gets a share of the voltage, or is there a more correct, technical explanation?

TOPIC	STUDY	REVISION 1	REVISION 2
Current			
Voltage			
Current and charge			
Resistance			
Ohm's Law			
Current and voltage			
Mains electricity			
Wiring a plug			
Fuses			
Power			
Paying for electricity			
Electric charge			
Electrolysis			
Electrical symbols			

WHAT YOU NEED TO KNOW

▶ **Current**   *'how to measure current in series and parallel circuits'* [4.1a]

'the current in a series circuit depends on the number of cells and the number and nature of other components' [KS3]

'current is a flow of charge' [KS3]

Electric current is the **flow of charged particles** around a circuit of conducting material such as metals; in solid metal conductors, current is a flow of **negatively charged electrons** from the negatively charged terminal to the positively charged terminal of the electrical supply. However, the conventional direction of current flow is usually shown by an arrow opposite to that of the electron flow.

The **energy** given to the **electrons** to push them round an electrical circuit is **transferred** from electrical sources such as **batteries**, solar cells and generators to **components** in a circuit, such as **lamps**, resistors, bells, motors, LEDs and buzzers; the energy transferred makes things happen in the circuit such as light, heat and sound.

Current is measured in **amperes (amps: A)** by using an **ammeter** in the circuit; the current will depend on the number of components, for example the number of cells (voltage). All circuits should be made from good conductors, such as metals, as these allow the charged particles to pass through easily. Poor conductors, such as wood, make good insulators. Figures 12.1 and 12.2 show you the position of an **ammeter** to measure **current** in a **series** and a **parallel** circuit. The current is the **same** in all parts of a **series** circuit.

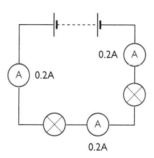

Fig. 12.1 Current in a series circuit

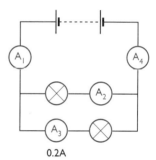

Fig. 12.2 Current in parallel circuits

Figure 12.2 shows two lamps connected in **parallel**. Each lamp glows brightly as it has the total voltage of the battery across it. In this circuit the lamps each take 0.2A (the readings on **A2** and **A3** are **0.2A**). The total current drawn from the battery is 0.4A (the readings on **A1** and **A4** are **0.4A**). The circuit with the current flowing into a junction is the same as the current flowing from the junction.

Advantages of a parallel circuit

▶   If one lamp is faulty the others stay alight. This is useful in wiring decorative lights, for example on a Christmas tree, or along a street. In a series circuit, if one lamp is faulty all the lamps go out.

▶   Most household power sockets are connected in **parallel** with the mains supply so that if one appliance is switched off the others continue to work; each appliance receives the mains voltage of 240V.

Disadvantage of a parallel circuit

▶   The circuit can be more complex to set up and use much more wire, which can be expensive.

▶ Voltage

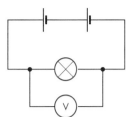

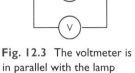

Fig. 12.3 The voltmeter is in parallel with the lamp

'energy is transferred from batteries and other sources to other components in electrical circuits' [4.1b]

'how to make simple measurements of voltage' [4.1e]

The **potential difference (p.d.)** or **voltage (V)** across a component in a circuit is the number of **joules of energy transferred** for each **coulomb of charge** passed.

Voltage is measured in **volts (V)** by using a **voltmeter** which is placed in a circuit in **parallel** with the component where the energy is being transferred as shown in Fig. 12.3. For example, when charge flows through a **lamp**, a voltmeter measures the **change of electrical energy** to **light** and **heat**. The voltage is the **same** across all components connected in **parallel.**

The **volt** is a **joule per coulomb**; the **joule (J)** is a unit of **energy**, for example: a **6V** **power supply** transfers **6 joules of energy** to each **coulomb** of charge:

energy transferred   =   potential difference   ×   charge
(joule, J)   (volt, V)   (coulomb, C)

For example, how many **joules** of electrical energy are changed into light and heat when a charge of **6C** is passed through a lamp which has a p.d. of **12V** across it? 12 × 6 = **72J**

Hint: This formula will be given in the exam paper when you need to use it.

Cathode ray oscilloscope (CRO)

A **CRO** can be used as a **visual voltmeter** for measuring voltage. A bright spot is produced on the oscilloscope screen by a beam of electrons. The vertical position of the spot can be altered by the voltage across the CRO. When the time base control is adjusted the dot moves across the screen and draws a visual graph of the **voltage** against **time**.

Figure 12.4 shows the waveform of a DC (**Direct Current**) supply. The gain control is set at 1 volt/cm and so the supply is positive + 4V DC.

Figure 12.5 shows the waveform of an AC (**Alternating Current**) supply.

The gain control is set at 4 volts/cm, so the spot is deflected 1 cm upwards for every 4 volts across the input terminals. The amplitude of the waveform is 4cm, so the **peak value**

   = 4cm × 4V/cm = 16V.

When a **diode** is placed in the circuit as shown in Fig. 12.6 then the current flows only in **one** direction and **halfwave rectification** occurs.

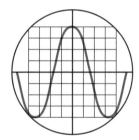

Fig. 12.4 The pattern produced by a DC supply (+4V)

Fig. 12.5 The pattern produced by an AC supply

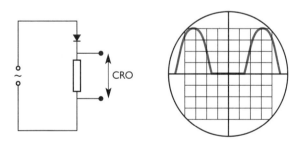

Fig 12.6 The pattern produced when a diode is placed in the circuit

▶ Current and charge

'the quantitative relationship between steady current, charge and time' [4.1p]

When an ammeter measures that **1 ampere** of current is flowing it means that in one second **one coulomb of charge** is passing that point. One coulomb is the amount of charge transported by an electric current of one ampere in one second. It is about the same charge as 6.2×10^{18} electrons.

The relationship between the amount of **electrical charge**, **current** and **time** is shown by:

charge   = current   × time $Q = I \times t$
(coulomb, C)   (ampere, A)   (second, s)

For example, calculate how many **joules** of electrical energy are changed to light and heat when a current of **2A** flows for **20s** through a lamp which has a p.d. of **12V**. First, work out the **charge in coulombs** = 2 × 20 = 40C; second, work out the **joules** = 40 × 12 = **480J**

The amount of current in a circuit depends on the **potential difference** (p.d.) or **voltage**, and the **resistance**.

The **current** in a circuit changes as a result of a change in **resistance**.

▶ Resistance

'resistors are heated when charge flows through them' [4.1c]

'the qualitative effect of changing resistance on the current in a circuit' [4.1d]

Resistance is a force which **opposes** the flow of an electric current so that **more energy** is needed to push the charged particles around the circuit. Resistance is measured in units called **ohms** Ω. A resistor has a resistance of one ohm if a voltage of one volt is required to push a current of one ampere through it. The **higher** the resistance the more voltage is required. Resistance, for example, in the **filament** of a light bulb, the long, thin wires **resist** the flow of electrons so energy is given out as **heat** and **light.** Other examples of the heating effect in resistors include hair dryers, immersion heaters, toasters, ovens and electric fires.

Four factors **increase** the **resistance** of a wire:

1. **diameter**: **thin** wires have **more** resistance than thick wires;
2. **length**: **long** wires have **more** resistance than short wires;
3. **material**: **iron** has **more** resistance than copper;
4. **temperature**: **hotter** wires have **more** resistance than cooler wires.

Resistors

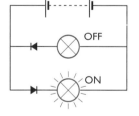

Fig. 12.7 Use of a variable resistor

Adjustable knob

Resistors are simply **conductors** which have a resistance. The value of a resistor is marked by colour bands on the outside which correspond to the value in ohms (Ω). These values can range from millions of ohms to a few ohms.

Resistors are devices which can be used to **control** the **current flowing** in a circuit, by offering **resistance** to the current. A **fixed** resistor is where there is a **constant** value of the resistor. A **variable** resistor (rheostat) is where the resistance can be **changed,** for example by sliding contact along a length of wire to vary the resistance. For example, in a food mixer the control knob can increase or decrease the speed of the mixer (Fig. 12.7). The knob is acting as a **variable resistor** and letting different amounts of current through. When the knob is turned to a **high** setting, the resistance is **decreased** and more current flows to the motor so the speed increases.

Uses of resistors

Variable resistors are used, for example to control the **volume** on a **television set**. In a laboratory a variable resistor can be used as a rheostat to control the current in a circuit, or as a potential divider to control the voltage (potential difference) across a component.

Diodes

Fig. 12.8 Use of a diode in a circuit

A special example of a device which uses resistance is a semiconductor **diode** which has a **high** resistance in **one** direction and a **low** resistance in the **other** direction allowing the current to flow.

Diodes are used to change **alternating** current to **direct** current. The diode only conducts during the part of the cycle when the current is flowing in the forward (positive) direction. This is known as **half wave rectification**. (See voltage above, Fig. 12.6.) Rectification or **smoothing** is necessary for many appliances which use d.c. only, such as **radios** and car battery chargers.

Internal resistance of cells

The **internal resistance** of a cell is the amount of energy that a coulomb of electricity has to use to get through the cell. This means that some of the electrical energy supplied by the cell is converted into heat in the supply and is not converted usefully in the circuit, and so becomes 'lost volts'.

energy available = energy converted externally + energy converted internally

In practice most power packs and batteries have very low internal resistance.

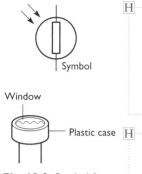

Fig. 12.9 Symbol for an LDR

Thermistor

The **thermistor** is a semiconductor device that changes its resistance as the **temperature** changes. The **resistance** gets **smaller** as it gets warmer. This change can be quite large, but the actual values depend on the type chosen.

The shape and size can vary from a small bead to a rod 10mm long. A large thermistor will obviously take more heat to change its temperature and might be unsuitable as the sensor for a thermometer, but would be stronger and cope with bigger currents.

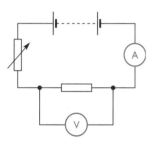

Light Dependent Resistor (LDR)

LDR stands for **Light Dependent Resistor**. It is a resistor that will change its resistance depending on the **brightness of the light** that falls on its window (Fig. 12.9). It will have a **smaller** resistance in **brighter** light. Different types from different manufacturers vary in the amount of charge produced, but one common type varies from a few hundred ohms in bright light to 100kΩ in the dark.

There are many uses for these devices, including **light meters** for photographers and **automatic switches** for security lights outside homes and factories. Usually the rest of the electronic circuit will need an output voltage that changes with the light, and this is often produced by putting the LDR in series with a suitable resistor to form a potential divider.

▶ Ohm's Law

'the qualitative relationship between resistance, voltage and current' [4.1f]

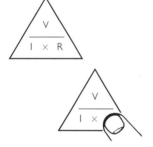

Fig. 12.10 You may have used a circuit like this to investigate Ohm's Law

Figure 12.10 shows a circuit you may have used to investigate Ohm's Law, the relationship between the voltage and the amount of current flowing in a resistor (at constant temperature). **Ohm's Law** states that the **current** passing through a **wire** (or **resistor**) at constant temperature is **proportional** to the potential difference (**voltage**) between its ends (across the resistor). It can be written as $I \propto V$.

For a given potential difference a **high resistance** wire passes a **small current** and a **low resistance** wire passes a **large current**.

Learn the formula:

$$\text{resistance (ohm, } \Omega\text{)} = \frac{\text{potential difference (volt, V)}}{\text{current (ampere, A)}}$$

also written as: **voltage (V) = current (I) × resistance (R) V = IR**

To help you remember this formula learn the triangle shown in Fig. 12.12; cover the unit you want to find to see the formula you need.

For example:

1. Calculate the **resistance** of a lamp when a p.d. of **12V** across it causes a current of 4A; use $R = \dfrac{V}{I} = \dfrac{12}{4} = 3\Omega$

2. Calculate the **p.d.** across a **15Ω** resistor carrying a current of 2A;
    $V = I \times R = 2 \times 15 = 30V$

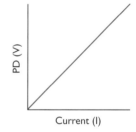

Fig. 12.11 This graph shows the relationship between current and voltage using a resistor in the circuit

Fig. 12.12 A useful way of learning the formula

▶ Current and voltage

'how current varies with voltage in a range of devices including resistors, filament bulbs, diodes, light dependent resistors (LDRs) and thermistors' [4.1g]

The **current** varies with **voltage** in different components, for example: **a resistor** at constant temperature, a **filament lamp** and a **diode**. This relationship is shown by **current-voltage graphs** as shown in Fig. 12.13.

▶   The resistance of a **filament lamp** increases as the **temperature** of the filament **increases**.

▶   The **diode** allows current to pass in **one direction** but current flow is almost zero in the **opposite direction** due to a very **high resistance**.

▶   In a **light dependent resistor** (LDR) the resistance **decreases** as **light intensity** increases, and in a **thermistor** the resistance **decreases** as **temperature** increases.

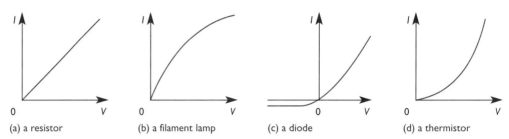

Fig. 12.13 Current–voltage graphs

▶ Mains electricity

'the functions of the live, neutral and earth wires in the domestic mains supply, and the use of insulation, earthing, fuses and circuit breakers to protect users of electrical equipment' [4.1k]

'the use of electrical heating in domestic contexts' [4.1l]

'the difference between direct current (d.c.) and alternating current (a.c.)' [4.1j]

Three key points to remember:

1. The voltage of the **mains electricity** in your home is **240 volts**.
2. The **direction** of flow changes **50 times per second** so its frequency is **50 Hertz**.
3. **Live** and **neutral** wires carry the **mains electricity**, and the insulation around the wires is colour coded so you know which is which.

Mains electricity can be **dangerous** if used incorrectly. A person could receive an electric shock which is sufficient to kill them if basic safety rules are ignored. You should learn some of these essential safety rules:

'Some important safety rules'

▶ always have **dry hands** and keep all electrical appliances and sockets completely dry;
▶ always **switch off** the electricity before putting a plug into a socket or removing a plug;
▶ always **check** that the cable or flex is in good condition and is not worn or damaged;
▶ always use a plug which is **correctly wired** (see Fig. 12.14) with the correct fuse.

Remember:

▶ **alternating current a.c.**: the direction of flow changes 50 times per second – its frequency is 50Hz; in the UK mains electricity is about 230/240V a.c.
▶ **direct current d.c.**: one-way flow; from batteries.

▶ Wiring a plug

Figure 12.14 shows the correct colour code for wiring a three-pin plug.

1. **Live wire: brown:** connected to **live** pin.
2. **Neutral wire: blue:** connected to **neutral** pin.
3. **Earth wire: green and yellow:** connected to **earth** pin to make sure current flows to **Earth** if appliance becomes **faulty**; for example, if the live wire touches part of the metal casing of the appliance; if the earth wire was not connected the current would flow to the person who touched the metal casing.

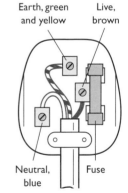

Fig. 12.14 Learn the colour code for the three-pin-plug

▶ Fuses

Each plug needs a **fuse** of the correct rating. The fuse is simply a thin piece of wire which melts and **breaks** the circuit if **too much current** flows. Always use a fuse with a slightly higher rating than the current which flows through the appliance, otherwise you would need to replace the fuse every time you switched on the appliance! To find out the size of the rating of the correct fuse use the following formula:

$$\text{power (W) = voltage (V)} \times \text{current (I)}$$
$$\text{current (I)} = \frac{\text{watts (W)}}{\text{volts (V)}}$$

For example to calculate the current (I) used by a 100W lamp (240V):

$$I = \frac{100}{240} = 0.4A \quad \text{a } \textbf{3 amp fuse} \text{ would be sufficient.}$$

An electric kettle using **8 amps** would require a **13 amp fuse**.

Magnetic (residual) circuit breakers are used instead of fuses as they can be **reset** once the source of the fault is located. **Double insulation** is plastic casing which **insulates** the user from the electric current if the appliance is faulty.

▶ **Power**   *'voltage is the energy transferred per unit charge'* [4.1h]

'the quantitative relationship between power, voltage and current' [4.1i]

The **rate** of **energy transfer (power)** is:

power   = potential difference ×   current;   P = VI
(watt, W)   (volt, V)   (ampere, A)

1 watt is the transfer of **1 joule of energy** in **1 second**; the higher the voltage, the greater the energy transferred for a given amount of charge; for example a lamp on a 240V household supply has a current of 0.25A passing through it, so the power is $240 \times 0.25 = \textbf{60W}$; this means that the lamp is transferring (changing) **60J of energy** into heat and light every second (see the section on Voltage above).

▶ **Paying for**   *'how measurements of energy transferred are used to calculate the costs of using domestic*
electricity   *appliances'* [4.1.m]

'electrical heating is used in a variety of ways in domestic contexts' [4.1.l]

The amount of electrical energy an appliance uses depends on how long it is switched on for and how fast it uses its energy (power). The power is measured in watts or kilowatts (1kW = 1000W). How much you pay depends on:

1.   how many appliances are in use;
2.   how long they are used for;
3.   what the power rating is of each appliance.

The **kilowatt hour (kWh)** is the basic unit used to calculate the cost of buying electricity. 1kWh means that 1kW (1000W) is being used by an appliance for 1 hour and costs approximately 10p.

kWh = power (kW) × time (h)
cost of electricity supplied (p) = **energy transferred** (kWh) × **price** per unit (p/kWh),

▶   An electric fire, rated at 2kW, which is used for 2 hours will use up 4 units or 4 kilowatt hours of electricity. The cost of using the fire for 2 hours is $4 \times 6p = 24p$.
▶   A table lamp, rated at 40W and switched on for five hours, uses 0.04×5 units = 0.2kWh. The cost of using the table lamp is $0.2 \times 6p = 1.2p$.

Energy used   = power   × time
(kilowatt hours)   (kilowatts)   (hours)

▶ **Electric charge**   *'about common electrostatic phenomena in terms of movement of electrons'* [4.1n]

'the dangers and uses of electrostatic charges generated in everyday situations' [4.1o]

Positive and **negative** electrostatic charges are produced on materials by **loss** and **gain of electrons**. There are forces of **attraction** between **unlike** charges and forces of **repulsion** between **like** charges.

Electrostatic charges (static) are generated in everyday situations, for example synthetic fabrics rubbing together. If a charge builds up on an object and causes a voltage (p.d.) between the object and Earth a **spark** can jump across the gap from the object to any earthed conductor and could be dangerous; for example, sparks from car doors to fuel pumps when putting petrol into the petrol tank.

▶ Electrolysis

'about electric current as the free flow of electrons in metals or ions during electrolysis' [4.1q]

Electric current is the free flow of **electrons** in metals or of **ions** during **electrolysis**. The electric current in **molten** or dissolved **electrolytes** is a flow of **negatively charged ions** (anions) to the **positive** terminal (anode) and **positively charged ions** (cations) to the **negative** terminal (cathode).

Electrolysis is one of those topics that comes up in different areas of the syllabus so look at Chapter 7, Ionic and Covalent Bonding and Fig 7.20, and Chapter 8, Extraction of Metals and Fig 8.5.

▶ Electrical symbols

Check you know most of these symbols so you can understand and interpret the components of a circuit diagram.

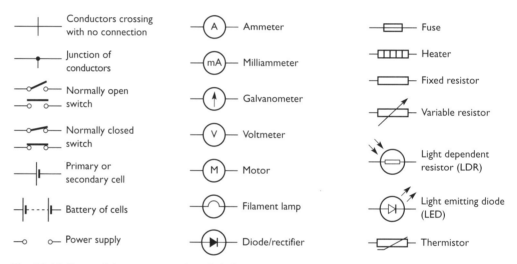

Fig. 12.15 Some of the conventional symbols for circuit diagrams

▶ Some useful definitions

current	a flow of charge, measured in amps
1 amp	1 coulomb of charge per second
voltage	the measurement of the energy of each charge
1 volt	1 joule of energy per coulomb
power	the rate of energy transfer, measured in watts
1 watt	1 joule of energy per second
power	current × voltage $P = I \times V$
resistance	$\dfrac{\text{voltage}}{\text{current}}$
charge	current × time $Q = I \times t$
Ohm's Law	current flowing is proportional to the voltage $I \, \alpha \, V$

▶ **EXAMINATION QUESTIONS**

Multiple choice

Q1 Which one of the following is the symbol for a switch in a circuit?

Fig. 12.16

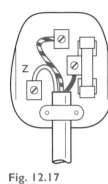

Fig. 12.17

Q2 The diagram (Fig. 12.17) shows a three-core cable connected to a three-pin plug.

What should be the colour of the cable labelled Z?

A blue   D green and yellow
B brown   E red
C green

Q3 Which of the circuits below (Fig. 12.18) would be suitable for measuring the resistance of a lamp?

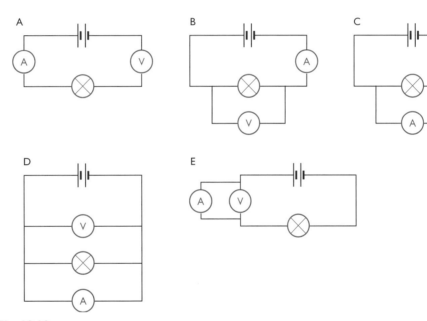

Fig. 12.18

Q4 Which one of the following is a unit of power?

A Ampere   D Watt
B Joule   E Volt
C Newton

Q5 When wiring a house, the switches and fuses should be connected in only one arrangement. This arrangement has:

A switches in the live side and fuses in the neutral
B switches in the neutral side and fuses in the live
C switches and fuses both in the live wire
D switches and fuses both in the neutral wire
E switches and fuses both in the earth wire

Q6   The diagram below (Fig. 12.19) shows a circuit in which one of the lamps is faulty. None of the other lamps in the circuit can work because of the faulty lamp. Which of the lamps is faulty?

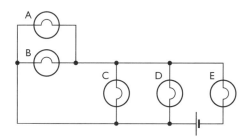

Fig. 12.19

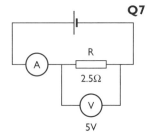

Fig 12.20

Q7   The diagram left (Fig. 12.20) shows a circuit. The resistor has a value of 2.5Ω and the reading on the voltmeter is 5V.

What is the reading on the ammeter?

A   0.5A   D   7.5A
B   2.0A   E   12.5A
C   5.0A

Q8   What is the frequency in Hertz of the mains electricity supplied to your home?

A 13; B 50; C 100; D 240; E 2,500

Q9   What is the cost of using a 2kW fire for 3 hours if a unit of electricity costs 6p per unit?

A 6p; B 12p; C 18p; D 24p; E 36p

Structured questions

Q10   (a)   Decorative tree lights can be arranged in two ways, as shown in the diagrams below (Fig. 12.21).

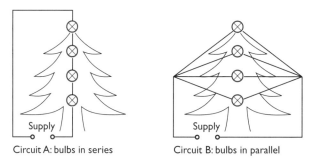

Fig. 12.21

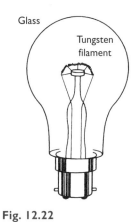

Fig. 12.22

(i) If one bulb blows in each of the circuits, in which circuit will the remaining bulbs stay alight?

_____   *(1)*

(ii) A set of lights has 20 bulbs in series, as in circuit A. Each is a 12V bulb. What is the total voltage required for the set? (2 lines)   *(1)*

(iii) Another set of lights has 20 bulbs in parallel, as in circuit B. The voltage supplied to the set is 240V. What is the voltage across each bulb? (3 lines)   *(1)*

(b)   A diagram of a typical light bulb is shown opposite (Fig. 12.22).

(i) In the light bulb, electrical energy is converted to _____

and _____   *(2)*

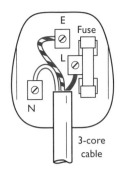

Fig. 12.23

(ii) Suggest **one** property which makes tungsten a suitable metal to use for the filament. _____ *(1)*

(c) The diagram left (Fig. 12.23) shows a three-pin plug.
    (i) What important safety feature, other than the top, is missing?

    _____ *(1)*

    (ii) The fuse used in a plug should be suitable for the appliance connected to it. Using the following relationship,

    Power measured in watts = Current in amps × Voltage in volts

Complete the table. Choose the most suitable fuse from 3A, 5A and 13A. *(2)*

Table 12.1

Appliance	Power rating in watts	Voltage supplied in volts	Current rating of the most suitable fuse in amps
Kettle	3,000	250	
Video recorder	50	250	

(MEG)

Q11 The kilowatt-hour is known as 1 unit of electricity. This is the amount of electricity used by a 1kW appliance in 1 hour. Suppose one unit costs 5p.

(a) What is the cost of using
    (i) a 1kW heater for 2 hours?

    _____ *(1)*

    (ii) a 3kW fire for 10 hours?

    _____ *(1)*

    (iii) a 1,500W iron for 2 hours?

    _____ *(1)*

(b) A student set up the circuit shown in the diagram below and then moved the contact to points **K, L, M, N** in turn.

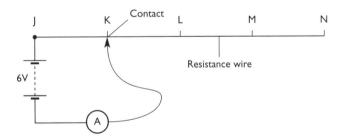

Fig. 12.24

The current was measured by reading the ammeter, and the results are given below.

Table 12.2

Contact made at	K	L	M	N
Ammeter reading	2	1	0.6	0.5

(i) What units are missing from the results table?

_____ *(1)*

(ii) As the wire under test becomes longer what happens to the electric current flowing in the circuit?

_____ *(1)*

(iii) If resistance = $\dfrac{\text{voltage}}{\text{current}}$

what is the resistance of the wire between **J** and **K**?

_____

(1)

(MEG)

Q12 Study the diagram of the hot glue gun (Fig. 12.25), then answer the questions below.

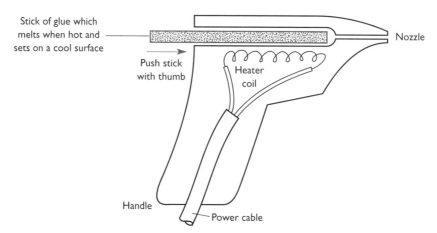

Stick of glue which melts when hot and sets on a cool surface

Push stick with thumb

Heater coil

Nozzle

Handle

Power cable

Fig. 12.25

(a) What happens to the solid stick of glue when the heater coil is switched on?

_____

(1)

(b) What should come out of the nozzle when the glue gun is working?

_____

(1)

(c) For the **wire** in the heater coil and the **wires** inside the power cable compare the following features and properties. Use words from the following list to complete the table below (Table 12.3). You can use the words once, more than once, or not at all.

high   copper   quite thick   none   plastic   low   thin

Table 12.3

Feature/property	Power cable wires	Heater coil wire
(i) thickness		
(ii) electrical resistance		
(iii) covering insulation		

(d) The label on the handle of the glue gun includes the following information:

> **V240**
> **W100**
> AC only 50HZ

(i) State what the following letters from the label stand for:

V_____   W_____

(ii) A battery will not operate this glue gun. Give **one** reason for this, *using information from the label*. (2 lines)

(iii) Name a very common electrical household object which is also rated at 100W.

_____

(3)

(WJEC)

Q13 (a) The diagram (Fig. 12.26) shows a hydro-electric power station.

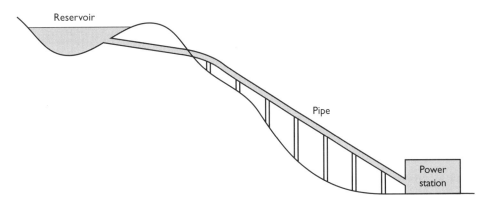

Fig. 12.26

What kind of energy does the water have
   (i) in the reservoir?   *(1)*
   (ii) just before it enters the power station?   *(1)*

(b) Electricity from power stations travels to your home, where it can be used for lighting. The diagram below shows part of a house lighting circuit. Each of the lamps carries a current of 0.25A.

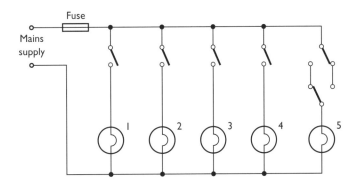

Fig. 12.27

Explain why a fuse of 1 amp is not large enough for this circuit.   *(1)*

(c) Electricity is also used to power appliances such as an electric kettle. Such an appliance is usually rated at 240V, 3kW. Calculate:
   (i) the current through the kettle, using the formula

$$\text{Power (W)} = \text{Voltage (V)} \times \text{Current (A)}$$ *(2)*

   (ii) the resistance of the kettle.   *(2)*
   (iii) the cost of using the kettle for 5 minutes if electricity costs 6p per kWh.   *(3)*
                                                                                                              (MEG)

Q14 (a) Maria's father has read a leaflet which tells him that his electric heating system should cost £400 a year to run. His annual bill totals £650.
Describe **four** ways by which he might save money on heating and still keep his house at a comfortable temperature.   *(4)*

(b) Maria was able to investigate the heating effect of an electric current at school. She used the circuit diagram overleaf (Fig. 12.28) to connect her apparatus.

Using this circuit, Maria took the following readings:

Table 12.24

potential difference V (V)	0	1.0	2.0	3.0	4.0	5.0	6.0	7.0	8.0	9.0
current I (A)	0	0.30	0.68	1.00	1.30	1.55	1.64	1.72	1.78	1.82

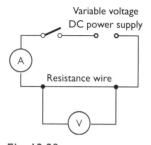

Variable voltage DC power supply

Resistance wire

Fig. 12.28

(i) Use the graph paper provided to plot a graph of potential difference V(V) (*y* axis) against current I(A) (*x* axis). (4)
(ii) Use your graph to find the potential difference when the current is 1.7A (1)
(iii) Calculate the resistance R of the wire at this value. (2)
(iv) Explain what is happening to the resistance of the wire as the current increases. (2)

(c) People often burn themselves on hot electric appliances like fires. Briefly describe how you would treat someone who had burned themselves badly on a hot electric fire.

(2)
(MEG)

▶ **EXAMINATION ANSWERS**

Multiple choice

A1 Symbol A is the switch, B is a resistor, C is a capacitor, D is a lamp and E is a cell.

A2 Key A. The colour should be blue to the neutral pin.

A3 Key B is the correct circuit. In option A the voltmeter is wrongly connected in series. In option C the ammeter is wrongly connected across the lamp. Remember a voltmeter should always be connected across the circuit component.

A4 Key D.

A5 Key C. The switches and fuses should both be in the live wire.

A6 Key E. If any of the other lamps went out the electricity could 'bypass' the fault.

A7 Key B. Use the formula current = voltage ÷ resistance.

A8 Key B. Option D is the mains voltage, not the frequency. Option A is the maximum current of a three-pin plug.

A9 Key E. Remember a kilowatt hour is 1kW for 1 hour. The fire uses 6kW, so the cost is 6p × 6 = 36p.

Structured questions

A10 (a) (i) circuit B (this is the parallel circuit)
(ii) 240V (20 bulbs × 12V = 240V)
(iii) 240V

(b) (i) light and heat
(ii) it has a high resistance and glows when hot

(c) (i) the cable grip
(ii) kettle 13A (current = watts ÷ volts, 3,000 ÷ 250 = 12)
video 3A (current = watts ÷ volts, 50 ÷ 250 = 0.2).

A11 (a) (i) 10p (1kW × 2 × 5p)
        (ii) £1.50 (3kW × 10 × 5p)
        (iii) 15p (1.5kW × 2 × 5p)

     (b) (i) amps or A
        (ii) it decreases
        (iii) 3 ohms (6 volts ÷ 2 amps).

A12 (a) The glue melts and is able to flow.

     (b) liquid glue

     (c) (i) quite thick; thin
        (ii) low; high
        (iii) plastic; none

     (d) (i) V is Volts, AC only 50Hz W is Watts
        (ii) The symbol on the label V 240, means that an alternating current is needed. Batteries only supply direct current, at a much lower voltage.
        (iii) a light bulb.

A13 (a) (i) gravitational potential energy
        (ii) kinetic energy
     (b) each lamp takes 0.25A. There are 5 lamps, so the total current is 1.25A. A 1 amp fuse would blow.

     (c) (i) current = power ÷ voltage
                = 3,000 ÷ 240
                = 12.5A
        (ii) resistance = voltage ÷ current
                  = 240 ÷ 12.5
                  = 19.2Ω
        (iii) cost for one hour is 6p × 3kWh = 18p
             cost for 5 minutes is 18 ÷ 12 = 1.5p

A14 (a) 1. By insulating the roof with insulating fibre material to trap air. Air is a poor conductor of heat.
        2. By double glazing the windows, using a secondary pane of glass to trap air in between the two panes.
        3. By having foam insulation put in the cavity walls.
        4. By draught proofing around doors to prevent cold air coming in and warm air escaping.

     (b) (i)

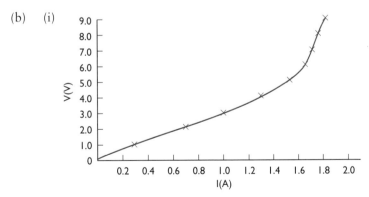

Fig. 12.29 Graph to show heating effect of an electric current

        (ii) 6.4V
        (iii) The resistance is 3.75Ω.
        (iv) As the current increases the resistance increases.

     (c) 1. Place burned area under cold water.
        2. Phone for doctor or take person to doctor or hospital.

A STUDENT'S ANSWER WITH EXAMINER'S COMMENTS

In this question part (d) is targeted at Higher Tier.
The diagram below shows an electric circuit.

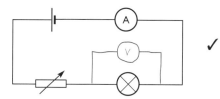

'Good – one mark for the symbol Ⓥ and one mark for the correct position across the lamp'

Fig. 12.32

(a) How could the voltage in this circuit be increased?

by adding another battery ✓   *(1/1)*

'Good'

(b) Add a voltmeter to the circuit in a position where it could be used to measure the potential difference across the lamp.   *(2/2)*

(c) What would happen to the current in the circuit if another lamp was added in series?

it would decrease ✓   *(1/1)*

'Good'

(d) Explain what is meant by the term electrical current.

current is measured by an ammeter. It is pushed round the circuit by

the battery ✗   *(0/2)*

'This is not asked for in the question and this does not explain what current is. The current is a flow of electrons from the negatively charged terminal to the positively charged terminal'

(Total 4/6 marks)
(Co-ordinated Science NEAB, WJEC, London)

SUMMARY

At the end of this chapter you should know:

▷ how to **measure current** in **series** and **parallel** circuits;

▷ that **energy** is **transferred** from **batteries** and other sources to other components in electrical circuits;

▷ that the **current** in a series circuit depends on the number of **cells** and the number and nature of other components;

▷ that **current** is a flow of **charge**;

▷ how to measure **voltage**;

▷ that voltage is the **energy transferred** per unit charge;

▷ the quantitative relationship between **steady current**, **charge** and **time**;

▷ that **resistors are heated** when charge flows through them;

▷ the quantitative **relationship** between **resistance**, **voltage** and **current**;

▷ how **current** varies with **voltage** in a range of devices including **resistors, filament bulbs, diodes, light dependent resistors (LDRs)** and **thermistors**;

▷ the qualitative effect of **changing resistance** on the **current** in a circuit;

▷ the difference between **direct current (d.c.)** and **alternating current (a.c.)**;

▷ the functions of the **live, neutral** and **earth** wires in the domestic mains supply, and the use of **insulation**, **earthing**, **fuses** and **circuit breakers** to protect users of electrical equipment;

▷ the use of **electrical heating** in domestic contexts;

▷ how measurements of **energy transferred** are used to calculate the **costs** of using domestic appliances;

▷ about common **electrostatic** phenomena in terms of **movement of electrons**;

▷ the dangers and uses of **electrostatic charges** generated in everyday situations;

▷ about electric current as the free **flow of electron**s in metals or of ions during **electrolysis**.

13

Electromagnetism

▶ **GETTING STARTED**

When a coil of wire is placed between two magnets, the coil turns when a current is passed through it. This effect was observed by Michael Faraday, who first realised that electric currents also have magnetic fields, just like ordinary magnets. When two magnetic fields interact, then movement can take place. This is the basis of the electric motor which is used in many household appliances, such as a record turntable, a hair drier, a food mixer, a vacuum cleaner and an electric oven fan. These motors have the ability to turn, owing to the **combined** effects of electricity and magnetism.

An electric current, flowing through a coil of wire, has the effect of making the coil act as a magnet, but when an iron bar is put inside the coil an **electromagnet** is made. The iron bar becomes a magnet only when the current is flowing, and so the magnetic effect can be switched on and off. Electromagnets are used in many machines, such as microphones, loudspeakers, radios, televisions and telephones.

TOPIC	STUDY	REVISION I	REVISION 2
Magnets and magnetic fields			
Electromagnets			
Electric motors			
Induced voltage			
Generators and alternators			
Transformers			
Generation and transmission of electricity			

WHAT YOU NEED TO KNOW

▶ **Magnets and magnetic fields**

'the field pattern produced by a bar magnet' [KS3]

'like magnetic poles repel and unlike magnetic poles attract' [4.1r]

The effect of a **magnetic field** around a **magnet** can be shown by using a **plotting compass** to find out which is the **north-seeking** or **N** pole of a magnet. If you place the plotting compass near the end of the magnet, the needle of the compass is **repelled** from the N pole, as shown in Fig. 13.1.

You can also show the magnetic field by shaking **iron filings** around a magnet. The iron filings line up along the **lines of force**. Figure 13.2 shows the pattern produced.

These patterns show the lines of magnetic force. The magnetic field patterns produced between two **attracting** (unlike) poles and two **repelling** (like) poles are shown in Figs 13.3 and 13.4 respectively.

When two magnetic fields come together there is either a force of **attraction** or a force of **repulsion**, and as a result there is a possibility of movement. Magnets are usually made from magnetic alloys, and attract other **magnetic** metals such as iron and steel. Magnets do *not* attract non-magnetic metals such as copper, tin and zinc.

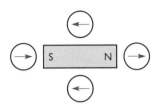

Fig. 13.1 The compass needle is repelled from the N pole of the magnet

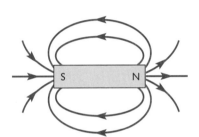

Fig. 13.2 The magnetic field pattern around a magnet

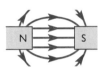

Fig. 13.3 Attraction between unlike poles of two magnets

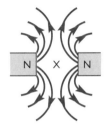

Fig. 13.4 Repulsion between like poles of two magnets

Remember:

▶   **magnets** have a **north** (N) pole and a **south** (S) pole;
▶   **unlike** magnetic poles **attract** (N–S);
▶   **like** magnetic poles **repel** (N–N)(S–S);
▶   a bar magnet has a **magnetic field** around it.

▶ **Electromagnets**

'how electromagnets are constructed and used in devices, e.g. electric bells, relays' [KS3]

A **magnetic field** is produced around a straight **wire** whenever an **electric current** flows through the wire. Plotting compasses or iron filings can be used to show this magnetic effect (see Figs 13.5, 13.6 and 13.7).

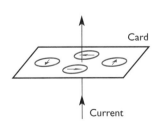

Fig. 13.5 Plotting compasses can be used to show the magnetic field around a current flowing through a wire

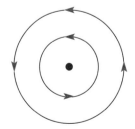

Fig. 13.6 The pattern produced for a single wire carrying current. The current is flowing upwards out of the page.

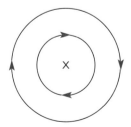

Fig. 13.7 The pattern produced for a single wire carrying current. The current is flowing downwards into the page

These magnetic fields are fairly weak, and the effect can be increased by using a **coil** of wire called a **solenoid.** The coil of wire acts like a **magnet** when an electric current flows through it. A **soft iron bar** placed inside the coil creates a more powerful magnetic effect and becomes an **electromagnet.** The strength of an electromagnet can be increased by:

▶   increasing the **number of turns** on the coil;
▶   increasing the **size of current** flowing through the coil.

Reversing the current in an electromagnet **reverses** the direction of the magnetic field around it.

Figure 13.8 shows the current flowing in a **clockwise** direction around the X end of the core. This end becomes the **south** pole.

When the current flow is **anti-clockwise** then X becomes a **north** pole as shown in Fig. 13.9. So the **polarity is changed** by reversing the current direction.

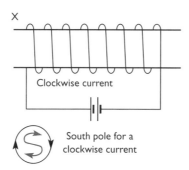

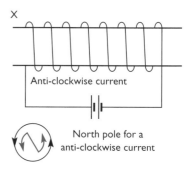

Fig. 13.8 The current flows in a clockwise direction around the X end of the core

Fig. 13.9 The current flows in an anti-clockwise direction around the X end of the core

Electromagnetic relay

A simple application of this principle is in the **electromagnetic relay**, shown in Fig. 13.10. The relay is a simple **switch**, operated by an **electromagnet**, in which a **small input current** controls a **larger output current**. Stages 1 to 4 below describe how it works:

1.   The **input** current causes the electromagnet to become **magnetised.**
2.   The electromagnet attracts a **soft iron armature**, which **closes the contacts** and causes a **greater current** to flow through the output circuit.
3.   The **output** circuit controls a device such as a **motor.**
4.   When the **input** current **stops** then the **output** current is switched **off** and the motor **stops.**

Remember: an **electromagnet** is produced when a soft iron bar is placed inside a solenoid (coil) which has an electric current flowing through it.

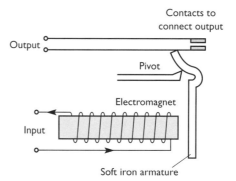

Fig. 13.10 An electromagnetic relay

▶ **Electric motors**   *'a force is exerted on a current-carrying wire in a magnetic field and the application of this effect in simple electric motors'* [4.1s]

Forces on currents in magnetic fields

When an electric **current** is passed through a length of copper **wire** which is placed in the field of a strong **magnet**, the wire **moves at 90°** to the **direction of the magnetic field**. If the **current direction** is reversed, then the **force on the current** is reversed and the wire moves in the opposite direction. The **direction** of force is always at right angles to the **current direction** and the **field direction**, as shown in Fig. 13.11.

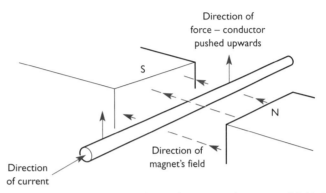

Fig. 13.11 The direction of force is at right angles to the current direction and field direction.

Some people learn this rule by using **Fleming's left-hand rule**, shown in Fig. 13.12.

If the thumb and first two fingers of the left hand are held at right angles to each other, then the **thumb** gives the direction of the **force**, the **first finger** points in the same direction as the **field**, and the **second finger** points in the direction of the **current**.

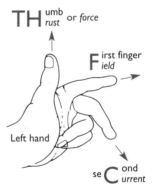

Fig. 13.12 Try this with your **left** hand to learn Fleming's rule for direction of current, field and force

[H]   The **size** of the force can be increased by:

▶   increasing the **strength of the magnetic field**;
▶   increasing the **size** of the **current**.

One important application of this effect is in the **moving coil loudspeaker** (Fig. 13.13).

Moving coil loudspeaker

Figure 13.13 shows the three main sections of the loudspeaker. When an **alternating current** is passed through the coil, the coil is pushed **backwards** and **forwards**, causing the paper cone to **vibrate** and give out **sound waves**. The frequency and amplitude of the alternating current which flows through the coil affect the type of sound produced.

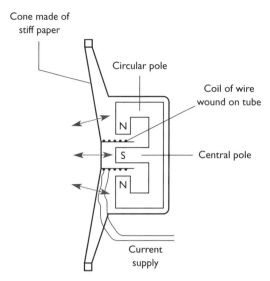

Fig. 13.13 A moving coil loudspeaker

A simple motor

A simple **motor** contains several **coils of wire**, wound on a **core** which is pivoted on an **axle** between two **permanent magnets**, as shown in Figure 13.14.

The coil is connected to a **power supply** by two carbon contacts called **brushes**. These are held in position against two halves of the **commutator**, which is a split ring made of copper. When a **direct current** (d.c.) is passed through the coil, the **magnetic field** created is attracted to the **opposite poles** of the permanent magnets and this causes the coil to **spin** in a **clockwise** direction. When the N and S poles of the coil lie opposite the S and N poles of the permanent magnets, the coil should **stop turning**, but it **carries on spinning** because the two brushes now press against the **opposite** half rings of the commutator. The current now flows in the **opposite direction** and this results in the N and S poles of the coil being **reversed**. The coil then spins round to the S and N poles of the permanent magnets, and once again the current direction is **reversed** as the coil is about to stop.

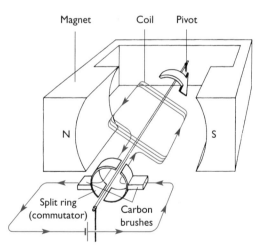

Fig. 13.14 The construction of a simple electric motor

More complex motors

Real motors which are used in everyday **appliances**, such as electric **drills**, **washing machines** and food mixers usually have several coils, each of which may have its own commutator. The purpose of these is to produce a **smoother** and more powerful turning effect, and thereby allow the motor to run more evenly without stopping. The coils are usually wound on a soft iron core, called an **armature**. The effect of this is to increase the strength of the magnetic field.

Remember:

▶ a **magnetic field** is produced by a **current** in (1) a **straight wire** and (2) in a **solenoid** (a coil);

▶ the **d.c. electric motor** is a result of the interaction between the magnetic **force** around a **current-carrying wire** and an external **magnetic field**.

▶ Induced voltage

'a voltage is induced when a conductor cuts through magnetic field lines and when the magnetic field through a coil changes' [4.1t]

Induced current

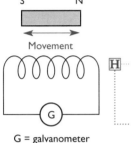

Movement

G = galvanometer

Fig. 13.15

When a **magnet** is **moved in** and **out** of a **coil of wire** which is part of a complete circuit a **voltage** (potential difference) is produced between the ends of the wire. This induced voltage causes a **current** to flow (Fig. 13.15). Similarly a voltage is **induced** when a coil of wire is moved in a **magnetic field**, i.e. the lines of magnetic force are cut by a conductor.

Three factors increase the size of the induced voltage:

▶ how **fast** the magnet or coil is moved;

▶ how **many turns** there are on the coil;

▶ the **strength** of the magnetic field.

Remember: a **voltage** is **induced** when there is relative **movement** between a **conductor** and a **magnetic field** and when the **magnetic field** through a coil changes.

▶ Generators and alternators

'how simple a.c. generators and transformers work' [4.1u]

You may have used a simple **generator** in the form of a **dynamo** to light the lamps on a bicycle. Generators transfer **kinetic** energy to **electrical** energy.

On an industrial scale, generators are used in power stations to supply **mains electricity** (see p. 253). Most generators work on the same principle that a current can be **induced** in a coil by electricity turning it in a **magnetic field**.

There are basically **two** types of generators:

'Generators produce electricity'

▶ **d.c. generators**, which produce one-way direct current.

▶ **a.c. generators** or **alternators**, which produce alternating current, such as those found in power stations and in cars.

H Alternators

'Alternators are generators which produce alternating current'

The **alternating current** is **included** as the coil **rotates** between the permanent magnets. The coil is linked to the outside circuit by two carbon brushes which press against two carbon slip rings which are fixed to the end of the coil, as shown in Figure 13.16 above.

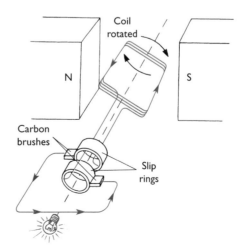

Fig. 13.16 The construction of a simple a.c. generator or alternator

The current can be increased by **four** factors:

1. having **more turns** on the coil;
2. using **stronger magnets**;
3. winding the coil on a soft **iron armature**;
4. rotating the coil at a **higher speed**.

Remember:

▶ electricity can be **generated** by (1) **rotating a magnet** inside a **coil** of wire and (2) by **rotating a coil** of wire in a **magnetic field**;

H··· ▶ this is the principle of an **a.c. generator** (**alternator**) – the rotation of a coil between permanent magnets **induces a voltage** (**p.d.**) which causes a **current** to flow;

▶ **d.c. generator** (**dynamo**) – the rotation of a coil of wire in a magnetic field to produce **d.c.** (one way) current; used to light bicycle lamps.

▶ Transformers

'the quantitative relationship between the voltages across the coils in a transformer and the number of turns in them' [4.1v]

Three important facts to remember:

1. Transformers **change voltage**.
2. Transformers only work on **alternating current**
H 3. Transformers contain an **iron core** and two coils of wire, a **primary coil** and a **secondary coil**.

Figure 13.17 shows a **step-up** and a **step-down** transformer.

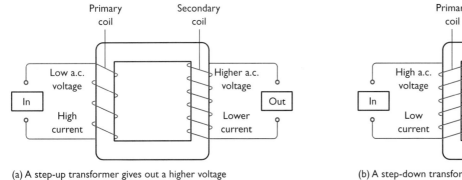

(a) A step-up transformer gives out a higher voltage than the input voltage

(b) A step-down transformer gives out a lower voltage than the input voltage

Fig. 13.17

A **step-up** transformer gives out a **higher** voltage than the input voltage and has more turns on the **secondary** coil than the primary coil. A **step-down** transformer gives out a **lower** voltage than the input voltage, so there are more turns on the **primary** coil than the secondary coil.

When the **primary coil** is connected to an alternating current, it acts like an **electromagnet** which is switched on and off very quickly. This sets up a changing magnetic field in the iron core, which **induces** alternating current in the **secondary coil**.

'Transformers change voltage'

H··· You can calculate the **voltage induced** in the secondary coil using the following formula:

$$\frac{\text{voltage across secondary coil}}{\text{voltage across primary coil}} = \frac{\text{number of turns in secondary coil}}{\text{number of turns in primary coil}}$$

In symbols $\dfrac{V_2}{V_1} = \dfrac{N_2}{N_1}$

For example, if a **step-down** transformer has **100** turns on the **primary** coil and **10** turns on the **secondary** coil, you can calculate the **output** voltage given that the input voltage is **240V**.

$$V_2 = \frac{10}{100} \times 240 = 24V$$

The output voltage is **24** volts.

One of the main uses of transformers is in the National Grid system, where **step-up** transformers **increase** the voltage and **lower** the current so that less electricity is wasted as heat. **Step-down** transformers are used in many household **appliances**, such as **televisions, computers**, radios and washing machines, in order to **reduce** the mains voltage to a **lower** voltage.

Remember: **transformers** contain an **iron core** and two **coils of wire, primary** and **secondary**; when an **a.c. voltage** is applied across the **primary** coil an **a.c. voltage** is **induced** in the **secondary** coil; voltage is either **stepped up** (increased) or **stepped down** (decreased).

▶ **Generation and transmission of electricity**

'how electricity is generated and transmitted' [4.1w]

Using fuels to generate electricity

Fuels such as coal and oil are used in a power station to **heat water** and convert it into pressure **steam**. The steam is then used to **turn** huge **turbines** which spin around and in turn drive a **generator**, causing it to **rotate** very rapidly, at about 50 times per second. It is the **generator** which produces an **alternating current** at a frequency of 50 Hertz. The electricity is generated at a **high voltages** of about 25,000 volts, and it is usually **increased** using a **transformer** to 400,000 volts when it is passed through the overhead transmission lines of the National Grid. The **high voltage** mean that a **low current** is used and, as a result, very **little power is lost** during transmission to people's homes. The voltage is then **decreased** to the 240 volts required for the home.

Any fuel can be used to produce the steam in a power station. In **nuclear** power stations, **nuclear fuel** is used to heat carbon dioxide gas, which in turn converts water into steam.

In power stations the process of generating energy is **inefficient** and some energy is lost to the environment as **heat**. The **efficiency** of the power station can be calculated using the formula

'See Alternative energy sources, pp. 326–329'

'Keeping warm uses energy'

$$\text{efficiency} = \frac{\text{useful energy out} \times 100}{\text{total energy in}}$$

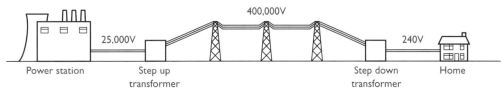

Fig. 13.18 How electricity gets from the power station to your home

Transmission of electricity

Electricity from a power station is **transmitted** across the country by the **National Grid** system. The commonest method is by **overhead power cables**, carried on pylons. Sometimes, **underground transmission lines** are used. The chart below summarises some of the main advantages (A) and disadvantages (D) of each method:

Overhead cables

▶ **cheaper** to install (A)
▶ **easier** to repair (A)
▶ **unsightly** (D)
▶ **dangerous** to people, especially those using kites, moving boats with high masts or carrying fishing rods (D)

Underground cables

▶ more **expensive** to install (D)
▶ more **difficult** to repair (D)
▶ **hidden** underground (A)
▶ **no danger** to people (A)

Electricity is transmitted from power stations at voltages of 400,000V. The reason for using such high voltages is that there is a very **low current** and the **energy loss** is very small. If electricity was transmitted at a lower voltage there would be a greater current, and more energy would be lost as **heat**. A simple model of this situation can be set up in the laboratory, using **12V** to represent a **low voltage** line, and 240V to represent a **high voltage** line. A short piece of high resistance wire is used to represent the actual power lines which are used in the transmission of electricity. Two circuits are set up as shown in Figs 13.19 and 13.20.

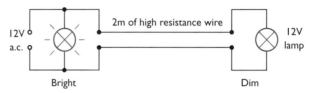

Fig. 13.19 A low-voltage power line

Fig. 13.20 A high-voltage power line

Energy is lost from the low voltage line (Fig. 13.19) as the second lamp glows only dimly. In the high voltage model in Fig 13.20, the second lamp glows very brightly.

The output power equals the input power minus the power loss.

$$P_{OUT} = P_{IN} - P_{LOSS}$$

Power loss is I^2R, so **low** currents therefore **reduce** power **loss**. **Step-down** transformers are used to **reduce** the high voltages used in the transmission of electricity to the 240V which is used in domestic electricity. The reason why alternating current (a.c.) is used in the transmission of electricity is that **transformers** work only on **alternating current**.

Remember: electricity is **transmitted** through power lines in the National Grid at **high voltages** (400,000V) so there is a **low current** and power losses are **reduced**; **step-down transformers** which work only on a.c. reduce the high voltage for domestic use.

▶ **EXAMINATION QUESTIONS**

Multiple choice

Q1 Which one of the following substances is used to make the core of a transformer?
A aluminium; B carbon; C copper; D iron; E steel

Q2 A step-down transformer has 300 turns on the primary coil and an input voltage of 240 volts. The secondary coil has an output voltage of 40 volts. How many turns must there be on the secondary coil?

A 40; B 50; C 100; D 250; E 400

Q3 What is the advantage of using an electromagnetic relay switch in a transistor circuit?

A A large input current controls a small output current.
B A large output current controls a small input current.
C A small output current controls a large input current.
D A small input current controls a small output current.
E A small input current controls a large output current.

Q4 Two bar magnets are placed so that their north poles are 2cm apart. Which of the following diagrams best represents the resulting magnetic field?

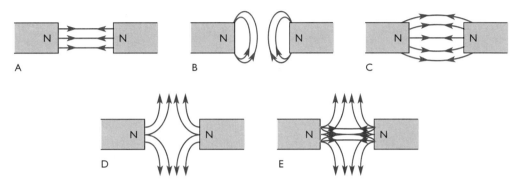

Fig. 13.21

Q5 In the National Grid system, the transmission of electrical energy is by means of overhead conductors. These conducting wires carry

A alternating current at high voltage
B alternating current at high frequency
C alternating current at low voltage
D direct current at low voltage
E direct current at low frequency.

Q6 The circuit below (Fig. 13.22) was set up as shown and connected to an oscilloscope. Which one of the following traces was produced on the oscilloscope screen?

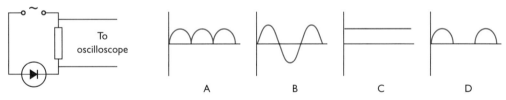

Fig. 13.22

Q7 The diagram opposite (Fig. 13.23) shows a horizontal wire carrying a current, placed between the poles of two magnets.
 In which direction is the force on the wire?

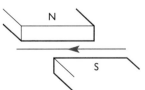

Fig. 13.23

A vertically downwards between the two magnets
B vertically upwards between the two magnets
C the same direction as the current flows in the wire
D from the north pole to the south pole of the two magnets
E from the south pole to the north pole of the two magnets.

Structured questions

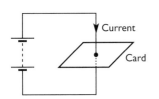

Fig. 13.24

Q8 (a) Some students set up the apparatus shown in the diagram opposite (Fig. 13.24) to show that a current flowing through a wire produces a magnetic field.

   (i) State **two** methods of detecting the magnetic field around the wire that they could have used.

      1. _____   *(1)*

      2. _____   *(1)*

   (ii) Sketch the magnetic field obtained.   *(1)*

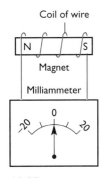

Fig. 13.25

  (b) The teacher then challenged the students to see if they could obtain electricity from magnetism. The students set up the apparatus as shown in Fig. 13.25.

       The apparatus was left lying on the bench but no reading was seen on the milliammeter.

   (i) What should the students do to get a reading on the milliammeter?

      _____

      _____   *(1)*

   (ii) State **two** ways in which they could increase the milliammeter reading.

      1. _____   *(1)*

      2. _____   *(1)*

  (c) A useful application of electromagnetism is the electromagnetic relay which is shown in Fig. 13.26.

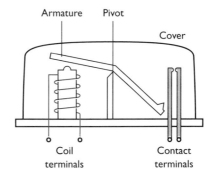

Fig. 13.26

   (i) What is the armature made of?

      _____   *(1)*

   (ii) Describe how the relay works when a current flows in the coil. (3 lines)   *(3)*

   (iii) Explain why relays are used in some electrical circuits. (3 lines)   *(2)*

                                                                      (MEG)

Q9 The diagram (Fig. 13.27) shows a simple motor which has been made by a student in a laboratory.

  (a) Describe what happens when the motor is connected to a DC supply. (2 lines)   *(1)*

  (b) What would happen to the speed of the motor if a resistor was added to the circuit between points X and Y? (2 lines)   *(1)*

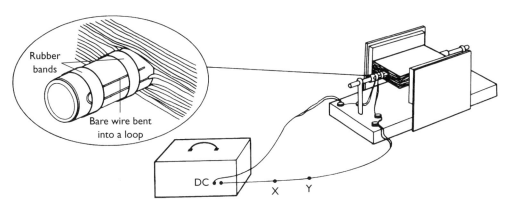

Fig. 13.27

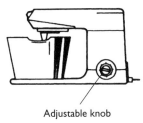

Adjustable knob

Fig. 13.28

(c) Many modern electrical appliances, such as the food mixer shown opposite (Fig. 13.28), have variable speeds.

Explain how turning the knob on the mixer causes the speed of the motor to increase. (4 lines)   *(3)*

(d) Explain the purpose of a commutator in an electric motor. (6 lines)   *(3)*

(e) Why do motors used in electrical appliances usually have at least three commutators and complex coils? (3 lines)   *(2)*

(f) When a tape recording is made, the microphone converts the energy in sound waves into changing electrical currents. Name the electrical device which receives these electrical currents and magnetises the particles on the tape.   *(1)*

(MEG)

Q10 Figure 13.29 shows the main parts of a meter designed to measure electric current. There are two iron bars inside a coil. One bar is fixed and the other is on the end of a pivoted pointer.

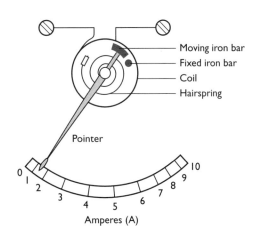

Moving iron bar
Fixed iron bar
Coil
Hairspring

Pointer

Amperes (A)

Fig. 13.29

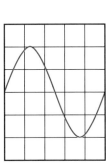

Trace 1

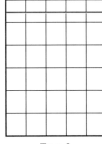

Trace 2

Fig. 13.30

(a) (i) Apart from heat, what will be produced inside the coil when electricity passes through it?

_____   *(1)*

(i) Explain what effects this will have on the two iron bars (6 lines)   *(4)*
Suggest what the hairspring does. (2 lines)   *(1)*

Another way of detecting electric currents is to use an oscilloscope. The diagrams left (Fig. 13.30) show two possible traces on the oscilloscope screen. Explain what each trace represents.

Trace 1 (3 lines)   *(2)*

Trace 2 (3 lines)   *(2)*

Q11 (Higher Tier) In this question notice how parts (a), (b) and (c) can be answered separately so if you are unable to do part (a), go on to (b).

(a) The relay circuit shown in Fig. 13.31 is used to switch on a car starter motor.

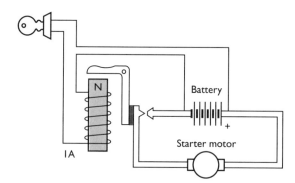

Fig. 13.31

    (i) Explain how this relay works when the key is turned. (6 lines)   *(3)*
    (ii) Name **two** other devices that use an electromagnet.

_____ and _____   *(2)*

(b) Another part of the car electrical circuit is used to light a 12V lamp. A constant current of 3A circulates around the circuit.

    (i) Explain what happens to the energy of the electrons as they flow through the lamp wire. (5 lines)   *(4)*
    (ii) How much energy is converted (used) by the lamp in 20 seconds? (Energy = watts × seconds). (4 lines)   *(2)*
    (iii) If the current flows for 20s, what is the **charge passed** in the circuit during this time? (3 lines)   *(3)*

(c) Explain what is meant by **electromagnetic induction** and state the factors that affect electromagnetic induction when moving a magnet into a coil. (10 lines)   *(6)*

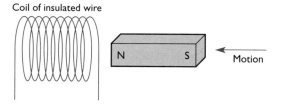

Fig. 13.32

(SEG Science)

▶ **EXAMINATION ANSWERS**

Multiple choice

A1 Key D, iron. The core of a transformer has to become magnetised and demagnetised very quickly. Iron is easily magnetised and loses its magnetism easily.

A2 Key B, 50 turns. The ratio of the input voltage to the output voltage is 6:1. So the number of turns is 300 ÷ 6 = 50.

A3 Key E. In using a relay switch in a transistor circuit, a small input current, such as that triggered by an electron sensor, controls a large output current, such as that used by a motor.

A4   Key D. The poles are both N poles so they repel each other. Option C shows the pattern of attraction which would be produced by two unlike poles.

A5   Key A. The National Grid carries a.c., and high voltages are needed to produce a low current and prevent loss of heat.

A6   Key D. The diode has the effect of half wave rectification.

A7   Key B. The force on the wire is upwards. Remember Fleming's left hand rule. Hold the thumb and first and second finger of the left hand at right angles to each other. The second finger points in the direction of the current, the first finger points in the field direction; and the thumb gives you the direction of movement.

Structured questions

A8   (a)   (i)   1.   iron filings sprinkled on the card
                      2.   a plotting compass placed on the card
              (ii) see Fig. 13.33

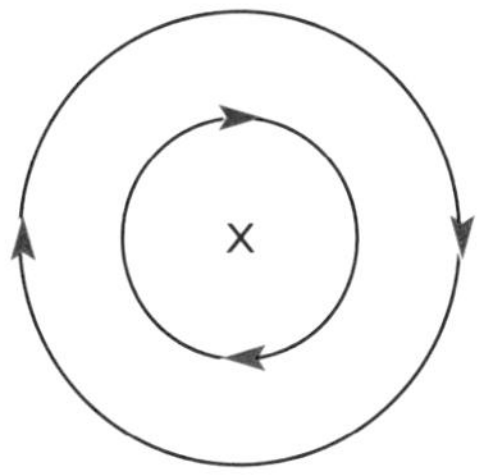

Fig. 13.33

     (b)   (i)   move the magnet in and out of the coil
              (ii) 1. put more turns on the coil 2. use a stronger magnet

     (c)   (i)   soft iron
              (ii) a magnetic field is produced when the current flows in the coil which attracts the armature. As the armature moves, it closes the contacts and completes the circuit.
              (iii) a relay is used because a small current controls a larger current.

A9   (a)   the motor spins

     (b)   the speed would slow down

     (c)   the knob is linked to a variable resistor. As the knob is turned, the resistance is decreased and more current flows, so the motor gets faster.

     (d)   the commutator changes the direction of the current flowing through the coil, so that the coil keeps on spinning.

     (e)   so that the motor is more efficient and runs smoothly

     (f)   an electromagnet

A10 (a)   (i)   a magnetic field
              (ii) The iron bars become magnetised temporarily and repel each other. The moving iron bar is fixed to a pointer, which moves along the scale. The higher the current the further the iron bars repel each other.

     (b)   The hairspring resists the rotation of the coil and prevents the pointer moving off the scale.

     (c)   Trace 1 shows an alternating current. The top of the wave shows the maximum forward current. The bottom of the wave shows the maximum reverse current. Trace 2 shows a direct positive current. The height of the line above the zero can indicate the voltage if the scale is known.

A11 (a)   (i)   When the key is turned the circuit is complete (1)
                   the electromagnet is switched on (1)
                   and attracts the armature (1)
              (ii) any two devices such as a tape-recorder, an electric bell (1)

     (b)   (i)   The electrons flow through the lamp wire due to the potential difference (1)
                   There is resistance to the flow of electrons in the lamp wire (1)
                   Some of the potential energy (1)
                   is transferred to heat and light (1)
              (ii) Energy = volts × amps × seconds (1)
                        = $12 \times 3 \times 20$ (1)

(iii) Q = I × t (1)
    = 3 amps × 20 seconds (1)
    = 60 Coulombs (1)

(c) There are four marks allocated for the explanation.

electromagnetic induction occurs when an electric current is induced (1)
by a changing magnetic field (1)
the size of the current depends on the number of turns on the coil (1)
and the rate of change of the magnetic field (1)

There are two marks allocated for giving this explanation in a logical sequence (1)
and for being precise. (1)

▶ **A STUDENT'S ANSWER WITH EXAMINER'S COMMENTS**

A student was working in a laboratory and needed to produce a 3V AC electrical supply to light a lamp. The only power pack available was set at a fixed output of 12V AC.
   The student drew a sketch of a transformer which could be made from two iron C-cores and some insulated wire.

(a) (i)   How many coils of wire should there be on each C-core?   (2)
    (ii) Explain how you calculated the number of coils on each C-core.   (2)

(b) Draw a diagram to show how the student could use the 12V AC supply, together with two iron C-cores, two lengths of insulated wire and the 3V lamp to produce a 3V supply and light the lamp.   (4)

(c) Explain how an output is produced from the secondary coil of the transformer.   (3)

(d) Why is it necessary to use an AC supply for a transformer instead of a DC supply?   (2)
          (MEG)

'Correct formula'

(a) (i)   *40 on the primary coil, 10 on the second coil*   'Good, over 10 coils used'
    (ii) *using the formula* $\dfrac{V_2}{V_1} = \dfrac{N_2}{N_1}$; $\dfrac{12}{3} = \dfrac{4}{1}$

The ratio of turns is therefore 4:1, so 40 turns on the primary 10 turns on the secondary.

'Clearly explained'

(b)

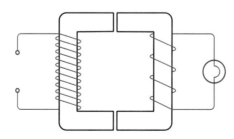

'You understand the circuit and the principle of a transformer. Also correct ratio of turns'

Fig. 13.34

'Good, a detailed account'

(c) *Current flows backwards and forwards through the primary coil, and sets up an alternating magnetic field in the core, which induces a current of the same frequency in the secondary coil.*

'Yes, you have established the main points'

(d) *An alternating current is needed which changes direction to induce an EMF in the secondary coil.*

SUMMARY

At the end of this chapter you should know:

▷ about the **field pattern** produced by a **bar magnet**;

▷ that **like magnetic poles repel** and **unlike magnetic poles attract**;

▷ that a **force** is exerted on a **current-carrying wire** in a **magnetic field** and the application of this effect in simple **electric motors**;

▷ that a **voltage** is **induced** when a **conductor** cuts through **magnetic field lines** and when the **magnetic field** through a **coil** changes;

▷ how **electromagnets** are constructed and used in devices e.g. relays;

▷ how simple **a.c. generators** and **transformers** work;

▷ the quantitative relationship between the **voltages** across the **coils** in a **transformer** and the **number of turns** in them;

▷ how **electricity** is **generated** and **transmitted**.

Force and motion

 GETTING STARTED

Walking, running, swimming, cycling and flying are all ways in which you may have moved at different **speeds**. The speed at which you travel depends on two factors: **how far** you have moved and **how long** it has taken. Light waves and sound waves also travel at **different** speeds, with both waves moving a large distance in a short time.

You have probably experienced **acceleration** when sitting in a car or bus which has started moving and then got faster and faster. You may also have experienced **deceleration** as friction from the brakes caused the car or bus to slow down. Forces are needed to change the **motion** of moving bodies. For instance, you will have worn a seat belt when travelling in a car, or when taking off and landing in an aeroplane.

TOPIC	STUDY	REVISION 1	REVISION 2
Speed and velocity			
Acceleration			
Balanced and unbalanced forces			
Friction			
Vehicle stopping distances			
Forces acting on falling objects			
Force and pressure on solids, liquids and gases			
Moments			

WHAT YOU NEED TO KNOW

▶ **Speed and velocity**

'*how distance, time and speed can be determined and represented graphically*' [4.2a]

'*the quantitative relationship between speed, time and distance*' [KS3]

'*the difference between speed and velocity*' [4.2c]

Speed is the **distance travelled in a unit of time**, such as metres per second, or kilometres per hour.

The formula is:

$$\text{speed (m/s)} = \frac{\text{distance travelled (m)}}{\text{time taken (s)}}$$

For example, a car travels 300km in 6 hours, its average speed = $\dfrac{300}{6}$ = 50km/h.

In the laboratory you may have made measurements to speed using a **ticker-timer**. This instrument is a type of clock which produces 50 ticks every second, equal to 5 ticks every 0.1 second. These ticks appear as dots on a strip of ticker-tape paper, which shows how far the tape has moved between each dot. The time interval between each dot is 0.02 seconds. When the dots are **close** together the tape has been moved **slowly**. When the dots are **far apart** the tape has been moved **quickly**.

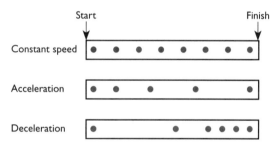

Fig. 14.1 Each piece of ticker tape shows a different type of movement

The ticker tape is usually attached to a moving trolley to study how the trolley moved. The tape shown in Fig. 14.2 was produced by a trolley moving down a runway.

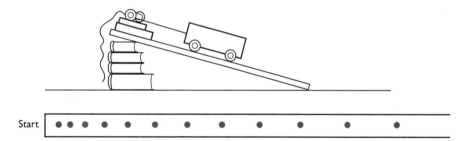

Fig. 14.2 The ticker tape shows how the trolley accelerated

When a long piece of tape is pulled through the ticker-timer, the tape can be cut up into **5-dot lengths**, each representing a time interval of **0.1s** and fixed on to paper as shown in Fig. 14.3.

The velocity for each piece of tape can be found by measuring the distance travelled in 0.1 seconds.

The length of strip 3 is 2.5cm, which means the trolley moved 2.5cm in 0.1s (25cm/s). In strip 4 the distance moved was 3.0 cm in 0.1 second (30cm/s), so the **change in velocity** is 5cm/s in 0.1 second and the acceleration is 50cm/s². The information from ticker tapes can be shown on a **velocity–time** graph.

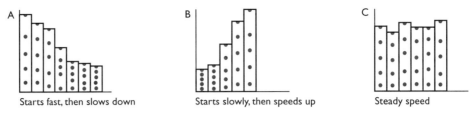

Fig. 14.3 The tape is cut into 5 dot lengths and made into a graph

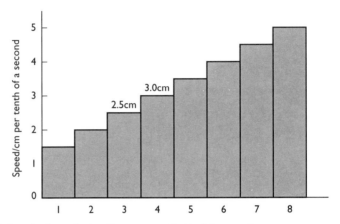

Fig. 14.4 Each length of tape is the distance travelled in 0.1 seconds

Speed is the distance travelled in a unit of time whereas **velocity** is the distance travelled in unit time in a stated direction. **Speed** is a **scalar** quantity and has **magnitude** but not direction; whereas **velocity** is a **vector** quantity (**vv**) and has **magnitude** (size) and **direction**; the direction must be stated, e.g. a force of 20N acting vertically downwards.

The **slope** of a **distance–time graph** represents **velocity**; for example, a car travelling with **uniform velocity** covers equal distances in equal times; on a distance-time graph this is shown as a **straight line** (Fig. 14.5).

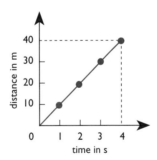

Fig. 14.5 A distance–time graph showing uniform velocity

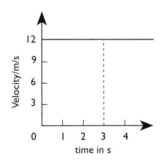

Fig. 14.6 A graph showing constant velocity

On this graph (Fig. 14.5) you can see the car travelled 40m in 4s, so the speed $\frac{40}{4} = 10$m/s

Velocity–time graphs show the **velocity** of a vehicle plotted against **time** (see Fig. 14.6). The **area** under a velocity-time graph measures the **distance travelled**; in the example shown in Fig. 14.6, the distance travelled = $12 \times 3 = 36$m.

Learn the formula:

$$\text{speed (m/s)} = \frac{\text{distance travelled (m)}}{\text{time taken (s)}} \qquad s = \frac{d}{t}$$

▶ **Acceleration**   *'about acceleration as change in velocity per unit time'* [4.2d]

'the quantitative relationship between force, mass and acceleration' [4.2f]

Acceleration of an object is the **change in velocity per unit time** (rate of change of velocity). In other words, the rate at which the speed in a particular direction changes.

H   The formula is:

$$\text{acceleration (m/s}^2) = \frac{\text{change in velocity (m/s)}}{\text{time taken for change (s)}}$$

$$a = \frac{v - u}{t}$$

Figure 14.7 shows a constant acceleration of 3m/s²

$$a = \frac{(12 - 0)}{4} = 3\text{m/s}^2$$

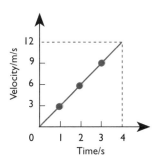

Fig. 14.7 A graph showing constant acceleration

Force and acceleration

When an object is at **rest**, a **force** such as a push or a pull must be exerted on the object to make it **move**. A force is required to make it go faster or accelerate. The **amount of force** required depends on the **mass of the object** and is given by the formula below:

H   force (N) = mass (kg) × acceleration (m/s²)
               F = ma
    or   a = F/m.

The amount of **acceleration** produced depends on **two** factors:

▶   the **size of the force**, measured in Newtons (N);
▶   the **mass of the object**, measured in kilograms (kg)

If the force **doubles**, or the mass is **halved**, then the acceleration is **doubled**. For example, if a force of 15N acts on a mass of 3kg, then its acceleration is 5m/s². If the force doubles to 30N, then the acceleration is 10m/s².

H   Remember:

$$\text{acceleration} = \frac{\text{change in velocity}}{\text{time taken for change}} \quad a = \frac{(v-u)}{t}$$

e.g. for a steady increase in velocity from 30m/s to 60m/s in 5 seconds:

$$\text{acceleration} = \frac{(60-30)\text{ m/s}}{5\text{s}} = 6\text{m/s per second}$$

positive acceleration = **increase** in velocity;

negative acceleration = **decrease** in velocity (**deceleration**).

▶ **Balanced and unbalanced forces**

'that balanced forces do not alter the velocity of a moving object' [4.2e]

'that unbalanced forces change the speed and/or direction of moving objects' [KS3]

'that when two bodies interact the forces they exert on each other are equal and opposite' [4.2g]

When two bodies interact, the forces they exert on each other are **equal and opposite**; this means when object A pulls or pushes object B then object B pulls or pushes object A with an **equal force** in the opposite direction. **Balanced forces** have no effect on the movement of an object; a stationary object will not move, a moving object will continue to move at the same speed and in the same direction.

If the forces acting on an object do **not** cancel each other out then an **unbalanced** force will act on the object. The direction and **size** of the unbalanced force affects the movement of the object:

▶ a **stationary** object will start to move in the direction of the unbalanced force;
▶ an object moving in the **direction** of the force will **speed up** (accelerate), the greater the force the greater the acceleration;
▶ an object moving in the **opposite** direction to the force will **slow down**;
▶ the greater the size of the unbalanced force, the faster the object will speed up or slow down.

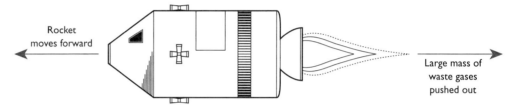

Fig. 14.8 The rocket accelerates due to the force of the gases being pushed out

▶ **Friction**

Friction is a force that **resists motion**. When you **push** an object to start it **moving**, the object will eventually slow down and stop due to the force of friction. The direction of the force of friction is always **opposite** to the direction in which the object is moving. When travelling in a car, friction between the **tyres** and road is essential to allow the tyres to grip the road safely and not to skid about. When riding a bicycle or motorbike, friction is essential between the brake pads and the wheels, and between the wheels and the road.

Energy must be used to overcome friction so there are ways of **reducing** friction as described below

▶ **oil** is used in car engines to reduce the friction of the parts rubbing against each other;
▶ **air** is used in hovercraft to reduce the friction between the boat and the water;
▶ **ball bearings** are used to reduce the friction between the wheel and the axle of a skateboard.

▶ **Vehicle stopping distances**

'about factors affecting vehicle stopping distances' [4.2b]

Friction between surfaces is needed to slow down and stop a moving vehicle. When a car brakes to stop, **kinetic energy** is transferred to the brakes and to the road. The amount of energy transferred is equal to the braking force times the distance taken to stop.

Factors affecting vehicle stopping distance

stopping distance = (thinking distance + braking distance)

'Travelling *twice* as fast needs *four* times the stopping distance'

'See Chapter 17, Kinetic energy, p. 331'

1. **Speed** of the vehicle: if cars A and B have the **same mass** but car A is travelling at **twice the speed** of car B, car A needs **four times** the **stopping distance** of B.
2. **Mass** of the vehicle: if cars A and B are travelling at same speed but car A has **twice the mass** of car B, car A needs **twice** the **stopping distance** of B.
3. **Friction** between the **wheels** and the **road** is important; wet or icy roads have less friction than dry roads.

4. **Friction** between the **tyres** and **brakes** is also essential; smooth tyres and worn brakes have less friction than tyres with a good depth of 'tread' on them.
5. The **reaction time** of the driver is another factor; the 'thinking time' before braking can be affected by concentration, alcohol intake, drugs and tiredness.

▶ **Forces acting on falling objects**

'the forces acting on falling objects' [4.2h]

'why falling objects may reach a terminal velocity' [4.2i]

Weight, mass and gravity

The force which is acting on free-falling objects is the force of **gravity** caused by the Earth's gravitational field. This is described as the **weight** of the object.

weight = mass × gravitational field strength

'See Chapter 17, Power, p. 331'

The weight of an object depends on how far it is from the Earth's centre. The gravitational pull of the Earth is **decreased** the further away an object is, so the weight is reduced. At the Earth's surface, the force acting on **1 kilogram** is **10 Newtons**. Therefore:

the weight of the 5kg mass is $5 \times 10 = 50N$
the weight of the 20kg mass is $20 \times 10 = 200N$

$$\text{acceleration} = \frac{\text{force}}{\text{mass}}$$

$$\text{for the smaller object } a = \frac{50}{5} = 10\text{m/s}^2$$

$$\text{for the larger object } a = \frac{200}{20} = 10\text{m/s}^2$$

(assuming negligible air resistance).

Fig. 14.9 Both the 5kg object and 20kg object would have the same acceleration

Free-fall

An object which is allowed to fall freely near the Earth's surface has a **constant acceleration** of 10m/s^2. For example, if two objects one of 5kg and one of 20kg were dropped from a weather balloon, they would both have the same acceleration. The larger object would need **more force** to accelerate its greater mass.

The **faster** an object moves through a gas or liquid the **greater** the force of **friction** which acts on it. Air resistance **increases** as the speed increases so the acceleration of the object is **reduced**. Air resistance (exerted upwards) equals the weight of the object (acting downwards). The resultant force eventually reaches **zero** and the body falls at constant velocity which is its **terminal velocity**. Factors affecting the terminal velocity are the **shape** of the object (streamlined objects move faster) and **air resistance** (drag), which opposes the motion of a falling object. For example, air resistance allows a **parachute** to slow down a falling sky-diver.

▶ **Terminal velocity**: this is the **constant velocity** reached by falling objects in air and fluids.

Satellites in orbit

The gravitational pull of the Earth provides the pull required to make a satellite follow a circular path around the Earth. For a satellite to orbit just above the atmosphere it needs to orbit at about 8,000m/s. The Moon, a natural satellite of Earth, orbits much further away from Earth at a speed of about 1,000m/s.

Ⓗ Gravitational potential energy

When an object is at a point above the ground it has **gravitational potential energy**. If you hold a book above your desk, the book has gravitational potential energy, equal to the amount of work which you did to lift it to that height, which is given by force × distance moved. On Earth the gravitational field strength is about 10N/kg.

The **gravitational potential energy** of an object is **mgh**, where **mg** is the upward force needed to lift the object, and **h** is the vertical height above the ground.

For example, if the book has a mass of 2kg, and is held 3m high, then:

$$\text{gravitational potential energy} = 2\text{kg} \times 10\text{m/s}^2 \times 3\text{m}$$
$$= 60\text{J}$$

H

▶ **Force and pressure on solids, liquids and gases**

'the quantitative relationship between the force acting normally per unit area on a surface and the pressure on that surface' [KS3]

'how extension varies with applied force for a range of materials' [4.2j]

'how liquids behave under pressure, including simple everyday applications of hydraulics' [4.2k]

'how the volume of a fixed mass of gas at constant temperature is related to pressure' [4.2l]

Pressure

Pressure is the effect of **force on an area**.
The formula is:

$$\text{pressure (Pa)} = \frac{\text{force (N)}}{\text{area (m}^2)} \quad P = \frac{F}{A}$$

The units of pressure are **newtons per square metre** (N/m^2), also called a **pascal** (Pa).

The **same** force acting over a **large** and **small** area will give a **smaller pressure** over the **large** area. The **greater** the force which acts on an area the **greater** the pressure. Large heavy animals such as camels and elephants have feet with a **large surface area** to **reduce** the pressure the animal exerts on the ground. You may be requested to calculate the pressure exerted by a person standing on the ground. For example, a person who weighs 500N stands on an area of shoes of about 250cm².

Therefore the pressure exerted on the floor is:

$$\frac{500}{250} = 2\text{N/cm}^2$$

There are 100×100 centimetre squares in 1m², so the pressure is:

$$2 \times 100 \times 100\text{N/m}^2 = 20\text{kN/m}^2$$

Extension and force

You may have carried out an investigation to study the relationship between the **extension of a spring** and the **force applied** by adding weights to a steel spring which was hanging from a retort stand. You probably measured the length of the spring before starting and as each weight was added, and then calculated the **extension** each time by subtracting the original length from the new length of spring. You may have observed that the spring may have exceeded its elastic limit and not returned to its original shape.

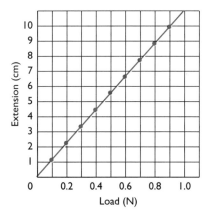

Fig. 14.10 A graph of extension against stretching force

When a force (such as hanging a weight) is applied to metal wire or spring, they stretch or extend. The greater the force, the greater the extension. **Hooke's Law** states that the **extension of the spring** is **proportional** to the **force** applied (provided that the force is not enough to stretch the spring permanently). If the **elastic limit** is exceeded, the spring will not return to its original shape and will be deformed.

Fluid pressure

Remember:
1. pressure increases with **depth**
2. pressure increases with the **density** of the fluid

Practical applications include **hydraulic machines** such as **hydraulic brakes**. These machines use **liquid pressure** to **transfer** a force from one place to another. They work on **three** basic properties of liquids:

1. They are **incompressible**, i.e. liquids cannot be compressed.
2. At the same depth, liquid pressure is the same in all directions.
3. Any change in liquid pressure is **transmitted** instantly to all parts of the liquid.

The diagram (Fig. 14.11) shows the basic principle on which hydraulic brakes and jacks work.

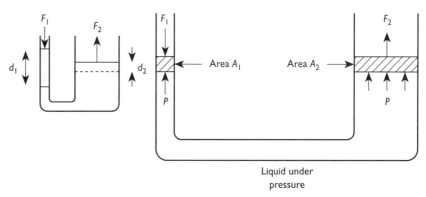

Fig. 14.11 Principle of hydraulic systems

Since A_2 is **greater** than A_1, a **small** force applied at the **smaller** cylinder is multiplied to become a **large** force applied at the **larger** cylinder. Although the force is made greater, energy is still **conserved** and at best work done by F_1 = work done by F_2. In Fig. 14.11

$$F_1 \times d_1 = F_2 \times d_2$$

So if the **force** is increased **10 times**, the **distance** moved is **decreased** in the same proportion.

This is the basic principle behind **hydraulic jacks** and **hydraulic brakes**.

Obviously if **air** entered the hydraulic fluid, the system would not work well since **gases can be compressed** and pressure would **not** be transmitted instantly from one side of the system to the other.

Dam walls are constructed with wide bases to resist the increased pressure at greater depth.

Pressure in gases

The gas laws

The particles in a **gas** are moving very fast. When these particles hit something they exert a **force** on that object. The combined effect of the many millions of particles in a gas acting on an area is its pressure:

Pressure = force per unit area

The pressure of a gas can be **increased** by **increasing its temperature** (heating). The gas particles will have more **kinetic energy** and so will be moving faster and striking the sides of a container harder and more often.

The pressure of a gas can also be **increased** by **reducing the volume** of that gas. The particles in the gas will be closer together, so they will strike the walls of the container more often.

Remember: the volume of a gas is equal to the volume of the container.

These ideas help to explain the '**gas laws**' or 'gas patterns':

'The gas laws'

▶   Pressure α temperature (provided the volume remains the same),
or P/T = a constant.
▶   Pressure α 1/volume (provided the temperature remains the same),
or P × V = a constant

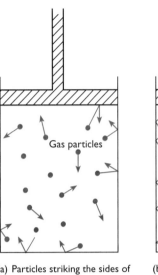
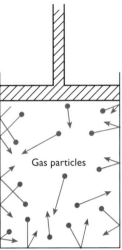
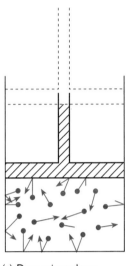
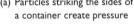

(a) Particles striking the sides of a container create pressure

(b) Increasing temperature increases pressure

(c) Decreasing volume increases pressure

Fig. 14.12

In order to make calculations using these gas 'laws', temperatures are measured on the **Kelvin** scale of absolute temperature, where 0K (Kelvin) is equal to –273° Celsius. 0K is known as **absolute zero**, or the temperature at which particles have **no kinetic energy**.

▶ Moments

'the principle of moments and its application to situations involving one pivot' [KS3]

The **moment** of a force is its turning effect.
The formula for moments is:

moments (Nm) = force (N) × perpendicular distance between the line of action and the pivot (m)

To reach **equilibrium**, when an object is not turning, the **total** moments of forces tending to turn it in **one** direction must be exactly **balanced** by the **total** moments of forces tending to turn it in the **opposite** direction. This can be expressed as:

'The equilibrium condition'

sum of clockwise moments = sum of anticlockwise moments

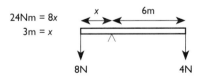

Fig. 14.13 Equilibrium is reached when *x* = 3m

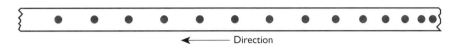

EXAMINATION QUESTIONS

Multiple choice

Q1   During an investigation into how objects move, the ticker-tape sample shown below was produced by a moving model vehicle.

Fig. 14.14

Which one of the following correctly describes how the vehicle moved?

A   got faster and then slowed down
B   steady, constant speed all the time
C   steady, constant speed and then slowed down
D   steady, constant speed and then got faster
E   started slowly and then got faster.

Q2   The graph below (Fig. 14.15) represents the journey of a car

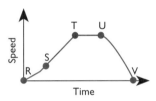

Fig. 14.15

During what part of the journey is the car braking?

A   R-S;   B   S-T;   C   T-U;   D   U-V

Q3   What is the average speed of a vehicle which travels 30 kilometres in 15 minutes?

A   2 km/h;
B   45 km/h;
C   120 km/h;
D   250 km/h;
E   450 km/h

Q4   The graph below (Fig. 14.16) shows how the speed of an object varies with time.

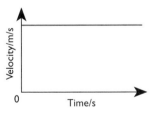

Fig. 14.16

The object is

A   falling freely
B   moving with constant speed
C   moving with constant acceleration
D   moving with constant deceleration.

Q5   The force on a 10kg mass is 25N. The acceleration is

A 0.4ms^{-2} C 25ms^{-2}
B 2.5ms^{-2} D 250ms^{-2}

Q6   Using the pattern

Energy$= \frac{1}{2} \times$ mass $\times$ speed^2

what is the energy of a car of mass 6000kg moving at a speed of 10m/s?

A   6,000J   D   300,000J
B   30,000J   E   600,000J
C   60,000J

Q7   The Moon's gravitational field strength is one sixth that of Earth. An object on Earth has a mass of 60kg and a weight of 600N. What is the mass and weight of the object on the Moon?

	Mass	Weight
A	10	100
B	10	600
C	60	100
D	60	600

Q8   Using the formula

gravitational potential energy = m g h,

what is the gravitational potential energy of an object which has a mass of 5kg and is 6m above the ground?

A 30J; B 50J; C 60J; D 300J; E 600J

Structured questions

Q9   Speed skiers can reach very high speeds by travelling down very steep slopes of snow. Fig. 14.17 shows a speed skier in a ski-run competition.

Fig. 14.17

(a) A drag force acts on the speed skier.
   (i) Explain why it is important for the drag to be reduced for a speed skier. (2 lines)
                                                                                          (2)
   (ii) State and explain **one** way the speed skier tries to reduce the drag. (2 lines)   *(1)*

(b) Figure 14.18 shows the run of the speed skier.

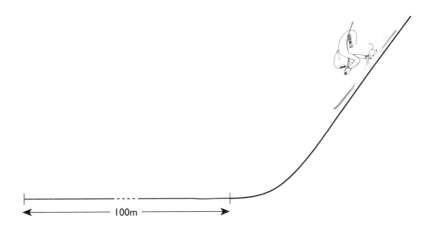

Fig. 14.18

(i) As the speed skier travels down the slope he loses potential energy.
     What happens to this energy? (2 lines)   *(2)*

(ii) The time for covering the 100m was found to be 1.80s.
      Calculate the average speed over this distance. (2 lines)   *(2)*

(c) Speed skiers use skis with a larger surface area than normal skis.
     Suggest an explanation for using these larger skis for a speed skier. (3 lines)   *(3)*

(Combined Science, London)

Q10 Higher Tier. A car of mass 1,000kg starts off from rest at traffic lights, and accelerates away uniformly, as shown in the graph below (Fig. 14.19).

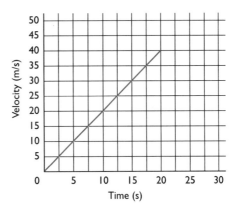

Fig. 14.19

(a) (i) What is meant by 'accelerates'? (2 lines)   *(1)*

(ii) Calculate the acceleration of the car and state the units. (4 lines)   *(3)*

(b) The kinetic energy of a moving body can be found from the pattern

     Energy = $\frac{1}{2}$ mass × (velocity)^2

     Find the kinetic energy of the car at 10 seconds after the start, stating the units.
     (4 lines)   *(3)*

(c) The input energy is produced by petrol burning in the engine. Car engines waste some of this input energy, because not all of it can be converted to kinetic energy.

(i) What is the other main form of energy produced?

                                                                             (1)

(ii) What use can be made of this energy? (3 lines)   *(1)*

The car has an input energy of 400kJ 10 seconds after the start.
The efficiency of the engine is found from the pattern:

$$\text{Efficiency} = \frac{\text{kinetic energy}}{\text{input energy}} \times 100$$

Calculate the efficiency of the engine after 10 seconds. (3 lines)   *(3)*

(d) 20 seconds after the start, the driver of the car puts on the brakes and comes to a stop in 5 seconds.

Force = mass × acceleration

Calculate the braking force, stating the units. (3 lines)   *(3)*

(London)

Q11 (Aimed at Foundation and Higher Tiers)   In this question parts (a) and (c) are common to both tiers. Parts (b) and (d) are only for level H.

The table below gives some details about a jet aircraft, and some information and two equations you will need to use to answer the questions.

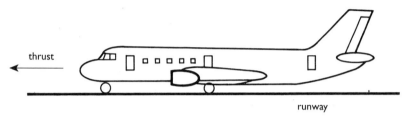

Fig. 14.20

Table 14.1

Maximum take-off mass	= 250t
Maximum take-off thrust force of all the engines	= 670kN
Total thrust force when cruising	= 290kN
Speed at take-off (rotation)	= 90m/s
Cruising speed	= 320m/s
Cruising altitude	= 11,000m
1t = 1,000kg 1kN = 1,000N Kinetic energy = ½ mass × (velocity)² Force = mass × acceleration	

(a) Calculate the acceleration at the start of the take-off when the aircraft is fully loaded. (3 lines)   *(3)*

(b) Calculate the kinetic energy of a passenger of mass 70kg when the aircraft is just about to lift-off. (3 lines)   *(3)*

(c) (i) What is the size of the force which acts against the motion of the aircraft when it is cruising at 11,000m? Give a reason for your answer. (2 lines)   *(1)*
    (ii) Give **two** reasons why the same aircraft flying at a lower altitude, in the same weather conditions, needs more thrust to maintain the same speed. (4 lines)   *(2)*

(d) The diagram below (Fig. 14.21) shows a turbojet used in high-speed passenger aircraft.

Turbojet

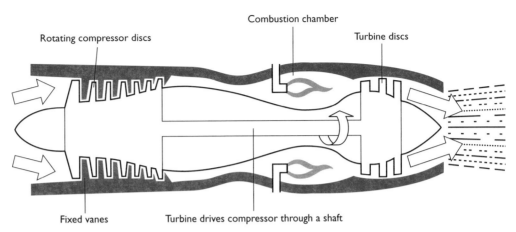

Fig. 14.21
With acknowledgements to *Flight in Focus* (1986), publ. Hobsons (Cambridge)

In the turbojet engine, air enters the front of the jet and is compressed, mixed with fuel and ignited. It then travels out of the exhaust as shown. Explain in terms of momentum **or** a law of forces how the action of the jet engine is able to give the aircraft a forward thrust when the pilot starts the take-off run. (5 lines) *(3)*

(Science Double Award, Modular, SEG/London)

 EXAMINATION ANSWERS

Multiple choice

A1   Key C, constant speed then slowed down. As the dots are not evenly spaced, option B is wrong. The direction the tape is moved indicates that it is slowing down instead of getting faster, so options A, D and E are incorrect.

A2   Key D, U-V. Options A and B show the speed increasing, and option C, region T-U, shows constant speed.

A3   Key C, 120km/h. The catch here is km/h. The distance travelled is for 15 minutes, so multiply by 4 to find the speed in one hour. Option A is for people who divide the 30 by 15 and this is wrong.

A4   Key B. The straight horizontal line shown on the graph represents moving with constant speed.

A5   Key B. Acceleration is force divided by mass, $25 \div 10 = 2.5$.

A6   Key D, 300,000J. Multiply 6,000 by $\frac{1}{2}$, then multiply the answer by 10×10.

A7   Key C. Remember the mass on the Moon stays the same, so it is 60kg. The weight is one sixth, so 600 divided by 6.

A8   Key D, 300J. Multiply $5 \times 10 \times 6$.

Structured questions

A9   (a) (i)   drag slows down the skier/reduces the speed (1)

less drag increases chance of winning competition (1)

(ii) Note: any reasonable statement and explanation would give you two marks; points referring to the skier's crouched position, the helmet, smooth clothing, etc. are all acceptable.
For example: streamline-shaped helmet (1)
so air flows around smoothly (1)

(b) (i)   the skier gains kinetic energy (1)
work done against drag (1)

(ii) $\text{speed} = \dfrac{\text{distance}}{\text{time}} = \dfrac{100}{1.80}$ (1)

$= 55.6$ (m/s)(1)

(c)   the weight of the skier is spread over a greater area (1)
skier does not sink into snow as much (1)
so can go faster (1)

A10   (a)   (i)   The velocity of the car increases.

(ii) $\text{acceleration} = \dfrac{\text{change in velocity}}{\text{time taken}}$

$= \dfrac{20-0}{10}$

$= 2\text{m/s}^2$

$= 2$ metres per second per second

(b)   (The mass of the car is stated above the graph, the velocity can be read from the graph.)

$\text{kinetic energy} = \tfrac{1}{2} \times 1000\text{kg} \times 20^2$

$= 500 \times 400$

$= 200{,}000$ Joules

$= 200\text{kJ}$

(c)   (i) heat energy
(ii) to heat the inside of the car
(iii) $\text{efficiency} = \dfrac{200\text{kJ}}{400\text{kJ}} \times 100$

The efficiency is 50%.

(d) $\text{force} = 1{,}000\text{kg} \times 8\text{m/s}^2$
$= 8{,}000$ newton

A11   (a)   Use the information in the table to convert the figures for mass from tons to kilograms, and the thrust force from kilonewtons to newtons by multiplying by 1000

$\text{acceleration} = \text{force/mass}$
$= 670{,}000/250{,}000$
$= 2.7\text{m/s}^2$ (2 marks with correct unit)

(b)   Higher Tier
use the formula given for kinetic energy
$\text{KE} = \tfrac{1}{2}\,\text{mass} \times (\text{velocity})^2$
$= 0.5 \times 70 \times (90)^2$
$= 283{,}500\text{J}$ (2 marks with correct unit)

(c)   (i) the force which acts against the motion of the aircraft is the total thrust force from the table $= 290\text{kN}$ (1)
(ii) at lower altitude there is more air resistance/drag (1)
net force is smaller for same speed (1)

(d)   Higher Tier
you are given a choice here; you can either answer in terms of momentum or in terms

of action and reaction (Newton's Third Law)

momentum before = momentum after (1)
the change of momentum of exhaust gases must equal
change of momentum forward (1)
change of momentum per second gives forward thrust (1)
OR

action and reaction are equal and opposite (1)
the exhaust gases provide the action force (1)
the reaction force on the jet gives the jet a forward thrust (1)

▶ # A STUDENT'S ANSWER WITH EXAMINER'S COMMENTS

1.   The graph below represents the movement of a car during a short journey.

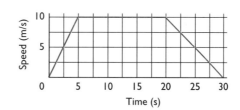

Fig. 14.22

(a) What is happening to the car
    (i)   in the first 5 seconds?

'No, it is better to write:
it has constant
acceleration'   →   *it is speeding up*   (0/1)

    (ii) between 5 seconds and 20 seconds?

'No, the car is travelling at
constant speed'   →   *it has stopped*   (0/1)

(b) How far does the car travel between 5 seconds and 20 seconds?

'it travels at 10 m/s for
15 seconds, 10 × 15
= 150 metres'   →   *15 seconds*   (0/1)

(c) Between 20 seconds and 30 seconds the car comes to rest without the use of
    brakes. Explain how this could happen.

'This is not an explanation
especially as the question
states "without the use of
brakes" a better answer is
"the person takes their
foot off the accelerator"
or "the car is going uphil"'   →   *the person stopped the car*

    (0/1)

'This is a difficult topic'   *(Total 0/4 marks)*
    (MEG)

SUMMARY

At the end of this chapter you should know:

▷ how **distance**, **time** and **speed** can be determined and represented graphically;

▷ the quantitative **relationship** between **speed**, **time** and **distance**;

▷ about factors affecting vehicle **stopping distances**;

▷ the difference between **speed** and **velocity**;

▷ about **acceleration** as **change in velocity per unit time**;

▷ that **balanced forces** do not alter the velocity of a moving object;

▷ that **unbalanced forces** change the speed and/or direction of moving objects;

▷ the quantitative relationship between **force**, **mass** and **acceleration**;

▷ that when two bodies interact the forces they exert on each other are **equal** and **opposite**;

▷ the forces on **falling objects**;

▷ why falling objects may reach **terminal velocity**;

▷ how **extension** varies with applied **force** for a range of materials;

▷ the quantitative relationship between the **force** acting normally per unit area on a surface and the **pressure** on that surface;

▷ how **liquids** behave under pressure, including simple everyday example of **hydraulics**;

▷ how the **volume** of a fixed mass of gas at constant **temperature** is related to **pressure**;

▷ the principle of **moments** and its application to situations involving one pivot.

GETTING STARTED

When you listen to the radio, watch TV, read a magazine, or sit by a fire, you are making use of the different effects of a group of waves known as electromagnetic waves. These waves, together with sound waves, seismic waves and water waves all transfer energy **without** the transfer of matter.

An earthquake is the result of a very large amount of energy travelling through the Earth. This energy can cause great destruction of buildings, roads and bridges, and great loss of life. Waves at sea also carry very large amounts of energy, and research is being carried out into ways in which this energy can be used to generate electricity.

TOPIC	STUDY	REVISION 1	REVISION 2
Characteristics of waves			
The electromagnetic spectrum			
Reflection			
Refraction			
Total internal reflection: critical angle			
The spectrum			
Lenses			
Sound and ultrasound			
The ear			
Interference, diffraction and polarisation			

WHAT YOU NEED TO KNOW

▶ **Characteristics of waves**

'longitudinal and transverse waves in ropes, springs and water' [4.3c]

'waves transfer energy without transferring matter' [4.3g]

'the meaning of frequency, wavelength and amplitude of a wave' [4.3e]

'the quantitative relationship between the speed, frequency and wavelength of a wave' [4.3f]

There are **two** types of waves, **longitudinal** and **transverse**. **Electromagnetic** waves and waves in **water** are examples of **transverse** waves. These are like the waves produced in a piece of rope when it moves up and down as shown in Fig. 15.1.

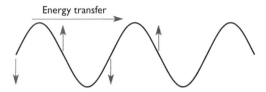

Fig. 15.1 Energy is being transferred along this transverse wave, but the particles only move up and down

Each part of the rope is oscillating up and down, as the **energy** is being transferred along the rope.

Sound waves are the *only* waves which are **longitudinal** waves. These waves are like the waves produced by a **long spring**, as shown in Fig. 15.2. The **energy** is being transferred along the spring, but the particles are oscillating from left to right.

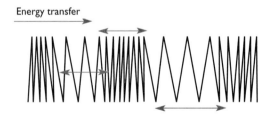

Fig. 15.2 Energy is being transferred along this longitudinal wave, but the particles are oscillating from left to right

Waves transfer energy without transferring matter.

Amplitude and wavelength

The length of each complete oscillation of the wave is the **wavelength**. The **size of the wave** is the **amplitude** as shown in Fig. 15.3.

The distance marked λ (lambda) is the **wavelength**, and is the distance between two troughs or two crests. The distance marked **A** is the **amplitude**, and is the amount by which a particle is displaced up or down.

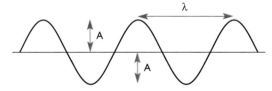

Fig. 15.3 The letter 'A' shows the amplitude of the wave. The letter 'λ' shows the wavelength

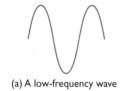

(a) A low-frequency wave

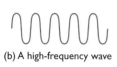

(b) A high-frequency wave

Fig. 15.4

Frequency

The **frequency** of the wave is the number of complete cycles per second, measured in Hertz (Hz). (Imagine standing on a beach and counting the waves as they come towards you. This would give you the frequency of the waves.) Figure 15.4(a) shows a wave with a **low** frequency and **large** amplitude, and Fig. 15.4(b) shows a wave with a **high** frequency and **small** amplitude.

Speed, frequency and wavelength

$$\underset{\text{(in metres per second)}}{\text{Speed (m/s)}} = \underset{\text{(in Hertz)}}{\text{frequency (Hz)}} \times \underset{\text{(in metres)}}{\text{wavelength (m)}}$$

For example, if a wave is travelling with a frequency of 30Hz and has a wavelength of 3m, its speed or velocity is 90m/s. The waves in the **electromagnetic spectrum** all travel at the **same velocity** of 300,000,000 metres per second, or 3×10^8m/s. **Sound waves**, however, travel much more **slowly**, at approximately 330 metres per second. For example, if a sound wave has a wavelength of 0.6m, and travels at 330m/s, its frequency is 550Hz.

$$\text{frequency} = \frac{330}{0.6} = 550\text{Hz}$$

▶ The electromagnetic spectrum

'that the electromagnetic spectrum includes radio waves, microwaves, infra-red, visible light, ultra-violet waves, X-rays and gamma rays' [4.3h]

'some uses and dangers of microwaves, infra-red and ultra-violet waves in domestic situations' [4.3i]

'some uses of radio waves, microwaves, infra-red and visible light in communications' [4.3j]

'some uses of X-rays and gamma rays in medicine' [4.3k]

Waves of the **electromagnetic spectrum** are:

▶ transverse waves with a **range of frequencies and wavelengths**;
▶ waves that all travel at the **same speed**: (300,000,000 metres per second);
▶ waves that travel through **vacuum** (no material medium required);
▶ all produced by changing **magnetic** fields and changing **electric** fields.

Table 15.1 shows the position, relative wavelength and frequency of the different electromagnetic waves.

Table 15.1 The chart summarises the waves of the electromagnetic spectrum

Type of wave	Uses	Source	Wavelength frequency
radio waves	radio communication, television	radio transmitters	long low
microwaves	cooking in microwave ovens, radar, satellite communication	electronic circuits	↑
infra-red waves	electric fires, remote control devices	any hot object	
visible light	electric light, optical fibres	very hot objects	
ultra-violet waves	sunbeds, fluorescent lamps, security devices	glowing gases	
X-rays	in hospitals to photograph bones, at airports to check luggage	X-ray tubes	↓
gamma-rays	kill cancer cells, irradiation of food and equipment	radioactive materials	short high

The different types of radiation have different effects on living cells:

▶ **microwaves** are absorbed by the water in living cells; the **heat** released may damage or **kill** the cells;
▶ **infra-red radiation** is felt as **heat** when it is absorbed by the **skin**;
▶ **ultra-violet (UV) radiation** passes through the upper layers of the skin to the deeper tissues; darker skin absorbs more ultra-violet so that less reaches the deeper tissues;
▶ **X-radiation** and **gamma-radiation** pass through most living tissue although some may be absorbed by the cells; low doses of UV, X-radiation and gamma-radiation can cause cells to become cancerous; higher doses may kill normal cells.

A more detailed look at X-radiation

'See Chapter 18, Radioactivity, p. 342'

X-rays are electromagnetic waves which have a very **short** wavelength between 10^{-9} and 10^{-12} of a metre. They are produced when a beam of high-energy electrons strikes a metal target, such as tungsten. The **penetrating** power of X-radiation depends on the wavelength of the radiation and the type of material the rays fall on. X-rays are able to **pass through** many materials and are used to 'see' through dense objects. For example, at many airports suitcases are passed through an **X-ray machine** to search for any dangerous objects. In hospitals, X-rays are used by a radiographer to identify where **bones** may be broken.

X-rays are also used by scientists to help determine the internal structure of materials such as crystals, and used in industry to show hidden flaws in metal.

▶ Reflection

'waves, including light and sound, can be reflected, refracted and diffracted' [4.3a and d]

'total internal reflection and its use in optical fibres' [4.3b]

When a wave hits a barrier it is **reflected** away from the barrier. If a plane wave hits the barrier at **right angles**, it 'bounces back' along its original path, at the same wavelength, frequency and velocity. If the wave hits the barrier at an **angle**, it is reflected at the same angle away from the barrier, as shown in Fig. 15.5.

The angle of incidence equals the angle of reflection, and the wavelength, frequency and velocity stay the same.

Reflection of light

'Light rays are reflected into your eyes'

You see the world around you because **light rays** are reflected from different objects into your eyes. When you look at yourself in the mirror you see an **image** of yourself reflected in the mirror. Your image appears as far behind the mirror as you are in front of the mirror. The image is described as a **virtual** or **imaginary** image. It is the same way up as you are but the left and right sides are reversed. Figure 15.6 shows how an image is formed by a plane mirror.

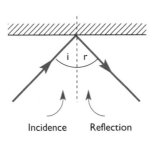

Incidence   Reflection

Fig. 15.5 The angle of incidence equals the angle of reflection

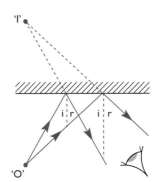

Fig. 15.6 The image 'I' of the object 'O' appears to be behind the mirror

▶ Refraction

Waves travel at a certain speed in air, but when they pass into a different medium, such as water, the speed **slows down**. The velocity of waves will also **decrease** as they pass from deeper to shallower water, i.e. their speed slows down.

Refraction of light

'Refraction is a change in direction'

When light rays cross the boundary from one substance to a different substance their **speed changes** and this may cause a change of direction known as **refraction**. For example, as light rays pass from **air** into **glass**, Perspex or water their speed **slows down**, their **wavelength** becomes **shorter** and their **direction** may be **changed**, unless their direction of travel is along the normal.

If a ray of light enters a glass block at 90°, then it leaves the block in the same direction. It is when the light ray enters **at an angle** that its direction changes, both on entering and leaving the glass.

Light refracts or **bends towards** the normal (an imaginary line at 90° to the glass surface) as it enters the glass, which is more dense than the air. The light ray then refracts or **bends away from** the normal as it leaves the glass and passes into the air, a less dense medium as shown in Fig. 15.7.

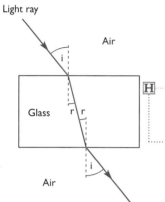

Fig. 15.7 The light ray is bent or 'refracted' as it enters and leaves the glass

Some common effects of refraction

If a thick glass block is placed over some print then the print and the bottom of the glass appear raised. If a stick is placed in water it appears to bend upwards. Both of these effects are due to the refraction of light rays away from the normal as they pass from a denser medium to another less dense medium.

Refractive index

Light is refracted as it enters and leaves the glass block because its speed changes according to the refractive index of the material.

$$\text{Refractive index (n)} = \frac{\text{Speed of light in air}}{\text{Speed of light in material}} = \frac{C_{air}}{C_{medium}}$$

'The greater the refractive index, the more the light is slowed down'

For example, light travels at 300,000km/s in air, but at 200,000km/s in glass. The refractive index of the glass is 3/2.

The greater the refractive index of the medium, the more the light is slowed down.

▶ Total internal reflection: critical angle

When light travels from a denser to a less dense medium, for example, glass to air, there is a strong refracted ray and a weak ray reflected back into the glass (Fig. 15.8(a)). When the angle of incidence reaches a certain **critical angle** of incidence the angle of refraction is 90° (Fig. 15.8(b)). As the angle of incidence is increased then **total internal reflection** occurs and all the light rays are reflected inside the glass block (Fig. 15.8(c)). The critical angle of incidence for glass is about 42° and for water about 48°.

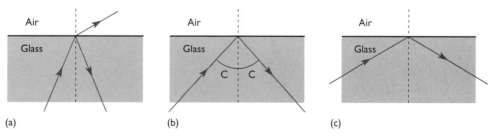

(a)   (b)   (c)

Fig. 15.8

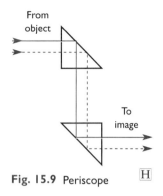

From object

To image

Fig. 15.9 Periscope   H

Periscopes and **optical fibres** are two ways in which total internal reflection is made use of as shown in the diagram (Fig. 15.9)

An optical fibre consists of **two** types of glass (the **core glass fibre** and the **cladding glass fibre**). When light passes through the optical fibre it is continually being **totally internally reflected**, 'bouncing' along the fibre; it does not matter if the fibre is coiled or knotted, the light will still get through. The two types of glass must be very pure, ensuring that this is so is the most difficult part of the manufacturing process.

Optical fibres are now being used instead of copper cable to carry **telephone messages**. The messages are carried as **pulses of light**. Optical fibres are better than copper cables in that they can carry **many more messages** for the same thickness of cable.

Optical fibres allow the rapid transmission of data using digital signals.

▶ The spectrum

White light is made up of **seven** different colours, each of which has a different **wavelength**. When a ray of white light enters a **prism**, each of the different wavelengths is **refracted** or bent by different amounts, because they travel through the prism at different speeds. This effect produces a **spectrum** of all the different colours which make up white light as shown in Fig. 15.10.

'The rainbow effect'

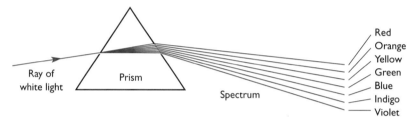

Ray of white light

Prism

Spectrum

Red
Orange
Yellow
Green
Blue
Indigo
Violet

Fig. 15.10 White light is split into a spectrum of colours as it passes through the prism

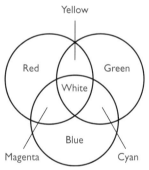

Fig. 15.11 The effect of coloured filters on white light

Coloured light

Red, green and blue are the three **primary colours** which **cannot** be made by mixing any other colours. All the other colours **can** be made from two or three of these primary colours.

When you **mix** two primary colours on a white screen, a new colour, called a **secondary colour** is produced. For example, mixing red and green light produces yellow light. If the third primary colour, blue, is now mixed with the yellow, white light is produced.

Colour mixing of paints

Coloured dyes in paints and clothes **absorb** parts of the spectrum of colours and **reflect** the other colours into our eyes so that we see a particular colour. For example, a red dress absorbs green and blue and reflects red, the colour we see. Green plants look green because the pigment in the leaves absorbs red and blue light and reflects the green.

When two coloured paints are **mixed together**, for example red and yellow, the paint appears to be orange, the colour that is **not absorbed** by either red or yellow. The red paint absorbs green and blue and reflects red and orange. The yellow paint absorbs red and blue and reflects orange, yellow and green. So **both** paints reflect orange.

How coloured pictures are produced on a TV screen

1. When a TV scene is filmed, light enters the camera, and is split into red, blue and green light.
2. These different signals then go to three different 'tubes', which then send out the corresponding signal on ultra-high-frequency waves, to the three electron guns at the back of the TV screen.
3. The electrons hit millions of tiny red, green and blue dots covering the TV screen, which glow when the electrons hit them.
4. Depending on which coloured dots glow, the different colours are produced on the screen.

▶ **Lenses**   There are two main types of lenses; **converging** (convex) and **diverging** (concave) (Fig. 15.12). Both lenses refract (bend) light but diverging lenses cause parallel rays of light to **spread out** (diverge) whereas converging lenses cause parallel rays of light to come **closer together** (converge).

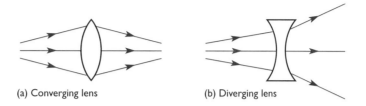

(a) Converging lens   (b) Diverging lens

Fig. 15.12

Focal length

When a convex lens is set up a few centimetres away from a small lamp the **image** of the lamp can be **focused** on a screen. The image is real (it exists in space) and inverted (upside down). If the object is moved closer to the lens, the screen must be moved further away to focus the image (Fig. 15.13).

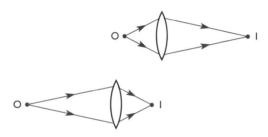

Fig. 15.13

When the object is moved far away, the rays reaching the surface of the lens are almost parallel and the image is formed close to the lens at a point called the **principal focus** (F). The distance from the centre of the lens to the principal focus is the **focal length** (Fig. 15.14).

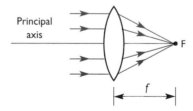

Fig. 15.14

You can **measure** the focal length of a lens by focusing rays from a distant object on to a screen and measuring the distance from the lens to the screen.

Finding the position of the image

If the focal length and the distance of an object from the lens is known, then the position of the image can be found by **scale drawing**. Two rays can be drawn from any point on the object; one ray is drawn parallel to the axis, and then, after it is bent by the lens, it must pass through the principal focus of the lens; the second ray can be drawn so it passes through the centre of the lens without being bent. The image is formed where the two rays meet; as shown in the diagram (Fig. 15.15).

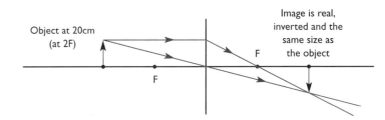

Fig. 15.15

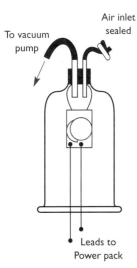

Fig. 15.16

Converging lenses as magnifying glasses

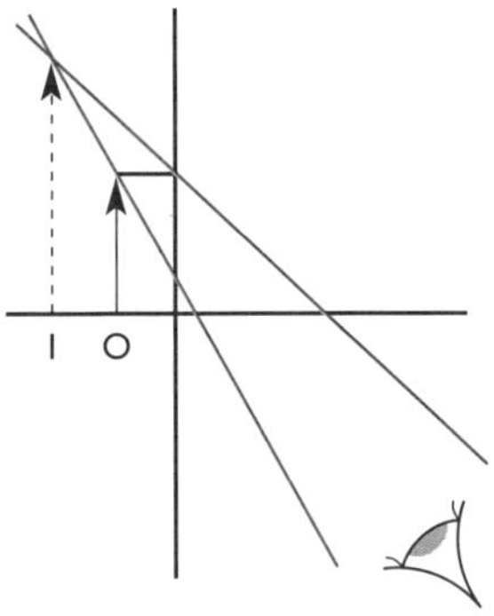

Converging (convex) lenses can be used as a **magnifying glass** if the object is closer to the lens than the focal length, as shown in the diagram (Fig. 15.16).

To the person looking at the object, the light rays appear to come from a point further away, so creating a **large upright image** because the light rays entering the eye are diverging. The image is described as **virtual** because no light rays originate from the image.

Converging lenses are also used in **cameras**, where they produce a small area inverted image; and in **projectors**, where a large real image is projected on to a screen.

▶ Sound and ultrasound

'about sound and ultrasound waves, and some medical and other uses of ultrasound' [4.3l]

Sound waves are **longitudinal waves** produced by **vibrating** sources such as a guitar, the human voice, a bell hitting a gong. Sound requires a substance or **medium** to travel through such as metal, air or water. The **particles** in the medium vibrate with the same **frequency** as the sound and along the same direction as the sound is travelling. The need for a medium can be demonstrated in the laboratory by hanging an electric bell in a glass jar and pumping all the air out of the jar. The bell can be seen to be hitting the gong but no sound can be heard. The sound waves **cannot pass through a vacuum**.

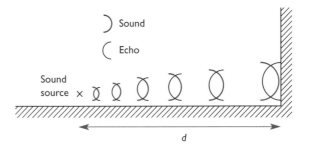

Speed of sound

You may remember a simple experiment you have done to determine the speed of sound. If you stand about 100 metres from a wall and clap your hands together, you can hear the **echoes** of the clapping. If you increase the rate of clapping until the echo corresponds to the next clap, you know that the sound has travelled to the wall and back, a distance $2 \times d$, in the time taken between claps. If you time the interval between 20 claps you can find the time for one interval (t). Knowing the distance (d) from the source of the sound to the wall enables you to find the speed of sound in air $= \dfrac{2d}{t}$.

Fig. 15.17

Fig. 15.18

The speed of sound depends on the material through which it is travelling; for example in **air** the speed is **330m/s**, whereas in sea **water** it is **1,200m/s** and in **steel** it is **2,500m/s**.

The **loudness** of a sound is determined by the size or **amplitude** of the vibrations. A musical note sounds louder if more **energy** is put into producing a note, for example, hitting a drum with more force **increases** the amplitude of the note and it sounds **louder**.

'Loudness depends on amplitude; pitch on frequency'

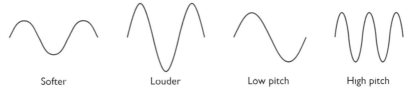

Softer   Louder   Low pitch   High pitch

Fig. 15.19

The **pitch** of a sound is determined by its **frequency**, i.e. the **number** of vibrations per second. A high pitch note has a **high** frequency and a **short** wavelength as shown in Fig. 15.19.

▶ **The ear**   The ear drum detects the **compressions** and **rarefactions** of the air which are caused when sound waves are produced from a **vibrating** source. The vibrations of the ear-drum are passed through the three **small bones** or **ossicles** in the middle ear which amplify the vibration (see Fig. 15.20). The fluid in the cochlea or inner ear then **vibrates** and impulses are passed via the auditory nerve to the **brain**.

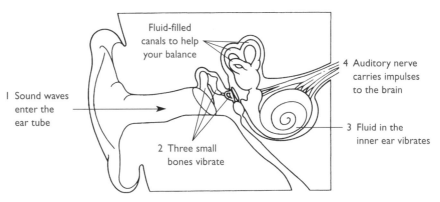

Fluid-filled canals to help your balance

4 Auditory nerve carries impulses to the brain

1 Sound waves enter the ear tube

3 Fluid in the inner ear vibrates

2 Three small bones vibrate

Fig. 15.20 The structure of the ear

Humans can detect sounds within the frequency of about 20Hz to 20,000Hz. The upper limit decreases with age. Sound is measured in **decibels** using a sound meter or decibel meter. One decibel is about the smallest amount of sound you can detect. Very loud noise over 100 decibels can be extremely unpleasant and may be **harmful to your ears**. People who are subjected to noise over 97 decibels for more than 2 hours a day can suffer from temporary or even permanent **deafness**. For example, listening to a personal stereo for several hours at a time can affect your ear-drums and may make you unable to hear higher-frequency sounds.

The harmful effects of noise pollution can be reduced by **double glazing** windows, using **acoustic tiles** to absorb sounds and wearing **ear defenders** when using noisy power tools.

Sound devices

Microphones convert **sound vibrations** into **electrical** vibrations of the same frequencies. The pattern of vibration can then be amplified and sent over long distances by radio waves, along wires or by optical fibres. **Loudspeakers** convert **electrical** vibrations into **sound waves** of the same frequencies.

'See Chapter 13, pp. 249–250'

Resonance

Objects which are able to vibrate or oscillate have their own **natural frequency of vibration.** If the object receives impulses from another vibrating system oscillating at the same frequency then the object can respond by vibrating sometimes at very large amplitudes. This can cause problems say, in a car, if the engine is vibrating at the natural frequency of the metal body work of the car and can cause large vibrations to be set up which weaken the metal.

H *Ultrasonic waves*

Sound waves with frequencies **higher** than 20,000Hz can be produced by **electronic systems**. One of the uses of these ultrasonic waves is in hospitals for **pre-natal scanning of a foetus**. An **image** of the foetus is produced on a screen so that the radiographer can check that the foetus has no abnormalities.

▶ Interference, diffraction and polarisation

Interference

When waves from two or more sources meet, a process known as **interference** takes place. Where two sets of light waves for example have the **same frequency**, **wavelength** and **amplitude** and are in time with each other (in phase) they combine with each other to give a **single wave** of maximum amplitude. This is known as **constructive interference**, and the amplitudes of the individual waves are **added** (Fig. 15.21).

Fig. 15.21 Constructive interference

Sometimes the waves are pushing the medium in **opposite** directions, so that the waves cancel each other. If two opposing 'peaks' (i.e. a peak and a 'trough') arrive at the same place at the same time, the waves are 'out of phase' and the amplitudes of the individual waves are **subtracted**. Indeed equal amplitudes would exactly cancel. This is called **destructive interference** (Fig. 15.22).

Fig. 15.22 Destructive interference

A similar effect can happen with sound waves from two **loudspeakers** in a large room. If the loudspeakers are connected to the same signal generator one can hear areas of '**sound**' and areas of '**silence**' as one moves across the room. The areas of **sound** represent **constructive interference** so the resultant amplitude is **high**. The areas of **silence** represent **destructive interference** so the resultant amplitude is **zero**.

H *Diffraction*

When waves pass through a **small opening** or around the edge of an obstacle they can change the shape of their wavefront so that they spread out from the edges. This effect is known as **diffraction**. The velocity, frequency and wavelength do not change. You may have seen this effect in a ripple tank. As plane waves approach a barrier or pass through a gap they spread out beyond the edges as seen in Fig. 15.23.

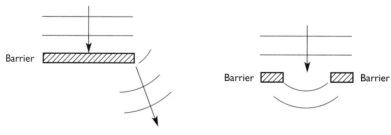

Fig. 15.23

Polarisation

Light is made up of transverse waves with vibrations in all directions at right angles to the direction of travel and is described as **unpolarised**. If a ray of unpolarised light is passed through a polariser then the vibrations are restricted to one direction only and the light is said to be **polarised** in that direction. A common polariser is a material called 'Polaroid' which is a thin transparent film made of sheets of plastics containing minute crystals. 'Polaroid' is commonly used in camera filters and sunglasses to reduce glare. Polarised light has many uses, for example in chemical analysis and in the measurement of stress in materials.

The list below summarises the main points of difference between electromagnetic waves, such as radio waves, and mechanical waves, such as sound waves.

Electromagnetic

- ▶ **transverse** waves
- ▶ travel through a **vacuum,** do not need a material medium
- ▶ travel **very fast** (3×10^8m/s)

Mechanical

- ▶ **longitudinal** waves
- ▶ need a **material** such as air to travel
- ▶ much **slower** speed (e.g. speed of sound in air is 300m/s approx.)

▶ EXAMINATION QUESTIONS

Multiple choice

Q1 Which one of the following is an example of a longitudinal wave?

A infra-red radiation   D sound waves
B microwaves   E X-rays
C radio waves

Q2 The diagram shows the position of the waves in the electromagnetic spectrum.

	microwaves		visible light		X-rays	P

What type of radiation is at position P?
A gamma; B infra-red; C radio; D sound waves; E ultra-violet

Q3 The diagram shows a simple wave form.
Which letter – A, B, C, D, or E – shows the wavelength?

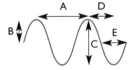

Fig. 15.24

Q4 Which one of the following waves has the longest wavelength and lowest frequency?
A gamma; B infra-red; C radio; D ultra-violet; E visible light

Structured questions

Q5 Waves were produced in a ripple tank as shown in the diagram (Fig. 15.25). A ruler was placed along the edge of the tank.

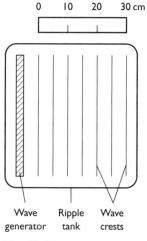

0   10   20   30 cm

Wave   Ripple   Wave
generator   tank   crests

Fig. 15.25

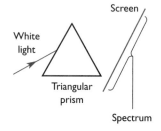

Screen

White
light

Triangular
prism

Spectrum

Fig. 15.26

The wave motion was frozen by a stroboscope set at 7 flashes per second.

(a)   (i)   What is the wavelength of the water waves in cm?

_____   (1)

(ii)   Suggest **two** possible frequencies of the wave motion.

1.   _____   (1)

2.   _____   (1)

(iii)   What would be the effect on the wavelength if the wave generator produced more waves per second?

_____   (1)

(b)   Light is also a wave motion and forms part of the electromagnetic spectrum. The following experiment was set up using white light and a prism.

(i)   Complete the diagram (Fig. 15.26), showing the dispersion and refraction of white light by the prism to form a spectrum.   (3)

(ii)   Show clearly where you would expect to find red light on the screen.   (1)

(c)   (i)   Name the types of radiation that would occur at A and B in the electromagnetic spectrum shown below.

radiowaves
microwaves

A   _____   (1)

visible light
ultra-violet light

B   _____   (1)

γ-radiation

(ii)   Which radiation shown in the spectrum has the shortest wavelength?

_____   (1)

Q6   Ultrasonic waves and X-rays can both be used to examine the interior of the human body.

(a)   Describe how each of them is produced
(i)   X-rays (8 lines)   (5)
(ii)   Ultrasonic waves (2 lines)   (1)

(b)   Explain fully why it is often preferable to use ultrasonic waves rather than X-rays to examine patients. (9 lines)   (6)

(Co-ordinated Science NEAB, WJEC, London)

Q7   (a)   (i)   How are sounds produced by a string instrument such as a guitar? (2 lines)   (2)
(ii)   How does the sound made by a string change if the string is shortened? (1 lines)   (1)
(iii)   The following diagram (Fig. 15.27) represents particles of air.

• • • • • • • • • • • • •
• • • • • • • • • • • • •
• • • • • • • • • • • • •
• • • • • • • • • • • • •

Fig. 15.27

Draw a diagram to show how the particles would appear as a sound wave passes through the air.   (1)

(b) The following diagram (Fig. 15.28) shows details of an ear.

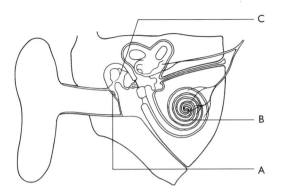

Fig. 15.28

(i)   Label parts A and B.   *(2)*
(ii) Describe **two** functions of the bones at C. (3 lines)   *(2)*

(c) The following diagram (Fig. 15.29) shows two people talking on mobile telephones.

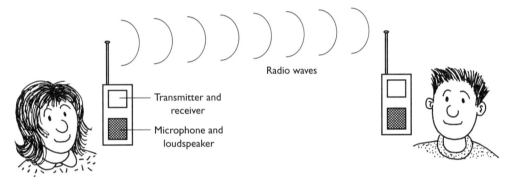

Fig. 15.29

(i)   What is the function of a microphone?

_____ *(1)*

(ii) Radio waves are part of a spectrum of radiations.
      What is this spectrum called?

_____ *(1)*

(iii) The diagram (Fig. 15.30) represents the energy changes which take place when
      the mobile telephones are used.

Fig. 15.30

Complete a similar diagram (Fig. 15.31) to show the energy changes which take place in a
system where the telephones are connected by optical fibres.

Fig. 15.31

(2)

(iv) Show a likely path for a light ray travelling down the following optical fibre.

Light
ray

Fig. 15.32

(d) A radiowave has a frequency of 92MHz and travels at 3×10^8m/s. Calculate its wavelength in metres. (3 lines)   *(3)*

(London)

Q8 (Aimed at Foundation Tier)

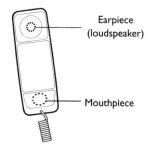

Earpiece
(loudspeaker)

Mouthpiece

Fig. 15.33

(a) (i) The diagram left (Fig. 15.33) shows part of a telephone.
Choose the words from the list in the box below which complete the sentence that follows.   *(2)*

chemical	electrical	gravitational	heat	light	nuclear	sound

The microphone in the mouthpiece changes _____

energy into _____ energy.

(ii) The earpiece contains a loudspeaker. The diagram below (Fig. 15.34) shows a sectional view of a loudspeaker.

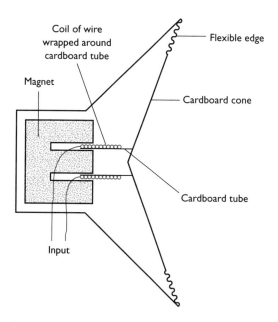

Coil of wire
wrapped around
cardboard tube

Flexible edge

Magnet

Cardboard cone

Cardboard tube

Input

Fig. 15.34

1. When an electric current flows through the wire of the coil the cardboard cone vibrates. Explain why. (4 lines)   *(3)*
2. Explain how the sound produced by the loudspeaker reaches the ear of a listener. (5 lines)   *(3)*

(b) Sound wave patterns can be shown as traces on the screen of an oscilloscope. The diagrams which follow (Fig. 15.35) show traces for two sound waves, **A** and **B**.

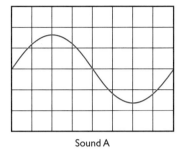 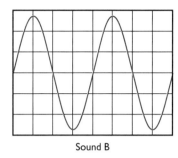

Sound A   Sound B

Fig. 15.35

(i) Which sound wave has the highest pitch? Give a reason for your answer.

Sound wave_____ because _____ (2)
(2 lines)

(ii) Which sound wave is the loudest? Give a reason for your answer.

Sound wave_____ because _____ (3)
(2 lines)

(c) (i) What equation should be used to find the **speed** of a wave from its **frequency** and **wavelength**?

_____ (1)

(ii) A sound wave has a wavelength of 0.25 metres (m). Use your equation to calculate its frequency. The speed of sound is 330 metres per second (m/s). (4 lines)   (4)

(d) Sounds above 20,000Hz are known as ultrasound. Some singers who can sing notes of very high frequencies are supposed to be able to break wine glasses when they make these high notes. People suffer great pain if 'kidney stones' grow in their kidneys. These stones are formed from calcium compounds. Doctors in some hospitals are trying to break up kidney stones using beams of ultrasound focused at the stones. Explain why the ultrasound beam could cause the break up of the kidney stones (4 lines).   (3)

(e) Smoke alarms are designed to produce a sound signal when smoke is detected. The graph below shows the different hearing abilities of a person aged 13 and a person aged 65.

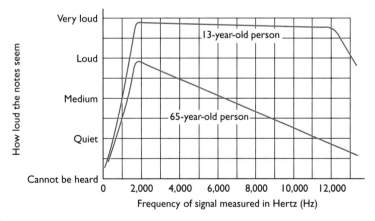

Fig. 15.36

(i) Use the information in the graph to suggest the best frequency for the signal produced by the smoke alarm. Give the reason for your choice.   *(2)*

Frequency _____

Reason _____

_____

(ii) Most smoke alarms set off a sound signal rather than a visual one, such as a flashing light.

(A) Give **four** different advantages of sound signals rather than visual ones. (6 lines)   *(4)*

(B) Explain why an alarm with both sound and visual signals is sometimes necessary. (6 lines)   *(2)*

(Science Double Award, Foundation Tier, SEG)

▶ EXAMINATION ANSWERS

Multiple choice

A1 Key D. Sound waves are the only longitudinal wave on the list, all the others are electro-magnetic waves and are transverse.

A2 Key A. Gamma radiation has a shorter wavelength than X-rays. The position of visible light and microwaves gives you a clue.

A3 Key A. The wavelength is the distance from one crest to another. Option B marks the amplitude.

A4 Key C, radio waves. Option A gamma rays have the shortest wavelength and the highest frequency.

Structured questions

A5 (a) (i) 5cm (measure the distance using the ruler above the diagram)
        (ii) 7Hz, 14Hz
        (iii) The wavelength would decrease.

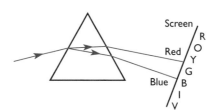

Fig. 15.37

(b) (i), (ii) see diagram (Fig. 15.37)
(c) (i) A infra-red
          B X-rays
     (ii) gamma rays
(d) (i) cooking food
     (ii) sterilising equipment

A6 This question is targeted at Higher Tier and is an example of extended writing. The number of lines available and the number of marks in brackets indicate the length of answer required. You should attempt to make specific points in your answer. Each point should gain one mark.

(a) (i) electrons gain energy (1)
leave heated wire (1)
accelerated by electric field (1)
hit metal target (1)
emit some of their energy as X-rays (1)
(ii) ultrasound is produced electronically (1)

(b) X-rays can damage living cells (1)
may cause cancers (1)
radiographers at risk (1)
X-rays suitable for viewing hard tissue, e.g. bone (1)
ultrasound used for soft tissue, e.g. organs (1)
does not damage living cells, e.g. foetus (1)

A7 (a) (i) the string vibrates (1)
causing vibrations in the air (1)
(ii) a shorter string produces sounds of a higher frequency/pitch (1)
(iii)

Fig. 15.38 (1)

(b) (i) A is the ear-drum/tympanum (1)
B is the cochlea (1)
(ii) the bones transfer vibrations from ear-drum to the oval window
(or: from the outer ear to the inner ear) (1)
the bones amplify the vibrations (1)

(c) (i) convert sound energy into electrical energy (1)
(ii) electromagnetic spectrum (1)
(iii) sound converted to light waves (1)
light waves converted to sound (1)
Note: use the same pattern as in the example given in the question.
(iv) draw straight lines showing the angle of incidence approx. equal to the angle of
reflection (1)
a mark is awarded for showing a large angle (1)

(d) $$\text{wavelength} = \frac{\text{speed}}{\text{frequency}} \quad (1)$$
$$= \frac{300,000,000}{92,000,000} \quad (1)$$
$$= 3.26 \text{ metres} \quad (1)$$

A8 (a) (i) In the mouthpiece sound energy (1) is changed into electrical energy (1).
Note: in the earpiece electrical energy would be changed into sound energy.
(ii) 1. The cardboard cone vibrates because the coil of wire becomes an electromagnet (1); the coil is in a magnetic field (1); interaction between the two
magnetic fields causes movement/attraction/repulsion (1).
2. The molecules of air vibrate (1); energy is passed on (1); mention of compressions where molecules are closer together or rarefactions where molecules are
further apart (1).

(b) (i) Sound wave B (1) has the highest pitch because it has a higher frequency (1)
(ii) Sound wave B (1) is the loudest because it has the highest amplitude (1)

(c) (i) speed = frequency × wavelength (1)
(ii) 330 = frequency × 0.25 (1)
frequency = speed/wavelength
= 330/0.25 (1)
= 1,320Hz (2) if units missing then (1)
Note: if you do not show your working here you would gain only 2 marks
instead of 4.

(d) This uses the principle of resonance (1); the frequency of the ultrasound waves should match the natural frequency of the stones (1); so the stones break up or disintegrate (1).

(e) (i) the best frequency is 2,000Hz (1)
          the sound seems loudest for both age groups (1)
     (ii) A   Note the question asks for four points;
               possible answers here might include
           1. you would be woken up by a sound if you were asleep
           2. you can hear a sound even if the door is closed
           3. sound travels through dense smoke
           4. people outside the house can hear the sound
           B   People who are deaf or who work where it is noisy (1) can see the visual signal (1)

▶ **A STUDENT'S ANSWER WITH EXAMINER'S COMMENTS**

(a) The diagram below shows an observer in an underground shelter.

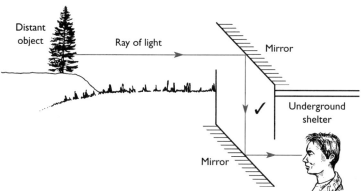

'Good. Right angles and arrows'

Fig. 15.39

(i)   Complete the ray of light from the object to the observer's eye.
(ii) Suggest another use for such an arrangement of mirrors.

     in a submarine ✓

'Yes, but state "periscope" and "to see the surface of the sea"'

                                                                    (2)

(b) (i) Complete the path of the ray in the diagram below.

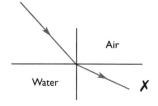

'No, the light ray bends towards the "normal"'

Fig. 15.40

(ii) Explain what is happening.

     the light ray bends away from the normal. ✗

'No, incorrect. As the light is entering a denser medium, it bends towards the normal'

(iii) What is the name given to this effect?

     Bending of light. ✗   (3)

'Refraction is the word required'

                                                          (Continued)

(c) (i) Complete the diagram below to show dispersion of white light as it passes through a prism.

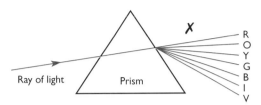

'Oh dear! See Fig. 15.10. The ray of light is split as it enters the prism'

Ray of light   Prism

Fig. 15.41

(ii) Visible light is part of the electromagnetic spectrum. Place the following in order of *increasing* wavelength:

radio waves, infra-red, visible light, X-rays

Shortest wavelength:

X-rays ✓

visible ✓

'Wrong order here'

{ *radio waves* ✗
{ *infra-red* ✗

(iii) Explain how selective absorption of light produces the following effects.

1. White paper: *it reflects all the light.* ✓

'Yes, but state it does not absorb light, as the question asks'

2. Black ink: *does not reflect any light.* ✓

'Yes, but it *absorbs* all the light'

3. A red apple: *absorbs green and blue, and reflects red.* ✓

'Good, well done'

(9)

(London)

SUMMARY

At the end of this chapter you should know:

▷ about **longitudinal** and **transverse** waves in ropes, springs and water;

▷ that waves **transfer energy** without transferring matter;

▷ that waves, including **light** and **sound**, can be **reflected**, **refracted** and **diffracted**;

▷ the meaning of **frequency**, **wavelength** and **amplitude** of a wave;

▷ the quantitative relationship between the **speed**, **frequency** and **wavelength** of a wave;

▷ the conditions for **total internal reflection** and its use in **optical fibres**;

▷ that the **electromagnetic spectrum** includes **radio waves**, **microwaves**, **infra-red**, **visible light**, **ultraviolet waves**, **X-rays** and **gamma-rays**;

▷ some uses and dangers of **microwaves**, **infra-red** and **ultraviolet waves** in **domestic** situations;

▷ some uses of **radio waves**, **microwaves**, **infra-red** and **visible light** in **communications**;

▷ some uses of **X-rays** and **gamma-rays** in **medicine**;

▷ about **sound** and **ultrasound** waves and some medical and other uses of ultrasound;

▷ the link between the **loudness** of a sound and the **amplitude** of the vibration;

▷ the link between the **pitch** of a sound and the **frequency** of vibration;

▷ that white light can be **dispersed** to give a range of colours;

▷ the effect of **colour filters** on white light;

▷ how coloured objects appear in white light and in other colours of light;

▷ that **sound waves** cause the ear-drum to **vibrate** and that different people have different **audible ranges**.

16

The Earth and geology

▶ **GETTING STARTED**

Every day the Sun rises and sets, at night the stars 'appear' in the sky, and the Moon seems to change its shape during the month. To understand how some of these events take place you need to know how the Earth orbits around the Sun, and how the Moon orbits around the Earth.

To investigate conditions in outer space, man has sent both manned and unmanned rockets on voyages of discovery. One day it is possible that people could be living in a space station instead of living on Earth.

Satellites are already in everyday use for observing the Earth and its atmosphere, and making a major contribution to weather forecasting. Although the weather in Britain seems very changeable, we are not usually affected by the extremes experienced in some parts of the world, where floods, droughts, earthquakes and volcanoes cause great suffering to many people.

TOPIC	STUDY	REVISION 1	REVISION 2
The solar system and wider universe			
The Earth			
The Moon			
Artificial satellites			
Stars			
Evolution of the Universe			
Structure of the Earth			
Plate tectonics			
Geological changes			
Changes to the atmosphere			

WHAT YOU NEED TO KNOW

The solar system and wider universe

'the relative positions of the Earth, Moon, Sun, planets and other bodies (such as stars) in the Universe' [4.4a]

'gravitational forces determine the movements of the planets, moons, comets and satellites' [4.4b]

'the Sun and other stars are light sources and planets and other bodies are seen by reflected light' [KS3]

▶ The **Sun** is at the **centre** of our **solar system; planets, asteroids** (rock debris between Mars and Jupiter) and **comets** orbit around the Sun.

▶ The **Sun** is the source of **light** and other forms of electromagnetic radiation.

▶ **Nine planets** have elliptical orbits around the Sun owing to **gravitational force of attraction** which exists between the Sun and planets; orbit time **increases** the further from the Sun; the orbits are in the same plane (exception: Pluto).

▶ The **planets** are non-luminous, they **reflect light** from the **Sun** (stars emit their own light).

▶ Some planets have **satellites** which orbit around them.

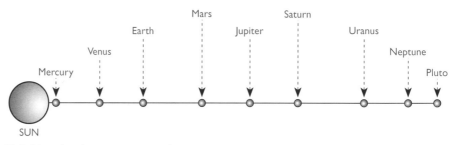

Fig. 16.1 How the planets are arranged

'Try to understand general patterns in the planets'

There are **two groups** of planets:

1. those **nearer** the Sun (Mercury, Venus, Earth, Mars) have **small diameters** and **high density;**
2. those **further** from the Sun (Jupiter, Saturn, Uranus and Neptune) have **large diameters** and **low density** (an exception is Pluto, the furthest away from the Sun, which has a small diameter)

Table 16.1 Some data about the nine planets in the solar system

The main members of the solar system										
Body	1 Diameter	2 Mass	3 Surface gravity	4 Density, in Kg m^{-3}	5 Period of spin			6 Angle of tilt between axis and orbit	7 Average distance from Sun (Sun–Earth=1)	8 Period of orbit, in years	9 No. of moons (*=plus rings)
(Earth=1)	(Earth=1)	(Earth=1)	(Earth=1)		days	hours	mins				
Sun	109.00	333,000.00	28.00	1,400	25	9		97°			
Mercury	0.40	0.06	0.40	5,400	58	16		90°	0.4	0.2	0
Venus	0.95	0.80	0.90	5,200	244	7		267°	0.7	0.6	0
Earth	1.00	1.00	1.00	5,500		23	56	113°	1.0	1.0	1
Moon	0.27	0.01	0.17	3,300	27	7		91°	1.0	1.0	0
Mars	0.53	0.10	0.40	4,000		24	37	114°	1.5	1.9	2
Jupiter	11.18	317.00	2.60	1,300		9	50	93°	5.2	11.9	16*
Saturn	9.42	95.00	1.10	700		10	14	116°	9.5	29.5	15*
Uranus	3.84	14.50	0.90	1,600		10	49	187°	19.2	84.0	5*
Neptune	3.93	17.20	1.20	2,300		15	48	118°	30.1	164.8	2
Pluto	0.31	0.0025	0.20	400	6	9	17	?	39.4	247.7	1

Hint: in the exam you are often asked to interpret tables of physical data about the planets, for example with reference to their masses and orbits in the solar system, so you don't need to learn the names of the planets and all the data shown in Table 16.1.

Problems of colonisation

'Would you like to live there?'

When considering the problems of living on any planet other than Earth, you have to think about factors such as the availability of **oxygen** and **water, temperature, pressure** and **radiation.** Conditions on the surface of the planets, with the exception of the Earth, are generally fairly **hostile.** For example, **Jupiter,** the largest planet in the solar system, has a solid rock core surrounded by layers of liquid **hydrogen** and is covered in a thick layer of **hydrogen gas.** The atmosphere is very **cold** since the planet is so far away from the Sun, and the planet is surrounded by zones of radiation. Trying to colonise this planet would cause astronauts several problems, such as protecting themselves from radiation and from the low temperatures, carrying sufficient oxygen to breathe, and moving about.

One of the factors which limit space travel is providing the amount of **fuel** required to accelerate to high speeds to escape from the Earth's **gravitational field.** Also, most journeys to other planets could take a number of years and problems of providing basic human needs such as water, food, oxygen, warmth and sanitation have to be solved.

▶ The Earth

Some important facts:

- ▶ **a year** (365 days): time taken for the **Earth** to orbit the **Sun;**
- ▶ **a day** (24 hrs): time taken for the **Earth to spin** on its own **axis;**
- ▶ **day** and **night** result from the Earth's rotation; the half of the Earth which faces the Sun is in daylight; the half which faces away from the Sun is in darkness (night).

The Seasons

- ▶ The **tilt of the Earth's axis** relative to its plane of orbit is the reason for the **seasons** and the change in the **length of daylight.**

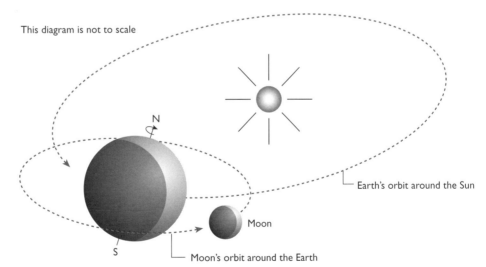

Fig. 16.2 How the Earth orbits the Sun

The 23° tilt of the Earth's axis means that different parts of the world get different amounts of sunlight, and this causes the **seasons. Winter** occurs in the half of the Earth which is tilted **away** from the Sun; **summer** occurs in the half of the Earth which is tilted **towards** the Sun. When it is summer in the **Northern** hemisphere, it is winter in the **Southern** hemisphere (see Fig. 16.3). This means that at places which are tilted towards the Sun the weather is **warmer** because more **energy** is received from the Sun. The period of daylight is **longer** than that of the nights and the Sun rises **higher** in the sky.

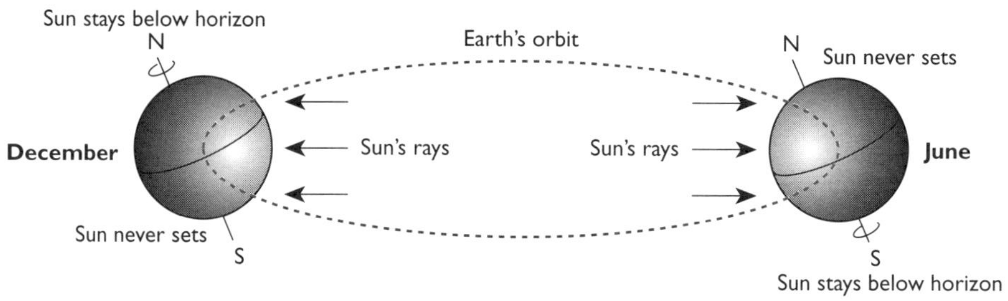

Sun stays below horizon

N

Earth's orbit

N

Sun never sets

December

← Sun's rays   Sun's rays →

June

Sun never sets

S

S

Sun stays below horizon

Fig. 16.3 How the seasons are caused

▶ **The Moon**

▶ A **lunar month** (28 days): time taken for the **Moon** (a **satellite** of Earth) to **orbit the Earth**.

▶ The **Moon** rotates on its own axis every **28 days** so the same side faces the Earth.

Figure 16.4 shows how the different phases of the Moon appear when the Moon is viewed from Earth. When the Earth is between the Sun and the Moon we can see all the light from the Sun which is **reflected** by the Moon, and the Moon therefore appears to be a full Moon.

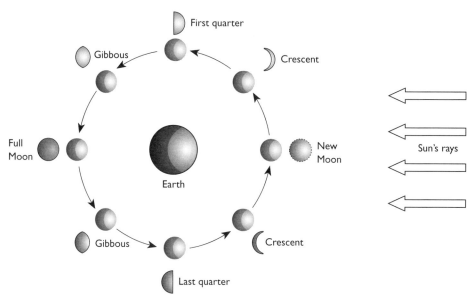

First quarter

Gibbous

Crescent

Full Moon

New Moon

Sun's rays

Earth

Gibbous

Crescent

Last quarter

Fig. 16.4 How the different phases of the Moon are caused

'Try to sort out the difference between an eclipse of the Moon and an eclipse of the Sun'

A lunar eclipse

An **eclipse of the Moon** happens when the Earth stops the Sun's rays from reaching the Moon, as shown in Fig. 16.5.

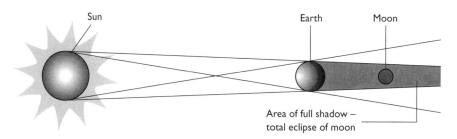

Sun

Earth   Moon

Area of full shadow –
total eclipse of moon

Fig. 16.5 In an eclipse of the Moon, the **Earth** blocks the light from the Sun

A solar eclipse

An **eclipse of the Sun** happens when the Moon passes between the Sun and the Earth, so the Sun appears to be covered, as shown in Fig. 16.6.

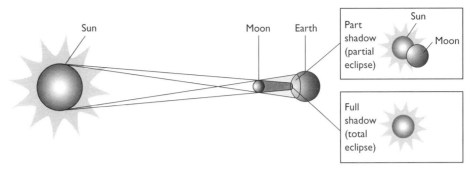

Fig 16.6 In eclipse of the Sun, the **Moon** blocks the light from the Sun

The tides

'See Tidal power,
p. 328'

The Moon exerts a **gravitational pull** on the water on the Earth's surface. The effect of this on the side nearest the Moon is to pull the water towards the Moon and thereby produce a **high tide**. Another high tide happens on the side of the Earth **furthest** away from the Moon. Owing to the rotation of the Earth, these high tides happen every 12 hours.

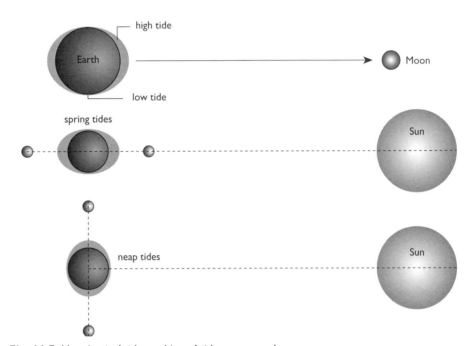

Fig. 16.7 How 'spring' tides and 'neap' tides are caused

Spring and neap tides

'Spring tides don't only
happen in the spring'

Although the Sun is much further away from the Earth, it too has a gravitational pull on the Earth. When the Sun and Moon are **in line**, about twice a month, their combined gravitational pull causes a very **high tide** or '**spring**' tide. These tides have very **large** tidal ranges, this means that they have 'very high' high tides and 'very low' low tides.

When the Sun and Moon are **at right angles** with each other, which happens about twice a month, the gravitational effect is cancelled out and weak tides, called '**neap**' tides, with small tidal ranges, are produced. These tides have 'low' high tides.

▶ Artificial satellites

'artificial satellites are used to observe the Earth and explore the solar system' [KS3]

Satellites

▶   **Artificial satellites** are used for observation of Earth, weather monitoring and exploration of the solar system.

▶ Geosynchronous satellites used for communication systems take 24 hours to go round the Earth.

Satellite pictures, like the ones shown on the TV weather news, are able to show the **position** and **speed** of the changing weather patterns. For example, a satellite could show the development of a cold front, or the position of a depression as it moved across the Atlantic Ocean, and how temperature varies vertically through the atmosphere. The **information** from satellites is used together with other information from more conventional methods of collecting data, such as using hydrogen-filled balloons which float in the atmosphere, and computer weather forecasts. Meteorologists are then able to pass information to national and local news stations as well as to aeroplanes and shipping.

H There are **two** types of weather satellites which are used: (1) **Earth-synchronous** satellites which use a **geostationary** orbit so that the satellite holds a **fixed point** above the Earth's **equator** and the speed matches that of the Earth; and (2) **Sun-synchronous** satellites which use a **polar orbit** so that the satellite **scans** the whole Earth each day as it spins beneath them. Some satellites are able to use both **infra-red** and **visible light** to collect **data**. This means that data can be collected during a 24-hour period as a frontal system develops, for example.

▶ **Stars**

'how stars evolve over a long time-scale' [4.4c]

'some ideas to explain the evolution of the Universe into its present state' [4.4d]

H ### *Evolution of a star*

▶ Stars **evolve** over millions of years and have a finite **life span.**
▶ The **Sun** is one of many millions of **stars** which make up the Milky Way **galaxy**; the **Universe** is a system of an enormous number of galaxies held together by gravitational forces.
▶ **Distances** in the Universe measured in **light years**: the distance travelled by **light** on one Earth year.
▶ **Stars**: very large clouds of hydrogen, helium and dust which collapse under gravity; **hydrogen** gas is converted to **helium** in process of **nuclear fusion;** thermal energy is released when small hydrogen nuclei are joined together to form helium nuclei; surface temperature 6,000°C.

'See Chapter 18, Nuclear fusion, p. 344'

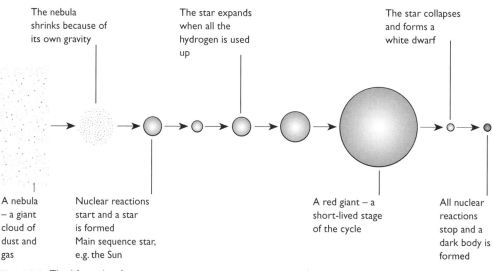

Fig. 16.8 The life cycle of a star

The Sun

The **Sun** is one of billions of stars which make up a **galaxy** known as the **Milky Way**. There are **billions of galaxies** like the Milky Way in the Universe. The Sun is about half-way through its **life cycle** of 9600 million years and is about a million times larger than the Earth. It is made of **hydrogen** and **helium gas,** and its temperature is about 6,000°C at its surface. At the centre of the Sun the temperature is much higher, and this is where **nuclear fusion** is taking place as the **hydrogen** is being converted to **helium.** Figure 16.8 shows the life cycle of a star such as the Sun.

▶ Evolution of H̄ the Universe

The '**big bang**' theory of the origin of the Universe suggests that an **explosion** may have occurred about 15 thousand million years ago to create the Universe. At one time the **galaxies** must have been much **closer** to each other and may even have been one big mass. It would seem that the galaxies are **moving away** from each other, possibly as a result of a massive explosion or 'big bang'. Evidence for this is suggested by the fact that the **light** from other galaxies has shifted to the **red end of the spectrum** the further away galaxies are, the **bigger** this '**red shift**'. The cause of the 'big bang' is not known.

▶ Structure of the Earth

(This section is often included with Sc 3 Materials and their properties.)
'*longitudinal (pressure) waves and transverse (shake) waves are transmitted through the Earth, producing wave records that provide evidence for the Earth's layered structure*' [4.3m]

The Earth is an almost spherical body about 6,400km in radius. Much of the **evidence** for the **layered** structure of the Earth comes from the behaviour of **earthquake shock waves** as they reach different zones. There are **two** types of earthquake waves:

H̄ 1. The **P waves** (pressure waves) are **longitudinal** waves which travel very **quickly** and will pass through liquids and solids, including the core; they travel more quickly through the core than the mantle.
2. The slower moving **S waves** (shake waves) are **transverse** waves which only travel through **solids.** An analysis of the behaviour of these shock waves has indicated the main regions of the Earth as shown in Fig. 16.9.

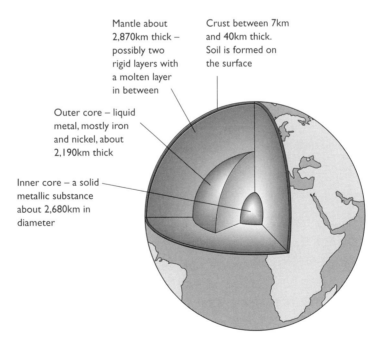

Mantle about 2,870km thick – possibly two rigid layers with a molten layer in between

Crust between 7km and 40km thick. Soil is formed on the surface

Outer core – liquid metal, mostly iron and nickel, about 2,190km thick

Inner core – a solid metallic substance about 2,680km in diameter

Fig. 16.9 The structure of the Earth

As can be seen in Fig 16.9, at the centre of the Earth is the **core,** a spherical zone about 3,500km in radius. The core is divided into an **inner core,** thought to be a **solid metallic** substance which has a radius of approximately 1,340km. The **outer core** is thought to be a **liquid mass** of **nickel-iron** with a radius of approximately 2,160km. This outer core is thought to create the **electric currents** which give rise to the Earth's magnetic field.

The average **density** of the Earth is about 5.5g/cm³ whereas the surface rocks average 3g/cm³. This observation means that the density **increases** towards the centre where it may be as high as 10–15g/cm³. **Temperatures** in the Earth's core are thought to be around 2,500°C.

Outside the core is the **mantle**, a layer about 2,870km thick thought to be composed of the mineral **olivine**.

The thinnest, outer layer of the Earth is the **crust**, about 7km to 40km thick. It is composed mostly of **igneous** and **metamorphic** rocks many of which contain **minerals** which exist as pure elements or as mineral ores. Earthquake waves change **velocity** very sharply at the boundary between the **crust** and **mantle**. Evidence indicates that the crust beneath the continents consists of **two rock layers** about 40km thick whereas beneath the oceans there is only **one thin layer**, mostly basalt, a few kilometres thick.

▶ Plate tectonics

'how plate tectonic processes are involved in the formation, deformation and recycling of rocks' [3.2z]

It is thought that the Earth's crust consists of a number of large '**plates**' and it is the interaction of these plates which is described as **plate tectonics**. The plates are thought to be moving at relative speeds of a few centimetres per year.

There are basically **three** ways the plates can move in relation to each other.

▶ The plates can **slide past** each other along a common boundary. The plane along which motion occurs is a vertical fracture or **fault**. **Earthquakes** can arise when there are sudden movements along these faults due to a build-up of energy. For example, the San Andreas fault in Southern California.

'Movement of the plates'

▶ The plates can **slide towards** each other so that the thinner, denser ocean plates are pushed beneath the more buoyant continental plates, forcing the continental crusts upwards. Strong **pressures** build up giving rise to **earthquakes** and **volcanoes**. For example, Chile, Japan and Alaska, as well as narrow zones around the Pacific Basin.

▶ The plates can **pull apart** from each other so that gaping cracks appear in the ocean crust. **Magma** continually rises to fill the gap and form **new ocean crust**. This is described as '**sea floor spreading**'. Earthquakes can also occur but are usually too small to be of significance, for example in the mid-Atlantic ocean ridges.

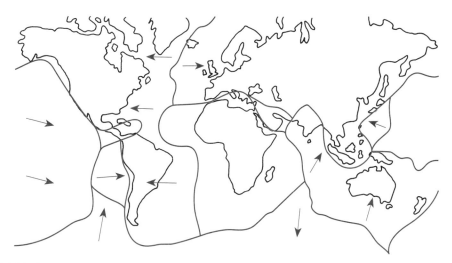

Fig. 16.10 The large plates of rock which form the Earth's crust

Continental drift

It can be seen from Fig. 16.10 that the edges of the continents have **shapes** which appear to **fit closely together**, even though they are now separated by oceans.

The theory that best explains this observation is that more than 300 million years ago the land masses formed a **super continent** called **Pangaea**. The Americas fitted closely against Africa and Europe, and the continents of Antarctica and Australia and the subcontinents of India and Madagascar were **closely grouped** around the Southern tip of Africa.

Two hundred million years ago the **separation** of the continents began as the Americas pulled away from the rest of Pangaea, leaving a great rift that became the Atlantic Ocean. Later, other fragments pulled away from Africa and from each other. The theory of **plate tectonics** helps to explain how the continents have moved apart in this way.

▶   In the mantle: **convection currents** as a result of heat released by radioactivity may be a possible cause of movement of plates.

Earthquakes

'Some effects of natural forces on humans'

Some of the visible effects of **earthquakes** are buildings falling down and large cracks appearing in roads. In mountainous regions earthquakes can be responsible for causing avalanches of snow, and in the oceans very large **tidal waves** can be produced. In 1988 a very powerful earthquake in Armenia destroyed whole towns and killed many thousands of people (see Fig. 16.11).

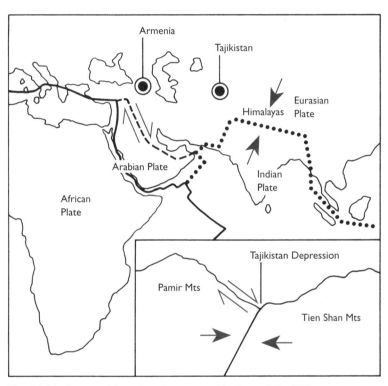

Fig. 16.11 A powerful earthquake occurred in Armenia in 1988

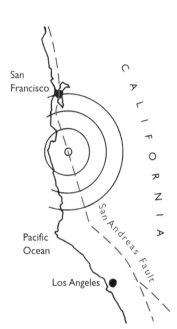

Fig. 16.12 The San Andreas fault in California

In 1989, the second-worst earthquake to hit the United States occurred in the San Francisco area of northern California along the San Andreas fault (Fig. 16.12), causing roads and bridges to collapse, landslides and gaping cracks in roads.

Volcanoes

A **volcano** is a large cone-shaped mountain which is formed when **steam, lava, rocks** and **gases** are pushed out from inside the Earth by the **pressure** of the gases and steam. The **magma** which flows out on the surface at a temperature of 1,000°C is a mixture of lava and volcanic gases (Fig. 16.13). Some eruptions produce large amounts of **volcanic dust** particles which enter the **atmosphere** and cause **cloud formation**. It is thought that the volcanic ash in the atmosphere may also cause cooling of the Earth as the particles prevent radiation from the Sun reaching the Earth. Some of the **effects** of volcanoes are the **destruction of towns** and villages, and the **removal of agricultural land** and forests. A major volcanic eruption took place in 1976 in China where more than 1 million people were killed. On the beneficial side: volcanic ash forms a very **fertile soil**, and molten rock underground heats underground water forming steam which can be used to generate electricity.

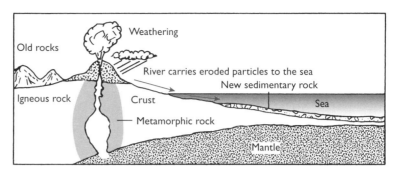

Fig. 16.13 Volcanoes are part of the rock cycle

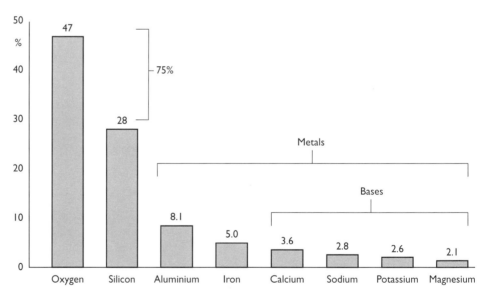

▶ **Geological changes**

'how igneous rocks are formed by the cooling of magma, sedimentary rocks by the deposition and consolidation of sediments, and metamorphic rocks by the action of heat and pressure on rocks' [3.2x]

'how the sequence of, and evidence for, these processes is obtained from the rock record' [3.2y]

The most important zone of the Earth for Man is the **thin outer crust** which contains the continents and ocean basins and is the source of the soil, the gases of the atmosphere and all the free water of the oceans, atmosphere and land. Figure 16.14 shows the eight most abundant elements of the Earth's crust.

The **oxygen**, which accounts for almost half the total weight, is combined with **silicon**, and is also a major element in organic substances.

The elements of the Earth's crust are present in **minerals** usually as compounds. A great variety of minerals exist and they are usually found in different combinations in rocks. Most rocks in the Earth's crust were formed millions of years ago but some are being formed now as lava from volcanic eruptions solidifies on contact with the atmosphere.

Fig. 16.14 The eight most abundant elements in the Earth's crust

Igneous, sedimentary, metamorphic rocks

There are **three** major categories of rocks in the Earth's crust:

Igneous rocks

'Look at some samples of rocks such as granite. Can you see the crystals?'

Igneous rocks are formed when molten **magma** from the mantle **cools** and solidifies. The size of the crystals which can be seen in igneous rocks indicates the **rate** of cooling of the magma. **Small** crystals are formed when the magma cools **rapidly**. Volcanoes occur when the molten rock forces its way to the surface, often through a weak part of the crust. **Granite** and **basalt** are examples of igneous rocks.

Sedimentary rocks

There are accumulations of **particles** from existing rocks formed in many different ways:

▶ by the action of moving water;
▶ by wind, ice and frost;
▶ by changes of temperature;
▶ by chemical action, such as acidic rainwater on limestone;
▶ by the action of living organisms, such as worms and plant roots.

These **factors** cause the existing rock to disintegrate physically or chemically and form small particles. Some of these particles become mixed with the remains of dead animals and plants and form **soil.** The soils formed will differ in their drainage properties, texture, acidity and mineral composition. Other particles such as gravels and sands are transported by streams, rivers, wind and ice and are deposited by streams and rivers as sediments on the sea bed, in estuaries, swamps and marshes where they form successive layers known as **sedimentary strata** over millions of years. These layers are usually laid down **horizontally** but as a result of movements in the Earth's crust they become **faulted** and **folded** (Fig. 16.15). You can sometimes see strata at the coast where uplifting of the ocean floor may have occurred.

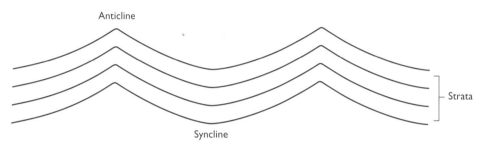

Fig. 16.15 Folding of rock strata

Larger, heavier particles settle out first and this fact affects the type of sedimentary rock which is formed; for example a mixture of particles of **salt and clay** with some **sand** forms the sedimentary rock **mudstone.** Other examples include **shale** – the most abundant sedimentary rocks, **sandstone,** and **limestone.**

Metamorphic rocks

These are **igneous** or **sedimentary** rocks which have been physically or chemically **changed** by the tremendous **pressures** and very high **temperatures** which accompany mountain-building movements in the Earth's crust. The metamorphic rock is so changed in appearance and may have formed new structures and minerals compared with the parent rock. For example shale, a sedimentary rock, is altered into **slate** which further changes into **schist;** limestone is changed into **marble** and so on.

Identification of rocks

The different rock types can be identified by their appearance:

'You can often identify the different rocks by their appearance'

▶ Rocks which have **random** interlocking **crystals** are usually **igneous** rocks. If the crystals are very **small** then the magma from which the rock is formed will have **cooled quickly.** These rocks will probably have originated from a volcano. If the crystals are **larger** then the magma will have cooled more **slowly,** probably within the crust.
▶ Rocks composed of **bands** of interlocking **crystals** are usually **metamorphic.**

'See Chapter 11, Patterns of Acid Reactions, and Chapter 5, Evolution'

▶ Rocks composed of **layers** of cemented grains or **fragments** are usually **sedimentary.** **Fossils** may also be present in sedimentary rocks with different layers of rocks containing fragments of plants and animals that lived at the time the sediments were laid down.

Remember: BIG (basalt, igneous, granite), SS (sedimentary sandstone), MM (metamorphic marble).

The rock cycle

All three types of rocks are continually being transformed from one rock to another over millions of years in a process known as the **rock cycle**. There is no record of the 'original' rocks that first formed the earth's crust as they will have been recycled millions of years ago.

▶ The **igneous** rocks are continually being affected by **weathering** and **erosion**.
▶ The resulting **sediments** are **transported** and **deposited** to form **sedimentary** rocks.
▶ High **pressures** and **temperatures** may cause some of these sedimentary rocks to be changed into **metamorphic** rocks, some of which may melt and form **magma**.
▶ The **magma** may rise into the **crust** where it cools and forms **igneous rocks**.

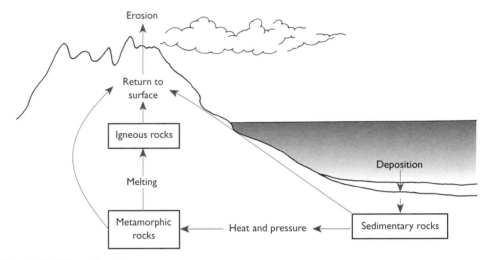

Fig. 16.16 The rock cycle

▶ Changes to the atmosphere

'how the atmosphere and oceans evolved to their present composition' [3.2v]

'how the carbon cycle helps to maintain atmospheric composition' [3.2w]

The surface of the Earth is surrounded by a thick layer of gases called the **atmosphere**. It is held to Earth by **gravitational attraction** and is densest at sea level and thins out rapidly at higher altitudes. About 97% of the atmosphere is within 30km of the Earth's surface, but the upper limit is about 10,000km. The atmosphere is essential in keeping the Earth's surface **temperature** more or less **constant**. In comparison the Moon, which is the same distance from the Sun as the Earth and has no atmosphere, has surface temperatures ranging from as high as 100°C in the sunlight falling to –150°C at night.

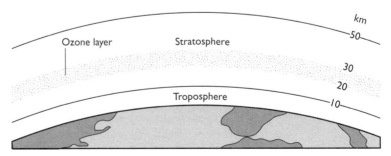

Fig. 16.17 The atmosphere

Composition of the atmosphere

The composition of the Earth's atmosphere is fairly uniform in terms of the proportions of gases it contains and is maintained by the **action of living organisms**, mostly green plants and micro-organisms.

The carbon cycle (see Chapter 6) maintains the composition of the atmosphere; CO_2 (carbon dioxide) is

1. added by respiration and combustion
2. removed by photosynthesis

The proportion of gases in the atmosphere is shown below:

'Proportion of gases in the atmosphere'

▶ nitrogen about 78%
▶ oxygen about 21%
▶ carbon dioxide about 0.03%
▶ inert gases, mostly argon, less than 1%
▶ impurities such as dust particles and very small amounts of other gases
▶ water vapour which varies from nil to about 5%

Evolution of the atmosphere

It is thought that **volcanic activity** during the evolution of the Earth released gases which formed the original atmosphere. This atmosphere probably consisted mainly of **carbon dioxide**, with some **water vapour, methane** and **ammonia.**

Changes due to the following processes are thought to have occurred which have resulted in the present atmosphere:

▶ the carbon from the **carbon dioxide** became 'trapped' in **sedimentary rocks** as **carbonates** and **fossil fuels;**
▶ the amount of **oxygen** increased due to **colonisation** by plants and the **ozone layer** developed to filter out harmful ultraviolet radiation from the Sun and allow development of **new organisms;**
▶ methane and **ammonia** reacted with **oxygen;**
▶ nitrogen gas was released into the air from reactions of **denitrifying bacteria;**
H ··· ▶ oceans formed as **steam condensed;**
▶ composition of oceans maintained by a **balance** between

1. **input** of dissolved salts in river water from weathering of rocks
2. **removal** of **dissolved salts** by:
    (i) shell formation by marine organisms
    (ii) chemical reactions to form sea floor sediment
    (iii) crystallisation to form salt deposits.

The water cycle

Water in the ocean is continuously being **evaporated** by the heat of the Sun, and this vapour condenses to form **clouds.** When the clouds are blown over hills and mountains, they release the condensation as **rain.** Some of the water drains through the ground and back to the sea by rivers, and some of it is absorbed through the roots of plants, and is evaporated from the leaves in the process of **transpiration.** Rain also dissolves some of the poisonous gases in the air, such as sulphur dioxide, and forms dilute sulphuric acid, which falls as **acid rain.**

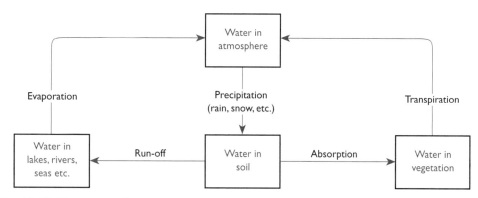

Fig. 16.18 The water cycle

The ozone layer

The **ozone layer** surrounds the Earth in the part of the upper atmosphere known as the **stratosphere**. The stratosphere is vital to life on Earth as it **shields** us from most of the harmful types of **ultra-violet radiation** from the Sun. Increased exposure to UV radiation may cause damage to crops and increase the incidence of **skin cancer** in humans.

'Benefits of ozone'

Ozone is a form of **oxygen** which has **three** atoms in each molecule (O_3) compared with the usual form of oxygen molecules which has only **two** atoms (O_2). In simple terms ozone protects us by a series of chemical reactions. Some types of UV radiation will split the oxygen molecules (O_2) to form **oxygen atoms**. These are very reactive and combine with oxygen molecules to form **ozone** (O_3). The ozone then **absorbs** other types of UV radiation which can convert ozone back into **oxygen molecules** (O_2) and atoms. These reactions normally **prevent** harmful UV radiation but this balance is being upset by the release of chemicals such as **chlorofluorocarbons** (CFCs) from aerosols and other sources, as well as **nitrous oxides** from car exhausts. These substances react with the ozone making **fewer** molecules available at any time to absorb the UV radiation. The result of this is to create 'holes' in the ozone layer through which **harmful UV radiation** can pass.

'See Chapter 17, p. 330'

▶ **EXAMINATION QUESTIONS**

Multiple choice

Q1   What is a year?

    A   the time taken for the Earth to rotate on its axis
    B   the time taken for the Moon to orbit the Earth
    C   the time taken between two solar eclipses
    D   the time taken for the Earth to orbit the Sun
    E   the time taken between summer and winter.

Q2   The flow chart below shows the possible life cycle of our Sun, a middle-aged star.

clouds of dust and gas → star contracts → main sequence star → star expands → X → white dwarf → dark body

Which one of the following should be at X?

    A   black hole   D   neutron star
    B   galaxy   E   red giant
    C   nebula

Q3   What happens during a total eclipse of the Moon?

    A   The Moon goes behind the Sun.
    B   The Moon is between the Earth and the Sun.
    C   Mars moves between the Sun and the Moon.
    D   The Earth is between the Sun and the Moon.
    E   The Sun is between the Earth and the Moon.

Q4 The diagram (Fig. 16.19) shows the approximate percentage of gases in the atmosphere. What gas is present in the largest percentage?

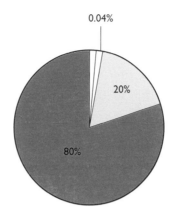

0.04%

20%

80%

Fig. 16.19

A   carbon dioxide   D   nitrogen
B   hydrogen   E   sulphur dioxide
C   oxygen

Q5 The diagram above (Fig. 16.20) shows the structure of the Earth.

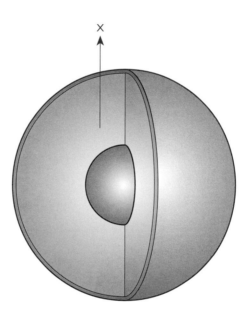

X

Fig. 16.20

What does area X represent
A   crust   D   outer core
B   inner core   E   continental plates
C   mantle

Q6 Which one of the following describes how igneous rocks are formed?

A   Existing rocks are broken down by changes of temperature.
B   Existing rocks are eroded by the action of water.
C   An earthquake cracks the Earth's crust.
D   Existing rocks are changed by high temperature and pressure.
E   Hot magma from the mantle cools and solidifies.

Q7   The diagram below (Fig. 16.21) shows the rock cycle.

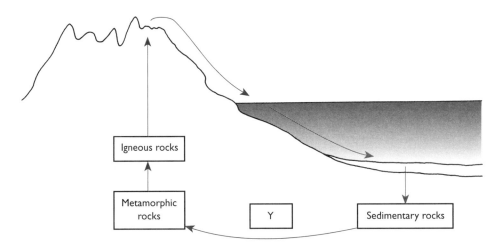

Fig. 16.21

Which one of the following should be in box Y?

A   deposition   D   melting
B   erosion   E   heat and pressure
C   evaporation

Structured questions

Q8   The diagram below (Fig. 16.22), which is not drawn to scale, shows the relative positions of the Sun, Moon and Earth.

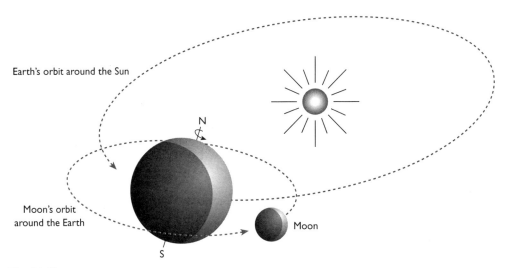

Fig. 16.22

(a)   State how the motion of the Moon and Earth gives us
    (i) a year (2 lines)   *(1)*
    (ii) a lunar month (2 lines)   *(1)*
    (iii) a day (2 lines)   *(1)*

(b)   Draw labelled diagrams showing the positions of the Sun, Moon and Earth when:

    (i) spring tides occur _____   *(1)*

    (ii) neap tides occur _____   *(1)*

    (iii) What phase of the Moon would you expect to see when there are spring tides?

    _____   *(1)*

(c) A list of planets is given below.
     Mercury
     Pluto
     Mars
     Saturn
     Venus
From the list choose which planet

(i) has the most moons _____ *(1)*

(ii) is the smallest planet _____ *(1)*

(iii) has the longest year _____ *(1)*

(d) If you attempted to live on Venus, describe two problems you might encounter other than those of getting there.

1. _____ *(1)*

2. _____ *(1)*

(MEG)

Q9   A study of some planets in a solar system has produced the following observations. They are listed in Table 16.2.

Table 16.2

Planet	Mass compared with Earth	Atmosphere	Nature of surface	Average temperature (°C)
A	one tenth	None	Very hard and rocky	−25
B	half	Traces of oxygen. Little carbon dioxide. Little clouds	Soft sand, some water	2
C	four times	Traces of oxygen. Nitrogen. Dense clouds	Mainly water. Swamp land	28

(a) (i) Suggest which planet may have the highest gravity.

_____ *(2)*

(ii) Give a reason. (3 lines) *(2)*

_____

_____

_____

(b) (i) Suggest which planet may support plant life.

_____ *(1)*

(ii) Give **two** reasons. (7 lines) *(2)*

(c) (i) Which planet is **most unlikely** to support life? *(1)*
     (ii) Give **two** reasons. (7 lines) *(2)*

(d) (i) What would happen to water spilled by an astronaut on planet A? (2 lines) *(1)*
     (ii) Give a reason for your answer. (2 lines) *(1)*

_____

_____

(e) Describe **five** benefits of space exploration to society. (10 lines) *(5)*

(f) State **two** disadvantages of space exploration.

1. _____

2. _____ *(2)*

(London)

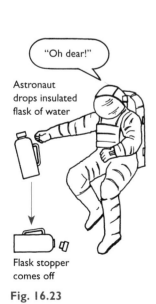

"Oh dear!"

Astronaut drops insulated flask of water

Flask stopper comes off

Fig. 16.23

Q10   Figure 16.24 is a map of California showing the San Andreas fault.

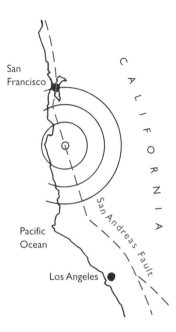

Fig. 16.24

(a) (i)   What is meant by a 'fault' in the Earth's surface? (2 lines)   *(1)*
     (ii) The San Andreas fault is known as a 'tear' fault. Draw a labelled diagram to
           illustrate how such a fault occurs in the Earth's surface.   *(3)*
     (iii) Explain why earthquakes are common in this area. (6 lines)   *(3)*
     (iv) Explain why volcanic eruptions are likely in areas of the Earth's crust like this.
           (6 lines)   *(3)*

(b) Earthquakes and volcanoes can give rise to destruction and enormous loss of human
     life. However, the San Andreas fault is in an area which is densely populated by
     people. Much of San Francisco was destroyed in 1906, and there is constant fear of
     further major earthquakes, yet still it is a densely populated region.
        Write a scientific account of why such active regions of the Earth's crust are still
     attractive for humans to live in. (12 lines)   *(6)*

Q11   The diagram below (Fig. 16.25) shows a section through a volcano.

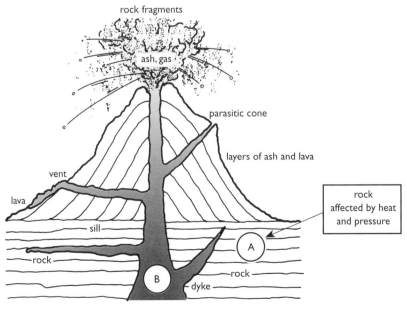

Fig. 16.25

(a) Name a type of rock you would expect to find at (A).

_____ *(1)*

(b) (i) What type of rock will eventually be formed at (B)?

_____ *(1)*

(ii) Explain how this type of rock is formed. (2 lines)   *(1)*

(Co-ordinated Science, NEAB, London, WJEC)

Q12 (Higher Tier)   This question provides you with data in the form of a map and gives you opportunity for extended writing. Note you are asked to use the theory of plate tectonics; the diagram (Fig. 16.26) gives you a clue to help you here by showing you the shape of the two continents.

The map below shows two of the continents bordering the Atlantic Ocean.

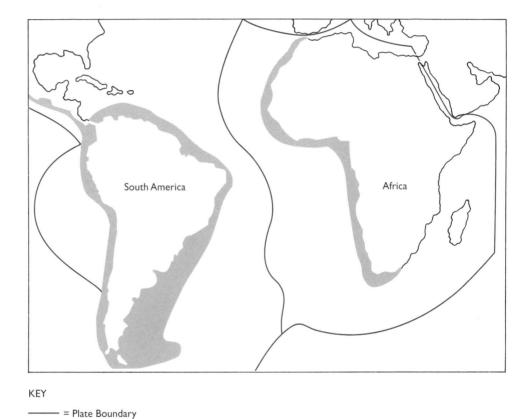

KEY

——— = Plate Boundary

▨ = Continental Shelf

Fig. 16.26

It is believed that 150 million years ago these two continents were joined.

Use the theory of plate tectonics to explain how these continents could have moved apart to reach their present positions. You may use diagrams if you wish.

Marks will be given both for showing knowledge and understanding and for the way in which your account is organised and expressed.

(space and 10 lines for the answer, and (10) marks)

(Co-ordinated Science, NEAB, London, WJEC)

▶ **EXAMINATION ANSWERS**

Multiple choice

A1   Key D. Option A is a day, option B is a lunar month.

A2   Key E, red giant. Option C, nebula, is the name of the gas cloud at the start of the life cycle. Option B is the name for a collection of many stars. Option D, a neutron star, is formed by some massive stars when they have exploded after becoming red super giants. but the question refers to the Sun.

A3   Key D. Remember, the Moon never goes behind the Sun as in option A, as the Moon is a satellite of the Earth.

A4   Key D, nitrogen. Option C, oxygen, is only present about 20%.

A5   Key C, the mantle.

A6   Key E describes the formation of igneous rocks. Options A and B are both descriptions of sedimentary rocks, and option D describes metamorphic rocks.

A7   Key E. Heat and pressure lead to the formation of metamorphic rocks.

Structured questions

A8   (a)   (i)   A year is the time taken for the Earth to go once around the Sun.
            (ii) A lunar month is the time taken for the Moon to go once around the Earth.
            (iii) A day is the time taken for the Earth to spin once on its own axis.

         (b)   (i)   diagram with the Sun, Moon and Earth in line
            (ii) diagram with the Moon at right angles to line of Earth and Sun
            (iii) full or new Moon

         (c)   (i)   Saturn
            (ii) Mercury (or Pluto)
            (iii) Pluto

         (d)   1.   no oxygen for breathing, so I would have to carry oxygen in cylinders
            2.   very hot, so I would have to wear protective clothing

A9   (a)   (i)   planet C
            (ii) four times the mass of Earth

         (b)   (i)   planet C
            (ii) 1. traces of oxygen for respiration
                 2. temperature similar to Earth

         (c)   (i)   planet A
            (ii) 1. no atmosphere
                 2. very low temperatures

         (d)   (i)   it would freeze
            (ii) temperature below freezing point of water, 0°C

         (e)   1.   minerals may be discovered
            2.   more space available for people to live
            3.   new sources of food may be discovered
            4.   alternative energy sources may be found
            5.   better understanding of effects of gravity if research carried out where there is little gravity
                 (Any similar answers acceptable.)

         (f)   1.   very expensive, the money could be used to cure diseases on Earth
            2.   dangerous: rockets explode and kill astronauts

A10 (a) (i) The pressure of the Earth causes the rocks in the crust to break or fault.

(ii)

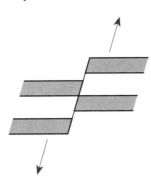

Fig. 16.27

(iii) Earthquakes happen near large faults, as two plates in the Earth's crust move past each other, aided by lubrication of a small proportion of molten material. Sudden fracturing releases energy, causing vertical and horizontal vibrations.

(iv) Volcanic eruptions occur at weak places in the Earth's crust, as molten rock forces its way to the surface. In this area, lava runs from long fractures or fissures to form basalt plateaux.

(b) The region may be very fertile and produce good crops. Other safer areas may be less fertile. The region may be on the coast and be accessible for trading, whereas other safer areas may be inland. There may be valuable minerals in the area which can offer employment to people involved in mining industries. The risk factor of earthquakes is being reduced, owing to their predictability. Buildings are being constructed to withstand the shockwaves.

(Any valid scientific suggestion would be acceptable here.)

A11 (a) the clue on the diagram is the label 'rock affected by heat and pressure' so the answer is metamorphic rock (1)

(b) (i) igneous rock (1)

(ii) magma cools and crystallises (1)

A12 This question is targeted at Higher Tier. The diagram should help you to remember the theory of plate tectonics. Note 10 marks are allocated but at least 3 of these will be for organising a logical account so you need to think about establishing 7 points in your answer.

A possible answer would include the following:

the Earth's crust is formed from a number of plates (1)
these are moving (1)
at a few centimetres per year (1)
as a result of convection currents (1)
these two continents are moving apart (1)
evidence comes from the formation of mid-Atlantic ridges (1)
formed from basaltic magma (1)

logical, concise, scientific account (3)
logical and concise but lacking in scientific terms (2)

▶ **A STUDENT'S ANSWER WITH EXAMINER'S COMMENTS**

Some facts about four planets in a different solar system are given in Table 16.3 below.

Table 16.3

Planet	Temperature range °C	Atmosphere	Surface conditions	Mass compared with Earth = 1
Helios	0 to 50	Nitrogen, oxygen, some carbon dioxide and cloud	Water and sandy soil	1.4
Rheagos	−25 to −10	Hydrogen, some CO_2. No cloud	Very hard rock with some powdered material	4.6
Solos	−10 to 12	Mainly CO_2 with a lot of cloud	Swamp-land and water	3.2
Carmel	−45 to 40	None	Very hard rock	0.9

(a) Study the table and then answer the following questions.
  (i) Which planet is most likely to support plant and animal life as we know it?

'Good'

  Helios ✔ _____ (1)

  (ii) Give **three** reasons for your answer to part (i).

  1. _water available on Helios_ ✔ _____

  _____ (1)

'Look at the information. What about oxygen?'

  2. _the temperature is like Earth_ ✔ _____

  _____ (1)

  3. _–_ _____

  _____ (1)

  (iii) Which planet has the greatest temperature variation?

'Look carefully. Carmel has a 95° range'

  Helios ✗ _____ (1)

  (iv) Why do you think Solos has a lot of cloud in its atmosphere?

  due to the CO_2, and water ✔ _____ (1)

  (WJEC)

SUMMARY

At the end of this chapter you should know:

▷   that the **Sun** and other **stars** are **light sources;**

▷   that **planets** and other bodies are seen by **reflected light;**

▷   the **relative positions** of the **Earth, Moon, Sun, planets** and other bodies (such as stars) in the Universe;

▷   that **gravitational forces** determine the movements of the **planets, moons, comets** and **satellites;**

▷   that **artificial satellites** are used to observe the Earth and explore the solar system;

▷   how **stars evolve** over a long time-scale;

▷   some ideas to explain the **evolution** of the **Universe;**

▷   that rocks are **weathered** by expansion and **contraction** and by the freezing of **water;**

▷   how rocks are classified as **sedimentary, metamorphic** and **igneous** on the basis of their **formation;** these processes affect their texture and minerals they contain;

▷   how **igneous** rocks are formed by **cooling of magma, sedimentary** rocks by the deposition and consolidation of **sediments**, and **metamorphic** rocks by the action of **heat** and **pressure** on rocks;

▷   how **plate tectonic** processes are involved in the **formation**, **deformation** and **recycling of rocks;**

▷   that **longitudinal pressure waves (P)** and **transverse shake waves (S)** are transmitted through the Earth, producing **wave records** that provide evidence for the Earth's **layered structure**, inner and outer **core, mantle,** and **crust**.

Energy resources and transfer

▶ **GETTING STARTED**

One of the most important topics in GCSE Science is the study of energy and fuels. In your home and at school you are using energy to heat and light the buildings you live and work in, to cook food and to make electrical appliances work. In industry, energy is being used to drive machinery to make many different types of consumer goods, such as cars and household items. Most of the energy which is used in this way is in the form of electricity which has been generated in a power station from a primary source of energy, such as the fossil fuels or nuclear fuel.

The **type** of fuel you use to heat your home may be affected by many different factors, such as how much a fuel costs, whether it is easy to store, and how cheap it is. Most people try to save money by reducing the amount of energy which is lost from their homes as heat, and you probably already know something about loft insulation and double glazing.

Fossil fuels, such as coal and oil, are finite and will eventually run out, so scientists and technologists are investigating **alternative** energy sources such as solar energy, tidal energy, wave energy and wind power.

TOPIC	STUDY	REVISION 1	REVISION 2
Energy transfer and efficiency			
Conduction, convection, evaporation and radiation			
Energy losses and insulation			
Energy resources			
Alternative energy sources			
Greenhouse effect			
Work, power and energy			
Kinetic energy			
Specific heat capacity			

WHAT YOU NEED TO KNOW

▶ **Energy transfer and efficiency**

'differences in temperature can lead to transfer of energy' [4.5a]

Energy efficiency

'the meaning of energy efficiency and the need for economical use of energy resources' [4.5.e]

Whenever you see something moving or happening you know that energy is being **transferred** from one form to another. Things move or happen only when energy is transferred. For example, a clockwork toy moves because the **potential energy** from the wound-up spring is transferred to **kinetic energy**, which turns the wheels of the toy.

There are many examples of **energy sources**, such as **chemical** energy in **fuel** and **batteries**, and **gravitational potential** energy in objects lifted above the ground. When a **fuel** is burned the **chemical** energy stored in it is **transferred** to **heat** (thermal energy). When an object falls to the ground the **potential** energy it had because of its position is transferred to **kinetic** energy.

One of the most useful sources of energy at home and in industry is **electrical energy** which is easily **transferred** into **light**, **sound**, **movement** (kinetic energy) and **heat** (thermal energy). You have many **electrical devices** at home which transfer electrical energy into other forms of energy, for example:

'Devices which transfer electrical energy into other forms of energy'

- ▶ an **electric lamp** converts **electrical** energy into **heat** (thermal energy) and **light** energy;
- ▶ an **electric kettle** converts **electrical** energy into **heat** (thermal energy);
- ▶ an **electric razor** converts **electrical** energy into **kinetic** energy and **sound** energy;
- ▶ a **radio** converts **electrical** energy into **sound**.

During the transfer of energy, some of the energy is transferred to where it is needed and some is **wasted**, for example as **thermal** (heat) energy or **sound** energy. In any device the **proportion** of energy which is usefully transferred is called the '**efficiency**' of the device. For example, an electric motor transfers electrical energy into kinetic energy but some heat and sound are produced as well. The efficiency can be calculated using the formula:

$$\text{efficiency} = \frac{\text{useful energy transferred by device (energy output)}}{\text{total energy supplied to the device (energy input)}}$$

This can also be considered as:

$$\text{efficiency} = \frac{\text{power output}}{\text{power input}}$$

You will be provided with this equation so don't learn it but understand how to use it.

'Energy cannot be created or destroyed'

For example, if a motor is supplied at **100W** and the power output is **60W** then its efficiency is 60/100 = **60%**. Note that when energy is transferred, the **total amount** of energy is **unchanged** but some energy is eventually **transferred** to the surroundings as **thermal** or **sound** energy where it is spread out and unavailable for further energy transfers. It is in this sense that the **40%** of energy can be regarded as '**wasted**' in the motor example above.

▶ **Conduction, convection, evaporation and radiation**

'how energy is transferred by the movement of particles in conduction, convection and evaporation' [4.5b]

'how energy is transferred by radiation' [4.5c]

Energy is transferred by **movement of particles** in four **processes**:

1. conduction;
2. convection;
3. evaporation;
4. thermal radiation.

Conduction is the **transfer of energy** through a substance without the substance itself moving. Heat energy is conducted as a result of **particles vibrating** in a **solid conductor** such as metals or non-metals; metals are very good conductors but non-metals (including glass) are poor conductors. Energy is transferred through a substance from where the temperature is **higher** to where the temperature is **lower**. Limited conduction takes place in liquids and gases.

Convection is the **movement of particles** in liquids and gases. Gases and liquids flow and **energy** is carried away from places where the temperature is **higher** to where the temperature is **lower**. Ocean currents and winds are a result of changes in density in liquids and gases which set up **convection currents**.

Evaporation is the **loss** of fast-moving **particles** from the **surface** of a **liquid**; the **rate** of evaporation of water depends on **surface area, temperature, humidity** and **movement** of surrounding air. The **rate** of evaporation can be **increased** by:

▶ blowing across the surface of the water, so that the vapour molecules are removed as they are formed;

▶ heating, thereby giving more molecules the energy to escape. If enough energy is transferred to the water, **all** the molecules will be able to escape. We call this **boiling**. Water boils at 100°C at sea level.

▶ by reducing the air pressure, thereby allowing the molecules to escape more easily. (This is why water boils at a lower temperature on mountains, where the air pressure is less than at sea level.)

Thermal radiation is the **transfer of energy** by **infra-red radiation** which can pass through a vacuum and be reflected. During radiation energy is transferred from all **hot objects**, which **lose heat** to their surroundings; the **hotter** the object the **more energy** it will radiate. **Dark, matt** surfaces emit more radiation than **light, shiny** surfaces; dark, matt surfaces are good absorbers (poor reflectors) of radiation; light, shiny surfaces are good reflectors (poor absorbers) of radiation.

▶ **Energy losses and insulation**

'insulation can reduce energy transfer from hotter to colder objects, and how insulation is used in domestic contexts' [4.5d]

During cold weather, about a third of the energy produced in Britain is used to heat people's homes to a comfortable temperature of about **20°C**. Some of this heat energy may come from using coal, oil or gas to heat up water in radiators in a **central heating system**, or from **burning fuel** in a fireplace in the room. Some houses are warmed using **heaters**, which in turn use **electricity** that has been generated in a power station from burning fuels. Figure 17.1 shows the ways in which heat energy is lost from an ordinary house.

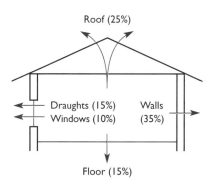

Fig. 17.1 How heat is lost from a house

Ways of reducing heat loss

(a) **Roof insulation**: laying an insulating fibre material which traps **air** in tiny spaces between the fibres. Air is a poor **conductor** of heat and reduces the heat escaping from the house.

'All these cost money but keep heat in'

(b) **Double glazing of windows**: putting a second pane of **glass** in each window, so that a layer of **air** is **trapped** between the two panes, greatly reduces the amount of heat which can escape. In most new houses the windows are **installed** as sealed double glazed units. These already consist of two panes of glass with a trapped layer of air to prevent heat escaping.

(c) **Cavity wall insulation**: most recently built houses have walls which are made of two layers of bricks with a gap in between. This gap can be filled with **insulating foam**, which again traps pockets of air and reduces heat escaping from the house.

(d) **Draught excluders**: putting strips of draught-excluding material around doors and windows can prevent **warm air escaping** and stop cold air from coming into the room. However, people who burn fuel in a fireplace need to check that there is a good flow of air to keep the fire burning, and to prevent the build-up of poisonous fumes within the room.

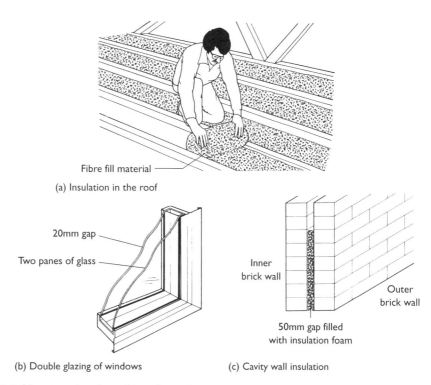

Fibre fill material

(a) Insulation in the roof

20mm gap

Two panes of glass

(b) Double glazing of windows

Inner brick wall

Outer brick wall

50mm gap filled with insulation foam

(c) Cavity wall insulation

Fig. 17.2 How to reduce loss of heat from a house

Remember: Insulation reduces the transfer of energy from hotter to colder objects; it works by trapping **air**, a poor conductor of heat, which is then warmed up.

Heat losses from **buildings** can be reduced by various methods of **insulation** such as: double glazing; cavity wall; and loft insulation.

▶ Energy resources

'See Chapter 4'

The importance of the Sun

The **Sun** is ultimately the major source of energy for Earth. Almost all the available energy comes from, or has come from, the Sun. Some of the Sun's energy is used by green plants in the process of **photosynthesis**. Over millions of years the remains of these plants and the animals which fed on them were changed into **fossil fuels** by the action of **heat** and **pressure**.

Fossil fuels

Fossil fuels are stores of **chemical** energy which is converted into **thermal** energy when the fuel burns. These fuels, such as **coal and oil**, were formed millions of years ago by the effect of **heat** and **pressure** on decaying plants and animals. Fossil fuels are described as **non-renewable** energy sources because once they are used up they cannot be replaced. Chemical energy is released as heat and light when the fuel is burned.

fuel + oxygen → **carbon dioxide + water + heat**

A **chemical equation** for this reaction would be:

$$CH_4 + 2O_2 \rightarrow CO_2 + 2H_2O + \text{heat}$$

'See Chapter 11, Acid Rain p. 214'

When fuels burn they may also produce **oxides of sulphur**, or **oxides of nitrogen** as well as **carbon monoxide**. These waste products are one of the main causes of **pollution**. For example, sulphur dioxide dissolves in water vapour in the air to cause 'acid rain', which damages trees, and harms animal life in rivers and lakes.

You may have **compared** the amount of heat energy released by different fuels by measuring the rise in **temperature** of a known volume of water in a test tube.

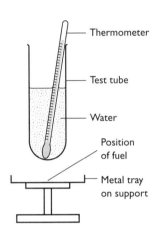

Thermometer

Test tube

Water

Position of fuel

Metal tray on support

Fig. 17.3 You may have used equipment like this to compare the amount of heat energy released by different fuels

What makes good fuel?

You should be aware of some of the factors which affect **why** a certain fuel is used for a particular job.

Some of these factors are:

1. How much it **costs** to obtain, and consequently the cost to the consumer.
2. How easy it is to **transport** and to **store**, which depends on whether it is solid, liquid or gas.

'Which factor is most important to you as a consumer?'

3. How easily it **catches alight** and **burns**.
4. How much **pollution** is caused, poisonous gases and dust particles being released into the atmosphere.
5. How much **energy** is released when it **burns**.

   For example the chart below shows how much **energy** is released when **1 kilogram** of fuel is burned:

Gas	55MJ per kg
Oil	44MJ per kg
Coal	29MJ per kg
Wood	14MJ per kg

Although gas may be the 'best' fuel as it releases the most energy, 1 kilogram of gas takes up much more **space** than 1 kilogram of oil, and is more bulky to transport and to store. So you have to take account of **all** the factors mentioned above, and the main interests of the **user** of the fuel, before you can make a decision as to the 'best' fuel for a particular task.

▶ Alternative energy sources

The supply of fossil fuels is limited and there is a need to obtain energy from **renewable** natural resources, such as the Sun as **solar** energy, the **wind**, **tides**, the rise and fall of **waves**, the flow of water from a higher to a lower level as **hydro-electric power**, and from the **heat of the Earth** itself.

Solar energy

'These are renewable sources of energy'

A common use of **solar** energy is to heat up water which is inside a **solar panel**. These panels are usually painted **black** so that they **absorb** as much heat as possible. The solar heated water is then pumped to a normal hot water tank where it can be used to **pre-heat** the cold water. The warmed-up water can then be further heated electrically. It is obviously much **cheaper** to heat water which has already been **warmed up** than to heat water from cold.

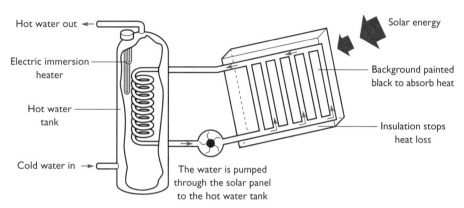

Fig. 17.4 A hot water system which uses solar energy

Solar cells

'Pollution free'

These are devices which absorb the **Sun's energy** and convert it into **electricity**. However, many thousands of cells are needed to produce useful amounts of electricity. One of their main uses is in **satellites**, where conventional batteries would be difficult to replace!

Hydro-electric power

'See Chapter 13, p. 253'

Hydro-electric power (HEP) is the result of fast-flowing water driving **turbines** in a hydro-electric power station and thereby producing electricity. There is no pollution, and the source of energy is free. The only costs involved are in the building of the power station and in maintenance.

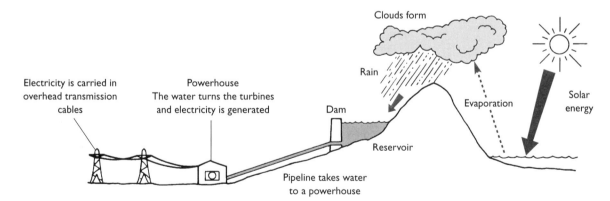

Fig. 17.5 How electricity is generated from hydro-electric power

Wave power

Waves are produced as the wind blows across the surface of the sea. A **wave power** machine converts the up and down movement of the waves into **electricity**. The potential for generating electricity is very great but there are many **technological** problems to be overcome.

Tidal power

'See Chapter 16, p. 303'

The **gravitational effect** of the Sun and Moon on the Earth cause regular **tidal movements** of the oceans. These tidal movements can be used to push water into reservoirs, which can then be used to drive **turbines** and so produce electricity.

Wind energy

Windmills which turn to generate electricity are called **aerogenerators**. A typical aerogenerator, capable of generating enough electricity for a small village, would need to have blades 20–25 metres long.

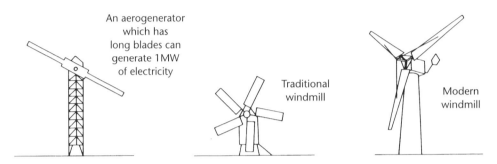

Fig. 17.6 Using wind energy to generate electricity

Geothermal power

Heat which is trapped in **hot rocks** deep in the Earth can be used to heat water and convert it into steam. The steam can then be used via a heat exchanger to drive **generators** and produce electricity.

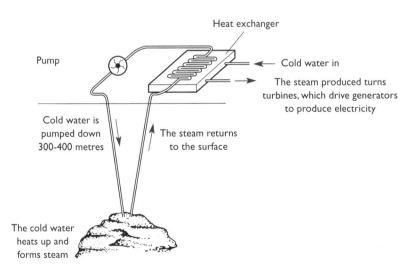

Fig. 17.7 Using hot water from the Earth to generate electricity

Why are alternative energy resources being developed?

Why are **alternative energy supplies** being developed? There are **three** main reasons:

'See Chapter 11, Acid Rain, p. 214'

1. Fossil fuels are '**finite**'. It has been predicted that in 600 years' time the known supplies of **coal** will have been **used up**.
2. Burning fossil fuels can cause **pollution**, especially **acid rain**.
3. There is an **increasing demand** for electricity from industry and from consumers. This may **exceed the supply** from existing power stations burning fossil fuels.

The chart below (Table 17.1) **summarises the main alternative sources of energy, and their advantages and disadvantages:**

Table 7.1

Energy source	Advantages	Disadvantages
Wind	• will not run out • no fuel costs • no pollution • useful for isolated communities	• windmills can spoil the environment • wind speeds may vary, so the generation of electricity is varied
Solar	• will not run out • no fuel costs • no pollution	• cloud cover blocks the Sun • difficult to store energy produced • huge solar panels needed
Tidal	• no fuel costs • no pollution	• expensive to build power stations • may cause silting up of rivers
Geothermal	• long-term supplies can provide hot water	• not easily available • costly to obtain
Wave	• will not run out • no pollution	• many technological problems • hazard to shipping
Hydro-electric power	• no pollution • cost of energy source is free	• high costs of building power station and maintenance • possible environmental damage if a valley is flooded to create a reservoir

Environmental problems

There are, however, **environmental** problems associated with all the different sources of energy. For example, burning fossil fuels generates **pollution** on a large scale (for one example of the pollution caused by burning fossil fuels: see Acid Rain, Chapter 11). However, using **renewable** energy sources such as **wind power** and **wave action** may seem environmentally 'friendly' but there is a huge **cost** of developing the technology to obtain energy in this way and to build the equipment required. The amount of electricity produced may be much **smaller** than that produced from a conventional power station so the cost per unit of electricity is relatively high.

Nuclear power

'One argument for and against nuclear power'

'See Chapter 18, Uses of Radioactivity, p. 344'

Nuclear power is another important source of energy. One of its main **disadvantages** is that the waste products are highly **radioactive** and are very difficult to dispose of **safely**. An **advantage** of nuclear power is that there are adequate supplies of **uranium**, and the nuclear power station does not release potentially harmful gases such as **sulphur dioxide**. Of course there is the **disadvantage** of the possible accidental release of radioactive substances into the atmosphere. Generally speaking, it can be said of nuclear power that although the **fuel** costs are relatively **low**, the costs of **building** nuclear power stations and the costs of **de-commissioning** them at the end of their useful life can be very **high**.

Remember: **Non-renewable** energy resources are finite and cannot be replaced, e.g. fossil fuels (coal, oil, gas), nuclear fuels (uranium).

Renewable energy resources are not finite and can be replaced, e.g. wood, wind power, solar power, hydro-electric power, wave power, geothermal.

▶ **Greenhouse effect**

'See Chapter 16, Changes to the Atmosphere'

The Earth is surrounded by an **atmosphere** which acts as a 'blanket' keeping it warm. On Earth the average surface temperature is +15°C, whereas on the Moon, which has no atmosphere, the surface temperature is −18°C.

Evidence has shown that the Earth is slowly warming up, caused by changes in the atmosphere. This gradual warming is called the '**Greenhouse effect**'.

During the past century man has been adding to the amount of **carbon dioxide** in the atmosphere as a result of **burning fossil fuels** (coal, oil, gas) and burning trees (as a result of deforestation to provide land for growing crops). This has disturbed the balance of carbon dioxide in the atmosphere; it is estimated to have increased over the past century from a 'pre-industrial' level of 0.275% to 0.350% today. This, in turn, has resulted in a slight warming of the Earth. In addition, other man-made gases have been released into the

'See Chapter 16, p. 312'

atmosphere which have been shown to add to the problem, for example chlorofluorocarbons (**CFCs**), methane, nitrous oxide and ozone. (Be careful – this is an increase in ozone in the lower atmosphere – do not confuse it with the ozone layer.)

How the greenhouse effect works

The Earth is warmed by **solar radiation** which passes through the **atmosphere** and is **absorbed** by the ground and oceans, warming them up. This energy is **re-radiated** (at a different wavelength) as **heat** into the atmosphere. Carbon dioxide, water vapour and the other gases mentioned absorb this heat energy and then re-radiate it **back** to the surface. Any increase in the amount of carbon dioxide will therefore increase the amount of heat 'trapped', resulting in a **gradual warming** (Fig. 17.8).

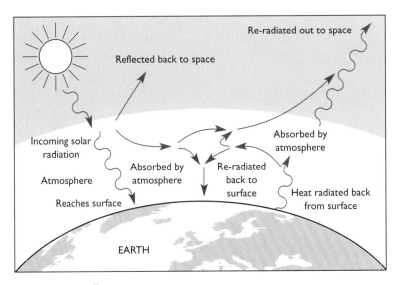

Fig. 17.8 The greenhouse effect

Implications

Many predictions have been made as to the effect that a slight warming of the Earth (1°C to 2°C) will produce, using many different computer models. Some of the suggestions put forward include:

▶ A **change in climate**; some areas will become drier, some wetter, some warmer. Drought may occur in parts of the Earth and floods in others.
▶ Polar ice caps will **melt** and this will itself affect the climate.

No one is certain what will happen – only that there will be changes.

The tables and charts used in many of the questions which follow provide extra detail on a number of the **principles** we have considered. This is true throughout the book. So, as well as answering the questions, take note of the relevant information.

▶ Work, power and energy

'the quantitative relationship between force and work' [4.5f]

'to calculate power in terms of the rate of working or of transferring energy' [4.5g]

'the quantitative links between kinetic energy, potential energy and work' [4.5h]

Work and energy

Work is done and energy is transferred whenever a **force** moves an object through a **distance**. The formula is:

work done (J) = force applied (N) × distance moved (m)

For example, if a person pushes a box with a force of 200N over a distance of 10m they have done $200 \times 10 = 2,000$J of work (Fig. 17.9).

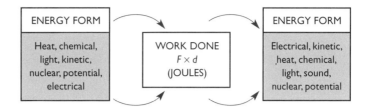

Fig. 17.9

Power

Power is the rate of doing work or the **rate of transfer of energy**.

The formula is

$$\text{power (W)} = \frac{\text{work done (energy transferred)}}{\text{time taken (s)}} = \frac{\text{Fd}}{\text{t}}$$

For example, if a person lifts 10 boxes on to a shelf 2m high using a force of 50N per box in 40 seconds, you can calculate their rate of doing work:

$$\begin{aligned} \text{work done} &= \text{ energy transferred} \\ &= 10 \times 50 \times 2 = 1{,}000\text{J} \end{aligned}$$

$$\text{power developed} = \frac{1000}{40} = 25\text{W}$$

'See Chapter 14, Weight, mass and gravity, p. 267'

In some calculations you may be given the **mass** of an object so you need to multiply the mass figure by **10**, as the force acting on **1kg** is **10N/kg**. For example, if a person has a mass of 65kg and climbs a flight of stairs 4m high in 5 seconds, then you can calculate the power developed as follows:

65kg weight (65 × 10) newtons
work done = 65 × 10 × 4 = 2,600J

$$\text{power developed} = \frac{2{,}600}{5} = 520\text{W}$$

▶ **Kinetic energy**

The **kinetic energy** (E) of a moving object depends on the mass (m) of the object and its velocity (v), as stated in the formula:

H   **kinetic energy $= \frac{1}{2} \times$ mass $\times$ (velocity)^2 $E = \frac{1}{2} m v^2$**

An object has **more** kinetic energy

'See Chapter 14, Vehicle Stopping Distances, pp. 266–267'

▶   the greater its **mass**
▶   the greater its **speed**

If a person of mass **60kg** is travelling with a velocity of **2m/s**, the kinetic energy =

$\frac{1}{2} \times 60 \times (2\text{m/s})^2 = \mathbf{120J}$

If the same person is travelling **twice as fast**, at **4m/s**, the kinetic energy =

$\frac{1}{2} \times 60 \times (4\text{m/s})^2 = \mathbf{480J}$

The **kinetic energy** has increased **four** times, as the **speed** has **doubled**.
If the **mass** of the person doubled to **120kg**, and the speed stayed at **2m/s**, the kinetic energy would be **doubled**:

$E = \frac{1}{2} \times 120 \times (2\text{m/s})^2 = \mathbf{240J}$

Momentum

The **momentum** of an object is a product of its **mass** and its **velocity**. The greater the mass of an object, and the greater its speed in a particular direction (its velocity), the more momentum an object has.

The formula is:

momentum (kg m/s) = mass (kg) × velocity (m/s)

In a collision the **total momentum after** a collision in a particular direction is the same as the total momentum in that direction **before** the collision. This is known as **conservation of momentum.**

▶ **Specific heat capacity**

When **energy** is supplied to a substance the temperature of the substance **rises** and the particles gain **kinetic energy**. The amount of heat energy required to raise the temperature of a substance depends on **three** factors:

▶ the **mass** of the substance being heated
▶ the **temperature** rise produced
▶ the **type** of substance

The energy required to raise the temperature of **1kg** of a substance by **1°C** is known as its **specific heat capacity.** For example the specific heat capacity of **water** is **4,200 joules per kilogram per degree Celsius** (J/kg °C). This means that to raise the temperature of 1kg of water by 1°C, **4,200 joules of energy** are required. The specific heat capacity of **copper is 380J/kg °C** so only **380 joules** are required to raise the temperature of copper by 1°C.

The amount of energy transferred to a substance when its temperature changes can be calculated using the formula

energy transferred = specific heat capacity × mass × change in temperature
(J)   (J/Kg °C)   (Kg)   (°C)

If you have to calculate the amount of energy transferred you will be given the relevant formula and all the measurements you need. One common error is being told that the mass of, say, water heated is 500g and inserting 500g into the formula. You need to convert the 500g to **0.5kg** before using it in the formula.

For example, 500g of water at 20°C was heated to 60°C. Calculate how much energy had been transferred to the water. (The specific heat capacity of water is 4,200J/kg °C.)

energy transferred = 0.5kg × 4,200 × 40°C = 84,000 joules = 84kJ

▶ **EXAMINATION QUESTIONS**

Multiple choice

Q1   Which one of the following is a fossil fuel?

A   coal   D   uranium
B   paper   E   wood
C   the Sun

Q2   What gas is released when coal is burned?

A   carbon dioxide   D   nitrogen
B   hydrogen   E   oxygen
C   methane

Q3   Which one of the following is an advantage of using coal, instead of wind energy, to generate electricity?

A   It is very cheap.
B   It will not run out.
C   It does not cause pollution.
D   It is very easy to obtain.
E   It can generate a lot of electricity.

Q4 The chart below shows some data on five different fuels. Which fuel, A, B, C, D, or E, costs the most to release 1,000 units of energy?

Fuel	Price per 100g	Energy released per 100g
A	10p	2,000
B	12p	3,000
C	18p	6,000
D	24p	4,000
E	25p	5,000

Structured questions

Q5 (a) Why is oil described as a fuel?

_____ *(2)*

(b) Suggest **two** reasons why gas is used to heat houses instead of solid fuel.

1. _____

2. _____ *(2)*

(c) Fossil fuels are non-renewable and will eventually run out. Name **two** sources of alternative energy which can be used to slow down the rate at which fossil fuels are being used.

1. _____

2. _____ *(2)*

Q6 Table 17.2 below gives some information about reducing heat loss in the home.

Table 17.2

Method of reducing heat loss	% of heat saved	Typical cost in £	Approx. time to recover cost (years)
Double glazing	15	1,000	30
Carpet underlay	20	200	8
Draught proofing	25	50	1
Roof insulation	30	150	3
Cavity wall insulation	35	300	5

(a) Which single method of reducing heat loss saves most energy?

_____ *(1)*

(b) Which is the most effective method of reducing heat loss at the smallest relative cost? Explain your answer.

Method _____

Explanation _____ *(3)*

(c) How much money do you save each year by using roof insulation?

_____ *(2)*

(NICCEA)

Q7 (a) Describe how you would use the apparatus shown below (Fig. 17.10) to compare the amount of heat released by three different samples of solid fuel. (7 lines)   (5)

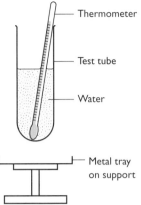

— Thermometer

— Test tube

— Water

— Metal tray
on support

Fig. 17.10

(b) State **three** factors which should be considered when choosing the best fuel to heat a house.

1. _____

2. _____

3. _____   *(3)*

(c) When fossil fuels burn they form sulphur dioxide gas. Describe and explain **one** effect that this gas has on the environment. (3 lines)   *(2)*

Q8 (a) Name **two** fossil fuels.   *(2)*

(b) Explain briefly how **one** of these fuels is formed and how it is extracted.   *(2)*

(c) When fossil fuels are burned in power stations sulphur dioxide and carbon dioxide are produced. These gases appear to be having an effect on our environment especially, with regard to the greenhouse effect and acid rain.
Explain how these gases affect our environment.   *(4)*

(d) Some varieties of plants have begun to show remarkable tolerance to high levels of sulphur dioxide in the air. Describe the mechanism that could lead to the evolution of these plant varieties.   *(3)*

(e) Nuclear power stations do not use fossil fuels.
  (i) Name a fuel that they use.
  (ii) Give **three** different environmental arguments for or against the use of nuclear fuels.
    (3)
    (MEG)

Q9 The diagram (Fig 17.11) shows the main parts of a solar heating system designed to provide hot water for a house. Heat energy from the Sun warms the water in the solar panel. This water is then pumped through a spiral of copper tube inside the hot water tank so that it can transfer its heat to the water in the tank.

(a) (i) State one reason why copper is used to make the spiral.

_____

  (ii) State one reason why a spiral tube is used and not a straight tube.

_____   *(2)*

(b) The pipes between the solar panel and the hot water tank are lagged.
  (i) Name a suitable material for the lagging.

_____

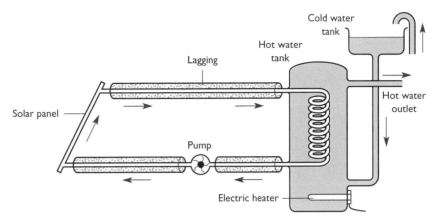

Fig. 17.11

(ii) State one reason why this should be done.

_____ *(2)*

(c) Explain why the hot water outlet pipe is at the top of the hot water tank. (3 lines) *(2)*

(d) The electric heater in the hot water tank is rated at 240V, 2,400W. Electrical energy is sold in units called kilowatt hours (kWh). Each unit costs 5p.

   (i) Calculate the electric current which will pass through the heater when it is switched on. (2 lines)

  (ii) How much energy is supplied by the heater if it is switched on for one hour? (2 lines)

 (iii) What is the cost of using the heater for two hours? (2 lines) *(6)*

                                                                        (SEG)

Q10 (Foundation Tier)   In this question notice how sub-questions (a), (b) and (c) can be answered independently so if you are unable to answer (a), go straight on to (b). Part (a) is targeted at level 6, part (b) at level 7, part (c) at levels 7 and 8.

(a) The diagram below (Fig. 17.12) shows the position of a hydro-electric power station.

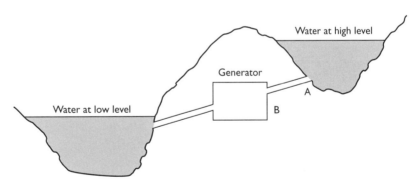

Fig. 17.12

 (i) What form of energy does the water have at the position marked A on the diagram?

_____ *(1)*

 (ii) What form of energy does the water have at the position marked B on the diagram?

_____ and _____ *(1)*

(iii) Give three advantages of a hydro-electric power station over a coal-fired powe station.

1. _____

2. _____

3. _____   (3)

(b) The diagram below (Fig. 17.13) shows an electrically heated hot water storage tank.

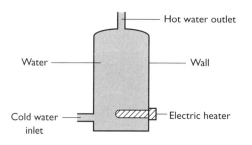

Fig. 17.13

(i)   Explain why the heater is placed at the bottom of the tank rather than at the top. (4 lines)   (2)

(ii) Explain how you would reduce the heat energy loss through the walls of the tank, naming any materials you might use. (4 lines)   (2)

(c) The diagram below (Fig. 17.14) shows a microwave oven.

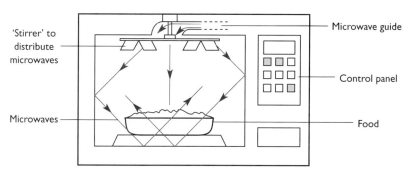

Fig. 17.14

Microwaves are absorbed by the water in the food. The specific heat capacity of water is 4.2kJ/kg/°C.

(i)   A plastic jug containing 500g of water at 20°C was placed in the microwave oven. The oven was switched on at full power. After two minutes in the oven the temperature of the water had risen to 44°C. Calculate how much energy had been transferred to the water in two minutes. (4 lines)   (3)

(ii) The output power of the oven is rated at 650W. How much energy does the cooker transfer from the electricity supply in two minutes? (2 lines)   (2)

(iii) Compare the amounts of energy you have calculated in (i) and (ii). Account for any difference. (3 lines)   (2)

(iv) The microwaves produced by the oven have a frequency of 2,450MHz and a velocity of 300,000km per second.
Calculate their wavelength. (4 lines)   (2)

(Co-ordinated Science, NEAB, London, WJEC)

> ### EXAMINATION ANSWERS

Multiple choice

A1   Key A, coal, is the only fossil fuel. A common distractor is option E, wood, which is a fuel made from trees but not a fossil fuel. Option D 'uranium' is a nuclear fuel, and options B and C are other **distractors**.

A2   Key A, carbon dioxide, is always formed when a fuel burns. Option C, methane, is the name for a fuel, natural gas, and option E, oxygen, is what all fuels need in order to burn.

A3   Key E, coal, produces a lot of electricity. All the other options, A to D, are advantages of wind energy, and disadvantages of fossil fuels.

A4   Key D is correct, as 1,000 units of energy at this rate would cost a quarter of 24, which is 6p. Options A and E cost 5p, option B costs 4p, and option C costs 3p.

Structured questions

A5   (a) oil is a fuel because it releases heat and light when it burns

   (b) 1. easy to transport through pipes to the house; 2. less dust, soot or ash

   (c) 1. wind power; 2. tidal power.

A6   (a) cavity wall insulation

   (b) Method – draught proofing. Explanation – cheapest method, recovers cost in 1 year, and 25% of heat saved. The most efficient method which saves 35% costs 6 times as much and takes 5 years to recover costs.

   (c) about one-third of the heating bill

A7   (a) These key points should appear in your answer:
        same mass of fuel used each time;
        same volume of water used at the same temperature;
        temperature of water measured before and after heating;
        method mentioned of preventing heat escaping;
        safety precautions such as wearing safety goggles;
        recording results in a chart;
        calculating and comparing temperature change.

   (b) 1.   the cost of the fuel;
        2.   whether it is a solid, liquid or gas;
        3.   how easy it is to transport and store.

   (c) Sulphur dioxide dissolves in the water vapour and forms acid rain. Acid rain can destroy trees and make water in lakes very acid, so killing the fish.

A8   (a) coal, oil

   (b) Coal was formed millions of years ago from trees and ferns which died and decayed, forming layers of peat. The peat layers were covered with mud and sand, and usually covered by the sea. This process was repeated many times over millions of years and the layers were pushed down. Owing to the pressure and the heat, the peat changed into coal seams. Coal is extracted by mining.

   (c) Sulphur dioxide forms acid rain when it dissolves in water vapour. The acid rain destroys trees and makes water in lakes very acid, so killing fish. Carbon dioxide in the atmosphere prevents heat escaping and produces the 'greenhouse effect', with a possible warming of the temperature of the Earth's surface.

   (d) A few plants may be more resistant to sulphur dioxide, and these grow well and form seeds which in turn produce plants which are resistant. By a process of natural selection those plants best adapted survive and others die.

(e) (i) uranium
     (ii) nuclear fuels produce radioactive waste which is difficult to dispose of safely;
           nuclear fuels do not pollute the atmosphere with harmful gases like fossil fuels,
           which produce sulphur dioxide; there is always the danger of an explosion which
           would be difficult to control in a nuclear power station.

A9 (a) (i) copper metal is a good conductor of heat;
             (ii)   to increase the surface area for exchange of heat.

        (b) (i) any material which has lots of air trapped in it, such as insulating foam, woollen
                  cloth, spongey tubing.
             (ii) to reduce the amount of heat loss from the water on its way to the tank.

        (c) Due to convection currents, hot water rises to the top of the tank and denser cold
             water sinks to the bottom of the tank, where it can be heated.

        (d) (i) Use the formula W = V × A (remember West VirginiA, i.e Watts = Volts × Amps)
                  So, to find the current, use $\dfrac{W}{V}$ = A

                  $\dfrac{2{,}400}{240}$ = 10 amps

             (ii) Energy supplied = power × time = 2.4kW × 1hr = 2.4kWh.
             (iii) In 2 hours the energy used = 4.8kWh. 1kWh costs 5p. The cost of using the heater
                   is 5p × 4.8 = 24p.

A10 (a) (i) At position A the water has gravitational potential energy. (1)
              (ii) At position B the water has kinetic energy and gravitational potential energy. (1)
              (iii) non-polluting (1)
                    cheaper running costs (1)
                    uses renewable energy source (1)

         (b) (i) A liquid expands and becomes less dense when it is heated (1), so the liquid at the
                   bottom of the tank therefore rises up towards the hot water outlet, creating a
                   warm convection current. (1) The cold water coming into the tank replaces the
                   warm water.
              (ii) The tank could be insulated (1) by wrapping padded fibre material around it. (1)

         (c) (i) energy transferred = specific heat capacity × mass × change in temperature (I)
                                       = 0.5kg × 4,200J × 24° (1)
                                       = 50.4kJ (1)
              (ii) 650W × 120s (1) 78kJ (1)
              (iii) More energy goes into the cooker than is transferred to the water. (1)
                    Energy may be absorbed by the inside of the cooker, or be released to the sur-
                    roundings (1)
              (iv) $\dfrac{300{,}000\text{km/s} \; (1)}{2{,}450\text{MHz}}$
                    = 1.2 × 10⁻⁴m (1)

▶ STUDENTS' ANSWERS WITH EXAMINER'S COMMENTS

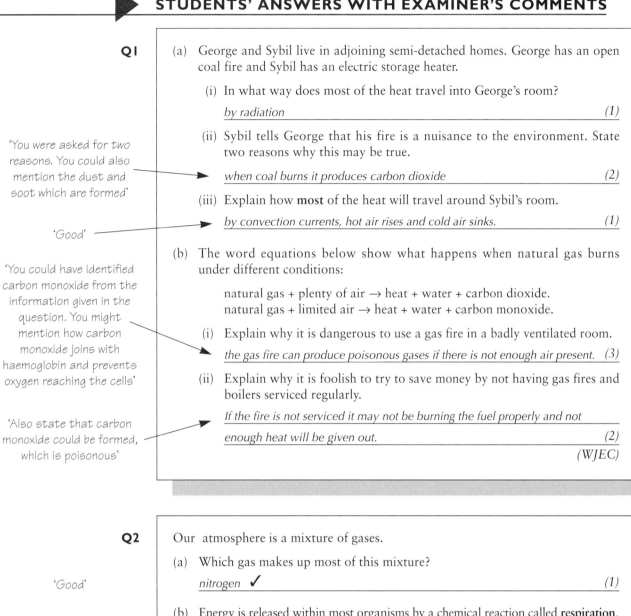

Q1

(a) George and Sybil live in adjoining semi-detached homes. George has an open coal fire and Sybil has an electric storage heater.

(i) In what way does most of the heat travel into George's room?

by radiation (1)

(ii) Sybil tells George that his fire is a nuisance to the environment. State two reasons why this may be true.

when coal burns it produces carbon dioxide (2)

'You were asked for *two* reasons. You could also mention the dust and soot which are formed'

(iii) Explain how **most** of the heat will travel around Sybil's room.

by convection currents, hot air rises and cold air sinks. (1)

'Good'

(b) The word equations below show what happens when natural gas burns under different conditions:

natural gas + plenty of air → heat + water + carbon dioxide.
natural gas + limited air → heat + water + carbon monoxide.

(i) Explain why it is dangerous to use a gas fire in a badly ventilated room.

the gas fire can produce poisonous gases if there is not enough air present. (3)

'You could have identified carbon monoxide from the information given in the question. You might mention how carbon monoxide joins with haemoglobin and prevents oxygen reaching the cells'

(ii) Explain why it is foolish to try to save money by not having gas fires and boilers serviced regularly.

If the fire is not serviced it may not be burning the fuel properly and not

enough heat will be given out. (2)

(WJEC)

'Also state that carbon monoxide could be formed, which is poisonous'

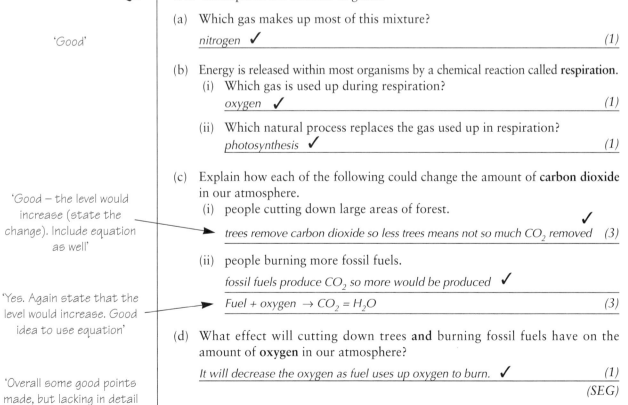

Q2

Our atmosphere is a mixture of gases.

(a) Which gas makes up most of this mixture?

nitrogen ✓ (1)

'Good'

(b) Energy is released within most organisms by a chemical reaction called **respiration**.
(i) Which gas is used up during respiration?

oxygen ✓ (1)

(ii) Which natural process replaces the gas used up in respiration?

photosynthesis ✓ (1)

(c) Explain how each of the following could change the amount of **carbon dioxide** in our atmosphere.
(i) people cutting down large areas of forest.   ✓

trees remove carbon dioxide so less trees means not so much CO_2 removed (3)

'Good – the level would increase (state the change). Include equation as well'

(ii) people burning more fossil fuels.

fossil fuels produce CO_2 so more would be produced ✓

Fuel + oxygen → CO_2 = H_2O (3)

'Yes. Again state that the level would increase. Good idea to use equation'

(d) What effect will cutting down trees **and** burning fossil fuels have on the amount of **oxygen** in our atmosphere?

It will decrease the oxygen as fuel uses up oxygen to burn. ✓ (1)

(SEG)

'Overall some good points made, but lacking in detail to gain still higher marks'

SUMMARY

At the end of this chapter you should know:

▷   that differences in **temperature** can lead to **transfer** of **energy**;

▷   how energy is transferred by the **movement of particles** in **conduction**, **convection** and **evaporation**;

▷   how energy is transferred by **radiation**;

▷   that **insulation** can reduce energy transfer from hotter to colder objects, and how insulation is used in domestic contexts;

▷   the meaning of **energy efficiency** and the need for economical use of **energy resources**;

▷   that there is a variety of energy resources, including oil, gas, coal, biomass, food, wind, waves and batteries;

▷   that the **Sun** is the ultimate source of most of the Earth's energy resources;

▷   that **electricity** is generated using a variety of **energy resources**;

▷   that some energy resources are **renewable** and some are **non-renewable**;

▷   the quantitative relationship between **force** and **work**;

▷   how to calculate **power** in terms of the **rate of working** or of transferring energy;

▷   the quantitative links between **kinetic energy**, **potential energy** and **work**.

Radioactivity

GETTING STARTED

You may have had an X-ray of your teeth at the dentist, or perhaps an X-ray of a broken bone at a hospital. When luggage is checked in at many airports, it is scanned by X-rays. This is done to detect the presence of illegal weapons or bombs which could cause problems on an aircraft.

In this chapter we will look at how unstable atoms break down to release heat and radiation and how radioactivity can be detected. We will see how radioactive isotopes are used in industry, medicine and food production. At the end of the chapter we will look at nuclear power and the processes of nuclear fission and nuclear fusion.

TOPIC	STUDY	REVISION 1	REVISION 2
Radioactivity			
Background radioactivity			
Radioactive emissions			
Half-life			
Beneficial and harmful effects of radiation on organisms			
Uses of radioactivity			

WHAT YOU NEED TO KNOW

▶ **Radioactivity**

'radioactivity arises from the breakdown of an unstable nucleus' [4.6a]

'Check back to Chapter 7, p. 140, for information on isotopes'

Radioactivity is the result of the breakdown of some **unstable nuclei** in atoms. Some **isotopes** are unstable and will emit **energy** in the form of heat and radiation to become more stable, for example, carbon 14 and uranium 235. Some of these isotopes are naturally occurring, like the two examples given, while others, such as plutonium 239, can be manufactured. Naturally occurring **radioactive isotopes** are usually found in the heavier elements, or are the isotopes of lighter elements which have more neutrons present in their nuclei.

▶ **Background radioactivity**

'there is background radioactivity' [4.6b]

We are constantly exposed to radioactivity from natural sources. This is referred to as **background radiation**. It arises from **cosmic rays** penetrating the **atmosphere, soil, rocks** (particularly granite in this country) and **building materials**, and from the **food** we eat (mainly owing to a radioactive isotope of potassium. In addition to these we receive small doses of radiation from **medical treatment**, such as chest and dental X-rays.

▶ **Radioactive emissions**

'there are three main types of radioactive emission, with different penetrating powers' [4.6c]

'the nature of alpha and beta particles and of gamma radiation' [4.6d]

When the **nucleus** in radioactive materials breaks down it can emit different types of radioactivity.

Table 18.1 shows the **three** main types of radioactive emissions.

Table 18.1

'Learn the characteristics of each type of radioactivity'

Type of emission	Description	Penetrating power	Deflection
alpha particles (α)	fast-moving helium nuclei (2 protons, 2 neutrons) H	absorbed by few cm of air or stopped by a thin sheet of paper	weakly deflected by a magnetic field
beta particles (β)	fast-moving electrons H	easily passes through air or paper; stopped by thin sheets of metal	deflected by a magnetic field
gamma-rays (γ)	short wavelength electromagnetic radiation	very penetrating; stopped by thick sheets of lead or thick concrete	not deflected by a magnetic field

When radioactive atoms **decay** and emit particles they change into other atoms. For example, when **uranium 238** loses an α particle: $^{238}_{92}\text{U} \rightarrow ^{234}_{90}\text{Th} + ^{4}_{2}\text{He}$

Similarly, when **carbon 14** loses a β particle: $^{14}_{6}\text{C} \rightarrow ^{14}_{7}\text{N} + ^{0}_{-1}\text{e}^{-}$

Radioactive atoms can be **created** by bombarding non-radioactive atoms with other particles. These could be α particles, β particles, or more often fast-moving neutrons.

Detecting radioactivity

'Check back to Chapter 15, p. 282, for a more detailed look at X-radiation'

Radioactivity was first discovered because of its ability to 'fog' **photographic plates** – in the same way as light affects photographic film. This is the way X-ray photographs are taken today (X-ray was the first name given to radioactivity). Radioactivity, however, also has the ability to ionise gases that it passes through, and it is this property that forms the basis of radiation detection techniques today. The **Geiger-Müller** tube is an example. The tube is filled with a gas that is mainly **argon**. When radiation passes into the tube, some of the gas atoms are **ionised**. This causes a tiny **electric current** to flow, the size of which can be measured and is proportional to the amount of ionisation produced (i.e. the radiation present).

▶ **Half-life** H

'*the meaning of the term 'half-life*' [4.6e]

'The half-life is constant for a particular radioactive material'

Over a period of time, any radioactive material will **decay** and become **stable** (non-radio-active). **When** any particular nucleus will decay and release its radiation and energy cannot be predicted. They decay in a **random way**. However, different substances decay at different **rates**, and the **rate of decay** of all radioactive material is measured in half-lives.

The **half-life** is the time taken for the radioactivity **to reduce by half**. For a particular radioactive material the half-life is **constant**, whatever the conditions. Radioactive decay is unaffected by temperature or pressure. Half-lives can be very **long** or very **short** (thousands of years to less than a second). If you plot a graph for the decay of any radioactive material it will always follow the same pattern, as in Fig. 18.1.

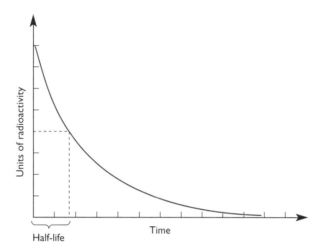

Fig. 18.1 The decay curve for radioactive materials

▶ **Beneficial and harmful effects of radiation on organisms**

'*the beneficial and harmful effects of radiation on matter and living organisms*' [4.6f]

The effect of radiation on living tissue depends on several factors:

1. the **strength** of the radiation;
2. the **length** of **exposure;**
3. how much of the **tissue** (how many cells) is exposed.

'Check back to Chapter 15, Waves, p. 282'

'Mutations were described in Chapter 5, p. 95'

The results of such exposure vary. There may be no serious effect if only a few cells are damaged, but in animals **cancer** may develop if the radiation dose is high enough. Radiation can also cause **genetic mutations**, so that future offspring are different in some way. In extreme cases, if enough cells are killed, the plant or animal may die.

▶ **Uses of radioactivity**

'*some uses of radioactivity, including the radioactive dating of rocks*' [4.6g]

Radioactive isotopes can be used in a variety of ways, for example in **industry**, in **medicine** for **food production** and for **radiocarbon dating**.

1. Manufacturers can check the **thickness** of metal containers, or the **amounts** of materials in packages, by measuring the amount of radiation that passes through. An example is measuring the amount of toothpaste in a tube.
2. All living things contain a large amount of carbon. Most of the carbon atoms are of the isotope **carbon 12**, but a small proportion are of the **radioactive isotope** carbon 14. This **proportion** of carbon 12 to carbon 14 is the same for all living things while they are alive. When the organism dies, the amount of carbon 14 **decreases** (half-life 5,736 years). By measuring the amount of radioactive carbon **left**, one can date the item by reference to the **half-life curve**. This technique of carbon 14 dating was recently used to date the Turin Shroud.
3. Small amounts of **radioisotopes** can be introduced into underground **water systems**. Geiger counters can then be used to detect the position of **leaks**.

'Another application of the half-life curve'

4. **Food irradiation** is a method of preserving food by directing **radiation** (usually gamma rays) on to **fresh food**. Such irradiation of food can **destroy bacteria** and prevent the growth of **moulds, sterilise the contents** of sealed packets, reduce the sprouting of vegetables or prolong the ripening of fruits. This irradiation does NOT make the food radioactive. However, it is not suitable for all food since it can change the taste.

5. Radiation can be used to **control pests**. Male insects are reared in the laboratory and are **sterilised** by being exposed to a controlled dose of **gamma-rays**. They are then released into the wild, where they mate, competing with normal males. The females with which the sterilised males mate do not reproduce, so the insect **population** is quickly **reduced**.

[H] ⋯ ### Nuclear fission

The atoms of radioactive material have **unstable nuclei** that break down releasing energy, either as radiation (**gamma-rays**) or as kinetic energy from **alpha** and **beta particles**. Nuclear **fission** is a process in which a radioactive **nucleus** splits into fragments; this occurs naturally in some elements which have very large unstable nuclei. When this happens often a few neutrons are released as well.

'Know how a chain reaction occurs'

The nucleus of a rare form of **uranium** (Uranium–235) will break down, at the same time releasing a few **neutrons**. These fast-moving neutrons can then strike another nucleus. When this happens the **second** nucleus will also immediately break down, releasing yet **more** neutrons. Each **fission** (breakdown) produces more **neutrons**, which in turn cause other breakdowns. This is called a **chain reaction**, and can happen very quickly. Each time a nucleus breaks down, a large amount of **energy** is released; this results in a rapid **rise in temperature** of the uranium and its surroundings. This type of reaction takes place in a **nuclear reactor**, which is fed with concentrated uranium–235.

Nuclear fusion

'See Chapter 16, Evolution of a star, p. 304'

Nuclear **fusion** is the **opposite** of nuclear fission. In nuclear fusion energy is released when small nuclei are **joined together** to form larger nuclei. This process is happening all the time in the **Sun**, and is the source of the Sun's energy. Scientists and technologist have been trying to produce nuclear fusion reactors on Earth for a long time but have still not overcome **two** major problems:

'Nuclear Fusion and Fission are opposites'

1. bringing the particles together fast enough;
2. building a 'container' for the reaction that can withstand the high temperatures involved.

The main advantage of nuclear **fusion** over nuclear **fission** is that it produces far less radioactive by-products and could use readily available **deuterium** (an isotope of hydrogen).

Nuclear power

'See Chapter 17, Alternative Energy Resources, p. 326'

The source of energy for **nuclear power** comes from the energy stored in the nuclei of a particular type of uranium, **uranium–235**, which has 92 protons and 143 neutrons in the nucleus. In a **nuclear power station**, the uranium is in the form of fuel elements in the reactor core.

During nuclear fission, the uranium nuclei are hit by slow-moving **neutrons** and the uranium nucleus splits into two smaller parts, giving out **energy** in the process. The neutrons which are released from the uranium nucleus are then used to split more uranium–235 nuclei in a chain reaction. In the **nuclear reactor**, this reaction is controlled by control rods, made of boron, which absorb neutrons. The heat produced by the reaction is carried away by a coolant liquid to a **heat exchanger** where it is used to generate steam which drives turbines to generate electricity (Fig. 18.2).

Nuclear power is an important source of energy as an **alternative** to fossil fuels. One of its main **disadvantages** is that the waste products are highly **radioactive** and are therefore very difficult to dispose of safely.

Two **advantages** of nuclear power are:

1. there are **adequate supplies** of **uranium** to last for a very long time;
2. nuclear power stations do **not** release gases such as sulphur dioxide and carbon dioxide which can harm the environment.

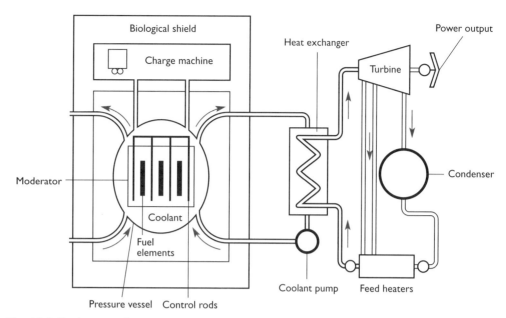

Fig. 18.2 Producing nuclear power

The accident at the nuclear reactor in Chernobyl, Ukraine, in 1986 was caused by the **control rods** being removed too far from the **reactor core**, so that the nuclear fission reaction produced **large amounts of heat** which could not be removed quickly enough from the reactor. The heat caused an **explosion** which exposed the top of the reactor core to the atmosphere, and ejected large amounts of **radioactive debris**. Some of the radioactive substances were carried by strong winds across into Europe, where heavy rainfall caused contamination of areas of Scotland, the Lake District and North Wales.

 EXAMINATION QUESTIONS

Multiple choice

Q1 Which type of radiation would be stopped by a few sheets of paper?

A   alpha particles
B   beta particles
C   gamma radiation
D   X-rays

Q2 A radioactive substance has a half-life of 15 years. What proportion of the substance would be left after 30 years?

A   a half
B   a third
C   a quarter
D   a sixth

Q3 The graph below shows how the activity of a radioactive substance changes with time.

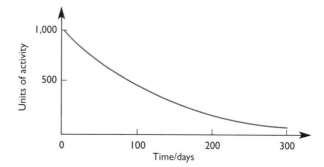

Fig. 18.3

What is the half-life of this substance?

A   50 days;
B   100 days;
C   200 days;
D   500 days;
E   1,000 days.

Structured questions

Q4   When a teacher discovers an unlabelled radioactive source, she uses the apparatus below to find out the activity of the source and type (or types) of radiation being emitted.

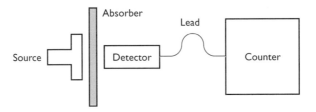

Fig. 18.4

(a)   What does 'activity of the source' mean?

_____   *(1)*

The number of counts with **no** absorber is recorded. When a thin piece of tissue paper is used as an absorber the number of counts drops noticeably?

(b)   What type of radiation has the tissue paper absorbed?

_____   *(1)*

A sheet of lead 2cm thick is now used as an absorber, but some radiation is still detected.

(c)   (i)   What is this radiation?   _____   *(1)*

        (ii)   Give **one** example of how this radiation can be used in either medicine or industry.

_____   *(1)*

_____   *(MEG)*

Q5   Tubes for toothpaste are filled as shown.
        The empty tube is placed between a radioactive source and a detector.
        Paste is put into the tube and, when the tube is full, it is moved along the production line for sealing.

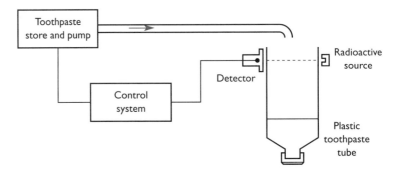

Fig. 18.5

(a)   When the tube is full what effect will this have upon the beam of radiation reaching the detector?

_____   *(1)*

(b)   What instruction will the detector pass to the filling mechanism?

_____   *(1)*

(c)   What type of radiation would most likely be used for this purpose?

_____   *(1)*

(d)   Name a suitable detecting device.

_____   *(1)*

(e)   (i)   This is an example of a feedback control system. Which of the two kinds of feedback, negative or positive, is being used here?

_____   *(1)*

   (ii)   Give one reason for your answer.

_____   *(1)*

   (iii)   Some years ago toothpaste tubes were made of lead. Why could this system not have been used then?

_____   *(1)*

(MEG)

Q6 (Foundation Tier)   This question is about some of the properties and uses of alpha, beta and gamma radiation.

(a)   (i)   Radiation is always present in the environment. What is the general name given to this radiation?

_____   *(1)*

   (ii)   Give one natural cause and one man-made cause of this radiation.

   1.   _____

   2.   _____   *(2)*

   (iii)   Name the instrument used to measure the radiation level.   *(1)*

(b)   The diagram shows alpha and beta particles passing between two charged plates.

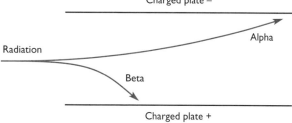

Fig. 18.6

   (i)   Explain why alpha particles are deflected upwards in the electric field, but beta particles are deflected downwards. (4 lines)   *(2)*

   (ii)   Some scientists investigating radioactivity bought a pure sample of thorium which gives out beta rays. When they examined the sample several days later they found that it contained protactinium. Why? (4 lines)   *(2)*

(c) Radioactivity is used in hospitals to investigate the inside of a person's body without having to cut them open. One substance used is Technetium – 99 (^{99}Tc) which gives out gamma (γ) rays.

   (i) What would be used to detect the gamma radiation? (3 lines)   *(1)*

   (ii) Why is it important to protect hospital workers from gamma rays? (5 lines)   *(3)*

   (iii) 99 is the mass number of Technetium. Explain what is meant by mass number. (4 lines)   *(3)*

(Integrated Science, NEAB, London)

Q7 (a) Carbon has a proton number (atomic number) of 6 and has three isotopes which are found naturally. The most common isotope is carbon 12. Another isotope is carbon 14 which is said to be a radioisotope.

   (i) Complete the table to show the particles that are found in an atom of each isotope.

Table 18.2

Isotope	Number of protons	Number of neutrons	Number of electrons
Carbon 12			
Carbon 14			

   (ii) How do the two isotopes differ in terms of their atomic structure? (2 lines)   *(1)*

(b) Radioisotopes decay to become more stable. Carbon 14 emits a beta particle when it decays. It decays according to the equation:

$$^{14}_{6}\text{C} \longrightarrow\ ^{14}_{7}\text{N} + ^{0}_{-1}\text{e}^{-}$$ *(1)*

   (i) What is a beta particle? (1 line)   *(1)*

   (ii) What change occurs in the nucleus of the carbon 14 atom when it decays? (3 lines)   *(2)*

   (iii) How can beta particles be detected? (1 line)   *(1)*

   (iv) In the diagram below (Fig. 18.7), a beam of beta particles is passing through an electric field. Complete the diagram to show what happens to the beam in the field.

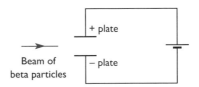

Beam of beta particles

Fig. 18.7

(1)

(Co-ordinated Science, London)

 EXAMINATION ANSWERS

Multiple choice

A1 Key A, alpha particles, are stopped by paper; Option B, beta particles, are stopped by thin sheets of metal, and option C, gamma radiation, is stopped by thick sheets of lead.

A2 Key C, a quarter. In 15 years a half would be left, so in another 15 years, a quarter of the original is left.

A3 Key B. It has taken 100 days for the activity to reduce from 1,000 units to 500 units (from the graph).

Structured questions

A4 (a) the number of particles emitted per second by the source

(b) alpha radiation

(c) (i) gamma radiation
(ii) to irradiate foods to kill bacteria

A5 (a) it will stop the beam

(b) to stop the filling mechanism

(c) beta radiation

(d) a Geiger-Müller tube

(e) (i) negative feedback
(ii) it stops the tube from becoming too full
(iii) beta radiation would be stopped by lead

A6 (a) (i) background (1)
(ii) a natural cause of background radiation is from radioactive rocks/minerals (1)
a man-made cause is from nuclear waste/fall-out/medical uses/TV (1)
(iii) a Geiger counter/Geiger-Müller/GM tube (1)

(b) (i) the alpha particles carry a positive charge and are attracted to the negative plate (1)
the beta particles have a negative charge and are attracted to the positive plate (1)
(ii) The nucleus is unstable (1)
and emits radiation/splits up (1)

(c) (i) photographic film could be used (1)
(ii) ionisation (1)
affects living cells/causes cancer (1)
causes changes in genes/mutations (1)
(iii) the mass number is the number of protons (1)
plus the number of neutrons (1) in the nucleus (1)

A7 (a) (i)

Table 18.3

Isotope	Number of protons	Number of neutrons	Number of electrons	
---------	-------------------	--------------------	---------------------	
Carbon 12	6	6	6	*(1)*
Carbon 14	6	8	6	*(1)*

(ii) they have different numbers of neutrons/carbon 12 has 6 neutrons but carbon 14 has 8 neutrons (1)

(b) (i) an electron (1)
(ii) when the nucleus of carbon 14 decays, the neutron splits (1)
into a proton and an electron (1)
alternative answer: the neutron number decreases by 1 (1),
the atomic number/proton number increases by 1 (1)
(iii) by using a Geiger counter or GM tube (1)
alternative answer: cloud chamber/photographic film
(iv) the beam of beta particles would be deflected towards the positive plate so draw the line bending towards the + plate (1)

▶ **A STUDENT'S ANSWER WITH EXAMINER'S COMMENTS**

Fig. 18.8 (with acknowledgements to 'The Observer')

Following the Chernobyl disaster in April 1986, the government in Britain started measuring the levels of radioactivity in sheep meat.

'Yes and state also that the radiation levels in meat had to be below a safe level for human consumption'

(a) Why was it considered important to measure the radioactivity in sheep meat?

The sheep would have eaten the grass which had radiation on it.   (2)

(b) State **two** methods of detecting radiation from the meat.

1. *Using a GM tube.*

2. *Using photographic film.*   (2)

(c) Complete Table 18.3 below about two radioactive particles.

Table 18.4

Name of particle	Description	Charge (+ or −)	How to identify each particle
Alpha	(i) *helium nuclei*	(ii) *+*	(iii) *stopped by paper*
Beta	(iv) *electrons*	(v) *−*	(vi) *stopped by lead*

'No. Thin metal sheets'

(d) The number of counts per minute from a radioactive source is recorded once every half hour. The results are shown in Table 18.4.

Table 18.5

Time/minutes	Corrected counts per minute
0	121
30	86
60	60
90	44
120	29
150	21
180	15

(i) What is the meaning of the term 'half-life'?

'Good'

time taken for radioactivity to be half   (2)

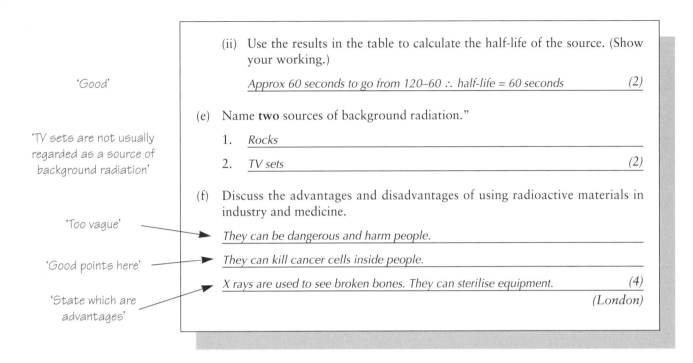

(ii) Use the results in the table to calculate the half-life of the source. (Show your working.)

'Good'

Approx 60 seconds to go from 120–60 ∴ half-life = 60 seconds   (2)

(e) Name **two** sources of background radiation."

'TV sets are not usually regarded as a source of background radiation'

1.   *Rocks*

2.   *TV sets*   (2)

(f) Discuss the advantages and disadvantages of using radioactive materials in industry and medicine.

'Too vague'   →   *They can be dangerous and harm people.*

'Good points here'   →   *They can kill cancer cells inside people.*

'State which are advantages'   →   *X rays are used to see broken bones. They can sterilise equipment.*   (4)

(London)

SUMMARY

At the end of this chapter you should know:

▷   that **radioactivity** arises from the **breakdown** of an **unstable nucleus**;

▷   that there is **background radioactivity**;

▷   that there are **three** main types of **radioactive emission**, with different penetrating powers;

▷   the nature of **alpha** and **beta particles,** and of **gamma radiation**;

▷   the meaning of the term '**half-life**';

▷   the **beneficial** and **harmful** effects of **radiation** on matter and living organisms;

▷   some **uses** of **radioactivity**, including the **radioactive dating** of **rocks**.

Index

Numbers in italics refer to illustrations.

Longman - for all your study guide needs

Addison Wesley Longman publishes a wide range of curriculum-related books to help you with your studies. If you have enjoyed using this book and have found it useful, you can now order others directly from us - simply follow the ordering instructions below.

Don't forget to tell your fellow students about *Longman Study Guides* - they might find them useful too!

HOW TO ORDER

A full list of titles is given overleaf. Decide which title(s) you require and then order in one of the following ways:

by post
Fill in the quantity alongside the title(s) you require, select your method of payment, complete your name and address details and return your completed order form and payment to:
Addison Wesley Longman Ltd
PO BOX 88
Harlow
Essex CM19 5SR

by phone
Call our Customer Information Centre on 01279 623923 to place your order, quoting mail number: HESG1

by fax
complete the order form overleaf and fill in your name and address details and method of payment, and fax it to us on 01279 414130.

by e-mail
E-mail your order to us on awlhe.orders@awl.co.uk listing title(s) and quantity required and providing full name and address details as requested here. Please quote mail number: HESG1. Please do not send credit card details by e-mail.

Mail no: **HESG1**

Your Name _____

Your Address _____

_____

Postcode _____ Telephone _____

Method of payment

☐ I enclose a cheque or a P/O for £ _____ made payable to Addison Wesley Longman Ltd
☐ Please charge my Visa/Access/AMEX/Diners Club card

Number _____ Expiry Date _____

Signature _____ Date _____

(please ensure that the address given above is the same as for your credit card)

Prices and other details are correct at time of going to press but may change
without notice. All orders are subject to status.

☐ *Please tick this box if you would like a complete listing of York Notes*
Literature Guides (suitable for GCSE and A-level English students)

LONGMAN   Addison Wesley Longman

LONGMAN HOMEWORK HANDBOOKS (KEY STAGE 3)

£7.99 each unless otherwise stated

QTY *(0582)*

1	_____ 29330 8	English (KS3)
2	_____ 29331 6	French (KS3)
3	_____ 30423 7	French pack*(KS3) (£12.99)
4	_____ 30425 3	French cassette (KS3) (£6.00)
5	_____ 29329 4	German (KS3)
6	_____ 30427 X	German pack*(KS3) (£12.99)
7	_____ 30428 8	German cassette (KS3) (£6.00)
8	_____ 29328 6	Mathematics (KS3)
9	_____ 29327 8	Science (KS3)

LONGMAN GCSE STUDY GUIDES

£9.99 each unless otherwise stated

10	_____ 30481 4	Biology
11	_____ 31538 7	Business Studies
12	_____ 30482 2	Chemistry
13	_____ 31539 5	Economics
14	_____ 30484 9	English
15	_____ 30483 0	English Literature
16	_____ 30485 7	French
17	_____ 03839 1	French pack* (£14.99)
18	_____ 03836 7	French cassette (£6.00)
19	_____ 30486 5	Geography
20	_____ 30487 3	German
21	_____ 03837 5	German pack* (£14.99)
22	_____ 03838 3	German cassette (£6.00)
23	_____ 30495 4	Higher Level Mathematics
24	_____ 30494 6	Information Technology (£10.99)
25	_____ 30496 2	Mathematics
26	_____ 30497 0	Music
27	_____ 31540 9	Physics
28	_____ 28700 6	Psychology
29	_____ 31542 5	Religious Studies
30	_____ 30498 9	Science (£10.99)
31	_____ 22651 1	Sociology
32	_____ 22652 X	Spanish
33	_____ 24509 5	Spanish pack* (£14.99)
34	_____ 24511 7	Spanish cassette (£6.00)
35	_____ 23771 8	Technology
36	_____ 30545 4	World History

LONGMAN GCSE EXAM PRACTICE KITS

37	_____ 30381 8	Biology £4.99)
38	_____ 30383 4	Business Studies (£4.99)
39	_____ 31191 8	English (£4.99)
40	_____ 30384 2	Geography (£4.99)
41	_____ 30385 0	Mathematics (£4.99)
42	_____ 30379 6	Physics (£4.99)
43	_____ 30380 X	Science (£5.99)

LONGMAN GCSE REFERENCE GUIDES *£6.99 each*

44	_____ 05788 4	Biology
45	_____ 05790 6	Chemistry
46	_____ 05072 3	English
47	_____ 05077 4	French
48	_____ 05074 X	Mathematics
49	_____ 05794 9	Physics
50	_____ 05076 6	Science

GCSE SURVIVAL GUIDE *£2.95*

51	_____ 05078 2

_____**YORK NOTES LITERATURE GUIDES** *(see overleaf)*

LONGMAN A-LEVEL STUDY GUIDES

£9.99 each unless otherwise stated

52	_____ 22569 8	Accounting (£10.99)
53	_____ 31545 X	Biology
54	_____ 31652 9	Business Studies
55	_____ 31546 8	Chemistry
56	_____ 05782 5	Computer Science
57	_____ 27688 8	Economics (£10.99)
58	_____ 31656 1	English
59	_____ 05784 1	French
60	_____ 24495 1	French pack* (£14.99)
61	_____ 24497 8	French cassette (£6.00)
62	_____ 05173 8	Geography
63	_____ 31654 5	German
64	_____ 24498 6	German pack* (£14.99)
65	_____ 24508 7	German cassette (£6.00)
66	_____ 28702 2	Government and Politics (£10.99)
67	_____ 31549 2	Law (£10.99)
68	_____ 31550 6	Mathematics (£10.99)
69	_____ 31551 4	Modern History
70	_____ 27690 X	Physics
71	_____ 31655 3	Psychology
72	_____ 27691 8	Sociology

LONGMAN A-LEVEL EXAM PRACTICE KITS *£6.99 each*

73	_____ 30386 9	Biology
74	_____ 30387 7	Business Studies
75	_____ 30388 5	Chemistry
76	_____ 30389 3	Mathematics
77	_____ 30390 7	Psychology
78	_____ 30382 6	Sociology

LONGMAN A-LEVEL REFERENCE GUIDES *£6.99 each*

79	_____ 06394 9	Biology
80	_____ 06390 6	Chemistry
81	_____ 06396 5	English
82	_____ 06398 1	Mathematics
83	_____ 06392 2	Physics (£7.99)

LONGMAN HANDBOOKS *£7.99 each*

84	_____ 09965 X	Botany
85	_____ 08810 0	Chemistry

LONGMAN PARENT'S AND STUDENTS' GUIDES

£2.99 each

86	_____ 29971 3	Longman Parent's Guide to Pre-school Choices and Nursery Education
87	_____ 29975 6	Longman Parent's Guide to Key Stage 1 of the National Curriculum
88	_____ 29974 8	Longman Parent's Guide to Key Stage 2 of the National Curriculum
89	_____ 29973 X	Longman Parent's Guide to Key Stage 3 of the National Curriculum
90	_____ 29972 1	Longman Parent's Guide to GCSE and Key Stage 4 of the National Curriculum
91	_____ 29978 0	Longman A-level Survival Guide
92	_____ 29969 1	Longman Students' Guide to Vocational Education
93 to	_____ 29970 5	Longman Students' Guide to Returning Learning
94	_____ 29976 4	Longman Students' Guide to Higher Education

* pack = book and cassette